Kunqu

Kunqu

A Classical Opera of Twenty-First-Century China

Joseph S. C. Lam

Hong Kong University Press
The University of Hong Kong
Pokfulam Road
Hong Kong
https://hkupress.hku.hk

© 2022 Hong Kong University Press

ISBN 978-988-8754-32-8 (*Hardback*)

All rights reserved. No portion of this publication may be reproduced or transmitted in any form or by any means, electronic or mechanical, including photocopying, recording, or any information storage or retrieval system, without prior permission in writing from the publisher.

British Library Cataloguing-in-Publication Data
A catalogue record for this book is available from the British Library.

Digitally printed

To Robert Walton

who galvanizes me with brotherly tenderness

Contents

List of Illustrations	x
Preface	xii
Acknowledgments	xv

1. Kunqu: A Performance and Discourse of Twenty-First-Century China — 1
   - An Overview — 1
   - An Ethnographic Report on a 2018 Kunqu Event — 4
   - Kunqu Appeals and Debates — 8
   - A Holistic Hypothesis on Twenty-First-Century Kunqu — 9
   - Chapters — 11

2. Kunqu Institutions, Practitioners, Terminology, and Theories — 13
   - Introduction — 13
   - Troupes and Practitioners — 14
   - Insiders' Keywords and Tropes — 17
   - Categories and Labels — 22
   - International Theories for Studying Kunqu — 25

3. Kunqu: A Heavenly Opera — 30
   - Introduction — 30
   - Kunqu Virtuosities — 31
   - Systematized Performance Practices and Materials — 36
   - The *Palace of Everlasting Life*: A Heavenly Entertainment — 47
   - Epilogue — 55

4. Kunqu: An Earthly Opera — 57
   - Introduction — 57
   - Kunqu and Earthly Practices — 58
   - Kunqu as a Cultural and Historical Root of Chinese Humanity — 59
   - A Pragmatic Narrative of Kunqu History — 61
   - The *Peony Pavilion*: A Malleable Opera — 72
   - Epilogue: Other Peonies — 78

5. Kunqu Lives, Dreams, Documents, and Character Models	81
Introduction	81
Kunqu Documents: Historical Scripts, Notated Scores, and Theoretical Treatises	82
Staged Ancestors	89
Dramatic Forefathers	91
Legitimizing Teachers	92
Visionary Patrons	98
Iconic Characters	103
Epilogue	108
6. Kunqu Operations: Resources, Stakeholders, *Yuescapes*, and Products	110
Introduction	110
Suzhou as a Kunqu *Yuescape*	111
Taipei as a Kunqu *Yuescape*	114
Mainland China as a Kunqu *Yuescape*	116
A Strategic Kunqu Operation in Nanjing	120
The *1699 Peach Blossom Fan*: A Sensational Product	124
Epilogue: Localized Operations and Individualistic Shows	126
7. Contemporary Kunqu: Creative Performers and Evolving Shows	128
Introduction	128
Kunqu Creativity and Re-creativity	128
The "Zither Seduction": A Case Study of Kunqu Creativities	134
Evolving Shows	144
Epilogue: A Diversity of Creativities, Expressions, and Selves	148
8. Kunqu as *Yue* Performance and Discourse: A Case Study of Kunqu Instrumental Music	150
Introduction	150
Kunqu as *Yue* Performance and Discourse	151
Kunqu Instrumental Music: A *Yue* Discourse of Contemporary China and *Qingchun* Selves	158
The *C-yue* of the *Young Lovers*	165
More *Yue* Discourses of the "Dark Silk Robe"	167
Epilogue	169
9. Kunqu as a Twenty-First-Century Chinese ICH and World Opera	171
Introduction	171
Overseas Kunqu Performances	171
Kunqu as a Chinese *Feiyi* and a World ICH	178
Other Chinese and Non-Chinese ICH	184
Epilogue: Bando Tamasaburo's Japanese-Chinese Du Liniang	190

Contents

ix

10. Kunqu at a Crossroads: Continuities, Changes, and Explorations   193
    Introduction   193
    Continuities   193
    Changes   196
    Explorations   204
    Epilogue   209
Appendix 1: Current Kunqu Scholarship: A Sketch   211
Appendix 2: Titles of Kunqu Dramas, *Zhezixi*, and *Qupai*   216
Appendix 3: Music Examples   220
Appendix 4: Links to Online Audiovisual Kunqu Recordings   240
Glossary   243
Works Cited   251
Index   273

Illustrations

Figures

Cover image: A kunqu moment at the University of Michigan, 2012

Figure 1.1: UNESCO honors kunqu	2
Figure 1.2: A curtain call by ShangKun performers	7
Figure 2.1: *Qingchun* kunqu characters	20
Figure 3.1: A stage backdrop that references heavenly music	31
Figure 3.2: A virtuoso act	32
Figure 3.3: A moment from *14:28*	34
Figure 3.4: A battle scene	40
Figure 3.5: A historical stage	42
Figure 3.6: A traditional kunqu instrumental ensemble	46
Figure 3.7: An imperial couple partying	50
Figure 4.1: Qiandeng children performing the *Peony Pavilion*	74
Figure 4.2: A grand dance, from the *Young Lovers*	77
Figure 5.1: Unveiling Wei Liangfu's bust	86
Figure 5.2: Zhao Kuangyin and Jingniang	91
Figure 5.3: Prime Minister Zhou Enlai congratulates kunqu performers	99
Figure 5.4: Woman Liu punishes her husband	104
Figure 5.5: Sekong and her young monk lover in "The Young Nun and Monk Leave for the Secular World"	106
Figure 5.6: Xian Yuzhi, the cheater and ignoramus	109
Figure 6.1: The Qianrenshi in Huqiu	112
Figure 6.2: A parade of beauties	125
Figure 7.1: A stage with panels of Chinese books	132
Figure 7.2: Pan Bizheng flirts with Chen Miaochang	139
Figure 9.1: Bando Tamasaburo as Du Liniang	191

Illustrations

Figure 10.1: Yang Yang performs Lin Chong — 206
Figure 10.2: "Dreams Long and Short" — 208

Musical Examples

Music Example 1: "Pink Butterfly," Aria 1 in "A Garden Party; Shocking News" — 221

Music Example 2: "Taking the Cloth Shirt Off," "Short Liangzhou," and "Repeat," Arias 4 through 6 in the "Lamenting" — 222

Music Example 3: "The Peddler, the Sixth Variation," Aria 8 in the "Ballad Singing" — 223

Music Example 4: "The Peddler, the Seventh Variation," Aria 9 in the "Ballad Singing" — 225

Music Example 5: "Sheep on the Slope," Aria 1 in the "Yearning for the Secular World" — 226

Music Example 6: "Geese Descending from the Sky" and "Being Victorious," Aria 6 in the "Flee by Night" — 229

Music Example 7: "Lazy Bird," Arias 1 to 4 in the "Zither Seduction" — 230

Music Example 8: "Pipa Tune," incidental music in the "Audience" scene of the *Fifteen Strings of Coins* — 234

Music Example 9: "Dark Silk Robe," Aria 4 in the "Strolling; Dreaming" — 237

Music Example 10: "Flower Angels' Dance" in the "Strolling; Dreaming" scene — 238

Tables

Table 8.1: Six types of *T-yue* commonly referenced in contemporary kunqu debates — 162

Table 8.2: Four types of *C-yue* commonly referenced in contemporary kunqu debates — 163

Preface

How does one tell the multifaceted story of kunqu, a 600-year-old genre of Chinese opera that was hardly performed in the late 1980s but is now frequently staged in theaters in China and around the world, mesmerizing audiences with literary lyrics, flowing melodies, and exquisite dances? This was the question I continuously wrestled with during the long process of writing this monograph. I finally chose to tell the story as I had experienced it as a devotee of kunqu, a music scholar and teacher, and a university administrator who had produced Chinese cultural shows on the campus of the University of Michigan, Ann Arbor. Thus, my telling of the kunqu story blends ethnographic and historical data, kunqu practitioners' inside knowledge, and academic analyses driven by international theories of opera as well as social and cultural theory.

I first encountered kunqu as a college student in Hong Kong. Sometime in 1974, I attended a performance of the "Flee by Night" ("Yeben") and found myself mesmerized by the music and dance. Being young and uninformed, I did not fully understand what the performance signified, but I will never forget how the hero of the story sang and danced with so much emotion as he found himself chased by assassins, vowing speedy vengeance.

Between the mid-1970s and late 1980s, I did not pursue kunqu systematically—I was busy studying ethnomusicology and musicology in Japan and in the US. During those years, I attended a number of kunqu shows in Hong Kong and Taiwan and listened to some cassette recordings by Mei Lanfang (1894–1961), Yu Zhenfei (1902–1993), and other legendary performers. I also read what I could find about the genre. In 1983, I briefly entertained the idea of writing a dissertation on kunqu, a proposal my wise mentor, Professor Rulan Chao Pian (1921–2013) of Harvard University, instantly vetoed. She told me that I had neither the cultural nor musical know-how to tackle that complex subject, nor did I have the time. I did not understand her reasoning then, but I do now.

So I gave up kunqu as a dissertation topic, but I did not forget the genre: its stories, arias, and dances continued to fascinate me. I continued to listen to kunqu music and read about it whenever and however I could. In 1988, I took kunqu singing classes for several months. In 1994, I published an article on the *Nashuying qupu* (Ye Tang's

Preface

library of kunqu scores) by Ye Tang (fl. 1780s–1790s), a seminal notated source of kunqu history. In 1999, I invited two scholars to write about Chen Shizheng's controversial production of the *Peony Pavilion* (1998–1999; *Mudang ting*) for an academic journal I edited. In 2004 and 2005, I attended Bai Xianyong's production of *Peony Pavilion*, a show that made kunqu a trendy subject for debates about traditional and contemporary Chinese culture. Four years ago, UNESCO had declared the genre a Masterpiece of the Oral and Intangible Cultural Heritage of Humanity.

In 2006, I decided to study kunqu systematically. Since then, I have been conducting fieldwork, attending kunqu shows and conferences in China and the US, teaching kunqu classes and seminars, publishing writings on the genre, and producing kunqu shows in Ann Arbor. Between 2009 and 2019, I visited China three or four times per year, attending shows and meeting with my kunqu research partners and friends. In the summers of 2016 through 2018, I taught kunqu as a visiting professor at Duke Kunshan University, using that opportunity to study the genre as it was produced in the cities of Kunshan, Suzhou, and Shanghai. In short, for almost fifty years, kunqu was in and out of my academic and personal life, affecting my emotional and intellectual being and shaping the ways I understand and write about Chinese music and music culture.

By the early 2000s, I felt an urgent need to find out how Ming dynasty (1368–1644) music actually sounded. I had studied the scores of historical Chinese music for more than twenty years, but I hardly knew what it had sounded like in the past. To explore Ming kunqu sounds as they were performed and heard, I began by examining the opera as it is performed today. Supposedly, contemporary kunqu performance practices faithfully continue the tradition established since, at the latest, the mid-Qing dynasty (1644–1911).

In 2006, I encountered kunqu as a microcosm of Chinese lives and dreams. That summer, I hosted an academic conference on late Ming music and culture. To render the event musically substantive, I had a kunqu show performed as a feature attraction. That production opened doors for me to a Chinese operatic world more artistic, discursive, and multivalent than anything I had experienced before. The production process brought to me the epiphany that I could hardly separate kunqu performers from the characters they enacted on stage. I could not tell which was more "real." I learned that off-stage, the actress who played a seductive young widow was in fact a plain-looking 60-year-old; yet on stage, she was as seductive as any man could imagine; her acting, singing, and dancing were all unforgettable. Then and there, I realized that I had got myself stuck in a hermeneutic dilemma: had I dismissed the staged widow as "unreal," I would have had to negate what I had learned/imagined about what a seductive Chinese widow is/should be; had I accepted the show as "real," I would be "fooling" myself—how could I allow a virtuoso performance to "mislead" me to accept something that could not be "true"?

That epiphany compelled me to explore kunqu as both a performance and a discourse of Chinese lives and dreams. To that end, I designed a hands-on course on kunqu in the winter of 2009 and invited Madame Zhang Xunpeng (b. 1941), a celebrated kunqu performer and pedagogue, to co-teach it. In the first eight weeks of the course, I lectured on kunqu history and theories. In the remaining weeks, she taught the class the basics of kunqu acting, dancing, speaking, and singing. She taught me how performance communicates what words and thoughts can only suggest, and her lesson was confirmed by my students. A female undergraduate student who took the course confided to me that only after she had learned from Madame Zhang how a Ming dynasty Chinese lady walked could she understand why kunqu was so charming.

At the end of the course, I produced a performance of "Autumn Farewell" ("Qiujiang") from the *Jade Hairpin* (*Yuzan ji*) featuring UM students as well as Madame Zhang and Maestro Cai Zhengren (b. 1941), a giant among twentieth-century kunqu performers. To provide instrumental music for the show, I hired instrumentalists from New York. Producing and marketing the show made me realize that kunqu serves the various needs of many stakeholders. My UM production, for instance, had to serve at least four contrasting groups of participants/stakeholders: the two kunqu master performers from Shanghai; the instrumentalists from New York; the UM students, who had only studied the operatic genre for two months and lacked well-honed skills to perform it; and Ann Arbor audiences, who had never seen a Chinese opera performed live—what kind of kunqu would appeal to them?

After 2009, I produced or co-produced a number of kunqu shows in Ann Arbor. In September 2010, I presented one with performers from the New York Kunqu Society. In September 2012, I collaborated with the University Musical Society of the University of Michigan to present two grand performances of kunqu by the internationally renowned SuKun (Jiangsu sheng Suzhou kunju yuan; Suzhou Kunqu Opera Theater of Jiangsu Province). In March 2017, I invited Danny Yung, Ke Jun, and other ShengKun (Jiangsu sheng kunju yuan; Jiangsu Province Kunqu Opera Theater) artists to perform traditional and experimental kunqu on the UM campus. In April 2019, I presented the *Lute: Cai Bojie* (*Pipa ji: Cai Bojie*), a contemporary kunqu that SuKun had premiered two years earlier. And throughout the 2010s, I invited many kunqu artists and scholars to visit Ann Arbor and give lecture-demonstrations.

As I got to observe kunqu from different angles, and as I learned more and more about its history and current developments, I began to comprehend the genre's underlying theories and performance practices. Kunqu blurs Chinese lives and dreams, an observation that the kunqu aphorism *yanhuole* (bringing characters alive on stage) underscores. Indeed, for many kunqu performers and audiences, life is but a dream, and opera affords them a stage to objectively and subjectively perform and negotiate their humanity. And to perform on this stage, one has to understand kunqu from different positions. To encourage such understandings, I offer this monograph.

Acknowledgments

I would like to thank friends who have generously supported my kunqu research and the writing of this monograph. Several anonymous reviewers offered criticisms and suggestions for revision. David Pears, Rachel Schneewind, and Matthew Kudelka edited earlier drafts. The staff at Hong Kong University Press guided the preparation of this publication. Many kunqu performers and critics, my research partners, have confided their insights to me; their names include but are not limited to Cai Zhengren, Cai Shaohua, Hong Weizhu, Danny Yung, Zhang Weidong, Zhao Shanlin, and Zhou Qin. Many individuals, whom I have yet to meet, have posted numerous audio-visual clips of kunqu performances and critiques on YouTube, Youku, Bilibili, and other websites, data that critically complemented what I had collected from published materials, fieldwork, and/or my own experiences. Publication of this monograph is made possible by two generous subventions from, respectively, the School of Music, Theater, and Dance and the Lieberthal-Rogel Center for Chinese Studies, both at the University of Michigan.

1
Kunqu

A Performance and Discourse of Twenty-First-Century China

An Overview

Twenty-first-century kunqu has a long and multifaceted history, one that needs to be approached from different perspectives. To holistically introduce kunqu, this chapter presents five accounts: (1) a bird's-eye view of kunqu history and its revival during the turn of the twentieth and twenty-first centuries; (2) an ethnographic report on a contemporary and representative kunqu event, demonstrating the ways in which the genre informs us about Chinese lives; (3) a critique of popular arguments about the genre's contemporary developments and significances; (4) a preview of the holistic interpretation of kunqu offered by this monograph; (5) and a brief outline of the chapters that follow.

Kunqu is a centuries-old genre of Chinese opera, one that first blossomed in Jiangnan, in central and coastal China, in the late 1500s. By the early 1600s, it had become a nationally popular form of operatic entertainment. From the late 1600s to the end of the 1700s, kunqu performance practices grew more diverse and refined, as well as virtuoso, securing the genre's historical reputation as a classical Chinese performing art. After the early 1800s, however, kunqu began to decline, gradually yielding center stage to regional operas and performing arts that had recently become fashionable throughout China. By the turn of the nineteenth and twentieth centuries, kunqu had ceased to be a viable genre of operatic entertainment; even so, its tradition was sustained by small but influential groups of educated and nationalistic patrons and connoisseurs in Beijing and Shanghai-Suzhou.

In 1921, a team of Suzhou kunqu patrons tried to revive kunqu by launching a modern school of kunqu performance. It recruited and trained fifty-five young students, who subsequently became vital teachers of the genre and are now celebrated as the Chuanzibei Masters. In 1956 a groundbreaking kunqu performance, the *Fifteen Strings of Coins* (*Shiwu guan*), premiered successfully in Beijing, generating national interest in the genre, and this led to the founding of seven government-supported troupes/schools of kunqu performance. Over the following decade, kunqu flourished;

the development was, however, cut short by the Cultural Revolution (1966–1976), a turbulent time during which kunqu performances were banned. From the late 1970s through to the mid-1990s, the genre was meagerly sustained by a community of dedicated performers, connoisseurs, and scholars, who strove to keep the genre alive. Their efforts, however, attracted little national attention or enthusiasm. As remembered by many kunqu actors, their shows staged in the late 1980s or early 1990s often had more singers and dancers on the stage than audience members in the seats.

In 1998–1999, Chen Shizheng, a Chinese-American theater director, staged an "authentic and complete" production of the *Peony Pavilion* at the Lincoln Center in New York City. That performance won praise from many Western audiences but also antagonized some Chinese kunqu practitioners. To assert their ownership of kunqu, and to demonstrate its "authentic" expressions and performance practices, they mounted their own version of the opera.[1]

Figure 1.1: UNESCO honors kunqu as a Masterpiece of the Oral and Intangible Cultural Heritage of Humanity. Source: Wu Xinlei, ed., *Zhongguo kunju dacidian*, front matter.

---

1. For further discussions on Chen's show, see Chapters 4 and 8.

A Performance and Discourse of Twenty-First-Century China   3

In May 2001, UNESCO designated kunqu a Masterpiece of the Oral and Intangible Cultural Heritage of Humanity. That honor prompted the Chinese government to generously promote the genre, which stimulated regular performances of new and traditional shows and nurtured new generations of professional performers and young urban fans. Since 2001, a number of seminal kunqu events have taken place, attesting to the genre's restoration as a form of classical Chinese opera. In 2002, two authoritative reference works on kunqu—*Zhongguo kunqu dacidian/A Dictionary of Chinese Kunqu Opera*, edited by Wu Xinlei, and *Kunqu cidian* (A dictionary of kunqu), edited by Hong Weizhu—were published in Nanjing and Taipei respectively. In November 2003, China launched the Kunqu Museum in Suzhou, thus making that city the centre of the genre's revival. Suzhou is now the permanent site of the national Kunqu Festival (*kunqu yishu jie*), held every three years. Each iteration of the festival offers an extensive program of traditional and new operas by professional kunqu performers and an international conference of kunqu scholars.

In 2004, efforts to revive kunqu shifted into high gear. In April and May of that year, the *Young Lovers* (*Qingchun ban Mudang ting; Peony Pavilion, the Young Lovers*), a groundbreaking performance that staged kunqu with its "original sauce and taste" (*yuanzhi yuanwei*), premiered in Taipei and Hong Kong. Over the following summer and fall, the show was presented in Beijing, Hangzhou, Suzhou, and Shanghai, mesmerizing tens of thousands of young, educated, arts-loving Chinese college students. Their enthusiasm for the show not only launched a national discourse about kunqu as part of China's cultural heritage but also a heated controversy over its *qingchun* (beautiful, classical, youthful) aesthetics and performance style.[2] Also in 2004, a grand new production of the *Palace of Everlasting Life* (*Changsheng dian*) premiered in Taipei and Suzhou, demonstrating the performers' vision of what authentic kunqu was, is, and should be.

In April 2005 the Chinese central government issued a national policy on safeguarding and developing kunqu: each year between 2006 and 2010, the ministries of culture and finance would invest an annual sum of RMB10,000,000 to support the genre's performance, training, and research. In March 2006 the *1699 Peach Blossom Fan* (*1699 Taohua shan*) premiered in Beijing, consolidating the *qingchun* aesthetics and performance practices that the *Young Lovers* had launched. In September and October of the same year, the *Young Lovers* was staged in Berkeley, Irvine, Los Angeles, and Santa Barbara, winning critical praise and nurturing international interest in kunqu. The year 2007 saw the premier of a Shanghai production, the *Palace of Everlasting Life*, demonstrating Chinese efforts to both preserve and develop the genre. In May 2008, a sensational Chinese–Japanese version of the *Peony Pavilion* was staged in Beijing, underscoring the extent to which the genre had attracted international attention. The artist who performed the leading female role in the production was Bando Tamasaburo (b. 1950), an internationally renowned Japanese kabuki

---

2. See Chapters 4 and 8 for further discussions of the show's innovative features.

onnagata (female impersonator), whose unique performance generated critical debate among kunqu fans.[3]

New and traditional kunqu performances are now regularly staged on Chinese and international stages. Domestic and overseas communities of kunqu fans are steadily expanding. These fans are now generating a demand for the genre and fostering the online circulation of audiovisual recordings of kunqu shows, performance scripts, music scores, and commentaries. Twenty-first-century kunqu is blossoming as a fashionable art form in China today.

An Ethnographic Report on a 2018 Kunqu Event

Kunqu is blossoming because it offers a stage for Chinese people to construct and negotiate their culture, history, and personhood, a fact that is palpable at grand performances, such as that of the *Palace of Everlasting Life* that ShangKun (Shanghai Kunju tuan; Shanghai Kunju Troupe) staged from May 10 to 13, 2018, at the Shanghai Oriental Arts Center.[4] A dramatization of the romance between Tang Minghuang (685–762), a Chinese emperor, and Yang Guifei (719–756), his beautiful consort, the performance unfolded as a sequence of four operas presented over four nights.[5] Each evening performance ran about 150 minutes, realizing scenes from a script that Hong Sheng (1645–1704) completed in 1688.[6]

The four parts together tell a romantic story with virtuosic acting, singing, and dancing; that story inspires debate over a number of Chinese issues. As scripted and performed, the first show includes two highly romantic scenes: "Pledging Love" ("Dingqing"), about how Tang Minghuang embraces Yang Guifei as his lover by presenting her with a golden hairpin and a bejeweled box; and "A Gift of Hair" ("Xianfa"), which shows how the consort, who has been banished from the palace for having displeased the emperor, wins back his love with a personal gift of her hair, a token of her femininity and charm.

The second installment features scenes that appeal to Chinese eyes, ears, hearts, and minds. The scene titled "Listening to Music; Notating Music" ("Wenyue; Zhipu"), for example, presents a fanciful story: the consort travels to the moon in a dream, where she listens to a rehearsal of the *Rainbow Skirt of Feather* (*Nishang yuyi qu*) and learns its melodies and rhythms. Upon her return to earth, she notates the

---

3. See Chapter 9 for further discussions of Bando Tamasaburo's performance.
4. For links to the online audiovisual clips of the show, see "Links to Online Audiovisual Kunqu Recordings."
5. For further details about the *Palace of Everlasting Life*, see Chapter 3.
6. For further details about the ShangKun production, see Shi Jian, *Nichang yayun yongting fangfei Shanghai kunju tuan tuanqing sishi zhounian jinian* (Shanghai: Shanghai Kunju Opera Troupe, 2017). On the production's claim of "returning to tradition," see Pan Yanna, "'Huigui chuantong' de linian yu shijian—Shanghai kunju tuan quanben *Changshen dian* yanjiu"/"The Idea and Practice of 'Returning to the Tradition'—a Case Study on the Full Version of the *Palace of Everlasting Life*, produced by the Shanghai Kunju Opera Troupe," dissertation, Shanghai Conservatory of Music, 2011.

A Performance and Discourse of Twenty-First-Century China 5

music she has learned, teaches it to the palace musicians, and has them perform it to entertain the emperor. Dramatically, the scene conflates historical memories with fictional imagination, a standard feature in kunqu operas. Yang Guifei was renowned as a talented musician and dancer, and the *Rainbow Skirt of Feather* is a celebrated work in Chinese music history. By tracing the work's provenance to supernatural forces, the scene underscores that kunqu is the music of heaven.

The third installment emphasizes how kunqu operates as opera (*xiqu*)—literally, the Chinese term means "theatre" and "songs"; conceptually, it defines Chinese opera as a performing art that tells stories with words, songs, and dances. The definition vividly manifests itself in the scene titled "A Garden Party; Shocking News" ("Xiaoyan jingbian"). Realistically, it presents the imperial couple drinking and flirting with each other, evoking games Chinese lovers play, and demonstrating the horrors that war would bring to the Chinese world. Kunqu audiences love this scene, and actor-singers yearn to perform it. Madame Zhang Xunpeng, a senior female kunqu performer, once told me that she loved the scene for its affective projection of the consort's charm and her love for the emperor, as well as for enabling performers to showcase their skills.

The fourth installment wraps up the heart-rending love story with a happy conclusion, a convention in traditional Chinese opera. The climax of the show is the scene titled "Ballad Singing" ("Tanci"), a masterpiece of kunqu music.[7] It presents an itinerant old balladeer, a former court musician, singing arias for a paying audience and relating key events in the imperial romance that he has witnessed. Melodically intricate and narratively dramatic, the arias in the scene include a set of nine variations. All were, and still are, popularly sung by old amateur male kunqu performers, who enjoy the tunes and use them to reminisce about their youthful dreams.

As noted earlier, the ShangKun performance of the *Palace of Everlasting Life* enabled kunqu audiences to vicariously experience, or imagine, romantic and historical Tang China. Even while empathizing with Tang Minghuang and Yang Guifei, they could not forget their contemporary selves and realities. The young cast of the performance reminded the audience that they were witnessing a transition between different generations of performers. Cai Zhengren, a celebrated kunqu actor, performed the leading role of Tang Minghuang in two scenes of the performance; in the other scenes, the role was performed by his students, young but accomplished ShangKun performers. Cai's sharing of the Tang Minghuang role in the 2018 production confirmed the passing of kunqu performance tradition from one generation of ShangKun performers to another.

Even while the audience enjoyed the young performers, they were reminded of kunqu's present-day social significance. The performance they attended was more than an operatic presentation—it was also a commercial and social event in

---

7. For a study of the scene and its music, see Joseph S. C. Lam, "A Kunqu Masterpiece and Its Interpretations: *Tanci* (the Ballad) from Hong Sheng's *Changsheng Dian* (*Palace of Everlasting Life*)," *Chinoperl* 33, no. 2 (December 2014): 98–120.

contemporary Shanghai.[8] The performance had been sold out five days before opening night. Ticket prices were barely affordable; the most expensive cost RMB¥800. Thus, the cost of attending all four evenings of the performance added up to one quarter or more of a typical Shanghai salaryman's monthly pay.[9] However, tickets could be scalped on-site at the last minute. An hour or two before 7:15 p.m. when the show began, scalpers were offering tickets by the entrance to the venue; prices dropped as showtime approached. Commercial activities also occurred inside the arts center. In its expansive lobby, sponsors had set up counters offering advertisement brochures, product samples, and souvenirs—all prominently marked with corporate sponsors' logos. Placed along aisles in the lobby were carts selling snacks and beverages, as well as books and media products about kunqu.

The commercial and social aspects of the performance were brazenly exposed by the empty seats at the "sold-out" event. At each of the four shows, around 20 percent of the seats were empty, and some seats were occupied by persons who were obviously not regular operagoers. This underscored the Chinese practice of giving out complimentary tickets in the kunqu world of contemporary and socialist-capitalist China. Only people/institutions with financial and social resources can afford to get or give complimentary tickets. Those who receive hard-to-get tickets are honored and are obliged to later return the favor somehow. Some gifted tickets had been passed on to the casual audience, who betrayed their unfamiliarity with kunqu in several ways. They squirmed in their seats throughout the performance, checking their smartphones, reading program notes, and showing their confusion or boredom. A few actually left before the performance was over. Those who stayed until the end might perhaps have become kunqu fans.

As indicated by the audience at the ShangKun performance, kunqu fans are diverse. Most of the audience at the shows appeared to be Chinese, most likely Shanghainese. Most were in their late twenties through to their fifties. Most dressed informally but neatly, indicating that they were financially and socially comfortable. A few among the audience wore formal evening dresses or suits, which made them stand out among the crowd, underscoring their business reasons for attending the shows. Many among the audience appeared to be regular operagoers, who responded positively or negatively to the performance. Some were serious connoisseurs who held in their hands performance scripts and/or notated scores of the opera being staged. A few among the audience were non-Chinese tourists exploring kunqu as Chinese culture and/or entertainment.

---

8. As listed in the program pamphlet of the shows, the institutional sponsors of the performance were: Center for Chinese Culture Transmission, Shanghai Headquarters, and Shanghai Hongwan Cultural Transmission Corporation.

9. As of 2018, average monthly salaries of mid-career college professors in Shanghai ranged between RMB¥6000.00 to RMB¥12,000.00.

All applauded enthusiastically right after the virtuoso scenes were performed, as well as at curtain calls. As they left the auditorium at the end of the shows, many chatted with their friends, exchanging comments on what they had just experienced. Arriving home, some posted messages on social media, telling friends how they enjoyed the shows, or not.[10] Commenting on storylines, performance styles, and particular arias and/or dances that individual performers delivered, the attendees discussed how and why the shows were operatically expressive and culturally realistic. Many also described what they disliked, revealing their personal preferences and social-political positions. For example, some asked whether the *Palace of Everlasting Life* was a moralist warning for men: male indulgence with female companionship leads to disaster, a common exhortation in patrilineal China. Others contemplated the issue of social responsibility and sacrifice: Should Tang Minghuang give up Yang Guifei for the empire? How were men and women to choose between serving the nation and their personal selves?

Figure 1.2: A curtain call by ShangKun performers of the *Palace of Everlasting Life*, 2018. Photograph by J. Lam, 2018.

---

10. For kunqu's presence in cyberspace, see Li Bin, "Hongqushu jieyuan hulianwang," on *Guanzhu xingjin zhong de kunju: Jiangsu sheng kunju yanjiu hui 2010 nian lunwen ji*, ed. Liu Junhong and Gu Lingsen (Beijing: Zhongguo xiju chubanshe, 2011), 154–172.

Kunqu Appeals and Debates

Searching for answers, the audience would promptly confront personal, social, and political issues in their own lives. At which point they would ask what the *Palace of Everlasting Life* or kunqu was, is, and should be, as well as who wanted to see kunqu performances now, and why. Many Chinese critics—in particular those who are knowledgeable about the genre's content and history, have formulated a number of useful but partial answers to these questions, clarifying some issues while obfuscating others. For example, most kunqu practitioners declare that the genre is being revived for its beauty (*mei*) and classicism (*dianya*).[11] While informative and self-explanatory for fans of kunqu, this point of view ignores the fact that kunqu is only one of many beautiful, charming, classical, and culturally as well as historically significant genres of Chinese opera. And above all, it does not answer why kunqu should be given a lion's share of the nation's attention and resources at the expense of other equally traditional and deserving Chinese operas, such as Cantonese opera and Shanghai opera. What makes kunqu uniquely significant in contemporary China?

Some kunqu professionals, such as Zhou Bing and Jiang Wenbo, proudly assert that the genre is being revived because it is the "mother of all Chinese operas."[12] History tells us that kunqu dramas, artists, and practices have strongly influenced Peking opera, Cantonese opera, and other "younger" genres of Chinese opera. However, the "mother" argument does not explain why and how kunqu has touched hearts and minds of Chinese today. Luo Zheng, a Peking University professor, reports that kunqu appeals directly to practitioners' artistic, emotional, and intellectual selves.[13]

Some kunqu practitioners, such as Zhou Qin, contend that kunqu's appeal stems from its Jiangnan roots.[14] There is some demonstrable truth to this argument. Kunqu stories, characters, aesthetics, and performance practices are closely aligned with Jiangnan biographies, histories, sentiments, and values. And many kunqu practitioners were/are sons and daughters of Jiangnan. Nevertheless, Jiangnan attributes did not prevent kunqu from declining in times past, nor have they endeared it to all Chinese today. Indeed, many contemporary Jiangnan sons and daughters do not find kunqu appealing; many would even dismiss it as an old-fashioned, even obsolete, form of Chinese opera.

Some critics have analyzed current kunqu developments in terms of theories about commodification, tourism, modernization, Westernization, and various other national and international forces. However insightful these analyses are, they can be factually and theoretically challenged. A case in point is the argument that greed and

---

11. This view appears in numerous introductions to kunqu. See, for example, Yu Dan, *Youyuan jingmeng: kunqu zhimei* (Taipei: Lianjing 2008).
12. See Zhou Bing and Jiang Wenbo, *Kunqu liubai nian* (Beijing: Zhongguo qingnian chubanshe, 2008), 80–91.
13. See Luo Zheng, "Wo he kunju," in his *Zhongguo kunqu ershi jiang* (Guilin: Guangxi shifan daxue chubanshe, 2007), 307–312.
14. See Zhou Qin, *Suzhou kunqu* (Suzhou: Suzhou daxue chubanshe, 2002).

A Performance and Discourse of Twenty-First-Century China   9

tourism are driving current developments in kunqu.[15] There is no denying that some kunqu producers and performers have kowtowed to market demands, thus compromising their artistic integrity. Yet few kunqu productions are staged merely for financial or political gain. Most are staged with some aesthetic and/or cultural goal in mind, such as to restore forgotten masterpieces or to revive cultural heritage. Shows produced with little more than sensational acting, singing, and dancing are often forgotten soon after they have premiered. Only kunqu performances that are artistically sophisticated and of cultural, social, and political value are performed repeatedly in contemporary China and perennially discussed by knowledgable fans.

Some critics suggest that the Chinese state has engineered the current rise of kunqu. As noted by Ke Fen, a young kunqu scholar, and Yang Shousong, a senior kunqu author and activist based in Kunshan, Chinese officials have played a vital role in shaping twenty-first-century kunqu.[16] However, Chinese officials and government institutions cannot totally dictate the genre's development and meanings. Officials who work with kunqu performers, critics, scholars, and fans may adjust the genre but they cannot single-handedly transform it.

A Holistic Hypothesis on Twenty-First-Century Kunqu

Kunqu is a multifaceted and multivalent performance and discourse of historical and contemporary China: thus, no single, linear description can comprehensively describe the genre's large repertory and diverse stories, its contrasting and iconic characters, its sophisticated performance practices and materials, or its diverse and evolving operations. And as analyses and interpretations driven by disciplinary theories or methodologies tend to highlight some facets of the genre at the expense of others, interdisciplinary and multiple perspectives are needed to holistically explain kunqu.

Kunqu practitioners are creative, informed, intellectual people. Even as they stage its performances, they debate its features and meanings with an insiders' vocabulary. Kunqu practitioners, be they fans, connoisseurs, celebrated performers, or authoritative critics and scholars, approach the genre with the following assumptions:[17]

---

15. The argument arises in many negative comments hurled at touristy kunqu shows, such as the abridged *Peony Pavilion*, which premiered in 2007 at the Imperial Granary Theater (Huangjia liangcang) in Beijing. For a more "neutral" view, see Colin Mackerras, "Tourism and Musical Performing Arts in the First Decade of the Twenty-First Century: A Personal View," *Chinoperl* 30 (2011): 155–182; see also his "Performance Review: The Imperial Granary Production of *Mudan ting (Peony Pavilion)*," *Chinoperl* 26 (2010): 209–216.

16. Ke Fan, *Shuying youlan—zhongguo kunqu de dangdai chuancheng yu fazhan* (Beijing: Wenhua yishu chubanshe, 2014), 61–66 and 203–205; Yang Shousong, *Kunqu zhi lu* (Beijing: Renmin wenxue chubanshe, 2009), 31–39, and 48–54.

17. My kunqu research partners repeatedly discussed these themes as their fundamental concerns/ understandings.

1. Kunqu is a microcosm of Chinese culture, history, and personhood—the genre both performs and reflects Chinese lives and dreams.
2. Kunqu is a genre of classical opera with a large repertory and a codified system of virtuoso performance practices—as such, it is a cultural heritage that today's China needs and should use to show its true self to the world.
3. Kunqu is a continuous tradition that has been faithfully transmitted through generations of mentors and disciples—artistic genealogy and legitimacy is thus a primary criterion in kunqu valorization and criticism.
4. Kunqu is a collaborative, recreative, and evolving art form—the genre's performances are collaboratively created/produced by regional schools/teams of artists over periods of time, and those performances evolve as the performers fine-tune their performances for audiences at specific times and sites.
5. Kunqu connects Chinese hearts and minds—much about kunqu performance and discourse is personal and subjective.

As kunqu practitioners passionately debate their genre, they tend to jump from topic to topic, generating a web of facts and interpretations, which include, to cite the obvious, documented data about historical developments; structural and expressive details about diverse dramas and performances; memories of past and present artists and their works, lives, and careers; and communal and personal experiences and feelings that kunqu performances and discussions continuously generate. Viewed close-up, the kunqu web of artistic-biographical-cultural-historical-political-social facts and claims indexes a bewildering conglomerate of objective and subjective Chinese lives and dreams.

Twenty-first-century kunqu resists linear description. That said, as a phenomenon it can be approached productively by way of the following holistic and heuristic hypothesis. As contemporary Chinese become more prosperous and self-confident, they yearn to present themselves as civilized, amicable, and responsible actors in world culture, economy, and politics. This desire, however, runs up against historical and negative images/memories of late imperial China, which Western and imperialist powers humiliated for two centuries. To counteract these negative images and memories, Chinese today seek cultural and historical evidence to legitimize and/or justify their contemporary selfhood. They find what they need in kunqu, a genre of Chinese opera six centuries old that presents characters who personify idealized Chinese society and values. Thus, contemporary Chinese eagerly reclaim kunqu as a means to perform and promote their reborn China and idealized selfhood. In doing so, they package kunqu into a classical opera of contemporary China, one that not only pleases their hearts and minds (*shangxin leshi*) but also serves their present and practical needs. Furthermore, as entertainment, kunqu is a "cultural heritage that can go out" (*wenhua zou chuqu*) to the world. It can rightfully claim a place in the global market for leisure.

A Performance and Discourse of Twenty-First-Century China 11

The artistic-cultural-economic-social-political phenomenon of twenty-first-century kunqu is not an isolated development. History has seen many comparable phenomena in the performing arts, such as French ballet, Japanese *noh*, and Wagnerian (German) opera. Contemporary kunqu is however a unique phenomenon; it presents *Chinese* aesthetics, emotions, facts, imaginations, and processes that Chinese have experienced and want to share with the globalized world. Examining it in this light, kunqu has something worthwhile to tell about twenty-first-century and global efforts to reclaim historical genres of performing arts around the world.

Chapters

This monograph has ten chapters, which discuss various interrelated facets of contemporary kunqu. The present chapter provides a historical and ethnographic introduction to kunqu, as well as a proposal that we understand it holistically. Chapter 2 introduces institutional and intellectual facets of the genre; to that end, it introduces troupes that stage formal and informal shows, explains key words and tropes that kunqu practitioners use to discuss the genre and its meanings, and expounds theories from around the world that have guided this interdisciplinary examination of contemporary kunqu.

Chapter 3 discusses how the Chinese have idealized kunqu as "heavenly" opera and describes its codified system of virtuoso performance practices and materials. To illustrate, three scenes from the *Palace of Everlasting Life* will be analyzed. Chapter 4 presents kunqu as an earthly and malleable heritage of China, using two retrospective accounts and an analysis of three contrasting productions of the *Peony Pavilion*. The first account describes the historical context in which demands for reclaiming kunqu arose. The second summarizes kunqu history as it is pragmatically told nowadays. The analysis demonstrates the ways in which kunqu staging practices have been adjusted to cope with evolving aesthetics and market demands.

Chapter 5 highlights biographical, historical, and technical sources and models that have shaped kunqu performance and discourse. It surveys the genre's preserved performance scripts, notated music scores, and theoretical treatises, and it traces the artistic genealogies that have guided its performers' aesthetics and performance styles. Artistic genealogies have played critical roles in shaping kunqu performance and discourse. Performers declare their artistic lineages to legitimize their performance artistry and expressions; connoisseurs reference the genealogies to evaluate the performers' performances and artistry. Kunqu shows stage many historical personages as dramatic characters. To illustrate this historical and dramatic facet of kunqu, this chapter sketches four representative and popular shows, namely "Kneeling by the Pond" ("Guichi"), "Yearning for the Secular World" ("Sifan"), "Flee by Night" ("Yeben"), and "Dog Exit" ("Goudong").

Chapter 6 describes contemporary kunqu operations in local, national, and global contexts. Kunqu is routinely described as a unique Chinese performance tradition, but in fact, it is an amalgam of localized/regionalized institutions and individual stakeholders, who strive to pursue their goals, making tactical use of available resources at particular times and sites, thereby asserting their individuality and values. To illustrate regional differences in the contemporary kunqu phenomenon, the chapter surveys kunqu's manifestations in Suzhou, Taipei, and Beijing. To demonstrate specific operations and distinctive results of localized kunqu troupes, the Nanjing production of the *1699 Plum Blossom Fan* will be examined as a case study.

Chapter 7 analyzes the collaborative and creative/re-creative processes whereby kunqu practitioners stage preexisting and/or original shows with known and/or unknown performance practices and materials, thereby eliciting diverse responses from connoisseurs. To illustrate kunqu creative and production processes, this chapter presents a historical overview of the *Jade Hairpin* and analyzes three contrasting productions of "Zither Seduction" ("Qintiao"), a popular scene from that drama.

Chapter 8 examines a controversy surrounding kunqu instrumental music that was triggered by the *Young Lovers* production of 2004. To contextualize the controversy and its arguments, this chapter begins with a historical overview of kunqu instrumental music and its model, *minyue* (Chinese instrumental music). The controversy will then be analyzed and illustrated with comparative analyses of musical renditions of the "Zaoluopao ("Dark Silk Robe") aria in "Strolling; Dreaming" ("Youyuan jingmeng").

Chapter 9 presents kunqu as a phenomenon of contemporary and globalized Chinese culture and society. Thus, the chapter discusses overseas performances of kunqu shows; the UNESCO ICH (intangible cultural heritage) policies and practices that China appropriated to justify their efforts for safeguarding and developing kunqu; kunqu's unique attributes as a mirror of an idealized China; and challenges from non-Chinese kunqu shows, such as Bando Tamasaburo's *Peony Pavilion*.

Chapter 10 ends this monograph by showing that twenty-first-century kunqu is at a crossroads. Today's kunqu practitioners face challenges to connect with the past and sustain the genre in the present and into the future. To illustrate this, this chapter examines a number of seminal kunqu activities and works from the 2010s, identifying overarching continuities, prominent changes, and bold explorations in kunqu. This volume ends with an overview of kunqu scholarship, musical scores of several arias discussed in the monograph, and other reference materials.

2
Kunqu Institutions, Practitioners, Terminology, and Theories

Introduction

The world of twenty-first-century kunqu is home to diverse practitioners—government officials, commercial entrepreneurs, professional performers, amateur players, discriminating connoisseurs, erudite historians and theorists, and enthusiastic audiences. They collaborate and/or compete with one another, arguing over what kunqu was, is, and should be and safeguarding and developing the genre in different ways. Their differences, however, have not splintered contemporary kunqu into warring camps; they are united by their shared acts, institutions, thoughts, and values and by an insider's language that reveals their intimate understandings of the genre. Contemporary kunqu becomes knowable when it is viewed with reference to historical and ethnographic data collected through library and fieldwork studies. This is particularly the case when international theories about music and culture are employed to illuminate kunqu practitioners' insider acts and utterances.

This monograph presents a holistic examination of twenty-first-century kunqu. It incorporates kunqu practitioners' insider perspectives, ethnographic observations, and international theories. Emphasis will, however, be placed on to the practitioners' acts and words. Kunqu is after all *their* operatic performance and discourse. To introduce twenty-first-century kunqu as a multifaceted phenomenon, this chapter offers four accounts. The first introduces eight national and professional institutions whose continuous production of kunqu performances has shaped the genre as it is practiced today. The second presents seven sets of aesthetic and cultural keywords that practitioners of kunqu use to express and negotiate their goals, operations, and results. The third provides technical terms about historical and contemporary kunqu repertories, divisions of artistic and discursive labor, and performance practices and materials; only in reference to these terms can kunqu acts and debates be meaningfully described and interpreted. The fourth explains international theories this author has consulted and employed to develop narratives that illuminate insider accounts.

Troupes and Practitioners

In terms of performance and production, contemporary kunqu is dominated by eight professional mainland Chinese troupes, which are government-supported and -supervised. All are staffed by a large group of administrators, executives, performers, and production specialists. These troupes' leaders have been appointed for their artistic expertise, after consultation with national and/or local government authorities. These troupes present weekly, monthly, or seasonal shows; regularly they premiere new or revised kunqu operas to celebrate local occasions. The eight institutions are officially known as:

1. BeiKun (Beifang kunqu juyuan/Kunqu Opera Theater of Northern China) of Beijing.
2. KunKun (Kunshan dangdai kunju yuan/Contemporary Kunqu Opera Theater of Kunshan City) of Kunshan, Jiangsu Province.
3. ShangKun (Shanghai kunju tuan; Shanghai Kunqu Opera Troupe) of Shanghai, Shanghai Municipality.
4. ShengKun (Jiangsu sheng kunju yuan/Jiangsu Province Kunqu Opera Theater) of Nanjing, Jiangsu Province.
5. SuKun (Jiangsu sheng Suzhou kunju yuan/Suzhou Kunqu Opera Theater of Jiangsu Province) of Suzhou, Jiangsu Province.
6. XiangKun (Hunan sheng kunju tuan/Kunqu Opera Theater of Hunan Province) of Chenzhou, Hunan Province.
7. Yongjia kunqu chuanxi suo (Yongjia Kunqu Academy of Zhejiang Province) of Wenzhou, Zhejiang Province.
8. ZheKun (Zhejiang sheng kunju tuan/Kunqu Opera Theater of Zhejiang Province) of Hangzhou, Zhejiang Province.

Complementing the eight mainland Chinese troupes are professional, semi-professional, and amateur kunqu institutions in Chinese and international cities. These institutions include the Concordia Kunqu Society of Hong Kong (Xianggang heyun qushe), the Taiwanese Kunju Opera Troupe (Taiwan kunju tuan), the Lanting Kun Opera Troupe of Taiwan (Taiwan Lanting kunqu she), the London Chinese Opera Studio, the New York Kunqu Society, the Wintergreen Kunqu (Dongqing kunqu she) of Washington, D.C., and the Western US Kunqu Society (Meixi kunqu she). All are financially supported by public grants, private donations, and ticket sales (if they stage commercial performances).

Professional and semi-professional troupes present performances in a variety of formats, ranging from commercial and formal shows for the general public to free and informal presentations/lecture-demonstrations for young students. Featuring kunqu star performers, commercial and formal shows present either a single operatic work or a group of three or more short and dramatically independent plays. Performance lengths range between 120 to 150 minutes. Some grand performances are, however, staged over three or four days, with performance times totalling seven or more hours.

Formal kunqu performances are collaborative efforts. For example, once the staging of a show is decided, its creative efforts will begin with the writing/editing of the performance script, casting, composition or making arrangements of the music and dance to be performed, and costume making. Rehearsals are held. Then, as the production takes shape, promotion campaigns begin. Advertising has become essential in contemporary kunqu performance and discourse. Shows with substantial artistic and financial investments hold meetings with the media, publicizing creative goals and strategies, introducing cast members, and specifying performance times and venues. A month or two before showtime, ticket sales begin. Online announcements proliferate. By the time curtains are raised, post-performance efforts have already begun. Large, stationary cameras and recording units in the auditorium would record the shows, which are then archived and posted online for global audiences. Their reactions—in particular, their written and circulated comments—will promote or undermine the recorded shows.

Informal kunqu shows can be casual affairs; most are either simple stagings of kunqu scenes or recitals of kunqu arias. Performance time can range from thirty minutes to two or more hours. Many recitals are artistic-cultural-social gatherings (*yaji*) attended by a variety of participants, many of whom do not perform. If they do perform, they sing to either live or recorded music; they neither act nor wear theatrical costume and makeup.

Indicative of the collaborative nature of kunqu performance and its division of artistic labor are the titles given to production members; grouped according to the members' creative specialties, the most commonly used titles are:

1. Dramatists (*zuojia*) and scriptwriters (*bianju*).
2. Actor-singers (*yanyuan*).
3. Artistic directors (*yishu zhongjian*), performance directors (*daoyan*), and producers (*jianzhi*).
4. Composers (*yinyue chuangzuo*), aria composers and arrangers (*changqiang chuangzuo, changqiang zhengli*), instrumental music and orchestration arrangers (*peiyue, peiqi*), and instrumentalists (*yueshi*).
5. Choreographers (*wumei sheji*), costume and makeup artists (*fuzhuang sheji*).
6. Sound and light designers (*yinxiang dengguang sheji*), and stage and prop technicians (*wutai*).
7. Advisers (*guwen*), who help producers and performers solve theoretical and practical problems in their productions.

The names and titles of the artists involved in a show are printed in its performance program as well as electronically projected on the stage at the beginning of the presentation. The order in which the names and titles appear reflects actual or nominal ranking of the artists involved. For example, names of dramatists and scriptwriters usually appear first, a practice that highlights traditional emphasis on dramatic libretti and their literary expressions.

In this monograph, people who participate in kunqu performance and discourse are called *practitioners*. To specify those who actively and professionally create or perform, they will be called actor-singers, composers, directors, dramatists, or other similar terms. To specify practitioners who do not actively perform but who play critical roles in kunqu activities, they will be classified into the following six types: (1) amateur performers (*quyou*); (2) connoisseurs/critics, who may or may not perform but who have much to say about kunqu expressions and meanings; (3) patrons, who aesthetically, financially, politically, and/or socially support kunqu activities—many are government officials and/or prosperous businessmen; (4) entrepreneurs, who market kunqu for material and/or non-material profits; (5) scholars (*zhuanjia*), who historicize and theorize kunqu repertory, performance, and developments; and (6) dedicated audiences/fans (*fensi*), who idolize performers and their individualized performance artistry or personae.[1] Collectively and individually, kunqu practitioners perform and discourse in one or more roles, shaping contemporary kunqu with their ideals and needs.

Different kunqu practitioners make different impacts on the genre; much depends on their social and political status, the contexts of their performance, and the nature of their discourse. Currently, actor-singers, who are now regarded as "people's artists" (*renmin yishu jia*), serve as active and authoritative gatekeepers. Wealthy patrons and discriminating critics are formidable movers and shakers. Dedicated fans and ticket-buying audiences make demands that cannot be ignored.

Social and power structures in contemporary kunqu differ from those of the past, when elite dramatists and patrons dominated the world of kunqu. Actor-singers were marginalized as socially low, uneducated, and thus unsophisticated participants, even though they were the very people who acted, sang, and danced on stage. Historical and contemporary fissures among practitioners often reveal themselves in heated debates. Not infrequently, kunqu performers—especially those who are young—are challenged with arguments about their lack of scholarly education. To fend off such challenges, some young performers acquire MA degrees in humanist fields in addition to their professional training in kunqu performance.

In historical China, kunqu performers were divided into *qinggong* and *xigong*, terms that indicate artistic and social divides. *Qinggong* refers to professional or amateur actor-singers who performed in the *qingchang* format—that is, they sang kunqu arias without acting or dancing and without wearing makeup and costume.[2]

---

1. For a pioneering work on Chinese opera audience, see Zhao Shanlin, *Zhongguo xiqu guanzhongxue* (Shanghai: Huadong shifan daxue chubanshe, 1990).
2. For a study on the *qingchang* format, see Zhu Kunhuai, *Kunqu qingchang yanjiu* (Taipei: Da'an chubanshe, 1991).

Institutions, Practitioners, Terminology, and Theories

Xigong were professional performers who wore makeup and costume to perform kunqu as commercial entertainment. Historically, *xigong* were often stereotyped as vulgar entertainers—indeed, some were also sex workers. Upon retirement from the stage because of age or for artistic or personal reasons, vocational performers might become professional composers/tunesmiths (*qushi*), music teachers (*paixian*), or acting and dance instructors (*taxian*).

Insiders' Keywords and Tropes

Keywords and tropes in kunqu discourse underscore the genre's aesthetics and history. Anyone who listens to kunqu practitioners' debates will quickly gather that they employ a culturally and historically developed insiders' language to communicate among themselves. The language is distinguished by a number of metaphoric/sensual/emotional terms, which the practitioners repeatedly use to express their acts, aesthetics, interpretations, and values as these relate to kunqu. Most of these terms are "self-explanatory" for kunqu insiders; as such, the terms cannot be rigidly defined, objectively verified, or adequately translated into English, as is clear from the following paraphrases of their utterances:[3]

> Kunqu is beautiful (*mei*) and classical (*dianya*).
>
> Kunqu looks good (*haokan*) and pleases the ears (*haoting*).
>
> Kunqu is a pleasure for the heart and a joyful thing to do (*shangxin leshi*).
>
> Kunqu is a mirror (*jingzi*) of Chinese culture and history.
>
> The actor-singer has brought the character alive on stage (*yanhuole*) with his/her pure singing and elegant dancing (*qingge miaowu*).
>
> Du Liniang lives, dreams, dies, and gets resurrected for genuine love.
>
> "Flee by Night" shows what a stalwart man (*haohan*) is.
>
> Kunqu is a UNESCO Masterpiece of the Oral and Intangible Cultural Heritage of Humanity; as such, it should be inherited, developed, and shared with audiences all over the world.
>
> Kunqu needs to be excavated (*wajue*), inherited (*chengji*), and developed (*fazhan*).
>
> Kunqu needs to be improved (*gailiang*) so that it can attract young audiences and have a sustainable future.
>
> That show is a fake (*jia*), a Chinese imitation of Western musicals paraded as kunqu!

Heard casually, these utterances seem to be simply subjective responses to kunqu performances and stereotypes. Analyzed pragmatically, however, the utterances underscore kunqu aesthetics and creative performance practices and materials as the

---

3. I frequently heard these utterances from my kunqu fieldwork research partners. For three representative publications by kunqu critics and performers, see Mu Fanzhong, *Kunqu jiushi* (Zhengzhou: henan renmin chubanshe, 2006); Chen Jun, *Jingdu lingqu lu* (Beijing: Shangwu yinshu guan, 2016), Cong Zhaohuan, *Cong Zhaohuan tanxi* (Taipei: Xiuwei zhixun keji, 2015).

practitioners understand them, besides serving as practical guides for deciphering what the practitioners are performing and negotiating. Heuristically, the metaphoric terms can be grouped into seven sets and clarified as follows; all will be used as paradigms for analyzing and describing kunqu performances and discourses in this study.

The first set involves the dyad of heaven (*tian*) and earth (*di*),[4] which evokes the Chinese cosmology that frames kunqu performance and discourse. Kunqu practitioners idolize the genre as heavenly music (*xianyue*), as music that is beautiful, desirable, and natural (*ziran*) and that angels in heaven might play for privileged audiences on earth—and the practitioners perceive themselves to be such fortunate individuals. As evidenced by the cosmological and tripartite Chinese term *tiandiren*, heaven, earth, and people are inseparably bound together. On the kunqu stage, characters travel freely between the supernatural world in heaven (*tianshang*), the human society on earth (*renjian*), and the underworld of the deceased and the spiritual (*yinjian*). In kunqu heaven, Chinese live their dreams; on kunqu earth, they lead fruitful lives, which can nevertheless be challenging at times; in the kunqu underworld, they atone for their sins or rescue someone they love. For many kunqu practitioners, the human world sandwiched between heaven and earth is a grand stage (*tiandi da wutai*), and the kunqu stage is a miniature cosmos of human affairs (*wutai xiao tiandi*).

The second set involves the practitioners' attitudes toward fact and fiction as told by history. Vividly, this set manifests itself with the following keywords: authentic and/or truthful (*zhen*); substantial and/or trustworthy (*shi*); deceptive and/or inauthentic (*jia*); and intangible and/or transient (*xu*). Kunqu offers many historical accounts about China and the Chinese people, but these do not always relate the past as it happened or has been documented. Kunqu tends to tell us what its practitioners accept as substantial, trustworthy, and representative of their historical experiences and cultural-social ideals, as well as what they objectively or subjectively reject as false, inauthentic, superficial, or transient. Kunqu may employ anachronistic expressions to highlight timeless principles or genuine emotions. For example, the *Young Lovers* employs young and physically attractive performers to enact handsome and beautiful characters from Southern Song China (1127–1279), projecting visually truthful images. The performers also sing lyrics more than four centuries old, set to tunes preserved in scores that are two centuries old; yet they also dance and act on stages equipped with the latest lighting and sound technologies. Their claims that they are performing kunqu with its "original sauce and taste" are assumptive and can neither be verifiably substantiated or refuted.[5]

---

4. For a standard discussion of heaven and earth as philosophical concepts, see Fung Yu-lan, "Philosophical and Religious Thoughts Prior to Confucius," in *A History of Chinese Philosophy*, trans. Derk Bodde (Princeton: Princeton University Press, 1983), 22–42.

5. For aesthetic and production details about the show, see Pan Xinghua, *Chunse ruxu: Qingchunban kunqu Mudanting renwu fangtan lu* (Singapore: Global Publishing, 2007); see in particular the interviews with Bai Xianyong, the project director (1–14); Cai Shaohua, the SuKun director (15–23); Wang Shiyu, the performance director (55–60); and Zhou Youliang, the music composer (69–74).

Institutions, Practitioners, Terminology, and Theories 19

The third set of keywords, which revolve around the expression "bring characters alive on stage" (*yanhuole*), underscores that kunqu practitioners understand dramatized characters both as historical personages and as models of and for their present-day lives and dreams. Characters are only "lifelike" to the extent that they realistically align with what the practitioners believe to be true, desirable, and/or representative of their personhood. Whether characters come alive on stage, and how, is a matter of negotiation between performers and audience, with reference to their Chinese and personal experiences and values.

The fourth set of keywords concerns performers and their artistry. In kunqu parlance, the greatest performances are presented by master performers (*dashi*), who possess and can execute at will their rare and/or unparalleled skills (*jueji*), delivering transcendental (*shen*) and exquisite (*miao*) expressions. Grandmasters' performance expressions and skills are the results of rigorous training under strict teachers (*yanshi*). This is why kunqu performers filially honor, or purposefully flaunt, their artistic genealogy (*shicheng*). And to underscore the length and intensity of their training, they often cite the aphorism that to deliver one minute of transcendental performance on stage, performers have to train hard (*kulian*) for ten years (*taishang yifen zhong, taixia shinian gong*).

The fifth set of keywords focuses on kunqu's artistic nature and social-political functions. Is kunqu a genre of opera/theatre (*xiqu*), or is it a genre of vocal music (*ge, qu*) that is sung (*chang*) for listening (*ting*) pleasure? Does kunqu represent and/or serve Chinese people as individuals or as a community (*xiaowo* or *dawo*; literally the small "I" and the big "I")? How? Should kunqu serve (*fuwu*) elite (*jingying*) or commoner (*dazhong*) audiences? Should kunqu be modernized so that it can serve contemporary China more effectively?

The sixth set of kunqu keywords revolves around Chinese theories of kunqu and practices for inheriting and developing it. These are discussed under the rubric of *feiyi*, an acronym of *feiwuzhi wenhua yichang*, a Chinese and literal translation of the UNESCO term "intangible cultural heritage" (ICH). *Feiyi*, however, signifies many Chinese ideals and actions that ICH does not define. For example, *feiyi* calls for a developmental sequence of Chinese actions: excavation (*wajue*), salvaging (*qiangjiu*), protection (*baohu*), transmission (*chuancheng*), inheriting (*chengji*), development (*fazhan*), reform (*gaige*), modernization (*xiandaihua*), creation of new works/performance styles (*chuangxin*), and being fashionable (*shishanghua*).

The seventh set of kunqu keywords consists of four Chinese words—*qing, chun, dian*, and *ya*—which can be uttered as either a catchphrase of four words or as two bisyllablic terms. All are flexibly uttered and diversely interpreted, and none can be rigidly defined or concisely translated. To avoid misinterpretation, Romanized forms of the keywords will be used in this monograph. Core meanings of the four words can however be sketched as follows.

Literally, *qing* means green; figuratively, it points to fresh young buds popping up in spring (*chun*), which is the season for planting, birth, rebirth, love, sex, and so on.

In Chinese vernacular, *qingchun* is often a euphemism for biological fertility, physical beauty, and sensual appeal. As a qualifier of twenty-first-century kunqu practitioners, the term paints them as young, beautiful, desirable, and productive. As a qualifier of contemporary kunqu, *qingchun* refers to performances that set out to attract youthful audiences with young and beautiful performers, fashionable and stylized costumes and makeup, updated performance practices, and electronic and multimedia staging.

As such, *qingchun* kunqu affords a stage for young urbanites to connect with their historical and idealized China, both past and present. This use is especially effective when its verbal, physical, and visual communications are complemented by sonic ones. Thus, *qingchun* kunqu performances often play contemporary Chinese instrumental music. Expressively and stylistically, they unfold with constantly changing tones, dynamic rhythms, orchestrated timbres, and symphonic textures, echoing Western and classical concert music, which many contemporary and Westernized Chinese musicians and audiences valorize as a lodestone.

The bisyllablic term *dianya* is similarly multivalent. Literally, *dian* refers to laws or canonized works that serve as institutionalized ideals for civilized and productive living, whereas *ya* literally means elegance, propriety, refinement, and sophistication.

Figure 2.1: *Qingchun* kunqu characters, from "Happy Time." Photograph by J. Lam, 2014. Courtesy of Lü Jia, Zhu Yinghuan, and Zhou Xuefeng.

Institutions, Practitioners, Terminology, and Theories   21

Ya is the opposite of *su*, which means common, vernacular, indulgent, and/or vulgar. Depending on the context in which it is uttered, *ya* evokes all kinds of ethnic, class, and political meanings in Chinese discourse. *Ya* is, for example, often discussed as a monopoly of Han Chinese.[6]

As an adjective for describing Chinese people, *dianya* refers to those who are materially and socially privileged, classically educated, intellectually astute, and politically connected and powerful. Praising people or their acts or possessions as *dianya* has long been a welcome form of flattery in China. As a qualifier of kunqu, *dianya* underscores the genre's long history and performative sophistication, attributes that have led it to be named part of the world's cultural heritage. For the sake of being recognized as *dianya*, many college-educated and upward mobile Chinese young men and women take kunqu lessons.

Kunqu practitioners use the word *dianya* a lot to characterize the genre and its performative activities, thus signifying their artistic merit and cultural-historical significance. To emphasize that the *dianya* in kunqu is a cultural and historical model for Chinese operas, the practitioners declare that the genre is the "mother of a hundred genres of Chinese opera" (*baixi zhi mu*).

Closely linked to the keywords *qingchun dianya* is the term *fugui*. Literally, *fu* means wealth and *gui* refers to nobleness. *Fugui* Chinese are people who enjoy or are destined to lead privileged lives. As paraded on the kunqu stage, *qingchun dianya* characters are often *fugui* sons and daughters of emperors, grand officials, and other noble persons. In traditional and contemporary China, *fugui* is not a hereditary attribute, though many people who possess it are members of privileged families. Others have to achieve *fugui* through hard work, perhaps with a good dose of luck. *Qingchun dianya* kunqu performances have many *fugui* features. Grand (*haohua*), elaborate, beautiful (*huali*) performances are staged with the best and latest technologies money can buy.

For kunqu practitioners, *qingchun*, *dianya*, and *fugui* attributes are attainable desiderata. Indeed, they are commonly found among, or ascribed to, top achievers in historical and contemporary China. In historical China, and on past and present kunqu stages, these top achievers appear as *caizi* or *zhuangyuan* and *jiaren* or *meiren*. *Caizi* are learned, talented, handsome men; simultaneously, they can be (or become) prodigal or filial sons, romantic partners, conscientious scholar-officials, stalwart heroes, or idealistic and virtuous gentlemen. Some are also *zhuangyuan* (top scholars), men who have passed the palace examinations with the highest scores and are now elite scholar-officials. Many subsequently acquire immense wealth, accomplish towering achievements, and bequeath monumental legacies to posterity. *Caizi* and *zhuangyuan* always marry *jiaren*—beautiful, smart, virtuous daughters of noble and

---

6. For further discussion of kunqu *ya*, see Joseph S. C. Lam, "Ya Kunqu in Late Ming and Early Qing China," *Chinese Arts Quarterly* 6 (September 2019): 68–94.

wealthy families. Many of the same successful men will, however, have romantic affairs with *meiren*, beautiful and desirable women, many of whom are courtesans.

Many *qingchun dianya fugui* men and women live in prosperous twenty-first-century China. Contemporary *zhuangyuan*, for example, are young people who have passed the university entrance examinations (*gaokao*) with flying colors and are now studying at top Chinese and/or non-Chinese universities like Peking University or Harvard University. Like their historical models, many eventually will become national officials, corporate CEOs, and social celebrities. They are beautiful, young, and productive and are making China a twenty-first-century superpower.

In short, *qingchun dianya fugui* kunqu characters are emblematic of not only the historical Chinese elite but also of contemporary Chinese high achievers. This is why when such characters "come alive" on stage, they confirm kunqu practitioners' hopes of being beautiful, civilized, prosperous, and youthful like their classical ancestors were, and their successful contemporaries are.

Categories and Labels

In addition to the keywords discussed above, kunqu practitioners' insider language includes various technical terms that either specify the genre's repertories, performance practices, and other practical concerns or evoke cultural-historical-social associations that define or nuance what is being discussed. The terms serve as convenient references for describing and analyzing kunqu acts and words in this study.

Kunqu, which literally means "songs of/from Kunshan," is one of two contemporary names for the genre. Popularized at the turn of the previous century, it replaced the earlier labels of *qu* (songs) and *kunqiang* (vocal music of Kunshan) and highlights the genre's provenance, history, and musicality, three core concerns in Chinese debates about kunqu. Currently, kunqu is the generic term for the genre/tradition as a classical opera and a cultural heritage. Kunqu is often translated as *kun opera or kunqu opera*; however, neither translation will be adopted here because neither evokes the genre as its practitioners perform and discuss it. In this monograph, the romanized term *kunqu* will be adopted, and the genre will be discussed as an opera (*xiqu*) in the Chinese sense—that is, as a performing art that tells stories with tightly integrated words, music and dance, and costume and makeup.

The other contemporary term for the genre is *kunju*, which literally means "theater performed with songs of Kunshan." Coined in the early 1900s, it defines the genre more as theater and less as a genre of songs. Contemporary kunqu performances tend to prioritize drama over music. Kunqu stories and scripts are derived from *chuanqi*, a literary/musical genre that first blossomed in Ming China. Literally, the term *chuanqi* means telling stories about the atypical or fanciful. As text, *chuanqi* dramas are complex literary works; many unfold over thirty or more scenes (*chu*). Complete realizations of *chuanqi* dramas were and still are infrequent; the human and material resources they require are prohibitive.

Institutions, Practitioners, Terminology, and Theories

To control production costs and to stage scenes that were popular with audiences, the practice of performing *zhezixi* (rearranged scenes) became the norm after the 1750s, by which time kunqu performance practices had become virtuosic and a repertory of 400 or more *zhezixi* had been established. Since then, *zhezixi* has become a focus of kunqu performance and discourse: *zhezixi* aesthetics, stories, scripts, characters, and performance practices are now being realized on-stage and discussed off-stage. Memoirs about past *zhezixi* and their performance history are critical references for contemporary kunqu practices.

Etymologically, *zhezixi* refers to playlists written on folded "menus" that hired performers would present to their patrons, indicating to the latter what shows they were prepared to stage; the patrons then picked from the menu what they wanted to see. As performed, *zhezixi* are short, stand-alone plays based on *chuanqi* scenes; they are textually and performatively structured as suites of arias (*liantao*) and speeches (*nianbai*). *Zhezixi* seldom realize *chuanqi* scripts literally. To stage dramatically effective shows, kunqu performers would abridge, rearrange, and/or rewrite *chuanqi* texts, creating dramatic times and places for acting, singing, and dancing. *Zhezixi* aesthetics and performance practices pushed kunqu to develop into the sophisticated opera that it now is. In this monograph, discussion of kunqu will focus on analyses of seminal and popular *zhezixi* and their performance practices and materials.

As realized nowadays, most *zhezixi* take between twenty-five to thirty minutes of performance time, and a medley of three or four *zhezixi* will fill a typical kunqu show. Some contemporary kunqu productions, however, play a selection of six or more scenes from the same *chuanqi* drama, thus generating a *strung-together version* (*chuanben*), or a *comprehensive version* (*quanben*). Either type of kunqu requires a performance time of at least 150 minutes; to keep performance times within practical lengths, some of the selected scenes are greatly condensed. A sample of a strung-together version is ShangKun's *Jade Hairpin* (1985), which consists of eight scenes/*zhezixi*. The original *chuanqi* drama has thirty-three scenes.[7]

With the recent demand for realizing *chuanqi* dramas as they are written, some kunqu productions have been staged as a sequence of three or four performances, each consisting seven to nine scenes/*zhezixi* from a *chuanqi* drama. In contemporary kunqu parlance, each show constitutes a *ben* (book; part) of the drama being staged. Kunqu presentations with multiple *ben* amount to theatrical spectacles. A prime example is ShangKun's *Palace of Everlasting Life*, which has four *ben*.[8] Such grand kunqu spectacles are truly, for lack of a better word, Wagnerian experiences.

As dramatic texts to be realized on stage, *chuanqi*/kunqu scripts are written in a number of literary forms. Each serves a particular dramatic function and thus needs to be performed in a codified way. For example, when characters come onstage, they introduce themselves by chanting (*nian*) short *shi* poems, which are written as stanzas

---

7. For further discussion of the opera, see Chapter 7.
8. For more details about the production, see Chapters 1 and 3.

of four rhymed phrases of five to seven words each. As dramatic situations develop, characters deliver monologues and dialogues, expository prose that explains what is happening; prose is spoken (*shuo*). To reveal their emotions and thoughts, characters sing arias (*qu*, *guoqu*), the lyrics of which are written in the *qu* literary form. Kunqu arias and their lyrics are composed according to specific *qupai*—preexisting patterns with a prescribed number of phrases, phrase lengths, and other linguistic-musical features.[9]

Kunqu speaking, reciting, chanting, and singing are distinctive but inseparable modes of oral delivery. Each is employed to maximize theatrical communications and/or effects. Smooth transitions between the oral deliveries are needed to ensure dramatic flow. In terms of tones and rhythms delivered and heard, kunqu reciting and chanting are performed with non-metric rhythms and flexible tones that constantly glide in and out of focused pitches. In contrast, kunqu singing is performed with focused pitches, pulsed rhythms, and florid melodies.

Kunqu performers speak, chant, and sing while acting, gesticulating, and dancing. Their bodily movements and expressions are conceptualized and discussed as *shenduan*. Literally, *shen* means body and *duan* signifies segments; *shenduan* means sequences of choreographed bodily gestures, pantomimes, and dances that seamlessly blend into one another, forming dramatically intelligible and kinetically and visually pleasing expressions. Kunqu *shenduan* is a systematized performing art. Many *shenduan* have established names and are used "tactically" to construct distinctive dramatic expressions that connoisseurs savor—and critique. The more a kunqu audience member can identify *shenduan* expressions and their dramatic functions, the more he or she can appreciate, or critique, the artistry of the actor-singers performing on stage.

Experienced kunqu practitioners recognize many codified *shenduan*, such as a beauty's orchid-like finger gestures (*lanhua zhi*), a ghost's walk (*guibu*), a gesture for opening doors (*kaimen*), and steps to end a scene (*yuanchang*). Whatever their codified names, all *shenduan* are creatively realized on stage. *Shenduan* cannot be routinely or mechanically performed, for performers have different bodies and because performance prescriptions are sketchy. Most *chuanqi* or kunqu scripts provide only rough prescriptions, such as "the female protagonist does the gesture of crying." Until recent years, *shenduan* was very much an orally transmitted art. Only after the 1960s did kunqu performers begin to publish illustrated books about *shenduan* practices (*shenduan pu*). And since the 1990s, performers have regularly used audiovisual recordings as teaching/learning aids.

Kunqu practitioners categorize and discuss kunqu shows and performance practices in terms of historical development. To evoke differences and similarities, various kunqu shows are classified as historical (*jiu*, *gudian*), traditional (*chuantong*),

---

9. For two informative discussions, see Wang Jilie, *Yinlu qutan* (Shanghai: Shangwu yinshuguan, 1934), and François Picard and Kar Lun Alan Lau, "Qupai in Kunqu: Text-Music Issues," in *Qupai in Chinese Music: Melodic Models in Form and Practice*, ed. Alan Thrasher (New York: Routledge, 2016), 119–154. See also discussions in Chapters 3 and 7.

contemporary (*xiandai, dangdai*), or experimental (*shiyan*). In this monograph, the historically qualified categories are heuristically defined as follows.

Historical kunqu refers to those works and performance practices that emerged before 1920. Historical kunqu is partly knowable through preserved performance scripts, notated sources, verbal descriptions of performances attended, and a small number of preserved photographs and audio recordings produced between the 1920s and the 1940s. Historical kunqu is what many nostalgic practitioners of the genre want to excavate, safeguard, and develop for twenty-first-century China.

Traditional kunqu refers to those shows and performance practices that current kunqu performers have learned from their twentieth-century mentors/models. Typical sounds and sights of traditional kunqu can be heard and seen through audiovisual recordings made between the 1950s and the early 1990s.

Contemporary kunqu refers to those shows and performance practices that have been created since the mid-1990s. These shows typically feature newly written or rewritten performance scripts, play orchestral music as overtures and interludes, and make use of elaborate stage designs and new staging technologies. As of this writing, contemporary kunqu is arguably the most commonly performed type of kunqu. *Experimental kunqu* refers to shows and performance practices that deliberately incorporate and/or highlight expressions that break away from tradition through the use of innovative or non-Chinese elements, such as Shakespeare stories, performance practices, and materials adapted from Western ballets, musicals, and operas.

Theoretically, experimental and contemporary kunqu sharply contrast with each other: the former prominently displays its innovations, while the latter adamantly emphasizes its traditionality, glossing over its new features. As realized on stage, however, the two types have more overlap than their practitioners would care to admit. By highlighting the types' differences at the expense of their similarities, performers and audience can gloss over theoretical and practical difficulties they cannot address in the present day.

Kunqu is often promoted as a single continuous tradition. For instance, its revival at the turn of the previous century was promoted as a national development. In fact, kunqu more closely resembles an amalgam of competing and local institutions and practitioners. Thus, three historically recognized branches of kunqu are *beikun* (northern kunqu), based in Beijing; *nankun*, flourishing in Suzhou, Hangzhou, Nanjing, and Shanghai; and *caokun* (grassroots kunqu), performed and enjoyed in rural China. Differences and similarities among kunqu branches are topics that kunqu performers and scholars vigorously debate.

International Theories for Studying Kunqu

Kunqu keywords and technical terms project an insider view of kunqu. That view is factually solid and intellectually meaningful, but it begs comparative analyses and interpretations. Indeed, kunqu practitioners' vocabulary becomes more intelligible and significant when it is compared to international and academic concepts and terms about performing arts outside China. To develop a comparative understanding of kunqu, this author has consulted a number of international theories on world music and culture. They are introduced below and will be discussed more thoroughly in later chapters.

Directly and indirectly, these "outsider" theories help address three fundamental questions about contemporary kunqu: (1) How and why do Chinese employ kunqu to stage their past and present lives and dreams, thereby asserting their feeling, thinking, and action-taking selves? (2) How does kunqu, a genre of collaborative, creative/re-creative, discursive performance art, construct or represent Chinese realities and imaginations? (3) How does kunqu singing/music serve practitioners' and stakeholders' operatic and cultural-social-political performance and discourse?

Publications on the Chinese and expressive self by Tu Weiming and other international sinologists prompted this author to conceptualize kunqu practitioners as intellectual, emotional, and practical beings. They express themselves and interact with others in order to advance their Chinese desires and needs.[10] Studies by Chinese historians and anthropologists helped me identify Confucian and cultural practices in kunqu performance and discourse.[11] Claims that kunqu is a refined genre of opera (*yabu*), one that gives pleasure to practitioners' hearts and minds, are unmistakably rooted in Chinese and Confucian experiences. Defining kunqu as *xiqu* and/or *yue* (music; multimedia performing arts) aligns with the ways traditional Chinese integrate words, songs, and dances to express themselves. The "Shi daxu" ("The great preface to *Classic of Poetry*") and the *Yueji* (*Record of Music*) declare that when people are stimulated by their surroundings, and want to express their emotions, they make verbal/literary utterances; when their words cannot adequately tell what they feel and think, they sing; when their sung words fail to fully express what they want to communicate, they dance.[12] To impress on his disciples that *yue* involved much more than making sounds, Confucius challenged them with an open question: "*yue*, oh, *yue*, is it

---

10. For theories on Chinese selves, see Tu Weiming, "Embodying the Universe: A Note on Confucian Self-Realization," in *Self as Person in Asian Theory and Practice*, ed. Roger T. Ames, Thomas P. Kasulis, and Wimal Dissanayake (New York: SUNY Press, 1994), 177–186. See also Harris M. Berger, "Horizons of Melody and the Problem of the Self," in *Identity and Everyday Life: Essays in the Study of Folklore, Music, and Popular Culture*, ed. Harris M. Berger and Giovanna P. Del Negro (Middletown: Wesleyan University Press, 2004), 43–88.

11. For a brief introduction to Confucianism, see Daniel K. Gardner, *Confucianism: A Very Short Introduction* (New York: Oxford University Press, 2014); see also Joseph S. C. Lam, "Musical Confucianism: The Case of 'Jikong yuewu,'" in *On Sacred Grounds: Culture, Society, Politics, and the Formation of the Cult of Confucius*, ed. Thomas A. Wilson (Cambridge, MA: Harvard University Asia Center, 2002), 134–172.

12. See "Shi daxu", accessed May 16, 2021, https://baike.baidu.com/item/%E8%AF%97%E5%A4%A7%E5%BA%8F#2; and "Yueji," accessed May 16, 2021, https://ctext.org/liji/yue-ji/zh. For an English introduction to the *Yueji*, see Scott Cook, "'Yueji'—Record of Music: Introduction, Translation, Notes and Commentary," *Asian Music* 26, no. 2 (Spring–Summer, 1995): 1–96.

merely an act of striking gongs and drums?"[13] And to impress on them that *yue* is a powerful force that must be handled properly, he told them about his personal experiences: he once was so mesmerized by an authentic performance of ritual music that he forgot the taste of meat for three months; and he was once incensed by a socially and politically transgressive dance performance.[14]

As they perform and discuss kunqu with *yue* ideals, kunqu practitioners render their opera a microcosm of their Chinese lives and dreams. Kunqu tells archetypal Chinese stories and presents iconic characters with literary lyrics, flowing melodies, and exquisite dances. Superficially, what kunqu is and how it works is distinctively Chinese. Underneath its Chinese facade, however, are principles that it shares with many genres of performing arts around the world. International scholarship on expressive cultures, histories, and societies has abundantly attested to this. For example, Howard Becker, Tia DeNora, Richard Schechner, and many other cultural and performance studies scholars have amply demonstrated that arts are intricately linked to the societies in which they are created.[15] And many ethnomusicologists, such as Timothy Rice, Anthony Seeger, and Thomas Turino, have offered insights and techniques for analyzing musics as performances and discourses of human objectivities and subjectivities.[16]

Among the many studies of artistic creativity, performance practices, and virtuosity, the following scholars' works have been instrumental to the writing of this monograph. Jeffery Alexander theorizes that when people set out to construct and communicate new meanings with known facts and ritual/ritualized acts, they fuse and re-fuse expressive elements in their shows for their target audiences.[17] Michel de Certeau contends that in their social-political endeavors, people develop tactics for achieving their agendas, thus bypassing or counteracting limitations imposed by authoritative others or contextual forces.[18] Yan Huang and other scholars of linguistic and social pragmatics have offered insights for deciphering what people explicitly and implicitly say and how their words can be meaningfully deciphered.[19] For example, when a kunqu critic declares that an actor-singer has brought a well-known character

---

13. D. C. Lau, trans, *Confucius: The Analects* (London: Penguin Books, 1979), 145.

14. D. C. Lau, trans, *Confucius: The Analects*, 67 and 87.

15. Howard Becker, *Art Worlds*, updated and expanded ed. (Berkeley: University of California Press, 2008); Tia DeNora, *Music in Everyday Life* (Cambridge: Cambridge University Press, 2000); Richard Schechner, *Performance Studies: An Introduction*, 2nd ed. (London: Routledge, 2006).

16. Timothy Rice, *Modeling Ethnomusicology* (New York: Oxford University Press, 2017); Anthony Seeger, *Why Suya Sing: A Musical Anthropology of an Amazonian People* (Urbana: University of Illinois Press, 2004); Thomas Turino, *Music as Social Life: The Politics of Participation* (Chicago: University of Chicago Press, 2008).

17. Jeffry Alexander, "Cultural Pragmatics: Social Performance between Ritual and Strategy," *Sociological Theory* 22, no. 4 (2004): 527–573.

18. Michel de Certeau, *The Practice of Everyday Life* (Berkeley: University of California Press, 1984); see esp. 29–44.

19. Yan Huang, *Pragmatics* (New York: Oxford University Press, 2007); Sun Huichu, *Shehui biaoyanxue* (Beijing: Shangwu yinshuguan, 2009).

alive on stage, her declaration communicates surface and hidden messages. Besides telling what the performer has sung, and why it pleases the critic, it displays her artistic agenda and values.

Murray Schafer's notion of soundscape in which sounds define and are defined by their environment, the players, and the listeners offers a practical approach to analyzing kunqu as a musical/*yue* performance and discourse of Chinese culture, history, and personhood.[20] Sound or music affords critics a means to critique similar performances of the same kunqu story. Rendering Schafer's concept of soundscape more effective in this author's analyses of contemporary kunqu is Arjun Appadurai's hypothesis of *technoscape*, in which technological flows are driven by complex relationships among stakeholders operating in fluid times and sites.[21] Kunqu is a technology of words, sounds, and sights with which contemporary Chinese perform and negotiate their local and globalized lives and dreams.

In analyses of kunqu as a *yue* performance and discourse, Christopher Small's hypothesis of musicking is key—music is not autonomous and fixed compositions; rather, it is performance that generates social meanings.[22] This provides a conceptual bridge to connect international theories on cultures and performing arts with Chinese and Confucian arguments that *yue* is a means for people to cultivate their virtues and build a harmonious society. With the bridge provided by Small, kunqu performance and discourse can be approached as a flexible sonic means to generate and activate interpersonal interactions and meanings.

Conceptually and heuristically, the hypothesis of kunqu as *yue* performance and discourse assumes that the genre's participants are *yue stakeholders* who deliberately organize *yue* happenings in complex and fluid *yuescapes* in which they maneuver *yue* as tangible or intangible objects/tools/expressions of sounds and non-sounds, thus advancing their communal and personal agendas and social-political interrelationships. *Yue* happenings are performative and discursive. They unfold fluidly as kunqu stakeholders compose/recompose, closely listen to, emotively respond to, and critique/interpret kunqu works/shows/performance features, which they deem instrumental for expressing their selves and advancing their agendas. This is possible because *yue* happenings take place in *yuescapes*, which are shaped by a confluence of biographical, cultural, historical, physical, and social-political forces and at the same time define what and how *yue* stakeholders perform and discourse among themselves and for/with their audiences.

---

20. Murray R. Schafer, *The Soundscape: Our Sonic Environment and the Tuning of the World* (Rochester: Destiny Books, 1977).
21. Arjun Appadurai, *Modernity at Large: Cultural Dimensions of Globalization* (Minneapolis: University of Minnesota Press, 1996), 34.
22. Christopher Small, *Musicking: The Meanings of Performing and Listening* (Middletown: Wesleyan University Press, 1998); see esp. "Socially Constructed Meanings," 130–143.

When examined through the hypothetical lens of kunqu as *yue* performance and discourse as just outlined, the genre's multiple facets become traceable and intelligible—there is a method in its madness! With literary lyrics, flowing music, and exquisite dances, kunqu, a six-century-old genre of Chinese opera, stages the historical and contemporary lives and dreams of *qingchun dianya* Chinese. As such, kunqu becomes a classical opera of twenty-first-century China and demands to be appreciated as such.

3
Kunqu

A Heavenly Opera

Introduction

To its practitioners, kunqu is heavenly music (*xianyue*), a historically and ideologically grounded concept, as corroborated by the genre's creative expressions and virtuosic performance practices. In historical Chinese cosmology, heaven is a supernatural and omnipotent force, one that shapes human lives in ways that people can hardly anticipate or resist.[1] Chinese language has many terms for heaven, its agents, and their control of human lives on earth. Seminal ones include: *tiandiren*—heaven, earth, and people, which together constitute the cosmos; *tianxia*—under the sky, which is the earth or the world of China; *tianyi*—heaven's will, which steers dynastic changes and critical turns in people's lives; *tianshen*—deities who involve themselves in human affairs; *tianxian*—angels, immortals, and, by extension, beautiful women; *tianzi*—a son of heaven who rules over China; and *tiancai*—prodigies or gifted people who perform at levels unachievable by average people. "Tian" appears in many kunqu names and terms, such as the Tianyun she, a kunqu singing club in Wuxi, Jiangsu Province, China, which was founded in late Ming China and has recently been revived. The institution's name literally means "a social institution of heavenly rhymes."[2]

In Chinese music aesthetics, "heavenly music" refers to exquisite, natural, and rare sounds (*tiannai*) that reveal cosmic forces, and/or to the transcendental songs of angels, or angelic musicians, that privileged audiences were able to experience from time to time at particular sites. The notion of heavenly music heard on earth arises in many Chinese musical and literary documents, but its most celebrated manifestation is a poem by Du Fu (712–770), who writes: "Everyday string and wind music is busily played in the prosperous city; breeze would bring half of its musical sounds to the

---

1. For a philosophical explanation on heaven, see Fung Yu-lan, *A History of Chinese Philosophy*, trans. Derk Bodde, Vol. 1, paperback ed. (Princeton: Princeton University Press, 1983), 30–31.
2. For further information on Tianyun she, see Zhongguo yishu yanjiuyuan yinyue yanjiusuo et al., ed, *Tianyun she qupu*, facsimile edition (Beijing: Wenhua yishu chubanshe, 2019); see esp. vol. 3, 147–228.

A Heavenly Opera

river [by the city] and the rest to the clouds above it. This music belongs to heaven, but it is occasionally heard by people living on earth." Du's poem is often cited in kunqu performance and discourse. A calligraphy representation of it appeared on the stage of a 2014 performance of the *Peony Pavilion*.

To delineate kunqu's aesthetics and performance of heavenly music, this chapter presents four accounts. The first is this brief introduction to the Chinese concept of heaven which shapes kunqu practitioners' historical and contemporary pursuit of expressive and performative excellence. The second surveys five types of kunqu virtuosities that render the genre's verbal and performative expressions aesthetically intelligible, sensuously pleasurable, and socially relevant. The third introduces the genre's systematized performance practices and materials, which are fundamental constituents of kunqu as a multimedia performance art. The fourth account analyzes three scenes from the *Palace of Everlasting Life*, a celebrated sample of heavenly kunqu.

Kunqu Virtuosities

Heavenly kunqu is ephemeral, and its transcendental performance practices and materials are intangible. Yet as a matter of course, these are witnessed and discussed by kunqu practitioners, who contend that master kunqu performers sing and dance

Figure 3.1: A kunqu backdrop with calligraphy of Du Fu's poem about heavenly music. Photograph by J. Lam, 2014. Courtesy of Qu Binbin and SuKun.

with rare and supreme artistry (*jueji*), thus generating transcendental expressions that afford them a heavenly means to live and/or dream as they want, bypassing earthly constraints. The performers and their transcendental artistry are comparable to those of artists who work with "spiritual axes and divine craft" (*guifu shengong*), producing results that "surprise gods and merge with nature" (*chushen ruhua*).

Kunqu practitioners' discourse of heavenly music and performance artistry is idiosyncratic; it unfolds with its own key terms and tropes. Its arguments and meanings, however, become more apparent when they are interpreted with reference to international theories of expressive and performance virtuosity.[3] As discussed in music and performance studies, virtuosity refers to skills that only gifted and trained creators/performers possess: these people can exercise those skills at will, generating expressions that are sensuously affective and intellectually self-explanatory. For example, kunqu singing of high, sustained notes in florid melodies, and seemingly impossible acrobatic leaps across the stage are unmistakably virtuosic and always earn thunderous applause from both connoisseurs and casual audiences.

Figure 3.2: A virtuoso act in a kunqu performance in New York. Photograph by J. Lam, 2011.

---

3. For a study about musical virtuosity, see Vernon A. Howard, "Virtuosity as a Performance Concept: A Philosophical Analysis," *Philosophy of Music Education Review* 5, no. 1 (1997): 42–54.

A Heavenly Opera

Most virtuoso kunqu performance practices and expressions are, however, more subtle. Kunqu performers diligently acquire and fine-tune these throughout their careers. That is why the pursuit and achievement of virtuosity is a core concern in kunqu performance and discourse. Audiences and critics always ask themselves whether the performers have done their best.

Kunqu virtuoso expressions and skills manifest themselves in five interrelated areas: (1) dramatization of Chinese experiences and values; (2) writing of literary scripts, and in particular poetic lyrics; (3) theorizing about kunqu features and issues; (4) valorizing and marketing the genre as a desirable expression; and (5) the transcendental performance practices of acting, chanting, dancing, singing, and speaking. None of these is unique to kunqu; what makes them exceptional is their seamless integration in the genre's past and present performances. Kunqu virtuosity involves much more than what audiences see and hear on the stage. In kunqu, much of the effort to pursue and deliver excellence takes place before and after the performance.

Chuanqi/kunqu dramas are purposefully constructed and interpreted. *Chuanqi* audiences/readers have traditionally savored stories that unfold in ways both expected and unexpected, crisscrossing historical and contemporary times with serious or playful episodes. A prime example of virtuoso kunqu storytelling is Tang Xianzu's (1550–1616) *Peony Pavilion*, which projects late Ming people's distinctive pursuit of human passion (*qing*) with a story about a Southern Song dynasty (1127–1279) woman who lives, dies, and is resurrected for love.[4] Kunqu scripts tell culturally and socially meaningful stories with literary words and dazzling acts of dancing, singing, costuming, and stage design. A prime example of such a kunqu script and its contemporary realization is the 2010 production of the *Dames in Love* (*Lianxian ban*). Presenting a story on heterosexual and same-sex love and marriage by Li Yu (1610–1680), the contemporary show not only entertained audiences with its fanciful costumes and sets but also spurred a thought-provoking debate about LGBTQ realities in historical and contemporary China.[5]

The virtuosity of kunqu storytelling/dramatic realization is most evident in its large repertory of *zhezixi*.[6] By the late 1760s, the genre had developed a repertory of at least 400 *zhezixi*.[7] By the 1870s, that repertory had expanded to more than 700 *zhezixi*.[8] As of today, the repertory has shrunk to around 300. Reflecting a variety of Chinese memories and desires, these inherited *zhexizi* tell archetypal Chinese stories,

---

4. "*Qing*" is a much-discussed topic in late Ming culture and history; for a scholarly description, see Martin W. Huang, "Sentiments of Desire: Thoughts on the Cult of Qing in Ming-Qing Literature," *Chinese Literature: Essays, Articles, Reviews* (*Clear*) 20 (1998): 153–184.

5. For an informative report on the production, see S. E. Kile, "Sensational Kunqu: The April 2010 Beijing Production of *Lianxiang ban* (*Women in Love*)," *Chinoperl Papers* 30, no. 2 (December 2011): 215–222.

6. A pioneer study on *zhezixi* is Lu Eting, *Kunqu yanchu shigao* (Shanghai: Wenyi chubanshe, 1980); see also Wang Ning, *Kunqu zhezixi yanjiu* (Hefei: Huangshan shushe, 2013).

7. See Qian Decang, *Zhui bai qiu* (1760s; reprint, Beijing: Zhonghua shuju, 2005).

8. Lu Eting, *Kunqu yanchu shigao*, 328–340.

such as "Taken Alive" ("Huozhuo")—a play about the ghost of a murdered woman returning to earth to take her former lover to the underworld; and "Zither Seduction" ("Qintiao)," in which a young scholar and a beautiful nun flirt with each other in the moonlit garden of a convent, taking turns playing *qin* (zither) music and testing each other's amorous intentions.

Following the genre's tradition of virtuoso storytelling, newly written and staged kunqu works dramatize contemporary Chinese lives and dreams, spurring vigorous debates. For example, the experimental kunqu opera *Earthquake at 14:28* (*14:28*) poignantly stages the suffering and survival the nation underwent in 2008. At 14:28 on May 12 of that year, a devastating earthquake struck Wenchuan in Sichuan Province,[9] killing or injuring more than 300,000 people. The following November, Shengkun premiered *Earthquake at 14:28*, a dramatization of Chinese people's suffering inside and outside the disaster area, with kunqu singing, speechifying, and a creative mix of traditional *shenduan* and contemporary acting and dancing. Since 2020, kunqu practitioners have created *zhezixi* and/or arias that dramatize Chinese struggles with COVID-19.

Chuanqi/kunqu dramatists/scriptwriters are master wordsmiths. They communicate Chinese emotions and experiences with both realistic and flowery words,[10] manifesting a variety of Chinese dramatic and rhetorical conventions and devices, which they have mastered through hard work and the persistent pursuit of excellence.

Figure 3.3: A "realistic" moment from *14:28*, when kunqu performers stare at a TV screen showing an earthquake victim crying for her lost. Courtesy of ShengKun.

---

9. Ke Jun, "Xie zai kunqu 14:28 yanchu zhi qian," in Gu Lingshen, *Yeben xiang liming: Ke Jun pingchuan* (Shanghai: Guji chubanshe, 2011), 162–163.
10. For an English description of *chuanqi* as dramatic literature and theater, see William Dolby, *A History of Chinese Drama* (London: Paul Elek, 1976), 71–156. For an insightful introduction to *chuanqi* drama, see Cyril Birch, "Introduction: To the Reader as Fellow Mandarin," in his *Scenes for Mandarin: The Elite Theater of the Ming* (New York: Columbia University Press, 1995), 1–20. For a literary-social account of *chuanqi* authors and scripts, see Guo Yingde, *Ming Qing chuanqishi* (Beijing: Renmin wenxue chubanshe, 2012). For a Chinese study of *chuanqi* performance practices, see Wang Anqi, *Mingdai chuanqi zhi juchang ji qi yishu* (Taipei: Xuesheng shuju, 1986).

Hong Sheng, the author of the *Palace of Everlasting Life*, for example, spent ten years perfecting the script of his drama, a sterling example of kunqu verbal virtuosity.

To achieve their dramatic goals, kunqu scriptwriters must somehow freely dramatize while abiding by the genre's conventions.[11] Kunqu performance scripts are built with alternating passages of prose and poetry. The former includes monologues and dialogues that realistically develop the dramatic action. To create dramatic realism, the texts often feature slang and dialects, which help locate the characters within specific ethno-geographic communities and/or social-political classes. For emotional moments, poetic texts are written as arias modeled after standardized *qupai* (aria patterns), that is, linguistic-musical patterns with relatively fixed verbal-linguistic-musical attributes. They include, for example, established rhyme schemes, fixed sequences of phrases with unequal lengths, and a "skeletal tune," the melodic contour of which cannot conflict with the linguistic tones of the words in the written lyrics. As expressions sung and heard, kunqu lyrics are only intelligible when the linguistic tones of their constituent words align with the melodic progressions with which they are vocally performed. Theories and practices of composing and singing kunqu aria lyrics with preexisting *qupai* melodies are vigorously discussed among kunqu practitioners and are realized by them in diverse ways.

Practitioners' oral and written debates have generated an intellectually formidable tradition of kunqu scholarship, one that manifests itself in the genre's seminal treatises. To name but a few, these range from Wei Liangfu's (fl. 1522–1573) historical *Qulü* (Principles of kunqu composition and singing) to Bai Yunsheng's (1902–1972) essays and insights on his performance experiences and Yu Zhenfei's (1902–1992) instructions and notated music for kunqu singing.[12] Each is a reminder that kunqu is very much a pursuit of musical and theoretical virtuoso excellence. This intellectual virtuosity is what makes kunqu stand apart from other historical and contemporary genres of Chinese opera.

Some efforts at theorizing about kunqu are clearly self-serving. This is particularly obvious with kunqu practitioners' valorization and marketing of the genre. Since early Qing, kunqu has been heralded as a *ya* (classical, elite) genre of Chinese opera. Defined narrowly, *ya* music refers only to court and ceremonial music; defined broadly, *ya* music includes kunqu and *qin* instrumental music, which Chinese elites claim as their own. In Confucian terms, *ya* music should be promoted, whereas its antithesis—that is, vernacular music (*suyue*) such as secular songs, dances, and operas—should

---

11. For a discussion of literary and dramatic conventions of kunqu scripts, see Li Xiao, *Kunqu wenxue gailun* (Shanghai: Wenhua chubanshe, 2014).

12. For two English translations of Wei's treatise, see Chen Fu-yen, "Principles of K'un-ch'ü Singing," *Asian Music* 8, no. 2 (1977): 4–25; and Koo Siu-sun and Diane Yue, *Wei Liang-fu: Rules of Singing Qu* (Hong Kong: Oxford, 2006). For Bai Yunsheng's essays, see Liu Yucheng, ed., *Bai Yunsheng wenji* (Beijing: Zhongguo xiju chubanshe, 2002); for Yu Zhenfei's prescriptions, see Richard E. Strassberg, "On Singing Techniques of K'un Ch'ü and Their Musical Notation," *Chinoperl Papers* 6 (1976): 45–81.

be dismissed.[13] By declaring kunqu to be a form of *ya* music, kunqu practitioners not only enjoy the genre without the risk of being stamped as libertines, but also use it to advance personal and social agendas. In late Ming and early Qing China, Li Yu (1611–1680) reported that some *nouveau riche* of his time had *ya* kunqu shows performed in their mansions, even though they neither understood nor enjoyed the genre's sophistication and virtuosity.[14] In early twentieth-century China, which was struggling to fend off the invasion of foreign cultures, including their music, kunqu was promoted as a classical and national opera, one that Chinese of the time needed to sustain in order to assert their national self. Today, kunqu is being marketed as a classical opera of China and as part of UNESCO's Intangible Cultural Heritage of Humanity.

Vigorous promotion of the genre has been an integral part of kunqu history. Indeed, some contemporary kunqu shows have become sensational hits in part as a result of successful advertising and publicity. A prime example of such a campaign was a stunt that ShengKun staged in 2006. It had young performers of its *1699 Plum Blossom Fan* ride the subway in their elaborate stage costumes and makeup. Their jarring presence in the newly built Nanjing subway system compelled commuters to wonder whether heavenly kunqu was relevant to their earthly lives.

Systematized Performance Practices and Materials

Kunqu's non-sonic and sonic aspects are largely stylized and self-explanatory. The non-sonic ones involve role-typing of characters, the costumes and makeup they wear, the stage design, and the execution of *shenduan*; the sonic ones include chanting, speaking, and singing of texts, as well as the playing of instrumental music. All were developed systematically in the past but are still to this day being creatively practiced and/or fine-tuned.

Kunqu involves set roles, which in turn set the standards for the genre's composition, performance, and reception. Each character "type" must perform according to established conventions; the more closely a performer abides by those conventions, the closer he can come to achieving an idealized image of the character he is playing and the more his performance will earn praise from critics. For example, a kunqu actor-singer enacting a *jinsheng* (a young commoner male) role will wear simple makeup and costume; he will act and dance in ways that cultural-theatrical China deems representative of such a character/man. In terms of his performance, he will speak and sing with a voice that constantly shifts between real and falsetto registers. Whatever and however he performs will be assessed according to models that master *jinsheng* performers have established. Kunqu role-typing is thus both limiting and

---

13. For further details about kunqu as *ya* music, see also Joseph S. C. Lam, "*Ya* Kunqu in Late Ming and Early Qing China," *Chinese Arts Quarterly* 6, no. 2 (2019): 68–94.
14. Li Yu, "Sizhu," in *Xianqing ouji* (Beijing: Yanshan chubanshe, 1988), 182.

A Heavenly Opera

enabling; it limits by setting clear criteria as to what and how actor-singers should perform; it enables by affording a framework within which performers can develop their virtuosity and audience members can formulate their critiques.

Kunqu today has five basic categories and twenty-plus subcategories of role-types, encompassing a wide range of dramatic characters and offering many specific performance prescriptions. The five categories are: the male (*sheng*) role, the female (*dan*) role, the painted face (*jing*) role, the old male (*laosheng*) role, and the clown (*chou*) role. The male role is further divided into five subcategories:

1. Grand and authoritative men (*da guansheng*): emperors, high officials, and other powerful men in imperial China.
2. Scholar-officials (*guansheng*): learned and wise men holding various court-appointed positions.
3. Young male commoners (*xiaosheng; jinsheng*): handsome, talented, and romantic young men who will go on to have successful careers and privileged lives.
4. "Down and out" men (*qiongsheng*): men with neither power nor positions; many will, however, eventually become successful.
5. Martial men (*wusheng*): generals and/or heroes.

In addition to the above male roles, there are boys (*wawasheng*), who are often played by young actresses.

The old male role-type includes three subcategories:

1. Mature males (*laosheng*): senior and wise men who usually confront life issues other than those of romantic love.
2. Male sidekicks (*wai*): adult men who serve minor dramatic and narrative functions.
3. Subordinate men (*fumo*): manservants or other socially marginalized male characters.

The female role-type is divided into five subcategories:[15]

1. Old women (*laodan*): nurturing mothers, and other senior and socially esteemed females.
2. Mature and married women (*zhengdan*): wives and women who are not romantically involved with any men.
3. Flowery women (*huadan*): beautiful young women pursuing love or being courted by men.
4. Young and supporting women (*liudan*): innocent and playful maids who serve *huadan* characters.
5. Martial women (*daomadan, cishadan*): female warriors or murderesses.

---

15. Theoretically, the *dan* role divides into six subcategories, which include the *zuodan*, boy characters enacted by actresses; the role is no longer considered a female role.

The painted-face role-type has three subtypes:

1. The fully painted-face role (*damian*): mature, martial, and usually righteous male characters.
2. The white-face role (*baimian*): treacherous and evil male characters.
3. The small white-face role (*xiao baimian*): supporting male and comical characters.

There are two types of clowns: the comical and harmless, and the evil and/or despicable. In addition to the above role-types/characters, kunqu features many soldiers, guards, palace maids, and passersby, whose stage presence is always brief and marginal. Collectively known as the corps (*longtao*), these marginal characters are played mostly by apprentices. With luck and hard work, some will graduate to perform as *xiaosheng* or *huadan*, the two primary kunqu role-types and dramatic protagonists. Those who distinguish themselves with transcendental skills become stars.

To enact role-typed characters, kunqu performers employ a battery of kinetic, material, musical, and visual performance practices and materials. Conceptually, all have been codified; in practice, each is creatively realized in different performances and by individual performers. For example, artistic directors and actor-singers use codified costumes and makeup designs as a base for their creative works and then collaboratively work out what specific characters in their shows will do and what they will look like. All details of their makeup, costumes, singing, and *shenduan* actions have to be fine-tuned to achieve the desired results.

The principles of makeup design are straightforward; their implementation is dynamic. Traditional designs, which symbolically project differences in characters' gender, age, social status, and emotional-intellectual attributes, will be consulted, emulated, and then judiciously adjusted during the long production and rehearsal process. For example, a clown is always marked by a white square painted on his nose. The size of the painted area is, however, creatively adjusted to match the eyebrows and other facial elements of the performer/character and to visually suggest his dramatic comicality.

The face of a tragic and/or evil character is routinely covered with white makeup. The whiteness of the face is, however, judiciously nuanced, as well as contrasted by facial elements in non-white colors. For example, Yang Guozhong, the abusive official whom rebels would lynch in the ShangKun production of the *Palace of Everlasting Life*, features an intensely white face with very black eyebrows and several lines of red and black "wrinkles."

Designing and donning kunqu costumes is an art that implements codified prescriptions.[16] Conceptually, kunqu apparel falls into four major types: (1) headgear;

---

16. A richly illustrated monograph on kunqu costume is Liu Yuemei, *Zhongguo kunqu yixiang* (Shanghai: Cishu chubanshe, 2010). Representative illustrations of kunqu costumes are available in Wu Xinlei, *Zhongguo kunqu dacidian* (Nanjing: Nanjingdaxue chubanshe, 2002); and Hong Weizhu, *Kunqu cidian* (Yilan: Guoli chuantong yishu zhongxin, 2002).

A Heavenly Opera 39

(2) full-length robes, half-length garments, and trousers; (3) shoes; and (4) handheld accessories. All are designed with symbolic colors and decorative patterns, and all are placed on actor-singers' bodies for specific dramatic meanings. For example, a performer playing an emperor holding court would wear ceremonial regalia. When he relaxes in private quarters inside the palace, he wears a full-body robe (*pei*). Martial and male *jing* performers appear on stage with their grand armor (*kao*) and headgear with two tall pheasant feathers. The feathers vibrate whenever the martial characters move, projecting their masculine vigor. Actors playing civil scholar-officials wear formal gowns (*guanyi*) in rank-appropriate colors. Performers playing down-and-out scholars wear their *fugui yi* (literally, a garment of the rich and noble), which is a long, dark dress with stitched-on patches. Buddhist monks, palace eunuchs, restaurant waiters, household servants, and other historically and socially distinctive characters wear role-specific costumes.

Performers playing imperial consorts and other elite female characters, for example, wear bejeweled headgear (*fengguan*) and fancy dresses that highlight their physical charms and elevated social status. Actresses playing abandoned wives or women in distress don plain dresses in subdued colors. Those who play young and innocent maids wear form-fitting dresses. Those enacting nuns wear a white and blue dress with a diamond pattern.

Costumes are integral to kunqu movements and dances. Many *shenduan* requires the virtuoso use of *shuixiu*—the term literally means long garment sleeves, which can be made to flow like water. To perform dramatically expressive and visually interesting *shenduan*, kunqu actor-singers swing their *shuixiu* in ways that kinetically extend their acting bodies and project their characters' emotions. Elegant *shenduan-shuixiu* acting renders kunqu kinetically, visually, and symbolically fascinating. In the "Nightly Rendezvous" ("Yougou") scene of the *Young Lovers*, for example, the male and female protagonists symbolically caress one another with their *shuixiu*, creating a virtuoso *pas de deux* of love.

Supported by elaborate costumes and makeup, kunqu artists use every part of their bodies to act and dance, generating a distinctive body language (*zhiti yuyan*).[17] Derived from everyday gestures, *shenduan* are, in principle, mimetic and thus self-explanatory. This is apparent with "entrance poses" (*liangxiang*), that is, the poses kunqu actors strike momentarily as soon as they enter the stage in a scene, revealing who they are and foretelling what they will do next. For instance, when military characters appear on stage, they pause by the *shangqiang* (stage entrance) and strike a martial pose, their limbs stretched out and the tall pheasant feathers on their headgear shaking.

---

17. For a richly illustrated study on Chinese opera actor-singers' craft, see Siu Wang-Ngai and Peter Lovick, *Chinese Opera: The Actor's Craft* (Hong Kong: Hong Kong University Press, 2014); see also Ding Xiuxun, *Kunqu biaoyan xue* (Nanjing: Jiangsu fenghua jiayu chubanshe, 2014).

Given that they are constituent gestures in kunqu acting and dancing, many *shenduan* poses and body movements have established names.[18] For example, *lanhua zhi* (orchid fingers) refers to the stylized hand and finger gestures that women characters make to project their feminine charms. Similarly, *guibu* and *aibu* refer respectively to the ways a female ghost and a male dwarf walk. *Guibu* presents a dead woman walking, her torso rigid and her feet gliding across the floor. *Aibu* dramatizes the short body of a male dwarf by having the performer stroll with a crouched torso and bent legs—a physically demanding but sensuously entertaining act.

Some *shenduan* are performed with realistic and/or symbolic props. For instance, a boatman steering his vessel would hold an oar-rudder. When passengers board his vessel, their bodies make rising and falling movements, suggesting the rocking of an boat. Similarly, when a character mounts a horse, he waves a symbolic horse crop (*mabian*), whereas those traveling by chariot hold embroidered panels with wheel designs. Battle scenes are marked by military flags and weapons. Kunqu generals usually fight with swords or spears. Their soldiers, by contrast, make martial gestures

Figure 3.4: A battle scene from a kunqu performance in Suzhou, 2014. Photograph by J. Lam, 2014.

---

18. For a checklist of codified *shenduan* with short explanations, see Wu Xinlei, *Zhongguo kunqu dacidian*. Many photographs and audiovisual recordings of contemporary *shenduan* performance and lecture demonstrations are published online.

A Heavenly Opera

and/or acrobatic somersaults, virtuoso movements that often win enthusiastic applause from the audience.

More subtle actions are performed to impress connoisseurs. For example, performers may roll their eyes or contort their faces to project characters' emotions. In the belief that eyes are windows onto human hearts and minds, kunqu artists have developed specific combinations of eyerolls and facial expressions to project all kinds of human emotions. One celebrated example of this is Zhang Jiqing's (b. 1941) "blank look," which portrays a madwoman's dreaming of her reunion with the husband she has forcefully divorced.[19]

In kunqu, such bodily expressions are most communicative when performed in intimate venues. This is, perhaps, why Ming and Qing kunqu venues were relatively small. As historically documented, an informal indoor stage might simply be an area covered by a piece of rug and flanked by a handful of spectators. Formal, outdoor stages were either stand-alone structures in gardens or other outdoor sites, or they were integral parts of large buildings. Such stages, which are now called *guxitai* (old stages), were open to the audience at the front, left, and right sides. The fourth (backstage) side had a backdrop and two doorways. The one on the audience's left was the *shangchang*, through which actors entered before striking their entrance poses. The one on the right was the *xiachang*, through which performers left the stage.

The kunqu *guxitai* is minimalist. Traditionally, it featured a table and two chairs, which besides serving as stage props symbolically marked the boundary between indoors and outdoors. Some *guxitai* were purposely built for musical performance; their elaborate ceilings helped project sounds. One such musical *guxitai* can be found within the Suzhou kunqu museum compound. Only a handful of *guxitai* built in historical China have been preserved and/or restored for contemporary performance. Many *guxitai* have, however, been recently built to satisfy nostalgia for kunqu.

Today, most traditional and contemporary kunqu performances are held on *modern stages* in cavernous auditoriums. These are open to the audience only at the front. Many such shows still feature the traditional minimalist set: one table and two chairs. Since the late 1970s, however, illustrative backdrops and realistic props have been coming into vogue. For example, the backdrop for the "Zither Seduction" scene in ShangKun's *Jade Hairpin* of 1985 was a painting of a moonlit treed garden, contextualizing the site where the protagonists play *qin* music to flirt with each other.

Until the early 2000s, kunqu lighting and sound projection involved flooding the stage with bright white light (*da baiguang*) and amplifying the performers with wired microphones and large speakers.[20] Since then, however, colorful spotlights, wireless microphones, sound mixers, elaborate speaker systems, and high-definition

---

19. For an audiovisual recording of Zhang's performance, see DVD attached to *Kunju Zhu Maishen xiuqi—Zhang Jiqing Yao Jikun yanchu banben*, ed. Lei Jingxuan (Hong Kong: Oxford University Press, 2007).

20. For a study on kunqu staging practices, see Ma Changshan, *Kunju wutai meishu gailun* (Shanghai: Shanghai wenhua chubanshe, 2017).

Figure 3.5: A historical kunqu stage in the Xiqu Museum compound in Suzhou. Photograph by J. Lam, 2012.

audiovisual recording units have become commonplace. This use of the latest staging and recording technologies has affected kunqu performances and their reception. For example, some *shenduan* are now choreographed and performed with close-up shots in mind. Some young performers rely on electronic amplification to compensate for weaknesses in their chanting and singing.

Modern stages have become more and more technologically advanced, and some have been transformed into *innovative stages*, where computer-assisted sounds and lights and tailor-made props are used to enhance the drama. For example, the innovative stage for ShengKun's *1699 Peach Blossom Fan* of 2006 featured a movable stage-on-stage and a semi-transparent backdrop.[21] The former facilitated rapid set changes. The latter, a giant reproduction of *Nandu fanhui jingwu tuquan* (A view of busy and prosperous Nanjing), intimated that the love story of the opera took place in Nanjing, the southern capital of late Ming China.[22] The age of virtuoso kunqu staging has arrived.

---

21. For further information about that distinctive stage, see Xiao Lihe, "Kunju *1699 Taohuashan* di yanchu kongjian ji wutai sheji shuoming," in Jiangsu sheng yanyi jituan, ed., *1699 Taohuashan: Zhongguo chuanqi dianfeng* (Nanjing: Fenghuang chuban chuanmei jituan, Jiangsu meishu chubanshe, 2007), 85–91.
22. For a brief discussion and images of the historical painting, see "*Nandu fanhui jingwu tujuan*," accessed January 15, 2021, http://old.chnmuseum.cn/Default.aspx?TabId=212&AntiqueLanguageID=220 &AspxAutoDetectCookieSupport=1.

A Heavenly Opera   43

But what integrates the verbal, visual, kinetic, and staging practices of kunqu into a heavenly performance is the music itself, which generates a sonically particularized time and site—an operatic mis-en-scène—on which actor-singers can bring characters alive. There, the performers as dramatized characters can theatrically interact with their audiences, negotiating each other's Chinese lives and dreams. Kunqu music performance practices and their sonic materials are traditionally divided into three related branches: (1) chanting and speaking (*nianbai*), (2) singing of arias (*chang*) and (3) playing of instrumental music.[23]

Though it mimics everyday communication, kunqu speaking is stylized and executed for operatic effects. Words are uttered as emotional exclamations, declarative comments, and expository monologues and dialogues. Kunqu chanting is similarly stylized. In theory, its melodies and musical contours are derived from the linguistic tones of the words delivered, and its rhythms are suggested by the scripted words and their syntactical structure. For example, in chanting the phrase "Bring wine here" (*qu jiulai*), the word "wine" (*jiu*) is performatively emphasized, while the directional verb and adverb of "to here"(*lai*) are melodiously and rhythmically drawn out. In practice, chanters creatively manipulate tones and rhythms to produce all kinds of expressive nuances.

Besides chanting and speaking, kunqu performers voice a variety of short oral/vocal expressions, ranging from calling names, laughing, and sobbing to affective utterances such as "*ah*," "*ei*," and "*ya*" and other vocables. When performed at the "right" moments and with the "proper" delivery, however, these vocables expose characters' feelings in ways that plain words cannot. In "Taken Alive" ("Huozhuo"), for example, the ghost of the murdered Yan Poxi calls her lover's name six times.[24] Each of these six is a sonically nuanced revelation of her changing emotions/actions, ranging from her tender love for him to her ruthless strangulation of him.

Kunqu oral delivery demands accurate and articulated elocution. Kunqu texts are meant to be vocalized according to Suzhou and dialectic pronunciation and/or Zhongzhou yun (Central Plain Tones and Rhymes), a historical system for pronouncing Chinese words that kunqu performers have preserved as a stage and musical language. To chant and speak at desired linguistic-musical pitch levels, many performers take as a reference the pitch of the small gong (*xiaoluo*), which is close to "A" (440). Given their communicative functions and improvisatory nature, kunqu speaking and chanting demand virtuoso skills and careful creative choices. Some kunqu practitioners suggest that if the artistic value/challenge of speaking and chanting weighs a thousand pounds (*jin*) of gold, that of singing is worth only "four ounces" (*liang*).

---

23. For an insightful introduction to kunqu music, see Fu Xueyi, *Kunqu yinyue xinshang mantan* (Beijing: Renmin yinyue chubanshe, 1996).
24. See Joseph S. C. Lam, "Musical Wantons, Chauvinistic Men, and Their Kunqu Discourse in Traditional China," in *Wanton Women in Late Imperial China*, ed. Wu Cuncun and Mark Stevenson (New York: Brill, 2017), 83–104; see esp. 94–102.

Setting aside such hyperbole, aria singing is still the core of kunqu performance and reception.[25] Kunqu's sung arias are heavenly, and their musical virtuosity is unmistakable. As performed sound, kunqu melodies are rhythmically regulated by *ban* and *yan* strokes. The singular *ban* strokes, which are played with wooden clappers (*ban*), are traditionally categorized as:

1. The beginning stroke (*touban*), which begins either a sung passage/aria or a rhythmic cycle that is repeatedly performed to structure kunqu music;
2. The ending stroke (*diban*), which marks the end of a sung phrase or aria;
3. The regular stroke (*zhengban*) which marks the beginning of a rhythmic cycle; and
4. The waist stroke (*yaoban*), which marks a tone sung with syncopated rhythm or at the midpoint of a rhythmic cycle/measure.

Yan strokes are played on a skin-covered wooden drum (*danpigu*). Alternating sequences of *ban* and *yan* strokes beat out pulses of the music being sung, generating rhythmic cycles that can be compared to metric measures in Western music. Besides regulating *yan* beats, rhythmically florid drum patterns can be played between *ban* and *yan* strokes to sonically "push" the melodies being sung.

Kunqu arias/sung phrases are regulated by five types of standardized rhythmic cycles:

1. The *sanban* (free *ban* strokes): a nonmetered and flexible rhythmic structure marked by the beginning and ending *ban* strokes; first phrases of long arias are usually sung with *sanban* rhythms.
2. The *liushuiban* (continuous strokes): a nonmetric rhythmic structure marked by a steady playing of clapper and/or drum strokes; it usually appears with narrative arias performed to quickly deliver a large amount of information about dramatic situations or actions.
3. The *yiban yiyan* (alternating clapper and drum strokes): a rhythmic cycle with alternating clapper and drum strokes; comparable to 2/4 time in Western music, it provides a steady rhythmic foundation for lyrical and narrative singing.
4. The *yiban sanyan* (one clapper and three drum strokes): a rhythmic cycle marked by recurring sequences of one *ban* and three *yan* strokes; not unlike 4/4 time in Western music, the rhythmic structure provides a steady rhythmic foundation for lyrical and narrative arias.
5. The *zengban* (the added *ban* stroke): an extended and recurring rhythmic cycle of eight pulses, in which the *ban* is struck at the first and fifth beats of the pattern, and the *yan* strokes, at the other beats; not incomparable to 8/4

---

25. For a study on kunqu singing, see Tian Shaodong, *Kunqu yanchang yishu yanjiu* (Hangzhou: Zhejiang daxue chubanshe, 2013).

A Heavenly Opera

time in Western music, this rhythmic cycle is used for lyrical arias sung slowly and with florid melodies.

Kunqu arias are noted for their flowing melodies. All are craftily composed and structurally articulated by distinctive melodic progressions, melismas, vocal ornaments, rhythmic fermatas, and modal/tonal progressions and cadences. When expressively performed, kunqu arias are profoundly pleasurable. Yu Zhenfei, the doyen of late twentieth-century kunqu music, noted that singers use sixteen specific techniques to achieve a smooth, intelligible, finely nuanced performance.[26] Three basic techniques with readily discernible results are:

1. *"Daiqiang"*: sing a main melodic note, take a short break, and then either repeat the note or add an auxiliary note before continuing on with the melody.
2. *"Dianqiang"*: add a tone between two main melodic notes separated by a third or more, smoothing the melodic progression.
3. *"Souqiang"*: expand a melodic main tone into a series of three fast notes—the first is an upper auxiliary to the following main note, which is sung twice.

Kunqu instrumental music complements aria singing through the systematic use of instruments, tunes, rhythms, textures, and timbres. Conceptually, kunqu instrumental music is played by either the *wenchang* (the civil ensemble) or the *wuchang* (the martial ensemble). The *wenchang* instruments include the *qudi* (kunqu flute), *erhu* (two-string fiddle) or *tiqin* (kunqu fiddle), *pipa* (pear-shaped lute), *xianzi* (kunqu lute), *sheng* (mouth organ), *yangqin* (dulcimer), *zheng* (zither), and other melodic instruments. Leading the *wenchang* is the *dizi*, which plays practically the same melodies that actor-singers perform. Currently, the *dizi* often shares its role of supporting the vocal line with the *erhu*, the fiddle that has practically replaced the *tiqin* and today is playing more and more solo parts in kunqu instrumental accompaniment or incidental music. The other *wenchang* instruments continue to perform their traditional roles, providing idiomatic and heterophonic lines of sung melodies. For example, the *xianzi* and the *pipa* are plucked and strummed to generate rhythmic and textural push for the vocal lines being sung, and the *sheng* is blown to produce sustained tones, which help blend different sounds/timbres of *wenchang* instruments into rich, harmonious sonorities.

The *wuchang* features the shawm (*suona*), the wooden clapper, the skin-covered wooden drum, and a battery of cymbals, drums, and gongs in small, medium, and large sizes; collectively, the percussion instruments are called *luogu* (literally, gongs and drums). The *wuchang* plays a variety of codified rhythmic patterns (*luogu dianzi*) to articulate oral deliveries and *shenduan* actions. Representative patterns include those for ending a scene, embarking on a boat, and so forth. Coordinating the playing

---

26. Yu Zhenfei, "Xiqu yaojie," in *Zhenfei qupu* (Shanghai: Wenyi chubanshe, 1982), 1–33; see esp. 15–23. See also Richard Strassberg, "On Singing Techniques of K'un Ch'ü and Their Musical Notation," *Chinoperl Papers* 6 (1976): 45–81.

Figure 3.6: A traditional kunqu ensemble performing in Ann Arbor, Michigan, 2009. Photography by J. Lam, 2009. The musical instruments are: first row, from the left: *erhu*, *xianzi*, *sheng*, *dizi*; second row: *ban*, *danpigu*, and *yangqin*.

of instrumental music with the actor-singers' singing and dancing is the *gushi* (the clapper and *danpigu* player). His playing of *ban* and *yan* strokes regulates the pulses and tempi with which actor-singers pace their singing and *shenduan*. In traditional shows—especially those with small instrumental ensembles—the *gushi* doubles as the conductor; in contemporary shows that feature orchestras with thirty or more instruments/instrumentalists, he performs under the conductor's direction.

Traditionally, kunqu instrumental music is categorized according to its affective/dramatic functions;[27] these functions are classified as dance music, military music, auspicious music, sad/funeral music, banquet music, and religious music. Each type features unique sounds, which can be identified as fixed *qupai* tunes, distinctive rhythms, and characteristic timbres and textures. For example, military music played by the *wuchang* includes piercing *suona* melodies, robust rhythms, and drum and gong playing. By contrast, sad music features downward-gliding tones in melodies played on string and/or wind instruments. Contemporary kunqu instrumental music does not fall neatly into the six types listed above. Many new compositions of kunqu music

---

27. Zhongyang yinyue xueyuan mizu yinyue yanjiu suo, comp., *Kunqu chuida qupai* (Beijing: Yinyue chubanshe, 1956); Wu Jinya, *Kunju luogu* (Suzhou: Guwuxian chubanshe, 2009).

A Heavenly Opera   47

are composed and performed as overtures, interludes, and postludes, heralding or
echoing dramatic developments with symphonic changes of sonic dynamics, timbres,
and textures. As such, they resist essentializing labels.

The *Palace of Everlasting Life*: A Heavenly Entertainment

All five types of kunqu virtuosity described above appear in Hong Sheng's *Palace of
Everlasting Life*, a classic in the kunqu repertory.[28] Among its many realizations, the
2007 production by ShangKun is representative[29] and has been much discussed.[30] As
introduced in Chapter 1, Hong's *chuanqi* fictionalizes the historical romance between
Tang Minghuang and Yang Guifei. It is, however, not the first creative telling of that
romantic story as a microcosm of Chinese lives and dreams. Soon after the imperial
couple's death, their romance grew into a myth and a literary trope. Du Fu (712–770)
and Bai Juyi (772–846), two leading Tang poets, penned their accounts, which are,
respectively, "A Procession of Beauties" ("Liren xing") and "A Ballad of Everlasting
Regret" ("Changhen ge"). Bai Pu (1226–after 1306) retold the story in his *Raindrops
on Paulownia Trees* (*Wutong yu*), a Yuan drama that Hong Sheng consulted as a model
for writing his *chuanqi* of fifty scenes. It offers a sanitized account of the historical
love story, dramatizing Tang Minghuang and Yang Guifei as icons of Chinese lovers
torn apart by forces beyond their control. Hong underscores the lovers' humanity by
exposing their emotional interiors, contrasting their happy times with sad ones. Their
marital bliss abruptly ends when a rebellious lord, An Lushan (703–757), attacks the
capital, forcing them to flee for safety. On the way, the army escorting them stages
a rebellion, compelling the emperor to let Yang Kuifei kill herself for him and his
empire, a choice he regrets for the rest of his life. Hong's *chuanqi* ends with the lovers
reunited in heaven.

Since 1688, the year Hong finished writing the *Palace of Everlasting Life*, the
chuanqi has been continuously staged as a kunqu opera. A number of its scenes had

---

28. There is a substantive collection of Chinese and English writings on the drama. For two recent essays
in English, see Ayling Wang, "Music and Dramatic Lyricism in Hong Sheng's *Palace of Eternal Life*," and
Judith Zeitlin, "Music and Performance in Hong Sheng's *Palace of Lasting Life*," in *Text, Performance,
and Gender in Chinese Literatrue and Music: Essays in Honor of Wilt Idema*, ed. Mahiel van Crevel,
Tian Yuan Tan and Michel Hockx (Leiden and Boston: Brill, 2009), 233–262 and 263–292.

29. Hong Sheng's opera is analyzed as it is realized in this production and as it is preserved in a commercially available audiovisual recording: *Changsheng dian* by ShangKun, 4 DVDs, ISRC CN-AA02-08-
0056-0/V.J9. For the original text of the drama, see Hong Sheng, *Changsheng dian* (Reprint; Beijing:
Renmin wenxue chubanshe, 1983).

30. For essays on the 2007 ShangKun production, see Liu Zhen and Gu Haohao, eds., *Changsheng dian
kunju quanben chuangzuo pinglun ji: Chahe qingyuan yu lishi xingwang di shendu chengxian* (Shanghai:
Guji chubanshe, 2014); Xie Boliang and Gao Fumin, eds., *Qiangu qingyuan: Changsheng dian guoji
xueshu yantaohui lunwenji* (Shanghai: Guji chubanshe, 2006); Ye Changhai, ed., *Changsheng dian
yanchu yu yanjiu* (Shanghai: Wenyi chubanshe, 2009); Tang Shifu and Guo Yu, eds., *Changsheng dian
wutai liuying*/Memories and Images from the Shangkun Performance of the *Palace of Everlasting Life*
(Shanghai: Wenyi chubanshe, 2009).

become favorite *zhezixi* by the mid-1700s. With its poignant dramatization of the historical love story, and for the literariness and musicality of Hong's lyrics—which can be sung with little adjustment by composers and actor-singers—Hong's masterpiece appeals to all kinds of kunqu practitioners, be they actor-singers, critics, or fans.

The ShangKun production is a pragmatic realization of Hong's drama, selectively staging its core scenes and cherished arias. Since its premiere in 2007, it has elicited different responses. Witnessing the consort's tragic fate dramatized by Hong, some traditional Chinese women would lament that such was/is their lot. Responding to the Shangkun production of the drama, some contemporary and feminist audiences challenge the chauvinistic messages of the historical romance. A senior female *huadan* performer, for example, once confided to this author that she did not like the way Yang Guifei dies in the drama. She asked what was wrong with a woman monopolizing her man's love. Challenging the traditional notion that Yang was a femme fatale, she enacted the consort as a truly feminine and innocent woman.

To illustrate the expressive and virtuoso performance that ShangKun has staged, analyses of three seminal scenes in the production will suffice.[31] The first is "A Garden Party; Shocking News," the fifth scene of the third evening of the ShangKun production. It marks the turning point in the love story, when the imperial couple's happy life is torn asunder by the rebels' siege of the capital. The scene unfolds with three episodes and nine rounds of speeches and arias.[32] Episode 1, flanked by Arias 1 and 3, sets up the autumnal time and scenic site of the garden party, where the emperor and his consort tenderly interact, revealing their genuine love for each other. Episode 2, anchored by Arias 4 and 6, features the imperial couple's indulgent games of flirting, drinking wine, and her dancing for him. Episode 3, framed by Arias 7 and 9, begins with an abrupt and alarming drumroll and ends with a terrified emperor wondering how his delicate consort will survive the court's retreat to the safe but faraway land of Sichuan.

The scene realistically portrays Chinese experiences and sentiments with poetic lyrics, touching music, and suggestive *shenduan*. The lyrics for Aria 1, for example, poetically project a romantic landscape. A translation:[33]

> Leisurely clouds drift through the pale-blue sky;
> Wild geese fly past in long rows.
> Inside the imperial garden, autumn colors are in full blossom:

---

31. For English translations of the scene scripts, see Yang Hsien-yi and Gladys Yang, trans., *Palace of Eternal Youth* by Hong Sheng (Beijing: Foreign Languages Press, 1955), 142–147, 188–195, and 228–238; Ben Wang, *Laughter and Tears: Translation of Selected Kunqu Dramas* (Beijing: Foreign Languages Press, 2009), 336–351 and 358–396.

32. Dramatic structures of Hong's drama, such as the number of arias, their appearance order, and their alternation with oral deliveries in individual scenes/*zhezixi*, will be analyzed as what the dramatist has scripted. Discrepancies between his script and the ShangKun production will be identified whenever they are pertinent to discussion.

33. Unless noted, English translations of Hong Sheng's lyrics presented in this chapter are adjusted versions of renditions by Yang Hsien-yi and Gladys Yan, and Ben Wang, cited earlier.

A Heavenly Opera 49

The willows' leaves have gained more yellow;
The duckweeds have lost a bit of green;
And the red lotus flowers have shed some petals.
By the long craved railings,
The blooming cassia flowers emit a pure and sweet fragrance.

Poetically, the lyrics describe emotions and experiences that Chinese literary readers and kunqu audiences know well: as beautiful as an autumn blossom/love is, it will soon wither! What the lyrics tell and evoke are rendered unmistakable by the performers' exquisite *shenduan*. For example, when Zhang Jingxian (b. 1947), who performed the Yang Guifei role, sings the second line of Aria 1, which describes geese soaring in the clear autumnal sky (1'40"–1'44"),[34] she tilts her head to look up at the sky and uses her right hand and fingers to guide audience attention/imagination to the flying birds. Similarly, when she and Tang Minghuang—as enacted by Cai Zhengren—sing Aria 2 (3'20"), they dance a *pas de deux*, enacting their stroll in the garden, exchanging words about the beautiful view they find, and gazing tenderly at each other. And to choreographically underscore the emperor's love for the charming consort, she does a *shenduan* of tripping (6'51"), so that he will do a *shenduan* of trying to prevent her fall. Throughout the scene, she sometimes crouches or swings, making her body look femininely delicate and her man look tall and strong.

The most entertaining *shenduan* in the scene are, however, those for drinking wine and holding emptied glasses high and bottoms up (10'24"; 16'08"–18'30"). As scripted and as performed, the emperor urges his beloved to drink more than she can hold, so that she becomes intoxicated, blushes, gets sleepy, and loses her courtly posture, thus making her physical beauty more striking. Being a responsive lover, she takes the chance to tease him back, flaunting her beauty and arousing his desire. As performed by Cai and Zhang, the game of flirting and drinking wine in the scene is kunqu performance and discourse at its best. It is an expressive and virtuoso performance that projects "entertaining but not licentious" (*le er bu yin*) Chinese intimacy. As dramatized, the game ends abruptly—and the second and tragic part of the scene begins unexpectedly. As the intoxicated Yang Guifei is being escorted out of the garden, a drumroll announces news of An Lushan's attack on the capital. This spurs Tang Minghuang into an emotional turmoil of anger, fear, and powerlessness, which Cai projects with wide-open eyes, drooping shoulders, and fallen limbs (22'29"–28'16").

---

34. The recording/performance times listed here specify the spots where the analyzed kunqu arias and *shenduan* can be located in the DVD recording of the 2007 performance, which is *Changsheng dian* by ShangKun, 4 DVDs, ISRC CN-AA02-08-0056-0/V.J9. Currently there is no online and complete audiovisual clip of the performance. With adjustments within 15 seconds, however, the times can be used to locate the same dramatic spots in online audiovisual recordings of the 2018 performance: *The Palace of Everlasting Life (Changsheng dian)*, 2018 version, by ShangKun, accessed May 16, 2021, Book 1, https://www.youtube.com/watch?v=qTzPhRUTnxQ&t=229s, Book 2, https://www.youtube.com/watch?v=28-5frwFYP8&t=7201s, Book 3, https://www.youtube.com/watch?v=Xjwr6xl28XM&t=4892s, Book 4, https://www.youtube.com/watch?v=xAUw7rFLn-4&t=267s.

Figure 3.7: An imperial couple partying: Tang Minghuang (Cai Zhengren) and Yang Guifei (Zhang Jingxian) toast one another in a ShangKun performance of "A Garden Party; Shocking New." Source: Tang Shifu and Guo Yu, eds., *Changshen dian wutai liuying* (Shanghai: Wenyi chubanshe, 2009), 107.

Yet what makes the *shenduan* dramatically affective is the vocal and instrumental music played in Episode 2. An example is the performers' chanting of the emotive words "please" (*qing*) and "bottoms up" (*gan*): with gliding tones and extended rhythms, these quotidian words become touchingly revealing. Accompanying the performers' musical utterances and *shenduan* are judiciously played *luogu dianzi* that sonically articulate their dramatic actions and expressions.

The arias in the scene are skillfully crafted literary-musical compositions. As demonstrated by Music Example 1, Aria 1, "Pink Butterfly" ("Fendie'er") is a through-composed song (1'07"). Its melodic melismas and pillar pitches expressively align with keywords in the lyrics—the *dol* and *mi* tones in the pentatonic scale of the tune articulate verbal phrasing and division. The wide range of the melody—an octave and a sixth—and the leisurely tempo of its performance sonically evoke the expansive landscape of the imperial garden. The high D and the low F# showcase the singers' masterful control of their voices.

Aria 5 of the scene projects the lovers' playfulness and Hong Sheng's literary-musicality (14'47"). Composed with reference to the *qupai* named "Fighting Quails"

A Heavenly Opera 51

("Dou anchun"), its lyrics feature extensive use of padding words (*chenzi*). Structured into verbal-musical units of three words/tones/rhythms—"*xiao yinyin*" (laughing and purring)—in which the first is accented and long and the second and third are short, light, and repeated, the units invite realizations with playful staccato sounds. Hong uses the same verbal-musical device in Aria 8, a noisy scene of soldiers fighting and commoners fleeing (unfortunately, this aria is skipped in the ShangKun production). Set to onomatopoetic words of war drums being struck and people falling and clashing with one another, the verbal-musical units of "long-short-short" render Aria 8 a dramatic contrast to Aria 5. The contrast is a testimonial to Hong's virtuoso skills at creating dramatic continuity and development. It is no accident that "A Garden Party; Shocking News" has long been a favorite *zhezixi* in kunqu; its appeal is self-explanatory and unmistakable.

Compared to "A Garden Party; Shocking News," "Lamenting" ("Kuxiang"), the fourth scene in the fourth book/show of the 2007 Shangkun production, is a very different type of dramatic-musical kunqu *zhezixi*. Structured as a sequence of three episodes and nineteen arias, "Lamenting" showcases virtuoso kunqu singing.[35] Episode 1, which goes up to Aria 6, shows Tang Minghuang regretting having left Yang Guifei. Episode 2, flanked by Arias 7 and 9, begins by introducing the imperial procession that escorts her statue to a newly built temple and ends with the emperor asking why she does not respond to his calls. Episode 3, which starts with Aria 10 and ends with Aria 19, tells how the old and mourning emperor makes three offerings of wine to the deceased consort, then finds tears falling from the eyes of her wooden statue. The teardrops highlight the traditional Chinese belief that sincere words and emotions can move even inanimate objects—heaven, earth, and people, or the supernatural, natural, and human, are inseparably linked in Chinese cosmology.

Despite being an abridged presentation of Hong's script, the "Lamenting" scene in the ShangKun production offers many opportunities for performers to showcase their virtuoso acting and singing, as well as their instrumental skills. As Episode 1 begins (0'0" to 1'49"), Tang Minghuang enters the stage, dressed in full regalia but appearing old and tired. Accompanying his entrance is a prelude featuring descending melodies played by the *dizi* (flute) and the *qin* (a seven-string zither) and isolated gong strokes. Kunqu connoisseurs will hear many "bitter tones" (*kuyin*), that is, downward-sliding pitches. Then the emperor chants a *shi* poem telling how he feels regret in his heart. Accompanied by *qin* music, the soft sounds of which are played to evoke the past, he delivers key words, such as "*jiaren*" (beauty) and "*nan*" (difficult), with affected tones, rendering their semantic and dramatic messages powerful. After the chanting, he delivers a monologue, explaining why he made Yang Guifei's wooden statue

---

35. The ShangKun production of 2007 performs only 12 of the 19 arias that Hong Sheng composed for the scene. Arias 2, 3, 7, 8, 9, 13, 16, and 18 are skipped for practical reasons, such as the limitations of performance time, the need to preserve performer's singing energies, and the need to gloss over dramatic and historical details, such as the traditional and ritual practice of three wine offerings, that contemporary and young audience might not understand.

and installed it in her new memorial temple (1'49" to 3'38"). Performing this monologue sitting on a chair—the only prop on the darkened stage—Tang Minghuang shakes his hand and fingers, accentuating the words he utters and the emotions he projects.

Many moments for performing coordinated sounds and *shenduan* appear in Episode 1 of the "Lamenting." Singing Aria 1 (3'44" to 5'27"), Tang Minghuang delivers many downward melodic phrases, which underscore his crying for the dead Yang Guifei. Performing Aria 4 (8'34" to 9'19"), he uses his *shuixiu* to wipe away his own tears. Shaking the same *shuixiu* up moments later, he projects his helplessness and hopelessness. To highlight keywords in the lyrics in Aria 5 (9'20" to 10'10"), he sings the *"fan"* ("offense") word in a rough tone, accompanying it with a throwing-up of his *shuixiu*—a gesture of failure and giving up. He then sings Aria 6, and closes Episode 1 by defiantly throwing his *shuixiu* up and to his right, asking how he can confront his regrets.

As Episode 2 begins (11'04"), Gao Lishi, the eunuch director, requests the emperor's permission to begin the procession of escorting Yang Guifei's statue to her temple. This procession presents a parade of palace maids dressed in beautiful costumes. As such, it makes not only "eye candy" for casual audiences craving visual delights, but also a repose that renders Tang Minghuang's crying in the beginning and ending of the scene more heart-rending. The procession is musical (12'15" to 13'55"): as Yang Guifui's statue is carried onto the stage, instrumental kunqu music is played. Then the palace maids and servants sing Aria 8 (12'40"), which concludes with another short postlude of drum and wind music. The procession is also theatrical: the statue is enacted by a female performer, who remains expressionless and motionless throughout the scene. Her "silent" act intrigues audiences and underscores the nature of performance virtuosity in kunqu. A living person enacting a lifeless wooden statue for thirty-some minutes is a performance stunt in itself! A wooden statue can be used in the scene, but there is no art or entertainment in that—some audiences find it thrilling to watch out for moments when the actor might blink or twitch. Episode 2 ends with a pantomime of installing the statue amid slow, plaintive incidental music (15'50" to 17'33").

Episode 3 of "Lamenting" begins with Tang Minghuang singing Arias 10 and 11 (17'34"to 21'40"), recalling how he and Yang Guifui pledged their love to each other in the past, and commenting on how they are now separated by life and death. Then Tang Minghuang begins his offerings of wine to Yang's statue. As he finishes the offering, he notices that the statue is shedding tears. He immediately points this out to Gao Lishi and the palace maids (23'14") and orders them to pay homage to the deceased consort. Accompanied by incidental music, they cry, kneel in front of the statue, and recall how graceful and kind she was. Episode 3 ends with Tang Minghuang singing Arias 17 and 19, while the palace maids and servants begin the return procession to the palace. The scene ends with a soulful *qin* solo.

A Heavenly Opera

Dramatic, literary, and musical virtuosities permeate "Lamenting," as Arias 4 through 6 eloquently demonstrate (see Music Example 2). Translated, its confessional lyrics run as follows.

Aria 4, "Taking the Cloth Shirt Off."
I cover my face in shame and sorrow.
I could not save my flowery beautiful consort.
It is my fault that I did not make the right decision.
It was wrong that I let her go so easily.

Aria 5, "Short Liangzhou"
Had I shielded her with my body,
The army might not have dared to attack me, the emperor.
But even if they had stuck me down, so what?
That would have at least kept me and my lover together.

Aria 6, "Short Liangzhou"
Now I live on alone, with a healthy body,
Without any happiness or pride,
But lines and lines of teardrops,
And sad faces.
In earth or heaven,
How can I stop this sadness and regret?

Through-composed songs derived from respectively the *qupai* of "Taking the Cloth Shirt Off" ("Tuo bushan") and "Short Liangzhou," the three arias demonstrate kunqu musicians' virtuoso alignment of *qupai* melodies, linguistic tones, literary expressions, and singing skills. Anyone who speaks Chinese and listens closely to the arias being sung will notice that the melodic contours closely coordinate with the rise and fall of the linguistic tones of the words in the lyrics. And by listening closely, she will also notice how rhythmically emphasized notes fall on the keywords of the lyrics, while modal cadences articulate rhymed words at the ends of phrases. And by tracing when and how an actor-singer judiciously accelerates or decelerates rhythmic pulses and tempi in the arias, kunqu connoisseurs can readily see/hear how Tang Minghuang comes alive on the stage.

Kunqu practitioners realistically perform and negotiate their Chinese lives and dreams on stage, a fact that the "Ballad Singing" ("Tanci") scene in Hong's drama attests.[36] Performed as the fifth scene in the fourth book/show of the ShangKun production, the *zhezixi* presents Li Guinian, a former court music director who survives the fall of the capital as an itinerant balladeer. He performs at temple bazaars, entertaining audiences with narrative songs about the love of Tang Minghuang and Yang

---

36. For further discussion about the scene and its creation, reception, and musical expressions, see Joseph S. C. Lam, "A *Kunqu* Masterpiece and Its Interpretations: *Tanci* (The Ballad) from Hong Sheng's *Changsheng Dian* (*Palace of Everlasting Life*)," *Chinoperl: Journal of Chinese Oral and Performing Literature* 33, no. 2 (December 2014): 98–120.

Guifei. In terms of structure, the scene unfolds with three episodes and twelve arias, nine of which constitute a set of variation arias (*jiqu*). As such, the scene is not only a masterpiece of kunqu dramatic and literary-musical composition but also a showcase of kunqu vocal performance.

The "Ballad Singing" makes a kunqu *zhezixi* par excellence for four reasons. First, Li Guinian, the balladeer, is a convincing character. He was historically known; he actually served the imperial lovers, and he witnessed the imperial romance; thus he could relate it as it happened. Second, the scene creates a dramatic-cultural-historical context to help audiences engage with the dramatic moment that Hong Sheng has authentically constructed. Just as he describes in the scene, Chinese in Ming and Qing times enjoyed ballad singing at ritual-social bazaars held outdoors around temples. Third, the scene creates an excuse for singing a long sequence of arias, with a minimum of *shenduan* dancing. Chinese balladeers sing and do not do elaborate *shenduan*! And being the only person singing, the performer of Li Guinian cannot bodily enact the multiple characters his lyrics reference. He needs to sonically bring them alive on stage. Fourth, the scene unfolds with its own *mis-en-scène*, one inhabited by five dramatic characters, and one that draws audiences into its operatic world. The characters personify five traditional Chinese archetypes—the intellectual elite, rich merchants, scholarly connoisseurs, simpletons, and female entertainers. The five characters render the staged ballad singing recital dramatically dynamic and realistic. They ask the balladeer questions that prompt him to sing songs describing more and more about the imperial lovers. Their responses to the songs shape the audience's responses to the arias the balladeer sings. For example, the simpleton's offer to take care of the courtesan who wonders if she will suffer like Yang Guifei did appeals to all who wonder what the future will hold. The offer is, however, instantly crushed by the rich and arrogant merchant, and this dramatic moment theatrically underscores gendered and economic fissures in historical and contemporary China.

The literary, narrative, and performative virtuosities the "Ballad Singing" scene demonstrates have to be experienced in situ—verbal descriptions can hardly do justice to their artistic meanings and operatic sophistication. To underscore the superlative creativity and skills involved in the scene's composition and performance, however, an analysis of the set of nine variation arias—Arias 3 through 11—will suffice. The arias are composed with reference to the same *qupai*, named "The Peddler" ("Huolang'er"), and they share some modally similar melodic phrases, codified melodic ornaments, and structurally required cadences (see Music Examples 3 and 4). As sung and heard sounds, the arias are, however, melodically quite different—to an uninformed audience, their musical connections are opaque. Only those who have studied the arias in great detail, and who are familiar with theories about kunqu *qupai* and compositional practices, will be able to specify how the arias are musically related.

Nevertheless, most audiences will hear that the music dramatically develops the scene of "Ballad Singing," affording them a soundscape to vicariously "witness" and negotiate what the imperial romance signifies. What and how kunqu practitioners hear and debate defies reductive analysis and description. It is, however, broadly comparable to what and how Chinese gardens are "read" by traditional aesthetes—kunqu practitioners claim that their genre shares with Chinese gardens something fundamental to Chinese aesthetics and sensitivities.[37] Meticulously designed and built, Chinese gardens are made to look "naturalistic," just as kunqu arias are "naturally" composed according to the rise and fall of the linguistic tones of the words in the lyrics. Just as garden connoisseurs know and can pinpoint underlying structures/patterns in gardens, kunqu connoisseurs can hear and identify the *qupai* with which individual kunqu arias or sets of variation arias are composed. However, neither Chinese garden nor kunqu connoisseurs care to direct their appreciative attention to how different gardens/arias are structurally patterned and/or related; they enjoy the gardens/arias by finding out how they look/sound as distinctive expressions—their shared structural patterns/elements are not ignored, but they are hardly the foci of appreciation. The arias in "Ballad Singing" are enjoyed more as individual arias and less as a set of variations.

Epilogue

Since 2007, ShangKun's *Palace of Everlasting Life* has been repeatedly performed. With each performance, some obvious and not so obvious adjustments have been made. All are necessitated by specific changes in the cast or contextual demands. All combine to make the productions fresh and appealing, each in its own way. It is no exaggeration to say that as ShangKun continuously fine-tunes its realizations of Hong's drama, it makes the opera more and more meaningful; and with each production, the performers polish their acting, dancing, and singing more and more meticulously. Thus, ShangKun's *Palace of Everlasting Life* makes a heavenly entertainment that stands apart from all other contemporary realizations of Hong Sheng's drama. For example, no one would mistake any of the sounds or images of the 2007 Shangkun production with those of the 2004 Sukun production directed by Gu Duhuang and performed by Wang Fang and Zhao Wenlin.[38] The latter makes heavenly kunqu with its own virtuoso performance practices and materials.

---

37. For an analytical study of Chinese gardens, see Francis Wood, trans., "The Traditional Gardens of Suzhou" by Li Dunzhen, *Garden History* 10, no. 2 (Autumn 1982): 108–141.
38. An audiovisual recording of the show is *The Palace of Everlasting Life* (*Changsheng dian*), 2004, by *by Sukun*, accessed May 15, 2019, https://www.bilibili.com/video/av12636683.

Figure 1.2: A curtain call by ShangKun performers of the *Palace of Everlasting Life*, 2018. Photograph by J. Lam, 2018.

Figure 4.1: A performance of the "Strolling; Dreaming" by children kunqu performers of Qiandeng, Jiangsu Province, China. Photograph by J. Lam, 2015.

Figure 4.2: A dance scene from the "Strolling; Dreaming" in the *Young Lovers*. Photograph by J. Lam, 2014. Courtesy of Shen Fengying and SuKun.

Figure 5.2: Zhao Kuangyin and Jingniang in the *Escorting Lady Jing Home*. Photograph by J. Lam, 2014. Courtesy of Shen Guofang and Tang Rong.

Figure 6.2: A parade of beauties, a historical painting as stage backdrop, and a movable stage-in-stage in the *1699 Peach Blossom Fan*. Courtesy of ShengKun.

Figure 7.2: Pan Bizheng flirts with Chen Miaochang in a ShangKun performance of "Zither Seduction" in New York. Photography by J. Lam, 2011. Courtesy of New York Kunqu Society.

Figure 10.2: A moment from "Dreams Long and Short." Photograph by J. Lam, 2015. Courtesy of Zhang Jun and Xu Sijia.

4

Kunqu

An Earthly Opera

Introduction

On December 30, 2005, Leehom Wang, a superstar of Asian-Chinese-Taiwanese popular music, released his "Beside the Plum Blossom" ("Zaimeibian"), a multimedia work of popular music and dance, which declared that young twenty-first-century Chinese do not have time to find love as *qingchun dianya* characters in the *Young Lovers* do.[1] On May 18, 2007, the Imperial Granary (Huangjia liangcang) premiered an abridged version of the *Peony Pavilion* at a historic Beijing building, a six-century-old imperial warehouse the company had recently refurbished as an entertainment complex.[2] The show catered to high-end tourists who wanted to experience privileged living in historical China. On September 9, 2010, Yang Xuejin, a Shanghai singer, performed the popular kunqu aria "Dark Silk Robe" ("Zao luopao") in the Golden Hall of the Musikverein in Vienna, accompanied by a full orchestra of Western musical instruments played by Viennese musicians.[3] The performance presented the kunqu aria as a sample of classical and historical Chinese music and Yang as a representative of Chinese musicality and femininity. Poignantly, the three events and many other similar happenings in contemporary China demonstrate, on the one hand, kunqu's artistic, cultural, and historical appeal, and on the other, how Chinese adjust the genre for practical purposes. For kunqu practitioners, the genre is more than a heavenly entertainment; it is also an earthly cultural heritage of China.

To discuss contemporary kunqu as a Chinese and earthly phenomenon, this chapter presents three accounts, detailing the genre's historical, intellectual, and performance dimensions. The first account sketches the practitioners' notions about

---

1. A recording of Wang's performance is accessible as "Zaimeibian," accessed January 20, 2020, www.youtube.com/watch?v=2YFDMXXf3ws.
2. See Colin Mackerras, "Performance Review: The Imperial Granary Production of *Mudan ting* (*The Peony Pavilion*)," *Chinoperl* 26 (2010): 209–216.
3. A DVD recording of Yang's concert is available as *The Lark from the East: Yang Xuejin Solo Concert at Vienna*; ISRC CMN-E02-12-318-09V-J6.

earth, which help justify their treatment of kunqu as malleable cultural capital/ heritage. The second account traces historical developments that gave rise to the genre's becoming a desirable source and effective tool for constructing a positive image of China. The third account relates a pragmatic narrative of kunqu history, one that not only historicizes the genre's past from Chinese and socialist perspectives but also drives nationalistic efforts to safeguard and develop the genre. Singularly and collectively, the three accounts demonstrate kunqu practitioners' performance and discourse of kunqu as Chinese culture, history, and personhood. To demonstrate their handling of kunqu as a malleable cultural heritage and an evolving genre of opera, this chapter analyzes three representative renditions of the "Strolling; Dreaming" scene from the *Peony Pavilion*.

Kunqu and Earthly Practices

As kunqu practitioners strive to objectively understand the genre's history and safeguard its repertory and performance practices, they work hard to develop the genre in ways that advance their contemporary Chinese agendas. Cognizant of the contradictions they face, most kunqu practitioners gloss over theoretical issues and focus on producing results that will serve their needs. To justify this approach, they evoke Chinese theories about heaven and earth.

In Chinese and philosophical discourse, heaven and earth are a cosmic pair of *yin* and *yang* forces, which constantly interact to shape human affairs. In everyday Chinese communications, heaven and earth often appear as a husband/father and wife/mother who are raising their children together. As the *yang*/father force, heaven is powerful but also authoritarian and rigid; as the *yin*/mother force, the earth is more accommodating, helpful, and practical. And it teaches its children to be practical. Traditionally, Chinese are taught to work hard and keep their feet on the ground (*jiaota shidi*). Should they need supernatural help, however, they can call upon the lords of the earth (*tudi gong*) and/or city gods (*chenghuang*), who appear in many kunqu dramas.

In imperial China, the earth is not simply the land where Chinese grow crops to feed themselves; it is also where the root of Chinese civilization and wisdom can be found. Chinese believe that by excavating these roots and learning from them, they will learn lessons and find materials for living successfully on earth in the present day. Prime examples of ancient roots serendipitously rediscovered, critically studied, and pragmatically packaged to serve contemporary China are the Marquis Yi Chime Bells, excavated in 1978. The discovery of those chime-bells has transformed Chinese understanding of their musical ancestors; it has also led to a "reconstructed" genre of ancient chime-bell music.[4] Chime bells are now commonly played in large kunqu orchestras, generating "ancient" sounds, and idexing the genre's historicity.

---

4. Many online audiovisual clips of Chinese music performance with chime-bells can be assessed with keywords like "ancient Chinese music," and "Zenghou Yi bianzhong."

Kunqu as a Cultural and Historical Root of Chinese Humanity

Twenty-first-century Chinese are confronting many challenges generated by painful memories of late Qing and early twentieth-century times. To come to grips with their recent history, Chinese people have had to ask: Who are they, and who do they want to be? How can they present themselves as *qingchun dianya*, or beautiful, civilized, and prosperous people within and outside China? What tools and evidence can they use to project Chinese culture and history in positive ways?

Chinese people harbor many anxieties about China and about themselves. Between 1839 and 1945, China lost many wars to the West, including the Opium Wars (1839–1842 and 1856–1860), the siege of Beijing by the Eight Nations Alliance (1900–1901), and the Sino-Japanese War (1937–1945).[5] Between 1840 and 1943, Guangzhou, Shanghai, and a number of coastal and inland cities operated as treaty ports that colonial governments ruled at the expense of Chinese sovereignty. By the 1930s, China had degenerated into a materially deprived and politically dysfunctional nation. Its pride as a civilization, a people, and a nation had collapsed.

To revive China, early twentieth-century Chinese strove to modernize their country and their culture. In the process, they renounced cultural and expressive practices from the past as obsolete and ineffective, while embracing Western ideologies and technologies as modern and productive. Between 1917 and 1921, the Chinese elite launched the May Fourth Movement, which generated a nationwide purge of native aesthetics and performing arts.[6] Chinese opera, which had been indispensable in Ming and Qing times, was declared outdated if not an actual hindrance to the nation's modernization.

In 1949, socialist China was established. Promptly, it strove to create revolutionary images/icons of Chinese people, such as Liu Sanjie, the commoner woman singer who outsmarts elite males, and Baimao nü, the young girl whose hair turns white after fighting with a landlord who abused her.[7] Personifying Chinese determination and capacity to deal with all kinds of difficulties, these revolutionary icons sharply contrasted with those now *personae non grata* in Chinese memory—despotic rulers, abusive officials, greedy landowners, layabout scholars, traitors, invaders from the West, and other corrupt and despicable persons.

---

5. For a general history of modern China, see Immaneul Hsu, *The Rise of Modern China*, 6th ed. (New York: Oxford University Press, 2000).

6. For a historical analysis of the movement, see Vera Schwarz, *The Chinese Enlightenment: Intellectuals and the Legacy of the May Fourth Movement of 1919* (Berkeley: Center for Chinese Studies, University of California, Berkeley, 1990).

7. For two insightful and informative articles on socialist China's construction of model personalities and icons, see Lydia Liu, "A Folksong Immortal and Official Popular Culture in Twentieth-Century China," in *Writing and Materiality in China*, ed. Judith T. Zeitlin and Lydia H. Liu with Ellen Widmer (Cambridge, MA: Harvard University Asia Center), 553–609; Alfreda Murck, "Golden Mangoes: The Life Cycle of a Cultural Revolution Symbol," *Archives of Asian Art* 57 (2007): 1–21.

The luster of revolutionary icons, however, did not last long. In the decade between 1966 and 1976, the Cultural Revolution generated massive turbulence throughout the nation. During those years, many Chinese experienced betrayal, injustice, humiliation, and even murder. To survive, some individuals turned against their loved ones; for others, especially the intellectual elite, suicide was often the only recourse to maintain their integrity. Many who suffered inhumane treatment began to wonder whether Chinese people were by nature barbaric, corrupt, and evil. Ironically, these negative views of Chinese people resonated with the racist labels that some nineteenth- and twentieth-century Westerners had imposed on Chinese people in general, and in particular on Chinese immigrants to the West. In some early twentieth-century and Western representations of China, such as the Fu Manchu novels and movies, Chinese were stereotyped as deceitful people hiding in opium dens. Even today, discrimination against Chinese people occasionally rears its ugly head in Hollywood movies and other international and popular media.

After the Cultural Revolution, China quickly set out to rebuild. In 1978, Deng Xiaoping launched a series of reforms (*gaige kaifang*) in China that triggered an economic, political, social, and technological transformation. Soon China was on its way to becoming a modern and prosperous nation. In the 1980s, China reinvented itself by learning from the West—again.

This soon had productive results, but new challenges promptly arose. Western ideals and cultural forms now flooded China. Popular music from Hong Kong, Taiwan, Japan, and the United States, for example, invaded mainland Chinese auditoriums and TV studios. Alarmed, some mainland Chinese intellectuals and officials began complaining about cultural and spiritual contamination (*wenhua wuran*; *jingshen wuran*).[8] Then in 1989, the Tiananmen Incident occurred, jolting Chinese confidence in their own humanity.

To restore confidence in their nation and their humanity, Chinese urgently needed to counteract painful memories of past horrors by highlighting what was beautiful, civilized, and noble in their culture and society. By the turn of the twentieth and twenty-first centuries, Chinese people's desire to present themselves in a positive light had grown powerful now that their country was on its way to becoming a prosperous modern nation; since 2010, it has boasted the second largest GDP in the world. Realizing their nation's newly acquired power and resources, Chinese people have made earnest attempts to display the past and present beauty, civility, and prosperity of their civilization.

In the process, they have unearthed many positive roots of Chinese culture and creativity, ranging from objects long buried in the ground, to calligraphy carved on Chinese lands, to memories preserved in manuscripts, paintings, and prints and/ or transmitted through rituals and the performing arts. An example is the newly

---

8. For an analysis of Chinese culture and politics in the 1980s, see Jing Wang, *High Culture Fever: Politics, Aesthetics and Ideology in Deng's China* (Berkeley: University of California Press, 1996).

An Earthly Opera   61

constructed Three Gorges Dam on the Yangzi River. Most tourists cruising the Yangzi and visiting the dam encounter a magnificent view of Chinese culture, history, and technology.[9] Less imposing than the river and its new dam, but equally influential in the Chinese search for positive roots, is a wealth of historical documents like those found in the *Siku quanshu* (Imperial Library). Here are preserved many images of beautiful, civilized, and productive Chinese people, one of whose glories is, needless to say, kunqu. In displaying talented scholars and charming beauties and their privileged lives on stage, the genre brings *qingchun dianya* ancestors alive. And with its virtuosic acting, dancing, and singing, the genre entertains both Chinese and non-Chinese audiences, generating all kinds of tangible and intangible profits for its practitioners.

A Pragmatic Narrative of Kunqu History

In other words, kunqu is a root par excellence of cultural and historical China, one that the genre's practitioners can use to inform on Chinese culture, history, and person-hood. Towards that goal, the practitioners explain the genre's rise and fall in ways that not only align with the nation's historical and modern development but also invigorate Chinese confidence in the genre and in themselves. The conventional history of kunqu the genre's practitioners recount to themselves and to their audiences does just these things. This conventional history can be labeled the *pragmatic narrative* of kunqu, a story that is still evolving with selective interpretations of historial facts and claims.[10]

A representative example of the narrative is *Six Hundred Years of Kunqu* (*Kunqu liubai nian*), from 2007, a CCTV documentary presented in both Chinese and English.[11] With attractive visuals, pleasing soundbites, established facts, and strategic interpretations, this documentary projects a panoramic view of the genre, highlighting Suzhou as the nexus of kunqu's development. Needless to say, the documentary was produced by a team of Suzhou artists, officials, and scholars, with generous support from the municipal and provincial governments.[12]

Viewed broadly, the pragmatic narrative constructs kunqu history along the following documented developments. In the mid-fourteenth century, a tradition of folk vocal music emerged in the Wu region of Jiangnan China; that tradition gave rise to a prototype of kunqu, a stylized genre of vocal music. By the late sixteenth century, the

---

9. For an ethnographic report on Chinese tourism along the Yangzi River, see Joseph S. C. Lam, "Chinese Music and Its Globalized Past and Present," *Macalester International* 21 (Summer 2008): 29–77.
10. For an authoritative account of kunqu development as Chinese music history, see Yang Yinliu, *Zhongguo gudai yinyue shigao* (Beijing: Renmin yinyue chubanshe, 1981), 856–978. For authoritative accounts of kunqu as Chinese opera, see Zhou Yibai, *Zhongguo xiju shi* (Beijing: Zhonghua shuju, 1953), 312–552; and Zhang Geng and Guo Hancheng, *Zhongguo xiqu tongshi* (Beijing: Zhongguo xiju chubanshe, 1981).
11. The TV documentary is accessible online as *600 Years of Kunqu Opera*, accessed May 15, 2021, https://www.youtube.com/results?search_query=600+years+of+kunqu.
12. The Suzhou bias of the TV documentary is so unmistakable that some critics have joked that it should be called the "Six Hundred Years of Suzhou Kunqu."

genre had become known as *shuimo qiang* (water-polished arias)—a term suggesting that kunqu melodies and singing are so finely polished that they flow like running water. By the mid-seventeenth century, kunqu had evolved into a nationally popular genre of opera and entertainment. Over the following century and a half, its repertory expanded rapidly and its performance practices became more and more sophisticated. Then, after the early 1800s, the genre began a gradual decline, losing audiences to more popular genres of opera and multimedia performing arts.

By the early 1900s, kunqu had sunk to its nadir. It could have died at that time, but it was resuscitated in 1921 with the launching of the Academy for the Teaching and Preservation of Kunju (Kunju chuanxi suo; hereafter the Academy). Launched in Suzhou by twelve kunqu patrons, this new school recruited a class of fifty-five students. Upon graduation, they became active kunqu performers in Republican China. After 1949, they became the genre's seminal pedagogues; their teaching in mid- and late twentieth-century China laid the foundation for contemporary kunqu composition and performance.

In the early 1950s, kunqu was rarely performed, a casualty of war and social-political unrest. Then in 1956, the genre was "salvaged" by a creative and politically significant show, the *Fifteen Strings of Coins*.[13] That show prompted the launching of seven national professional troupes/schools of kunqu. Over the following decade (1956–1966), a number of successful shows were produced, promising a bright future for the genre. This, however, was cut short by the Cultural Revolution, during which the troupes were forcefully disbanded and performances of kunqu were banned. But this did not kill kunqu; it was sustained clandestinely by a small community of dedicated professionals and connoisseurs. In 1978, shortly after the unrest ended, they strove to return the genre to the public. In the 1980s and 1990s, while they managed to put on some critically acclaimed shows, they failed to develop a national audience. Then in 2001, UNESCO declared kunqu a Masterpiece of the Oral and Intangible Cultural Heritage of Humanity, an international honor that prompted Chinese national and local authorities to support kunqu with official patronage and national resources. In the mid-2000s, a number of groundbreaking kunqu shows were performed, mesmerizing young Chinese operagoers and garnering praise from international audiences. By the late 2000s, six-century-old kunqu had become fashionable again in China.

As outlined here, the pragmatic narrative has been constructed with a wealth of documented and/or orally transmitted data as well as historiographic assumptions. Broad and nationalistic in nature, the assumptions generate pragmatic arguments. For example, kunqu practitioners assume that China has a continuous tradition of employing ritual and performing arts to negotiate cultural, social, and political agendas and that kunqu is integral to that tradition. The practitioners' assumptions are anchored by cultural memories and historical documents. In the *Classics of Poetry* (*Shijing*), for example, we find recorded a multitude of banquet and state sacrificial songs and dances

---

13. For further information on the work and its historical significance, see Chapter 8.

An Earthly Opera 63

that were performed in ancient China. The *Record of Music* (*Yueji*) posits that ritual, music, and law are all pillars of human societies.[14] Many Ming and Qing authors, describing kunqu performances as expressions of personal and communal lives,[15] have provided a wealth of documented facts about creative kunqu agents, seminal works, and transformative events. Examining data culled from dramatic scripts, biographies, historical writings, and theoretical treatises, historians paint the genre's past as a linear process of broad developments, glossing over performance practices and expressions that are too ephemeral to have been preserved with words.

Tracing the genre's provenance, the historians identify *zaju* (variety drama) and *nanxi* (southern drama) as immediate models. The former was a genre of Chinese theater that blossomed in Yuan China (1271–1368). It boasted a large repertory of literary and realistic scripts,[16] many of which became source materials for kunqu plays. Some traditional kunqu shows, such as the *Injustice Done to Woman Dou E* (*Dou'e yuan*) and the *Story of Guan Yu's Entering His Rival's Camp Barely Armed* (*Guan dawang dandou fuhui*), are based on Yuan drama scripts. *Zaju* is also the source of a number of foundational practices in Chinese opera, such as the structuring of scenes (*chu*) with suites of arias (*liantao*) and the systematization of role-types. The four *zaju* role-types—young male, young female, painted faces, and clowns—are continued and expanded in kunqu. *Zaju* arias, namely northern arias (*beiqu*), are one of the two repertories and styles of vocal arias that kunqu sings.

Nanxi, which first developed during the transition between the Southern Song (1127–1279) and Yuan dynasties, instilled in kunqu a practice of staging socially and politically sensitive stories. The genre began as a grassroots theater that commented on current events with freely structured songs and dances.[17] One of the earliest and best-known *nanxi* plays is, for example, the *Lute* (*Pipa ji*),[18] a dramatized negotiation of gendered roles and virtues in imperial China. Like *zaju*, *nanxi* bequeathed to kunqu a repertory of southern arias (*nanqu*) and a system of performance practices and materials. Historical records tell us that southern arias were sung in southern dialects and with flexible tones and rhythms. Traces of such musical flexibility are still noticeable in non-metric kunqu arias and recitations.

Regarding kunqu's musical provenance, the pragmatic narrative posits that the genre's immediate predecessors were the *sida shengqiang* (four grand operatic

---

14. For an English translation of *Yueji*, see Scott Cook, "'Yueji'—Record of Music: Introduction, Translation, Notes and Commentary," *Asian Music* 26, no. 2 (Spring–Summer, 1995): 1–96.
15. For representative samples, see Zhao Shanlin and Zhao Tingting, *Mingdai yong kunqu shige xuanzhu* (Taipei: Xiuwei zixun keji, 2014).
16. For a standard reference on Yuan drama, see Chung-wen Shih, *The Golden Age of Chinese Drama: Yüan Tsa-chü* (Princeton: Princeton University Press, 1976).
17. See Mei Sun, "Performances of *Nanxi*," *Asian Theatre Journal* 13, no. 2 (1996): 141–166.
18. For a translation of the drama, see Jean Mulligan, trans., *The Lute: Kao Ming's P'i-p'a chi* (New York: Columbia University Press, 1980). For a history of the drama's performance in the last 600 years, see Yang Baochun, *Pipaji di changshang yanbian yanjiu* (Shanghai: Sanlian shuju, 2009).

64   *Kunqu*

traditions) of mid-Ming China.[19] A *qiang* refers to a distinct repertory of vocal music and its performance practices.[20] Musical data about the four grand traditions are scarce: only a handful of historical notated scores have been preserved, and discussions about repertory and performance practices are sketchy at best. There are, however, many descriptions of the four *qiang* being widely sung all over mid-Ming China until the 1580s, when the kunqu *qiang* became dominant; supposedly, its melodies were more "flowing and florid" (*liuli*) than those of the other three.

Strategically, the claim highlights kunqu's musicality by collapsing complex cultural-musical events into a simple development, one that allows kunqu practitioners to aesthetically, and conveniently, rank their opera above others. Any scrutiny of available data about the four *qiang*, such as their names, which reference specific geographic communities, point to a web of entangled developments. *Yuyao qiang* refers to music of Yuyao County in Ningpo Prefecture, Zhejiang Province; *haiyan qiang*, to music of Haiyan County in Jiaxing Prefecture, Zhejiang Province; *Kunshan qiang*, to music of Kunshan County in Suzhou Prefecture, Jiangsu Province; and *yiyang qiang* to music of Yiyang County in Shangyao city, Jiangxi Province. In other words, if *Kunshan qiang* "rose above" the other three *qiang* as conventionally claimed, it won not only a musical battle but also a series of cultural and geographical competitions within the Jiangnan region.

This is clear from the limited evidence the pragmatic narrative presents to substantiate the rise of *Kunshan qiang*.[21] Reportedly, the first Ming emperor, Zhu Yuanzhang (1328–1398; r. 1368–1398), once summoned an old Wu area man to his court and asked him about songs sung in his hometown in the Wu dialect. Expediently, kunqu historians interpret the anecdote from a social-political perspective: they surmise that what the man sang must have been been musically sophisticated and nationally known; otherwise, the emperor would not have asked about it. And since the emperor ruled from 1368 through 1398, the meeting took place before the emperor's death. In other words, kunqu is at least six centuries old and had evolved into a sophisticated genre by the 1550s.

This account of kunqu's provenance is confirmed by another story uncovered in the 1960s. Reportedly, a commoner musician named Gu Jian helped develop a prototype of kunqu with a group of local artists in the mid-1300s.[22] A native of Qiandeng,

---

19. The claim has yet to be musicologically substantiated. The *locus classicus* on the rise of kunqu as southern arias is Xu Wei, *Nanci xulu*, in *Zhonggu gudai xiqu lunzhu jicheng*, vol. 3., 235–256. For a historical survey of the four traditions, see Liao Ben, *Zhongguo xiqu shengqiang yuanliu shi* (Taipei: Guanya wenhua shiye youxian gongsi, 1992); and Liao Ben and Liu Yanjun, *Zhongguo xiqu fazhanshi*, vol. 3 (Taiyuan: Shanxi jiaoyu chubanshe, 2003), 31–90.

20. In Chinese music theory and practice, repertory and performance practices are distinctive but inseparable: they constitute one another.

21. For a discussion of the anecdote and its incorporation in contemporary kunqu history, see Wu Xinlei, *Kunqu shi kaolun* (Shanghai: Guji chubanshe, 2015), 42.

22. For a scholarly account of the Gu Jian case, see Wu Xinlei, "Kunshanqiang xingcheng shiqi di Gu Jian yu Gu Ying," in *Kunqu yanjiu xinji* (Taipei: Xiuwei zixun keji, 2014), 472–488.

a small town about ten miles from Kunshan and forty miles from Suzhou, Gu Jian worked with Gu Dehui (1310–1369), a rich and proud Kunshan native who promoted southern aria, and left a collection of literary writings and reports about his cultural activities. The same group included Yang Tiedie, a flutist, and an unnamed musician who played musical accompaniment on the *ruan* lute. Though sketchy, this Gu Jian story makes a convincing argument about kunqu provenance and artistic excellence. Like the anecdote discussed previously, it points to historical provenance, approval by elite/imperial personages, and regional identities and functions, three standard criteria in Chinese and traditional assessment of operas. Realizing what the story is claiming, contemporary Qiandeng and Kunshan city authorities have been proudly promoting their towns as the birthplaces of kunqu. In Qiandeng, they have built a Gu Jian museum and invited kunqu devotees and tourists to visit.[23] Kunshan, a prosperous city in twenty-first-century China, has developed itself into a new center of kunqu activities;[24] KunKun, the local kunqu opera troupe, was founded in October 2015. And to commemorate Gu Dehui and his promotion of local arts and culture, a contemporary Kunshan tycoon, Shen Gang, has developed Yushan shengjing, a lakeside community of luxury villas in the Bacheng district of Kunshan; within the resort is his palatial mansion and garden, where he has been hosting kunqu performances and conferences since 2007.

Gu Jian is not the only kunqu ancestor whose biography, or hagiography, has driven the pragmatic narrative of the genre. Before the Gu Jian story was uncovered, kunqu practitioners worshipped Wei Liangfu (fl. 1522–1573) as a *qusheng* (sage) of aria. They still do, asserting that he developed the contemporaneous composition and performance of arias into a virtuoso practice that would later define kunqu as we now know it.[25] A medical doctor by profession, Wei lived in Taicang, a town about thirteen miles from Kunshan and forty miles from Suzhou. There, he allegedly holed himself up in his studio for ten years to work out compositional and performance practices, which he described in his *Qulü* (Principles of kunqu composition and singing).[26] Wei did not, however, leave any notated examples of his music.

Wei's creative work was triggered by his own personal desire and made possible by contextual forces, the pragmatic narrative reports. A southerner, he realized that he could not sing northern arias like a native, but he could transform the northern and southern arias he had learned into something musically distinctive, something that he could claim as his own. He achieved his goal by learning from different musics

---

23. Some skeptics have questioned whether the Gu Jian story has been promoted by contemporary Qiandeng and/or Kunshan authorities and personalities.

24. For a study of kunqu in Kunshan, see Chen Yi, *Zhengsheng jibaisui*, in *Kunshan chuantong wenhua yanjiu kunqu quan*, Vol. 1 (Shanghai: Renmin chubanshe, 2009).

25. For an analytical account, see Hu Ji and Liu Zhizhong, *Kunqu fazhan shi* (Beijing: Zhongguo xiju chubanshe, 1989), 54–61.

26. Wei Liangfu, *Qulü*, in *Zhong guo gudian xiqu lunzhu jicheng*, vol. 5, 1–14. For an English translation, see Koo Siu-sun and Diana Yue, *Wei Liangfu: Rules of Singing Qu* (Hong Kong: Oxford University Press, 2006).

and musicians performing in Taicang, a port where northern and southern Chinese peoples, cultures, and trades converged in sixteenth-century China.

Based on circumstantial evidence, the pragmatic narrative asserts that two Taicang musicians greatly contributed to Wei's success. The first was Guo Yunshi, a local music critic, whose suggestions for improvement Wei would seek. The second was Zhang Yetang, a soldier and a renowned singer of northern arias from Shouzhou, Anhui Province, who was dispatched, as a punishment, to Taicang. Having recognized Zhang's talents, Wei made him a son-in-law and a music collaborator. Supposedly, it was Zhang who developed the *xianzi*, a small lute, for accompanying kunqu singing. Its plucked sounds support Wei's elegant tunes and delicate singing with a soft but rhythmically forward-driving texture.

Whether they are factual or mythical, these stories about Emperor Zhu Yuanzhang, Gu Jian, and Wei Liangfu are credible for the genre's practitioners. Like the nation's social historians, they assume that kunqu and other Chinese operatic genres were created and developed largely by commoner artists. These people created or developed distinctive genres of performing arts in their hometowns and then took their practices and traditions to wherever they went to make their living, attracting both elite and commoner audiences throughout the nation. With such a process, kunqu became a national opera and a revealing mirror of Chinese lives and dreams.

To substantiate this interpretation, historians reference the historical labeling of Wei's music as *shuimo qiang*. Figuratively and associatively, the term connects kunqu to Jiangnan in a number of specific ways. It references the extensive web of waterways that meander through the forested hills in the Wu region. It points to the Wu dialect, which many Chinese would hear as melodious and soft.[27] It compares kunqu arias with a type of finely polished luxury wood furniture that late Ming Suzhou craftsmen produced, and that businessmen profitably marketed throughout the nation.

Historians also wrote biographies that illustrated how the forces of culture, land, and people converged to develop kunqu.[28] Thus, the pragmatic narrative showcases the biography of Liang Chenyu (1521–1591), who wrote the *Story of Washing Silk* (*Wansha ji*) and staged it as a kunqu opera. This biography makes the kunqu pragmative narrative convincing by aligning it with traditional paradigms for assessing Chinese opera.[29] First, though it is a multimedia performance art, Chinese opera has traditionally been judged in terms of its literary and narrative attributes. Liang's text of the

---

27. Many contemporary Chinese who are familiar with different Chinese dialects opine that the Wu dialect is more "musical" than those spoken in northern and northwestern China.

28. For a Chinese musicological theory on interrelationships among music, culture, and geography, see Qiao Jianzhong, *Tudi yu ge—chuantong yinyue wenhua ji qi dili lishi beijing yanjiu* (rev. ed., Shanghai: Shanghai Conservatory of Music, 2009); see esp. 261–297. For a historical interpretation that links the rise of kunqu with late Ming brothel culture—a topic that the pragmatic narrative glosses over, see Xu Peng, "The Music Teacher: The Professionalization of Singing and the Development of Erotic Vocal Style during Late Ming China," *Harvard Journal of Asiatic Studies* 75, no. 2 (2015): 259–297.

29. Liang Chenyu, *Wanshaji*, in *Liang Chenyu ji*, ed. Wu Shuyin (Shanghai: Guji chubanshe, 1998), 445–582. See Chapter 5 for a discussion of Liang's drama and role in kunqu history.

An Earthly Opera 67

Story of Washing Silk is literarily sophisticated and dramatically intriguing, and it was widely circulated and read. Second, Chinese grand operas project lives and dreams. Liang's story dramatizes beautiful women and heroes and anti-heroes who personify national values; they are the ancestors whom Chinese people—in particular Jiangnan daughters and sons—like to stage for themselves and international audiences. Third, Chinese operatic connoisseurs prescribe that the musical and verbal aspects of operas should be seamlessly coordinated. The linguistic aspects of Liang's lyrics closely match the perceived musical attributes of the *qupai* featured in his libretto.

Liang is not the only hero showcased by the pragmatic narrative of kunqu. Another prominent figure is Tang Xianzu (1550–1616), whose dramatic works are masterpieces of kunqu and whose literary-musical practices generated a historical controversy over kunqu lyrics and music—one that is still being debated by scholars of Chinese literature and kunqu.[30] A dramatist and philosopher, Tang wrote four *chuanqi* operas, including the *Peony Pavilion* (1598). All provocatively express human desires, dreams, and realities through literary lyrics. All can be sung as kunqu, yet Tang did not write them specifically for kunqu singing. The debate over how Tang's dramas could be performed as kunqu eventually divided late Ming and elite dramatists, performers, and theorists into two rival camps. Tang and his supporters prioritized dramatic-literary expression over musical performance. Tang declared that for the sake of dramatic and literary effects, he would break any rules for writing lyrics according to specific *qupai*—he would not even mind if performing his arias damaged actor-singers' voices. Shen Jing (1553–1610), a celebrated mid-Ming dramatist and theorist, and the leader of the other camp, demanded that aria lyrics be written in ways that could be musically and intelligibly sung—that the literary-linguistic-musical features of the lyrics not conflict with those of their *qupai* models. To make the *Peony Pavilion* "singable" as kunqu, Shen "edited" Tang's lyrics, which angered the author and his followers.[31]

Needless to say, the Tang-Shen controversy involved more than aesthetic, compositional, and performance concerns; it was also driven by personal, ideological, social, and political forces, a fact the pragmatic narrative clearly indicates. In the turbulent world of late Ming China, elite men used operatic activities to express themselves, exercise their energies, and vent their frustrations. Many kunqu practitioners, such as Gao Lian (fl. 1573–1620) and Zhang Dai (1597–1689), were talented scholars and privileged gentlemen who had failed to pass national examinations and rise to court positions. Others, such as Tang Xianzu and Liang Chenyu, were scholar-officials who retired early in order to maintain their personal integrity. To entertain themselves, or

---

30. There is a wealth of scholarly studies on Tang Xianzu and his dramatic works and theories; two recent and representative studies are: Hua Wei, ed., *Tang Xianzu yu Mudanting* (Taipei: Zhongyang yanjiuyuan zhongguo wenzhe yanjiusuo, 2005), and Zou Yuanjiang, *Tang Xianzu xinlun* (Shanghai: Renmin chubanshe, 2015).

31. For information on Shen Jing and his dramatic works, see Gu Lingshen et al., eds., *Shen Jing yu kunqu wujiang pai* (Shanghai: Wenyi chubanshe, 2005).

to soothe their damaged spirits, these elite gentlemen maintained household troupes (*jiaban*) for private performances. These troupes were also marks of conspicuous consumption and elite social networks. Some household troupes performed at the highest artistic level. For example, Shen Shixing (1535–1614), a grand councilor in late Ming China, kept a distinguished household troupe. Its lead actress-singer and pedagogue, Madame Shen, was noted for her performance skills.[32]

Some late Ming elites even traveled with musician-servants, an indulgence that helped spread kunqu. By the early 1600s, kunqu was regularly being performed in the palace in Beijing, a result of imperial patronage and a reflection of the capital's place as a cultural and political center. *Ming History* (*Mingshi*) reports that Emperor Shenzong (r. 1572–1620) had two theatrical troupes in his palace, one of which performed kunqu as a fashionable entertainment of the time. His grandson, Emperor Xizong (r. 1620–1627), was an enthusiastic amateur performer. One summer, he donned a fur coat to perform "Emperor Taizu Visits Zhao Pu on a Snowy Night" ("Fang Pu"), a favorite *zhezixi*. Fuwang (1607–1646), who briefly ruled the short-lived Southern Ming, was also a kunqu fan. One of Fuwang's senior officials, Ruan Dacheng (1587?–1646?), wrote the famed *Swallow Letters* (*Yanzi jian*), a romantic story of love and mistaken identities.[33] In early Qing China, Emperors Kangxi (1654–1722) and Qianlong (1711–1799) were known to be connoisseurs of kunqu. Many records of Ming and Qing court performances of kunqu have been preserved; some have recently become available for scholarly examination. How the resulting findings will impact the current pragmatic narrative of kunqu history is not yet known.[34]

By mid-Qing, kunqu had become a national pastime. Annual singing competitions were held at Huqiu near Suzhou and on the evenings when people celebrated the Mid-Autumn Festival.[35] Small bands of kunqu singers and instrumentalists called *tangming* were often hired to provide music for the Jiangnan elite's ritual and social gatherings. Regional traditions of kunqu had developed in Guiyang in Hunan Province, Wenzhou in Zhejiang Province, and other regional cities.[36] Commercial

---

32. Two informative studies on household troupes are Liu Shuiyun, *MingQing jiayue yanjiu* (Shanghai: Gujichubanshe, 2005), and Zhang Faying, *Zhongguo jiayue xiban* (Beijing: Xueyuan chubanshe, 2002). For a case study of late Ming kunqu patrons and their contributions to the genre's development, see Joseph S. C. Lam, "Zhang Dai's (1597–1680) Musical Life in Late Ming China," in *Ming China*, ed. Kenneth Swope (New York: Routledge, 2019), 343–365.

33. For more details about Ruan Dacheng and his *Yanzi jian*, see Guo Yingde, "Ruan Dacheng: Yuyi zizhao, qingwen wanzhuan," in *Ming Qing chuanqishi* (Beijing: Renmin wenxue chubanshe, 2012), 341–346.

34. For kunqu performance inside the Qing court, see Liana Chen's *Staging for the Emperors: A History of Qing Court Theatre, 1683–1923* (Amherst, NY: Cambria Press, 2021).

35. See the historical report by Zhang Dai, "Huqiu Zhongqiu ye," in *Tao'an mengyi*, 122.

36. For studies on the two kunqu branches, see Tang Xiangyin, *Lanyun jiumeng: wo di xiangkun yishu shengya yu qingjie* (Beijing: Zhongguo xiju chubanshe, 2010); and Shen Buchen, *Kuntan ouyun: Yongjia kunju renwu pingzhuan* (Shanghai: Guji chubanshe, 2011).

An Earthly Opera   69

performances became commonplace. For example, Li Yu (1610–1680),[37] a celebrated novelist-dramatist, had his household troupe perform for a fee in Hangzhou and Nanjing.

National developments converged to generate a golden age of kunqu between the 1680s and the 1860s; so the pragmatic narrative tells us.[38] The period began with the composition of two *chuanqi/kunqu* masterpieces, namely, the *Palace of Everlasting Life* (1688) by Hong Sheng and the *Peach Blossom Fan* (1699) by Kong Shangren.[39] Setting new standards for script writing and elaborate performance, these dramas pushed the kunqu genre toward the apex of its development. As kunqu historians have noted, after the early 1700s, Chinese dramatists no longer wrote long *chuanqi* plays in the manner of Hong and Kong. Also, performers began to focus their creative energy on *zhezixi* as short but dramatically self-contained and cost-effective shows.

The rise of *zhezixi* was a turning point in kunqu's development as a Chinese opera and cultural heritage, as the pragmatic narrative emphasizes. By the 1760s, *zhezixi* performances had become the norm. At that time, more than 400 kunqu *zhezixi* were being staged for the public, as attested by the publication of performance scripts.[40] Many of these *zhezixi*, such as "Strolling; Dreaming" and "Yearning for the Secular World," are still performed regularly.

The success of *zhezixi* had an enormous impact on kunqu's development; three of these can be highlighted here.[41] First, *zhezixi* performance made maximum use of minimal available resources, rendering kunqu an entertaining and sustainable genre of opera. Most *zhezixi* involved only one or two performers, who began their *zhezixi* shows by explaining who their characters were and what dramatic situations they faced. Second, repeated performances of the same *zhezixi* allowed performers to polish their performance skills and nurture their audiences so that they became more refined connoisseurs. Third, *zhezixi* accumulated to form an extensive repertoire of entertaining and impactful shows; their continuous performance and discourse rendered kunqu an integral part of artistic, cultural and social living in historical China.

After the 1860s, kunqu begun to decline noticeably in Beijing, a process expedited by two historical forces. The first was the Taiping Rebellion (1854–1862), which devastated Jiangnan, the source of many professional kunqu performers. The second was the rise of Peking opera, which by the 1840s had become a distinctive and popular genre of Chinese opera. As a consequence, kunqu gradually lost its place in Beijing. The last Beijing-based kunqu troupe, the Jixiu ban (Troupe of Gathered

---

37. There is a wealth of studies on Li Yu; for a representative study, see Patrick Hanan, *The Invention of Li Yu* (Cambridge, MA: Harvard University Press, 1988).
38. For a comprehensive account of the development, see Liu Ben, *Zhongguo xiqu fazhanshi*, Vol. 4 (Taiyuan: Shanxi jiaoyu chubanshe, 2003), 1–216.
39. See Chapters 3 and 7 for detailed discussions of the two dramas.
40. Qian Decang, *Zhui bai qiu* (1760s; reprint, Beijing: Zhonghua shuju, 2005).
41. See Lu Eting, *Kunju yanchu shigao* (Shanghai: Shanghai wenyi chubanshe, 1980); and Wang Ning, *Kunqu zhezixi yanjiu* (Hefei: Huangshan chuban chuanmei gufen youxian gongsi, 2013).

Stars), disbanded in 1827. After that year, kunqu shows were staged under the auspices of Peking opera troupes.

Kunqu fared better in the south. It found a temporary haven in Shanghai, a treaty port since 1842. Energized by an influx of domestic immigrants who had diverse expressive needs, the city quickly became a center of urban culture and commercial entertainment.[42] In 1851, the Sanya yuan (Theater of Three Elegances), Shanghai's first dedicated teahouse/entertainment center (*chayuan*), opened its doors and began presenting kunqu shows. Then in the early 1860s, two Suzhou kunqu troupes, the Dazhang (Great Expressions) and Daya (Great Elegance) troupes, moved their operations to Shanghai. By the 1880s, the city had overtaken Suzhou as a center of kunqu.

Kunqu was not, however, the only game in Shanghai. At the turn of the nineteenth and twentieth centuries, Peking opera and other fashionable genres flooded into the treaty port and began competing for audiences. In 1890, the Sanya yuan closed for good. In 1922, the Wenquanfu Ban (Kunqu Troupe of Civility and Fortune) gave its final performances in Shanghai. From then on, until 1956, Shanghai had no dedicated kunqu opera troupe, even though many professional performers and fans of the genre lived in the city. The presence of the former nevertheless left a legacy.[43] Audio recordings of Yu Shulu's (1847–1930) kunqu singing, some of the earliest sound documents of the genre, were produced in 1921 in Shanghai. A number of seminal kunqu scores, which notationally preserve nineteenth-century kunqu creative and performance practices, were published there during the 1920s and 1930s.[44] Kunqu in semi-colonial Shanghai was a multifaceted phenomenon that encompassed both change and continuity, a story the pragmatic narrative has yet to comprehensively report.

As kunqu declined more and more in the early 1900s, its classicism became socially and politically significant. The conservative and patriotic kunqu elite—men like Wu Mei (1884–1939) and Xu Zhiheng (1877–1935)[45]—promoted the genre as the "essence" of cultural and ethnic China and as a tool of soft power that could be wielded to combat Western and colonial arts and cultures. To sustain kunqu and cultural China, they organized kunqu associations, or music clubs, at universities and colleges, where members learned to sing classic arias of the genre and discussed its Chinese attributes and significance. Some members of these associations later became leaders of twentieth-century kunqu. These people included Wang Jilie (1873–1952), Xu Lingyun (1888–1966), Zheng Zhenduo (1898–1958), and Fu Xihua (1907–1970), as well as others.[46]

---

42. For an introduction to the Shanghai kunqu tradition and its preserved documents, see Shanghai shi lishi bowuguang, comp., *Shuimo chuanxing: Haishang kunqu wenwu shuzhen* (Shanghai: Xuelin chubanshe, 2011).
43. For historical recording of Su Yulu's kunqu singing, see "Yu Sulu Sings Kunqu," accessed May 17, 2021, www.youtube.com/watch?v=4LVNuNvrJ-g.
44. See discussion of kunqu notated sources in Chapter 5.
45. For their biographical sketches, see Wu Xinlei, *Zhongguo kunqu dacidian*; and Hong Weizhu, *Kunqu cidian*; see also Chapter 5 for discussions of early twentieth-century kunqu personages.
46. For biographical information on these kunqu practitioners, see Wu Xinlei, *Kunqu cidian*.

An Earthly Opera   71

However, what saved kunqu from its predicted death at the turn of the previous century was the founding of the Academy in 1921. A pioneer institution in kunqu history, the Academy recruited fifty-five students and had them trained by authoritative teachers like Shen Yuequan (1865–1936) and You Caiyun (1887–1955), former members of the renowned Wenquanfu ban.[47] Soon after its launch, the Academy ran into financial difficulties; it was rescued by Mu Ouchu (1876–1943), a Shanghai industrialist, who supported the institution and its students from 1921 until 1926.[48]

The Academy introduced a new method of teaching and learning kunqu. It not only trained students with the skills they required for multiple roles but also educated them in Chinese history, literature, and various practical subjects. By the time the students graduated in 1926, they commanded a sizable repertory and were ready to perform as modern professionals. Subsequently, they became master performers and influential pedagogues; their students would dominate late twentieth-century kunqu. They were collectively honored as the Chuanzibei Masters; they did not, however, have the good fortune to fully develop their own careers.

The war-torn China of the 1930s and 1940s could not provide the masters with sustainable stages. Indeed, in their short careers as professional kunqu performers, they encountered one disaster after another. During the Japanese invasion of Shanghai in 1937, the theater they performed in was bombed and all their costumes and props were destroyed. By the end of World War II, the masters had scattered, some meeting horrible ends—at least one starved to death. By 1949, only twenty-three of the Chuanzibei Masters survived. In the early 1950s, they lived precariously as kunqu tutors or performers in small regional theaters. As reported in the pragmatic narrative, the personal struggles of the Chuanzibei Masters and their timely transmission of classical kunqu become not only an allegory of early twentieth-century Chinese people's sufferings and struggles but also a justification for reviving the genre as a tool for presenting a beautiful, civilized, and productive China.

Kunqu was hardly known in socialist China of the early 1950s. Then it was "salvaged" by an epoch-making show, the *Fifteen Strings of Coins*, in 1956.[49] A sensational success and a pragmatic model for making traditional operas serve the needs of socialist China, the show led to the launching of seven kunqu troupes/schools, whose graduates have shaped the practice of kunqu since 1956.

In the early 1960s, kunqu showed many signs of a bright future. But darkness returned with the Cultural Revolution (1966–1976), during which kunqu was banned as a "feudalist" and obsolete genre of Chinese performing arts and its troupes/ schools were shuttered. In 1978, after the Cultural Revolution ended, a group of kunqu professionals led by Yu Zhenfei pleaded for permission to reopen the schools

---

47. For a biographical account of the Chuanzibei Masters, Sang Yuxi, *Kunju Chuanzibei pingzhuan* (Shanghai:Shanghaiguji chubanshe, 2010). See also discussion in Chapter 5.

48. See Chapter 5 for a discussion of Mu Ouchu's kunqu activities.

49. See further discussion of the opera in Chapter 8.

and stage kunqu again. Their appeal was granted but given little material support. The China of the early 1980s could scarcely afford the resources to promote the genre.

Over the next fifteen or so years, kunqu struggled on. Things only began to improve in the mid-1990s, when China was becoming prosperous and found the means to address its cultural needs. In 2001, UNESCO declared kunqu a Masterpiece of the Oral and Intangible Cultural Heritage of Humanity, and this prompted Chinese authorities to generously support the genre again. In 2004, Bai Xianyong and SuKun produced the *Young Lovers*; its sensational success triggered a tsunami of interest in the genre.[50] In 2005, China launched a series of large-scale programs to preserve and develop kunqu.[51] Three operating principles were declared and implemented:

1. Reinvigorate the seven nationally supported kunqu troupes: BeiKun in Beijing; ShengKun in Nanjing; ShangKun in Shanghai; ZheKun in Hangzhou; SuKun in Suzhou; XiangKun in Zhenzhou, Hunan; and Yongjia kunqu in Wenzhou, Zhejiang.
2. Designate Suzhou a center for safeguarding and developing kunqu, where an international festival of kunqu performance and scholarly discussions will be held every three years.
3. Support kunqu performances and training workshops with national grants.

In 2006, ShengKun staged the *1699 Peach Blossom Fan*. The following year, ShangKun produced the *Palace of Everlasting Life*. By then, twenty-first-century kunqu had taken shape as a classical opera of contemporary China. With heavenly and earthly attributes, it tells Chinese lives and dreams the ways kunqu practitioners desire to tell them.

The *Peony Pavilion*: A Malleable Opera

Kunqu is earthly malleable, and the genre's practitioners are pragmatically creative. Any comparison of popular shows, such as the "Strolling; Dreaming" *zhezixi* from Tang Xianzu's *Peony Pavilion*, will attest to this.[52] In the following pages, three contrasting and representative renditions of the *zhezixi* are analyzed: a 1960 production

---

50. For a document on the production's successful performance tour in China in 2004, see Bai Xianyong, ed., *Chazi yanhong kaibian: Qingchunban Mudang ting xunyan jishi* (Taipei: Tianxai yuanjian chuban, 2005).

51. See Wenhuabu, "Wenhuabu caizhengbu guanyu yinfa 'guojia kunqu yishu qiangjiu, baohu he fuchi gongcheng shishi fangan' di tongzhi," accessed February 23, 2016, https//:e.cacanet.;cn/cpll/law 7292.shtml.

52. For a monograph on three late twentieth-century productions of *The Peony Pavilion*, see Catherine Swatek, *The Peony Pavilion on Stage: Four Centuries in the Career of a Chinese Drama* (Ann Arbor: Center for Chinese Studies, University of Michigan, 2002). See also Chen Kaihua, *Cong antou dao qushu: Mudanting MingQing wenren zhi quanshi gaibian yu wutai yishu zhi dijin* (Taipei: Taida chuban zhongxin, 2013). For further research data on the drama, see Xu Fuming, *Mudanting yanjiu ziliao kaoshi* (Shanghai: Shanghai guji chubanshe, 1987).

An Earthly Opera 73

featuring Mei Lanfang, Yu Zhenfei, and Yan Weizhu; a 1987 show featuring Zhang Jiqing; and the *Young Lovers* of 2004, featuring Shen Fengying, Yu Jiuling, and Shen Guofang.

Based on scenes ten, eleven, and twelve of Tang Xianzu's original *chuanqi* script, "Strolling; Dreaming" relates a romantic encounter between the two protagonists, Du Liniang and Liu Mengmei.[53] An entertaining spectacle of fanciful storytelling, poetic lyrics, flowing melodies, and elegant *shenduan*, the *zhezixi* has been popularly performed since the late sixteenth century. Since the late 1800s, this *zhezixi* has been staged with a more or less standardized script, which in terms of structure falls into four episodes of fourteen arias and speeches.[54] Episode 1, Arias 1 through 3, presents Du Liniang as a young elite lady readying herself to venture into the family garden for the first time. Episode 2 begins with Du Liniang and her maid, Chunxiang, arriving at the garden. There, they sing Aria 4, "Dark Silk Robe," which describes what they see and how they feel strolling in the garden. Episode 3 begins as Du Liniang returns to her boudoir, takes a rest, falls asleep, and dreams of meeting Liu Mengmei, her future husband. Episode 4, structurally a coda, begins with Du Liniang calling her lover's name in her dream. At that very moment, her mother appears, wakes her, and asks what she is saying. Trying to cover up her calling of her future husband, she tells the mother that she was dreaming about embroidering; then she sings Arias 13 and 14, wrapping up the *zhezixi*.

"Strolling; Dreaming" offers many opportunities for kunqu practitioners to creatively realize the romantic story, highlighting or suppressing its eroticism. What producers and actor-singers realize on stage depends not only on the performance scripts and practices they employ but also on who the performers are and for whom they are performing. Superficially, all productions of this *zhezixi* look and sound similar. Du Liniang always appears as a beautiful and elite woman, Liu Mengmei as a handsome and talented commoner. Heard and viewed closely, however, the productions are expressively particularized. This is especially true with Episode 3, in the course of which Du Liniang and Liu Mengmei meet and make love. The episode needs to be dramatically projected but not realistically enacted—kunqu does not stage erotically explicit acts. To realize the episode, different producers and performers devise contrasting solutions, each a demonstration of their creativity and the genre's malleability.

In 1960, Mei Lanfang and Yu Zhengfei shot an opera-movie (*xiqu dianying*) version of the "Strolling; Dreaming" *zhezixi*, realizing Episode 3 (33'48") from

---

53. For a modern edition of the drama, see Tang Xianzu, *Mudanting*, ed. Xu Shuofang and Yang Xiaomei (Reprint, Beijing: Renmin wenxue chubanshem 2005). The standard English translation of the drama is Cyril Birch, the *Peony Pavilion (Mudang ting)* by Tang Xianzu, paperback edition (Boston: Cheng and Tsui Company, 1994).

54. The "standard version" used for this analysis is Yu Zhenfei's version; see his *Zhenfei qupu* (Shanghai: Wenyi chubanshe, 1982), 135–152.

Figure 4.1: A performance of the "Strolling; Dreaming" by children kunqu performers of Qiandeng, Jiangsu Province, China. Photograph by J. Lam, 2015.

a mid-twentieth-century Chinese perspective and using the latest staging and cinematographic techniques.[55] Thus, the episode begins with Du Liniang falling asleep by a table in her boudoir—a mise-en-scène realistically staged with luxurious furnishings. Soon after that, a beautiful angel comes to the sleeping Du Liniang, traveling through the clear sky and announcing her destiny with Liu Mengmei—audiences familiar with *The Wizard of Oz* (1939) will find the angel's entry reminiscent of the way Glinda the Good Witch comes to Dorothy's rescue. In response to the angel's words, Du Liniang's soul leaves her body, flies through the window of her boudoir, and descends to the garden to meet Liu Mengmei, who is being led into the garden by a flower angel. Meeting Du Liniang, Liu Mengmei announces his love for her. The couple then disappears into the back of the garden to consummate their love.

Instead of showing the couple being intimate, the screen introduces a group of twenty flower angels, who perform an extended sequence of song and dance, a choreographic realization of Aria 10. Suggestively, its lyrics describe the beautiful scenery in the garden (42'40"–49'50") and compare the couple to bees and flowers. The angels' singing and dancing is ambiguously intriguing: it is either an abstract, albeit elaborate, representation of the love/sex the lovers are experiencing or a kinetic and visual tool to divert the audience's attention from the eroticism being evoked. As the flower angels finish their dance, the young lovers reappear on stage/screen.

This choreographic and cinematographic realization of Episode 3 revealingly performs and negotiates mid-twentieth-century Chinese biography and culture. At that time, China was materially and technologically impoverished, and its precious resources were reserved for stars like Mei. He was one of a handful of nationally celebrated performers who could command all the human and technical resources

---

55. See *The Peony Pavilion (Mudanting)*, 1960 performance by Mei Lanfang, Yan Huizhu, and Yu Zhenfei, accessed May 16, 2021, https://www.youtube.com/watch?v=nNydt77MhzQ&t=2759s. Episode 3 begins at 33'48".

An Earthly Opera

they needed for their shows. Mei's opera-movie was made to serve personal and national agendas. It permanently preserved Me's superlative singing and chanting, accompanied by traditional kunqu instrumental music. Mei died in August 1961, not long after the screen work premiered. The movie-opera can now be shown repeatedly to a multitude of audiences throughout the nation, promoting Mei's artistry while advancing socialist China's cultural, social, and political agendas. Screening the opera-movie is also much cheaper than staging a live performance of the *zhezixi*.

In the 1980s, Zhang Jiqing performed Du Liniang to national acclaim. In 1987, an opera-movie version of her performance was produced by ShengKun and the Nanjing Movie Company.[56] Compared to Mei's 1960 show, Zhang's performance manifests a more traditional staging of the love story. It makes, however, an equally poignant commentary on China and Chinese people of the time. As filmed, Episode 3 (1:37'00") in Zhang's opera-movie begins with the appearance of a garden god dressed in red and holding a fan in each of his hands—a very traditional enactment of the supernatural character. Singing and speaking as scripted, he invites the young couple into the garden. Expressing desire for one another, the couple perform a sequence of walking *shenduan* to instrumental music, while moving toward the exit at the back of the stage. As they disappear, a flower god comes on stage, accompanied by eight flower angels. To the music of shawms and drums, the flower god sings to explain the couple's destined union, and orders the flower angels to wake them from their lovemaking. The angels then do a simple dance, singing a brief new song and commenting on the couple's destined love. When the angels finish their singing and dancing, the lovers reemerge on stage and perform their aria and speech sets as scripted. The eroticism in Episode 3 is dampened.

This 1987 production of "Strolling; Dreaming" was made to showcase Zhang Jiqing's exquisite but traditional enactment of Du Liniang.[57] A virtuoso performer, Zhang used her sweet singing and elegant *shenduan* to project Chinese femininity as she and her Shengkun partners envisioned it. Her singing is full of nuanced tones, rhythms, and timbres, and her poses and dances are choreographed to echo images of Chinese beauties found in traditional paintings. Zhang's Du Liniang sharply contrasts with the Chinese woman warriors who dominated China's cultural scene during and soon after the Cultural Revolution. The instrumental music that accompanies Zhang's singing and *shenduan*, however, sounds like typical post–Cultural Revolutionary *minyue*.[58]

---

56. *The Peony Pavilion*, 1987 performance by Zhang Jiqing, accessed May 16, 2021, June 28, https://www.youtube.com/watch?v=VWuEZkjK7ak.
57. For a biographical study of Zhang Jiqing and her artistry, see Zhu Xi and Yao Jikun, *Qinchu yulan: Zhang Jiqing kunqu wushiwunian* (Beijing: Wenhua yishu chubanshe, 2009).
58. See further discussion of *minyue* in Chapter 8.

In 2004, Bai Xianrong produced the *Young Lovers*, presenting the classic story with both modernistic touches and the genre's "original sauce and taste."[59] As performed, it faithfully realizes the popular *zhezixi's* story line—it features no new lyrics or prose. Nevertheless, the acting and dancing realized in the *zhezixi* are as *qingchun dianya* as contemporary Chinese can be. It begins with symphonic Chinese instrumental music, setting a dramatic soundscape for Du Liniang to fall asleep in.[60] Then the stage lighting darkens, directing the audience's attention to a troupe of male and female flower gods and angels entering the stage from its back right corner. The angels are dwarfed by a gigantic backdrop painted in impressionistic colors and visual patterns. The performers' dance movements with outstretched arms and their flowing silk costumes make them look as if they are floating in air. Once they take up their stage positions, they do a three-and-a-half minute (24'10" to 27'45") spectacle of group dance, one that evokes Western grand ballet. The evocation is unmistakable when the audience observes that the orchestra is playing with recurring melodic motifs, rich textures, and changing timbres. As the spectacle unfolds, a male flower god leads Du Liniang to center stage, where she meets Liu Mengmei, who is being escorted there by another male flower god. The couple meet, and he takes her to the back of the garden, leaving the flower gods and angels behind. To comment on the couple's lovemaking and happiness, the flower angels sing the choral arias (33'54" to 37'36) that Mei Lanfang's 1960 production popularized, while executing another grand dance. The young lovers then reemerge on stage, and the flower angels exit. He bids her farewell and is led away by a male flower god, leaving her to wake up alone in the garden.

As staged, Bai's production packages Episode 3 to kinetically and visually please young and contemporary Chinese. The flower angels paraded in the show look as young and beautiful as the production's fans are or want to be. The angels' makeup shows contemporary colors and patterns—they are not "exaggerated" as on traditional performers. This departure from traditional aesthetics and practices is significant in that it underscores the updated Chinese aesthetic and cosmopolitan experiences of Bai and his collaborators. The dance movements and formations choreographed for the angels are formalist, and traces of French-Russian ballet are quite discernible to those familiar with Western dancing—cosmopolitan Chinese embrace Western ballet as classical and expressive dance. The grand dances in Episode 3 are, however,

---

59. Complete recordings of *The Young Lovers* (about eight hours of performance time) are accessible online as at: *Peony Pavilion*, 2004 performance by SuKun, accessed May 16, 2021,
Book 1: https://www.youtube.com/watch?v=kn1du7m-vj8&t=3637s;
Book 2: https://www.youtube.com/watch?v=rcYkExD7Szc&t=50s;
Book 3: https://www.youtube.com/watch?v=MwFUbkkbuDQ&t=106s.
For a Chinese American scholar's take on the production, see Daphne Lei, "The Blossoming of the Transnational Peony: Performing Alternative China in California," in *Alternative Chinese Opera in the Age of Globalization: Performing Zero* (London: Palgrave Macmillan, 2011), 98–141.
60. See Chapter 8 for discussion of this music.

An Earthly Opera

Figure 4.2: A dance scene from the "Strolling; Dreaming" in the *Young Lovers*. Photograph by J. Lam, 2014. Courtesy of Shen Fengying and SuKun.

not without innovative touches. The waving of long banners by the two male flower gods makes a realistic dance. Some critics, however, find it mundane. They have jokingly compared it to the banners that Chinese tourist guides wave as they guide their international, and in particular Japanese, clients around crowded sites in contemporary China. The instrumental music that accompanies the group dance is symphonic, sounding just like Chinese concert music does.

Bai's realization of "Strolling; Dreaming" is representative of the *qingchun dianya* kunqu he has envisioned and popularized with the *Young Lovers*. A mesmerizing show and an eloquent statement on contemporary China, it has charmed many young Chinese and non-Chinese kunqu fans but offended a good number of conservative connoisseurs. Some critics have dismissed it as hybridized kunqu; a few have even disparaged it as more Broadway than kunqu. Such harsh words, however, ignore the ways in which malleable kunqu opens itself to creative realizations. Unless they are creatively and pragmatically staged, kunqu cannot tell Chinese lives and dreams as they were and are.

Epilogue: Other Peonies

The *Young Lovers* was successful because it packaged kunqu into a performance and discourse of *qingchun dianya* China and Chinese people. Bai had grasped kunqu's expressive malleability and realized its earthly potential. His packaging of kunqu for artistic and personal goals was by no means an isolated case. One international artist who saw kunqu as a tool for realizing his artistic vision and understanding of opera/multimedia performance arts was Peter Sellars. In 1998 he produced an innovative version of the *Peony Pavilion*,[61] featuring traditional and nontraditional acting and music by, respectively, Hua Wenyi (b. 1941) and Tan Dun (b. 1957). Hua is a former kunqu star and director of ShangKun who immigrated to the US in 1989. Tan is an Oscar-winning composer born in China but trained in the US as well as in China. He now lives in New York, composing music that blends traditional Chinese musical elements with Western and avant-garde ones. Sellars's show has earned praise from world theater critics and audiences, but it has barely been noticed by kunqu practitioners. They do not find their Chinese selves in the American director's production.

In 1998–1999, Chen Shizeng, a Chinese-American theater director, produced for Lincoln Center a historically informed version of the *Peony Pavilion*,[62] presenting all fifty-five scenes of the drama penned by Tang Xianzu. This was a herculean effort that had not been attempted since the late Ming. To sonically project the drama's historicity and multitude of expressions, Chen's production played not only notated kunqu music from the *Nashuying qupu* (Ye Tang's library of kunqu scores) of the 1780s and 1790s but also songs and dances from *huagu xi* and *Suzhou pingtan*. The former is a vernacular genre of operetta referred to as "flower drum song" in the West; the latter is Suzhou narrative music, a traditional and commoner's way of telling stories through ballads and the spoken word. To render his production realistic, and to assert his contemporary aesthetics and interpretations, Chen's stage featured a pond with live ducks.

Many New York critics, as well as the audience, found Chen's production innovative and entertaining. However, Shanghai municipal authorities, who had originally supported the production, condemned it as vulgar and as misrepresenting Chinese culture and history. Shortly before its scheduled premiere in New York in 1998,

---

61. Catherine C. Swatek, "Peter Sellars' Efforts to Reawaken Kunqu Opera," in *The Peony Pavilion Onstage: Four Centuries in the Career of A Chinese Drama* (Ann Arbor: Center for Chinese Studies, University of Michigan, 2002), 203–230. See also Min Tian, "Intercultural Theatre at the New Fin de Siècle: Peter Sellars' Postmodern Approach to Traditional Chinese Theatre, in *The Poetics of Difference and Displacement: Twentieth-Century Chinese-Western Intercultural Theatre* (Hong Kong: Hong Kong University Press, 2008), 113–137.

62. For a report on Chen Shizeng's production, see David Rolston, "Tradition and Innovation in Chen Shi-Zheng's *Peony Pavilion*," *Asian Theatre Journal* 19, no. 1 (Spring 2002): 134–146. See also Catherine Swatek, "To Perform 'Chuanqi' We Will Recreate a Chuanqi," in *The Peony Pavilion Onstage: Four Centuries in the Career of a Chinese Drama*, 231–256. For a comparison of Chen's production with other staging of the *Peony Pavilion*, see Judith Zeitlin, "My Year of Peonies," *Asian Theatre Journal* 19, no. 1 (2002): 124–133.

An Earthly Opera

they torpedoed it by preventing costumes and props needed for the performance in New York from leaving Shanghai, thus generating an incident in China-US cultural exchange history. The Lincoln Center's administrators struggled to have the show performed as scheduled, but the Chinese authorities refused to budge.[63] Chen had no choice but to postpone his performance for a year, until he could find an alternative group of kunqu performers and have their costumes made. Chen presented his production in 1999 and attracted much media attention in the West. In China, it was dismissed as an aberration. Most Chinese kunqu practitioners found Chen's use of "lowbrow" music and regional and vernacular genres unacceptable, arguing that kunqu is a *dianya* opera and cannot be performed with *su* (vulgar) and/or *tu* (rustic) sounds and sights like those of "flower drum songs."

Another equally controversial packaging of the *Peony Pavilion* is the dinner show at the Imperial Granary in Beijing, a luxury theater-restaurant establishment converted from a six-century-old warehouse of the imperial court. Presenting what was essentially an expanded version of the "Strolling; Dreaming" *zhezixi*, the show charged its small audience of fifty or so clients a high but not unreasonable admission fee—in 2013, tickets for the best seats cost RMB1,980 each; those for the cheapest seats, RMB580 each. Produced by Wang Xiang, a creative entrepreneur, and Wang Shiyu, the renowned kunqu actor and artistic director of the *Young Lovers*, the dinner show opened in May 2007 and closed in the summer of 2014. During its run, the show generated much commentary, both positive and negative. Many critics attacked it for its explicit commercialism. Many tourists who attended the show, however, left the venue fully satisfied, feeling that they had had a taste of Ming China luxury. However one argues about the merits and demerits of the production, it was a textbook example of twenty-first-century Chinese packaging of kunqu as both a heavenly entertainment and an earthly cultural heritage.[64]

The most recent trend in packaging kunqu is "garden shows" (*yuanlin ban*) or "shows in natural and outdoor settings" (*shijing ban*). Many take place in historical or newly developed Chinese gardens, with or without formal stages, again underscoring that kunqu is malleable, in that its practitioners dutifully learn from the genre's factual and fictive past. Many kunqu stories unfold within gardens, where ponds, man-made hills, pavilions, trees, and flowers serve as naturalistic backdrops for lovers to physically or imaginatively indulge their passions. Currently, the two most talked-about garden shows are Zhang Jun's presentation at Zhujiajiao in Shanghai and SuKun's presentation in the garden stage built on its own campus. With their advanced sound amplification and lighting techniques, evening garden shows have delighted many casual audiences and tourists. Many kunqu connoisseurs, however, find garden shows

---

63. For an analysis of the conflicts, see Elizabeth Wichmann-Walczak, "Ma Bomin and the Question of Creativity Authority in the Peony Pavilion Controversy," *ACMR Reports* 11 (1998): 107–110.

64. For an overview of Chinese tourism and operas, see Colin Mackerras, "Tourism and Musical Performing Arts in the First Decade of the Twenty-First Century: A Personal View," *Chinoperl* 30 (2011): 155–182.

unsatisfactory. Seated away from the open-air stage or performance area, they complain that they cannot clearly see or hear what is being performed. Thus, some critics have declared that garden shows have no magic, for they leave little room for the imagination. Kunqu garden shows have reached beyond Chinese borders. One favorably received production was the one presented, in November 2012, at the Astor Court, a Chinese garden within the Metropolitan Museum of Art compound in New York.[65]

To please diverse audiences, contemporary kunqu practitioners are staging many earthly shows, experimenting with a variety of staging methods and strategies. They have staged, for instance, "exemplary versions" (*chuancheng ban*), which master performers would like to see preserved; "essential versions," (*jinghua ban*), which present condensed versions of masterpieces for both connoisseurs and casual audiences; and cost-effective "recitals," in which performers sing and speak on stage without *shenduan* and without makeup or elaborate costumes. New formats of kunqu performance are always emerging. For example, single kunqu arias, with or without costume and *shenduan*, have become popular on TV variety shows. Such shows popularize kunqu and confirm what the genre's pragmatic narrative argues: kunqu is a classical opera with commoner roots. To some critics, however, these populist shows vulgarize kunqu with inexcusable indulgences, such as dramatically fragmented acts and intrusive backdrops/backscreens with "live" images. For example, a 2017 TV show had backup performers dressed in white ballet tutus dancing in front of a gigantic LCD monitor showing animated and colorful images, but behind kunqu actor-singers performing in traditional costume and facial makeup. Welcomed by TV audiences, these populist shows are what many Chinese TV audiences take as kunqu. This is one reason why some concerned kunqu critics lament that the genre is being short-sightedly exploited. They fear that its classical tradition will implode, sending its canonized repertory and cherished performance practices back to their graves.

---

65. *Peony Pavilion*, 2012 performance by Zhang Jun at the Astor Court, NY Metropolitan Museum, accessed September 2016, https://metmuseum.org/media/video/concerts/peony-pavilion.

5
Kunqu Lives, Dreams, Documents, and Character Models

Introduction

Opera is life and life is opera; both are real and illusive like dreams. So claim kunqu practitioners.[1] Carved into the stage in the restored Zhengyici Theater in Beijing is a couplet that reads: "Performing human sadness, happiness, separation, and reunion on stage, actors show that current affairs repeat historical ones; watching protagonists being suppressed, promoted, praised, and criticized on stage, audiences find the same characters sitting among themselves."[2] Many kunqu operas have been created, performed, and understood as lives or dreams. In the *Peony Pavilion*, Du Liniang dreams of Liu Mengmei, her future husband. In *Chenyu Fen's Dream (Nanke meng)*, an ambitious young man falls asleep under a tree and experiences life as a successful man; everything vanishes as he wakes up.[3] In the *Butterfly Dream (Hudie meng)*, Zhuangzi, a Chinese philosopher, dreams about his wife as a widow and finds human fickleness and tragedy.[4]

Kunqu performances tell archetypal stories and present iconic characters that Chinese culturally and historically know and personally and communally identify

---

1. For an insightful discussion of Chinese life, dream, and opera, see Zheng Chuanyin, "Renshen rumeng: Xiqu yu menghuan di goulian," in his *Chuantong wenhua yu gudian xiqu* /Traditional Culture and Classical Drama (Taipei: Yangzhi wenhua, 1995), 275–318. Many kunqu dramas and biographies have the word *meng* (dream) in their titles. And many others reference past lives; see, for example, Guo Chenzi, *Kunqu: Jinsheng kandao de qianshi* (Beijing: Xinxing chubanshe, 2006). For a scholarly analysis of dreams as human experiences in Chinese history and culture, see Lynn A. Struve, *The Dreaming Mind and the End of the Ming World* (Honolulu: University of Hawai'i Press, 2019); see esp. "Introduction" and "Epilogue," 1–15 and 243–257.
2. For information on the theater, google: http://theatrebeijing.com/theatres/zhengyici_theatre.
3. See Tang Xianzu, *Nanke meng*, in *Tang Xianzu xiquji*, ed. Qian Nanyang (Shanghai: Shanghai guji chubanshe, 1981), 509–698.
4. For historical information on *The Butterfly Dream* and the making of its current version, see Lei Jingxuan, ed., *Kunju hudiemeng: yibu chuantongxi di zaixian* (Hong Kong: Oxford University Press, 2005).

with.[5] Many kunqu stories have been developed from Chinese historical events, and many iconic characters are modeled after Chinese historical figures. All are realistically staged with virtuoso performance practices that generations of master kunqu practitioners have created and polished. As they perform or attend kunqu, the genre's practitioners have to decide for themselves whether what a show tells is true or untrue, representative or not, relevant or irrelevant to their own lives and dreams. As they answer such questions, the practitioners encounter still more questions: How should a historical story or person be performed on stage, and why? What historical/biographical facts and memories can be employed to substantiate interpretations and performances? However kunqu practitioners answer these, the stories and characters they enact on stage are simultaneously lifelike and dreamlike.

To elaborate on how Chinese biographical and historical facts are learned, interpreted, and then dramatized as successful kunqu productions, this chapter surveys the genre's material and human resources, ranging from preserved scripts and notated scores to practitioners' biographies and treatises. To highlight the transmission of kunqu memories and skills from one generation to the next, this chapter also sketches out the genealogies of seminal kunqu individuals: primordial ancestors, prominent performers and pedagogues, and influential patrons, critics, historians, and theorists. All have played critical roles in shaping the genre's performative features and discursive meanings. To demonstrate the kunqu blending of Chinese past and present lives and dreams on and off stage, four favorite *zhezixi* will be analyzed.

Kunqu Documents: Historical Scripts, Notated Scores, and Theoretical Treatises

Kunqu performances are scripted, and many historical scripts have been preserved, providing models and sources for the genre's contemporary performance practices and materials. Singularly and collectively, the scripts demonstrate how dramatists constructed realistic stories in the past and how their texts have been repeatedly copied and printed, interpreted, and realized on stage. Many historical kunqu scripts have been published with informative introductions that explain why the stories and characters were created and what they tell us about Chinese culture and history.[6]

An authoritative collection of kunqu scripts from Ming and Qing China is the *Guben xiqu congkan* (Collection of historical manuscripts and prints of Chinese dramas).[7] Compiled and published in the 1950s and early 1960s, this collection preserves more than 1,000 *chuanqi* scripts, many of which were repeatedly staged in Ming

---

5. Many kunqu performers personally identify with the characters they enact. For example, Cai Zhengren has told me after performances of scenes like "Lamenting" that he felt sad like Tang Minghuang, a man who had lost his beloved and regretted having done something wrong.
6. For a collection of these introductions, see Cai Yi, ed., *Zhongguo gudian xiqu xuba huibian* (Jinan: Qilu shushe, 1989).
7. Zheng Zhengduo et al., *Guben xiqu congkan*, 10 series and multiple volumes (Beijing: Guojia tushuguan chuabanshe, 2020).

Lives, Dreams, Documents, and Character Models   83

and Qing China. Many scenes from these dramas are still being performed as *zhezixi*. An equally significant collection is the *Shanben xiqu congkan* (Rare books of Chinese dramas), comprising 104 volumes of facsimile copies of performance scripts that have been preserved in Western libraries and museums.[8] The quantity and global spread of these scripts suggests that they were widely circulated in late imperial China. Many kunqu performance scripts were anthologized in China in the early twentieth century. A representative collection is Yi'an zhuren's *Huitu jingxuan kunqu daquan* (A comprehensive and illustrated collection of selected kunqu plays and scenes), published in 1925.[9]

Many traditional kunqu performance scripts include informative illustrations. A celebrated example is a woodblock print of the "Painting a Self-Portrait" ("Xiezhen") scene in a Ming printing of the *Peony Pavilion*.[10] It shows three faces of Du Liniang—her physical face, its reflection in a mirror, and its representation on a scroll. Graphically, the print underscores the realism with which kunqu characters were, and still are, constructed and staged. Since the turn of the previous century, many kunqu photographs have been taken, providing a visual record of historically celebrated kunqu performers and performances.[11] Collectively, woodblock prints and early photographs indicate visually how kunqu was performed a hundred or more years ago. This information is now regularly consulted and interpreted to strengthen creative productions in the present day. For example, Beikun's 2016 production of the *Dames in Love* was billed as a historically informed show; it featured stylized costumes and makeup designs modeled after documented Qing samples.

A wealth of historical kunqu scores have been preserved. A detailed system for kunqu/*gongche* notation had been developed by 1746, the year in which a seminal and notated anthology of 4,466 kunqu arias was published. Since then, many kunqu scores with *gongche* musical notation have been produced.[12] Kunqu practitioners today sing arias and play instrumental pieces according to historically established scores; proudly, they announce the titles they consulted for their historically informed performances.[13] The following are three eighteenth-century sources that kunqu practitioners cherish:

---

8. Wang Chiu-kui, comp., *Shanben xiqu congkan*, 6 series and 104 volumes (Taipei: Xuesheng shuju, 1984).
9. Yi'an zhuren, *Huitu jingxuan kunqu daquan* (Reprint, Taiyuan: Shanxi renmin chubanshe and Sanjin chubanshe, 2018).
10. For an insightful study on the print, see Wu Hung, "The Painted Screen," *Critical Inquiry* 23, no. 1 (1996): 37–79.
11. Many of these historical photographs have been reprinted in kunqu references, such as Wu Xinlei's *Zhongguo kunju dacidian* and Hong Weizhu's *Kunqu cidian*.
12. For a survey of kunqu scores, see Isabel Wong, "The Printed Collections of K'un-Ch'ü Arias and Their Sources," *Chinoperal* 8, no. 1 (1978): 100–129.
13. A thought-provoking case on kunqu scores and authentic interpretation concerns Zhou Xuehua's claim that Zhou Chuanying and Yu Zhenfei, her mentors, entrusted to her the task of accurately transmitting and transcribing kunqu music preserved in Ye Tang's *Nashuying qupu*. See her *Kunqu—Tang Xianzu Linchuan simeng quanji Nashuying qupuban* (Shanghai: Shanghai jiaoyu chubanshe, 2008).

84 *Kunqu*

1. The *Jiugong dacheng nanbeici gongpu* (A comprehensive and notated formulary of northern and southern arias in nine musical modes) of 1746, a court compendium of 4,466 operatic arias prepared under the supervision of Prince Yun Lu (1695–1767).[14]
2. Feng Qifeng's *Yinxiang tang qupu* (A kunqu score from the Studio of Music and Fragrance) of 1789, which preserves the earliest available and complete *gongche* scores for the *Peony Pavilion* and the *Palace of Everlasting Life*.[15]
3. Ye Tang's (fl. 1740s–1790s) *Nashuying qupu* (Ye Tang's library of kunqu scores), published between 1784 and 1792, a collection of notated kunqu music that Ye Tang, a legendary kunqu musician, composed or arranged for Tang Xianzu's four dream operas and more than 360 *zhezixi* culled from various *chuanqi* dramas.[16]

The following four authoritative notated sources have preserved late nineteenth-century kunqu music:

1. The *Eyunge qupu* (Kunqu scores of the Studio of Soaring Singing), published by Wang Xichun in 1893,[17] which preserves kunqu arias and speeches from eighty-seven *zhezixi* often performed in late Qing China.
2. The *Zengji liuye qupu* (Expanded collection of kunqu scores from the Studio of Cosmic Principles), which Zhang Yusun published in Shanghai in 1922,[18] preserving the music of 204 *zhezixi*. Zhang sourced the music from Yin Guishen (1825?–after 1896), a legendary late-Qing performer and pedagogue who produced and bequeathed to posterity a wealth of *gongche* music scores.
3. The *Jicheng qupu* (A comprehensive collection of kunqu scripts and scores), compiled by Wang Jilie (1873–1953) with the help of Liu Fuliang (1875–1936) and published in 1925.[19] A scholarly compendium, this document has preserved edited and notated performance scripts for 416 *zhezixi*; it includes

---

14. Yun Lu, ed., *Jiugong dacheng nanbeici gongpu*, in *Shanben xiqu congkan*, vols. 87–104 (1746; facsimile; Taipei: Xuesheng shuju, 1984). For a current study on this important kunqu source, see Wu Zhiwu, *Xinding jiugong dacheng nanbeici gongpu yanjiu* (Beijing: Renmin yinyue chubanshe, 2017).
15. Feng Qifeng, *Yinxiang tang qupu*, 1789, facsimile, accessed May 15, 2021, http://www.guoxuemi.com/shumu/3031690.html.
16. Ye Tang, *Nashuying qupu*, in *Shanben xiqu congkan*, comp. Wang Chiu-kui, Vols. 82–86 (Taipei: Xuesheng shuju, 1984). For an account of the historical reception of Ye's scores, see Joseph S. C. Lam, "Notational Representation and Contextual Constraints: How and Why Did Ye Tang Notate His Kunqu Opera Arias?", in *Themes and Variations: Writings on Music in Honor of Rulan Chao Pian*, ed. Bell Yung and Joseph S. C. Lam (Cambridge, MA and Hong Kong: Department of Music, Harvard University, and the Institute of Chinese Studies, Chinese University of Hong Kong, 1994), 26–35.
17. Wang Xichun, *Eyunge qupu* (Shanghai: Zhuyi tang, 1893).
18. Zhang Yusun, *Zengji liuye qupu* (Reprint, Taipei: Zhonghua shuju, 1977).
19. Wang Jilie, *Jicheng qupu* (Shanghai: Commercial Press, 1925).

Lives, Dreams, Documents, and Character Models   85

several substantive theoretical essays by Wang, who explains kunqu music with reference to Western musical concepts and practices.[20]

4. Yu Sulu's (1847–1930) *Sulu qupu* (Yu Sulu's scores of kunqu arias), published by his son and musical successor, Yu Zhenfei, in 1953.[21] A small collection of arias taken from twenty-nine *zhezixi*, this score is now considered an authentic representation of Ye Tang's nineteenth-century kunqu practices, the foundation of the twentieth- and twenty-first-century Yu School of kunqu music and singing.

Since late Ming China, scholarly kunqu practitioners have been writing and publishing formal and informal treatises on the genre, bequeathing a wealth of creative theories and performance practices to posterity. All have become source materials for contemporary kunqu aesthetics, history, performance practices, and reception. Five seminal kunqu treatises are included in the *Zhongguo gudian xiqu lunzhu jichen* (A compendium of classical treatises on Chinese operas) of 1959.[22]

Xu Wei's (1521–1593) *Nanci xulu* (An account of southern arias) is one of the earliest historical accounts of kunqu's rise as a genre of southern opera. Xu's account is considered authoritative and reliable because he was a prominent Ming scholar-official, author, dramatist, and painter who had witnessed the rise of kunqu.

Wei Liangfu's (fl. mid-1540s) *Qulü* (Principles for kunqu composition and singing) has been preserved as a set of eighteen short prescriptions for kunqu musicians, which can be summarized as follows.[23] Singers should accurately enunciate the lyrics; otherwise, their flowing melodies will be artistically and intellectually worthless. Singers should perform with energy from their abdomens and with poise; they should coordinate their rhythms with the drum and clapper strokes. To sing accurately, singers should use their muscles properly so that their faces do not turn red, their neck veins do not show, and their heads do not shake—all are signs that they are misusing their bodies and vocal apparatus.

Singers should develop their skills by practicing arias one by one for extended periods. They should realize that every *qupai* is a unique model. For example, the melody of "Huangying'er" ("Yellow oriole") unfolds steadily, while that of "Ji xianbin" ("Gathering of virtuous guests") moves with sudden leaps and dips in pitch. Insights learned from a particular *qupai* can apply to singing in general. Singers should study

---

20. One of the theoretical essays has been published as a standalone kunqu treatise; see Wang Jilie, *Yinlu qutan* (Shanghai: Commercial Press, 1934). Wang had been trained as a physicist.

21. Yu Zhenfei, ed., *Sulu qupu* (Reprint, Shanghai: Cishu chubanshe, 2011).

22. Zhongguo xiju yuan, comp., *Zhonguo gudian xiju lunzhu jicheng*, 10 vols. (Reprint, Beijing: Zhongguo xiju chubanshe, 1980). Li Yu's *Xianqing ouji* is in Vol. 7, 1–114; Shen Chongsui's *Duqu xuzhi* is in Vol. 5, 183–319; Wei Liangfu's *Qulü* is in Vol. 5, 1–14; Xu Dachun's *Yuefu chuansheng* is in Vol. 7, 145–188; Xu Wei's *Nanci xulu* is in Vol. 3, 233–256.

23. Wei Liangfu, *Qulü*, in *Xiqu yanchang lunzhu jishi*, ed. Zhou Yibai (Beijing: Shogun xiju chubanshe, 1962), 67–111.

Figure 5.1: Unveiling of Wei Liangfu's bust installed in the lobby of the new SuKun theater, 2014. Photograph by J. Lam, 2014.

the *Lute* (*Pipa ji*) and other dramatic masterpieces in order to grasp kunqu repertory, styles, and performance practices.

They should sing northern arias as rhythmic and energetic tunes accompanied by plucked string instruments. By contrast, they should sing florid southern arias with rhythmic articulations marked by drum and clapper strokes. The compositional and singing rules for both repertoires of arias must be followed faithfully. The same applies to instrumental kunqu music. Instrumentalists should play idiomatically and complement vocal singing judiciously; instrumental melodies that mechanically rise or fall to match high or low notes in vocal lines are musically confusing and offensive to the ear.

Singers should develop their talents as best as they can. Accomplished artists need not discuss their music with those who neither understand nor enjoy kunqu. Experienced audiences should listen calmly and critically, noting how the performers enunciate the lyrics and handle complex melodic and rhythmic twists. Audiences should also take note of expressive performers' mentors—knowledge of artistic genealogy has for centuries been essential to kunqu appreciation. Wei's eighteen practical prescriptions are still consulted today as authoritative guidelines for kunqu singing and composition.

Shen Chongsui's (d. ca. 1645) *Duqu xuzhi* (Essential knowledge for composing and singing arias) is a detailed discussion of twenty-four kunqu topics, ranging from the genre's historical development to its enunciation practices. Shen's meticulous prescriptions make him a model kunqu theorist; his tradition of theorizing kunqu music in terms of accurate and virtuoso performance practices, semantic intelligibility, and expressive sophistication still thrives.

Li Yu's (1611–1679) *Xianqing ouji* (Occasional notes on leisurely living) of 1671 is a general treatise on artistic and leisure life in early Qing China.[24] It includes two sets of systematic and practical comments for dramatists and performers. The former set can be summarized as follows. To construct effective dramas, librettists should develop their plots with logically and tightly connected dramatic developments. Thus, the opening scenes of a drama should provide the gist of the story and introduce the protagonists. The middle scenes should introduce unexpected twists, and the ending scenes should wrap up the drama with a grand and happy finale. The characters should speak role-appropriate words. A Buddhist nun, for instance, would not utter words with Daoist associations. Similarly, a southern male character should speak with a masculine southern voice.

Librettists should organize their arias and speeches into literarily and musically coherent scenes. The lyrics of an aria should follow one and a same rhyme scheme; the words in the lyrics should closely align with the literary-musical features of the *qupai* the lyricists have chosen as compositional models. The linguistic tones of the words in the lyrics should perfectly match the rise and fall of the *qupai* melodies. Otherwise, the lyrics will be neither intelligible nor performable. Speeches should be simple and straightforward, as well as witty. Comedic words can, however, be uttered at timely moments to underscore the characters' social roles and expressions.

In his comments on operatic performance, Li Yu offers the following guidelines. A show should meet the audience's needs and tastes—sophisticated performances are wasted on uninformed and unappreciative audiences. Performers should study the words they speak on stage, noting semantic meanings and linguistic attributes. Singers must choose their roles and arias according to the voices they were born with. Those with clear and sustained voices can sing the arias of young male roles; those with thick and dark timbres can sing the arias of painted-face roles. They must sing in the proper Wu dialect even if they are not native Wu speakers.

Actor-singers must internalize their characters so that their acting is natural and realistic. For example, to convincingly act out the roles of scholar-officials on stage, actors must cultivate themselves by learning to read, acquiring historical and literary knowledge, and mastering calligraphy, chess, painting, and instrumental music.

---

24. Li Yu, *Xianqing ouji* (Beijing: Yansan chubanshe, 1988); see also Li Yu, *Xianqingouji*, in *Zhongguo gudian xiju lunzhu jicheng* (Reprint, Beijing: Zhongguo xiju chubanshe, 1980), vol. 7, 1–114.

Performers should try to live like the historical figures/dramatic characters they are enacting. Actor-singers should guard themselves against common mistakes. These include wearing costumes made with inappropriate materials, excessive use of dialects to please regional audiences, mechanical use of rhetorical words or vocables, and vulgar use of bodily gestures, such as servant characters flashing their bottoms to show their displeasure with their masters.

Kunqu instrumental music should enhance the actor-singers' performances. Thus, flutists and fiddlers must melodically complement what the actor-singers are vocalizing. And percussionists should refrain from striking drums or gongs at "wrong" moments, thereby rendering the actor-singers' words inaudible and creating dramatically unintelligible moments.

Xu Dachun's (d. ca. 1778) *Yuefu chuansheng* (Traditional *qu* aria singing) of 1748 is a treatise on linguistic-singing performance practices, such as methods for uttering words in each of the four categories of Chinese linguistic tones, and the skills required for breathing and manipulating rhythmic and dynamic expressions. Like Shen Chongsui's treatise described earlier, Xu's work is a core reference for contemporary and scholarly debates on *qupai* compositional and performance practices.

In addition to the five treatises just described, there are many other informative documents on kunqu theory and practice. One that merits discussion here is the *Mingxin jian* (A mirror for actors' heart-minds), a rare treatise written by Qing professional actor-singers. As anthologized by Zhou Yibai,[25] this treatise categorizes eight types of Chinese personhood and four emotional states; all continue to be realized on kunqu stages. The eight types of Chinese personhood are as follows:

1. the powerful and dignified
2. the rich
3. the poor
4. the despicable
5. the idiotic
6. the mad
7. the sick
8. the drunk.

The four emotional states and their bodily manifestations are as follows:

1. happiness—the performers should slightly move their heads left and right
2. anger—the performers should pop their eyes out
3. sadness—the performers should shed tears
4. fear—the performers should open their mouths.

The *Mingxin jian* offers much practical advice for performers. For example, they should roll their eyes to prepare for their own stage movements and to help the

---

25. Yu Weichen and Gong Ruifeng, *Mingxin jian*, in *Xiqu yanchang lunzhu jishi*, ed. by Zhou Yibai (Beijing: Shogun xiju chubanshe, 1962), 176–208.

Lives, Dreams, Documents, and Character Models 89

audience understand what they are enacting; they should make small head movements and hand gestures to kinetically illustrate characters' emotions; and they should rehearse poses and *shenduan* routines in front of a mirror. The treatise includes a list of ten mistakes that novice kunqu performers regularly make:

1. bent legs
2. exaggerated recitations
3. misunderstanding of words in the lyrics
4. erroneous enunciation of scripted words
5. weak and unclear recitations
6. stiff necks
7. protruding shoulders
8. tense waists
9. hurried steps
10. expressionless face and eyes.

Clearly, verbal and notated sources of kunqu provide a wealth of facts, insights, and inspirations for contemporary kunqu producers, actor-singers, critics, and audiences, who are scholarly, and would diligently study documents relevant to their performances. More and more historical kunqu documents are appearing online, providing more and more cultural and historical connections between historical and contemporary kunqu practitioners.

Staged Ancestors

Through such connections, dramatized historical Chinese figures become discursive personifications of Chinese memories, values, fears, and desires. When performed well, the figures come alive on stage and become staged ancestors of Chinese history. For lack of a better term, these models can be referred to heuristically as the *staged ancestors* of kunqu. To illustrate how they tell Chinese lives and dreams and shape kunqu performance and discourse, the following description of three seminal *zhezixi* will suffice.

The first is "Wu Yuan Entrusts His Son to a Friend" ("Jizi"), a popular *zhezixi* from the *Story of Washing Silk* (*Wansha ji*) by Liang Chenyu, a *chuanqi* drama of heroes and anti-heroes, heroines and femmes fatales.[26] In the story, Wu Yuan (d. 484 BCE), a loyal and conscientious official, asks a friend to take care of his son so that he can warn his tyrannical ruler of the danger the state is facing; as expected, Wu is killed for telling the truth. As enacted on the kunqu stage, Wu Yuan exemplifies the unswervingly patriotic men who populate Chinese history—those who face moral

---

26. For the libretti of *The Story of Washing Silk*, see Liang Chenyu, *Wanshaji*, in *Liang chenyu ji*, ed. Wu Shuyin (Shanghai: Guji chubanshe, 1998), 445–582. For a representative performance, see "Wu Yuan Entrusts His Son to a Friend," performed by Zheng Chuanjin and Fang Chuanyi, accessed November 23, 2021, https://www.youtube.com/results?search_query=%E5%B4%91%E6%9B%B2%E5%AF%84%E5%AD%90.

90   *Kunqu*

and political dilemmas in China; who serve their nation or their family; and who either die for doing the right thing or live with regret for not doing so.

The second *zhezixi* is the *Story of the Mountain of Rotten Axe Handle* (*Lanke shan*), a dramatization of the marital nightmare that Woman Cui (Cui shi) and Zhu Maichen (?–115 BCE) experienced. As performed on contemporary kunqu stages, this *zhezixi* portrays Woman Cui as a short-sighted person; selfishly, she divorces her husband so that she can remarry for a more materially comfortable life.[27] The second marriage does not work out as she has planned. Then, when her divorced husband, a late bloomer, becomes a rich and powerful official, she wants him to take her back. To demonstrate that she cannot undo what she has done, he throws water on the ground and asks whether she can pick it up. She cannot, and he would not take her back. As a morality play, the tragedy of the *Story of the Mountain of Rotten Axe Handle* appeals strongly to Chinese audiences facing marital conflicts. Having seen the performance, many Chinese would ask themselves what they would do if they found themselves in a situation as fraught as the one that Woman Cui and Zhu Maichen encounter.

The third *zhezixi* we discuss is *Escorting Lady Jing Home* (*Qianli song Jingniang*), a story that presents Zhao Kuangyin (927–976), the founder of the Northern Song dynasty, as an ambitious young man who sacrifices romantic love to serve the nation. Created for China when it was on the brink of the Sino-Indian war in 1962, this *zhezixi* portrays an ambitious young hero who would eventually found a Chinese dynasty; in doing so, it underscores what socialist China demands from its young men—that they prioritize protection of the nation above personal happiness, just as Zhao Kuangyin did.[28]

Not all kunqu staged ancestors are heroes and heroines. In fact, many are aggressive or devilish characters whom righteous Chinese would condemn, thereby venting their frustrations at evils and social inequalities. For instance, Qin Hui (1090–1155), a notorious official in early Southern Song China (1127–1279), who had the victorious patriotic general Yue Fei (1103–1142) executed for treason—a groundless accusation– appears in "Scolding Qin Hui" ("Sao Qin"). A favorite scene from the *Story of Exposing a Crime Plotted by the East Window* (*Dongchuang shifa*), this *zhezixi* presents a righteous deity disguising himself as a monk to reprimand Qin Hui, thus soothing Chinese anger at evil and treacherous people.[29]

---

27. For a collection of studies on the drama, see Lei Jingxuan, ed., *Kunju Zhu Maichen xiuqi: Zhang Jiqing Yao Jikun yanchu banben* (Hong Kong: Oxford, 2007). For an online audiovisual clip of Zhang Jiqing's performance, see *The Story of the Mountain of Rotten Axe Handle*, performance by Zhang Jiqing, accessed September 23, 2019, https://www.youtube.com/watch?v=rLqhmPPr1V8.

28. For further discussion of the *zhezixi*, see Joseph S. C. Lam, "Escorting Lady Jing Home: A Journey of Chinese Gender, Opera, and Politics," *Yearbook for Traditional Music* 46 (2014): 117–141.

29. For a video clip, see "Scolding Qin Hui," 1998 performance by Wang Chuansong, accessed March 20, 2018, https//:www.youtube.com/watch?v=QbcuUwPcOJ0.

Lives, Dreams, Documents, and Character Models 91

Figure 5.2: Zhao Kuangyin and Jingniang in the *Escorting Lady Jing Home*. Photograph by J. Lam, 2014. Courtesy of Shen Guofang and Tang Rong.

Dramatic Forefathers

Unlike staged ancestors from China's distant past, *dramatic forefathers* of kunqu are historical figures who played significant roles in the genre's development. Their biographies and works are viewed as essential sources and models for kunqu performance and appreciation. Some dramatic forefathers have become kunqu characters; many have served as models for iconic characters. For example, Wei Liangfu, the kunqu master mentioned earlier, has been dramatized as a leading character in the *Kunqu Sage: Wei Liangfu* (*Qusheng: Wei Liangfu*), a new kunqu opera that KunKun premiered in 2017.[30]

One dramatic forefather who has inspired many male kunqu characters is Liang Chenyu (1521?–1592?), the librettist of the *Story of Washing Silk*, a celebrated exemplar of Chinese author-scholar-officials. As described in historical documents,[31] Liang was an imposing person, heavily built and with a spectacular beard. Disgusted

---

30. For a comprehensive study on *Qusheng: Wei Liangfu*, see Wei Juhua, "Kunqu in Practice: A Case Study" (PhD diss., University of Hawai'i, 2019).
31. For an interpretative account that blends Liang Chenyu's biography with his *Washing Silk*, see Guo Yingde, *Ming Qing chuanqishi* (Beijing: Renmin wenxue chubanshe, 2012), 145–150.

by the corruption he saw, he gave up his ambition of serving the nation as a dutiful scholar-official, returned home, and indulged in travel, music-making, and frolicking with beautiful girls. He built himself a mansion, where all kinds of artists and literati gathered. To his admirers, he was a demigod on earth. To kunqu practitioners, he was a prototypical *qingchun dianya* Chinese man.

Another leading dramatic forefather is Tang Xianzu (1550–1616), whose biography and dramas constitute a core component of contemporary kunqu performance, reception, and scholarship.[32] A native of Linchuan in Jiangxi Province, Tang grew up in a scholarly and privileged family, studying under leading teachers of his time. He acquired his *juren* degree at the early age of twenty-one but did not advance to the *jinshi* rank until he was thirty-four. He had only a brief career as an official—for five years (1593–1598) he served as a magistrate in Suichang County in Zhejiang Province. After that, he devoted himself to writing dramas. Tang was a creative storyteller and a philosopher whose dramatic works are simultaneously literary masterpieces and social-philosophical manifestos, which kunqu practitioners diligently study, dutifully applying what they have learned to their performances and discussions. According to scholarly practitioners, no conscientious actor-singer would perform a male character in Tang's four dream operas without having thoroughly studied his biography.

A late Ming and early Qing man who engaged with kunqu as life and dream was Zhang Dai (1597–1689). In his posthumously published *Tao'an mengyi* (Zhang Dai's dreams and reminiscences), Zhang wrote many vivid reports on elite late Ming kunqu practitioners, who contributed much to the genre's performance artistry.[33] Peng Tianxi, for example, spared no expense or effort to perfect his shows and performance skills. Zhang reports that the evil characters Peng enacted were vicious, their faces ugly and demonic, their words hurtful.

Legitimizing Teachers

Kunqu characters modeled after staged ancestors and dramatic forefathers are brought to life on stage by master performers who have trained under authoritative mentors, whose names they proudly declare. Artistic genealogy is of great importance in kunqu performance and reception. Declarations of artistic provenance are salient features of kunqu biography, criticism, and reviews. Kunqu genealogies are, however, complex in human terms. Actor-singers travel and learn from a multitude of teachers throughout their long years of training and performing. Since the late 1950s, China has been organizing conferences and workshops for actor-singers, where performers

---

32. For a recent study on Tang Xianzu's biography and career, see Zou Yuanjiang, *Tang Xianzu xinlun* (Shanghai: Shiji chubanjituan, 2015).

33. See, for example, Zhang Dai, *Tao'an mengyi*, annotated by Lin Bangjun (Shanghai: Shanghai shiji chuban gufen youxian gongsi, 2014), 41–42, 87–88, 133–124, and 159. See also Joseph S. C. Lam, "Zhang Dai's (1597–1680) Musical Life in Late Ming China," in *Ming China*, ed. Kenneth Swope (New York: Routledge, 2019), 343–365.

Lives, Dreams, Documents, and Character Models   93

from different troupes can learn from authoritative teachers as well as one another. Making long journeys to learn specific *zhezixi* or roles from celebrated masters is now common practice. Nevertheless, kunqu genealogies and stylistic differences between northern kunqu (*beikun*) and southern kunqu (*nankun*) are still noted, as the following account relates.[34]

In the early decades of the twentieth century, northern kunqu was led by Pu Tong (1877–1952), Han Shichang (1898–1976), Hou Yushan (1893–1996), Bai Yusheng (1902–1972), Mei Lanfang, Hou Yongkui (1911–1981), and other local masters. Pu Tong was a Manchurian nobleman, a versatile amateur performer, and an influential pedagogue.[35] His performance of Li Guinian, the itinerant singer in "Ballad Singing," is still fondly discussed. After 1929, he taught kunqu at a number of universities, training a group of kunqu artists and connoisseurs, including Xu Yanzhi (1898–1989), who moved to Taiwan in 1948 and there nurtured many kunqu performers and audiences.

Han Shichang was a professional female impersonator noted for his performances of "Yearning for the Secular World" ("Sifan"), "Raising a Ruckus in the Classroom" ("Naoxue"), and other popular *zhezixi*, playing young female roles.[36] Han was also one of the first kunqu masters to tour overseas; his performance in Japan in 1928 was a milestone in kunqu history. His stardom challenged that of Mei Lanfang. His legacy was powerful and is still felt. Han learned diligently from and actively collaborated with Wu Mei (1884–1939), Cai Yuanpei (1868–1940), and other early twentieth-century cultural and educational leaders. These relationships helped elevate kunqu performers' social status. In 1957, Han joined BeiKun as a director, and in that role he nurtured many youths who later became master performers. One of them was Li Shujun (1930–2011), who became a kunqu celebrity in the 1960s.[37] A long-time performance partner of Han was Bai Yunsheng (1902–1972), a celebrated performer of many male and female roles, who joined BeiKun as a faculty member in 1957. Bai

---

34. For three informative accounts of northern kunqu, see Liu Zhen, Liu Yuzhen, and Cong Zhaohuan, eds., *Beifang kunqu lunji* (Beijing: Wenhua yishu chubanshe, 2009); Chen Jun, *Jingdu kunqu wangshi* (Taipei: Xiuwei zixun chubanshe, 2010), and Zhu Junling, *Kunqu zai beifang di liuchuan yu fazhan* (Beijing: Zhongguo shehui kexue chubanshe, 2015). For a representative account of southern kunqu, see Liu Junhong and Gu Lingsen, eds., *Guanzhu xingjin zhong de kunju* (Beijing: Zhongguo xiju chubanshe, 2011). Due to space limitations, subsidiaries developed in Yangzhou, Wenzhou, and other secondary kunqu centers will not be discussed here.

35. Pu Tong's kunqu legacy is notationally preserved in his *Hongdou guan baizheng ciqu yicun* (facsimile, Beijing: Shuangwu yinshuguan, 2012).

36. For a study of Han's biography and artistry, see Lin Ping and Wang Weimin, *Han Shichang kunqu biaoyan yishu* (Beijing: Zhongguo xiju chubanshe, 2012). For a historical recording of the two masters' performance, see *The Jade Hairpin*, 1950s performance by Bai Yunsheng and HanShichang, accessed September 28, 2019, https://www.bilibili.com/video/av13811300.

37. For Li Shujun's biography, see Chen Jun, *Xianyue piaomiao: Li Shujun pingzhuan* (Shanghai: Guji chubanshe, 2011).

was also a scholar of kunqu who published many insightful articles on performance that today are considered standard references.[38]

Hou Yushan, who grew up among a northern clan of opera actors, excelled in the martial kunqu male role.[39] His enactment of Zhong Kui, a ghost character who escorts his living sister to her groom, still serves as a model for current renditions. Another teacher from the Hou clan of actors was Hou Yongkui (1911–1981), whose performance of "Flee by Night" won him the honor of being recognized as a "living Lin Cong."[40] Hou was the father of Hou Shaokui (b. 1939), who is currently the most respected kunqu teacher and performer of the kunqu *wusheng* role.[41] Hou Shaokui has taught many students, such as Fei Yanling (b. 1947) of Hebei Bangzi Opera Troupe, and Tang Rong, a star performer and vice-director of SuKun. The Hou genealogy and legacy is now nationally cherished.

Mei Lanfang, the legendary performer of Peking opera, holds a unique position in twentieth-century kunqu transmission and development.[42] Though remembered today mainly as a Peking opera artist, Mei learned, performed, and promoted kunqu throughout his career. When he toured in Russia, Japan, and the US in the 1920s and 1930s, his programs included popular kunqu *zhezixi* like "Yearning for the Secular World," "Strolling; Dreaming," and "Killing a Warlord" ("Cihu"). Mei's kunqu legacy is now preserved in audiovisual recordings and in treasured memories. Many senior kunqu masters who performed minor roles in Mei's productions proudly describe how they directly and indirectly learned from him.

Like its counterpart in the north, southern kunqu has its own lines of legitimizing mentors and successful disciples; for convenience, they can be organized into four related lines. The first is a known but under-studied line personified by Yin Guishen (1825?–?),[43] a versatile performer who not only performed many roles but also excelled in playing the flute and drum, delivering music that melodically and rhythmically defines kunqu instrumental music. After retiring from the stage, Yin became a

---

38. See Liu Yuchen, ed., *Bai Yunsheng wenji* (Beijing: Zhongguo xiju chubanshe, 2002).
39. For Hou Yushan's autobiography, see his *Youmeng yiguan bashinian* (Beijing: Zhongguo xiju chubanshe, 1991). For his performance photographs and notated music, see Guan Dequan and Hou Ju, eds., *Hou Yushan qupu* (Beijing: Shogun xiju chubanshe, 1994).
40. For an autobiographical account of Hou Yongkui, see his "Wo de kunqu wutai shengyai," in *Yandu yitan*, comp. Anonymous (Beijing: Beijing chubanshe, 1985), 50–58.
41. For a biography of Hou Shaokui, see Hu Shaokui and Hu Mingming, *Dawusheng-Hou Shaokui kunqu wushi nian* (Beijing: Wenhua yishu chubanshe, 2007).
42. There is a wealth of publications on Mei Lanfang. For a recent study of his operatic artistry and career, see Zou Yuanjiang, *Mei Lanfang biaoyan meixue tixi yanjiu* (Beijing: Renmin chubanshe, 2018). For an oral history of his early career, see Mei Lanfang, *Wutai shenghuo sishi nian*, documented by Xu Jichuan (Reprint, Hong Kong: Open Page Publishing, 2017). For an autobiographical account of Mei's performance of "Strolling; Dreaming," see Mei Lanfang, "Wo yan 'Youyuan jingmeng,'" in *Mei Lanfang wenji* (Beijing: Zhongguo xiju chubanshe, 1982), 60–79.
43. For a concise biography of Yin Guishen, see Wu Xinlei, *Zhongguo kunqu dacidian*; for studies of his kunqu scores, see Lu Eting, "Yin Guishen and *Yuqingtang qupu*," in *Zhongguo kunqu luntan* (2003), 180–185.

music teacher-transmitter who prepared the *gongche* notated scores for more than 500 *zhezixi*. The music preserved in Yin's scores, however, has yet to be analytically and historically investigated. The story of Yin's kunqu genealogy and achievements has yet to be comprehensively told.

The second line in the southern kunqu genealogy is headed by Xu Lingyun (1886–1966), an elite kunqu connoisseur, performer, and writer.[44] He performed a variety of male and female roles. In the 1930s, he began to publish on his performance insights and experiences. His *Kunju biaoyan yide* (Insights on performing kunqu) and *Kanxi liushi nian* (Sixty years of attending kunqu shows) are now seminal documents on kunqu history and traditional performance practices.

The masters who defined the lineage of late twentieth-century Shanghai kunqu are Yu Zhenfei and the Chuanzibei Masters. How Yu and the masters collaborated is a story that has yet to be fully told. Current discussions, however, tend to discuss them as distinct but related branches. Needless to say, Yu's branch has received the lion's share of discussion for artistic as well as social reasons. Yu had a perfect pedigree and career, one that his formal and informal disciples would proudly delineate, thus honoring their teacher and legitimizing their own artistry. Yu learned kunqu from his father, Yu Sulu (1847–1930), who was not only an acclaimed kunqu singer and pedagogue but also a master of Chinese calligraphy and painting and an authority on antiques.[45]

Yu Zhenfei (1902–1993) debuted as an amateur performer at the age of fourteen. By his early twenties, he was already a celebrated performer. In 1930, he became a professional performer of Peking opera and kunqu, and over the following decades his brilliant career won him many awards. In 1988 he received an honorary doctorate from the Chinese University of Hong Kong. The following year, he was awarded the Gold Prize of the China Record Company.

As a kunqu actor-singer, Yu was handsome and talented. He mesmerized his audiences with distinctive performance practices and materials. Celebrated are his exemplary enunciating of scripted words, his effortless shifts between natural and falsetto registers, and his expressive melodic ornaments and phrasing. Yu performed a large repertory and brought many characters to life on stage. His signature performances and characters include Liu Mengmei in the *Peony Pavilion*, Li Bai in "Li Bai Composes Poetry While Drunk" ("Taibai zuixie"), Pan Bizheng in the *Jade Hairpin*, and Tang Minghuang in the *Palace of Everlasting Life*. Preserved audio and audiovisual recordings of Yu's shows are now treasured as historical references on kunqu history and performance practices.

Yu shaped contemporary kunqu aesthetics and performance practices with his personification of *shujuanqi*, a distinctive cultural aura that traditional China finds

---

44. Xu Lingyun, *Kunju biaoyan yide; kanxi liushinian* (Suzhou: Guwuxuan chubanshe, 2009).

45. For a concise biography of Yu Sulu, see Wu Xinlei, "Kunqu Yupai changfa yanjiu," in *Kunqu shi kaolun*, 348–377.

96   *Kunqu*

in elite, erudite, and romantic scholar-officials.[46] Literally, "*shu*" means books; "*juan*," rolls of manuscripts; and "*qi*," the "aura" a person emits. In imperial China, many elite males lived among mounds of scholarly works and artistic objects that taught them Confucian and other lofty ideas and *qingchun dianya* practices. Many of their descendants live similarly in contemporary China. And many kunqu practitioners emulate Yu's *shujuanqi* model. They know that on stage, Yu enacted idealized Chinese men, and offstage, he lived like one. Yu the man and his idealized manhood survive in his paintings, calligraphy, and manuscripts; all are now collected as historical mementos, *objets d'art*, and profitable investments.

Yu's impact as a kunqu pedagogue was immense. Between 1957 and 1966, he served as the director of the Shanghai Opera Academy (Shanghai shi xiqu xuexiao). There, he personally supervised the education of an entire generation of professional Shanghai kunqu performers. Many of his students later became kunqu stars.[47] Their names include Cai Zhengren (b. 1941) and Yue Meiti (b. 1941). Yu's legacy has been perpetuated by many audiovisual recordings and publications from the 1960s and 1970s; many of these are now available online. In 1985, a collection of Yu's writings was published. Yu's kunqu life and artistry have been detailed by Tang Baoxiang, his official biographer.[48] Yu's school of kunqu singing is becoming more and more authoritative in twenty-first-century China.

Compared to the wealth of information about Yu's life and achievements, data about the Chuanzibei Masters and their legacies is relatively limited.[49] Current knowledge about the masters can be sketched as follows. Wang Chuansong (1906–1987) was a multitalented artist. His virtuosity has been immortalized by his performance of Lou the Rat in the 1956 opera-movie of the *Fifteen Strings of Coins*, and by his memoir, *Zhou zhongmei—Wang Chuansong tanyi lu* (A clown's charm: Wang Chuansong on his performance artistry).[50] Wang taught many students; among them are Liu Yilong (b. 1940) and Lin Jifan (b. 1946), who are universally acclaimed as the greatest clown

---

46. For a discussion of the ways kunqu performers project *shujuanqi*, see Yue Meiti, *Jinsheng jinshi— kunqu wushi nian* (Beijing: Wenhua yishu chubanshe, 2008), 272–282.
47. For an account of Yu's students who became ShangKun stars, see Ye Changhai and Liu Qing, eds., *Hunqian kunqu wushinian* (Beijing: Zhongguo xiju chubanshe, 2000).
48. For Yu Zhenfei's biography and career, see Tang Baoxiang, *Qingfeng yayun bo qianqiu: Yu Zhenfei pingzhuan* (Shanghai: Guji chubanshe, 2010).
49. For an autobiographical report of the Chuanzibei Masters and late Qing kunqu performers, see Lindy Mark, trans., "Argosies of Wonder on the Rivers and Lakes: Memories of the Quanfu Troupe by Yunhe Zhang and Qixiang Tan," *Chinoperl* 14 (1986): 77–95. For two biographical accounts of the Chuanzibei Masters, see Suzhou kunju chuanxisuo et al., *Suzhou kunju chuanxisuo jinian ji* (Suzhou: n.p.; 2006); and Sang Yuxi, *Youlan yanyun lai chuancheng: kunju chuanzibei pingzhuan* (Shanghai: Guji chubanshe, 2010). For two accounts of Chuanzibei Masters' students, see Suzhoushi wenhua guangbo dianshi guanli ju ed., *Sukunju chengjibei* (Suzhou: n.p. 2007), and Qian Ying and Gu Duhuang, eds., *Shengshi liufang: Jizibei congyi liushi nian qinghe yanchu jinian wenji* (Suzhou: Gu Wuxuan chubanshe, 2015).
50. Wang Chuansong, *Chouzhong mei*, documented by Shen Zuan and Wang Deliang (Shanghai: Wenyi chubanshe, 1987).

Lives, Dreams, Documents, and Character Models   97

performers of their generation. Wang's son, Wang Shiyao (b. 1939), is also a famous kunqu performer and a former director of ZheKun.

Shen Chuanzhi (1906–1994) was a legendary performer and teacher who represented the third generation of a kunqu family from Wuxing, Zhejiang Province. The first kunqu performer in the family was the grandfather, Shen Shoulin (1825–1890), originally a merchant who transformed himself into a top professional kunqu performer of the young male role. Following his footsteps, his four sons all became kunqu performers, specializing in different roles: the eldest son specialized in the painted-face role; the second, the young male role; the third, the *fu* role; and the fourth, the old man role. The second son was Shen Yuequan (1865–1936), the principal teacher of the Chuanzibei Masters and father of Shen Chuanzhi (1906–1994). In 1954, Shen Chuanzhi began teaching at the Shanghai Opera Academy; many of his students there are now preeminent kunqu artists and pedagogues. Their names include Liang Guyin (b. 1942) and Shi Xiaomei (b. 1949).

Zhu Chuanming (1909–1974) also came from a family of kunqu performers. A female impersonator admired for his singing and *shenduan* artistry, Zhu achieved stardom in the late 1920s and early 1930s. He was the principal teacher for a number of celebrated twentieth-century *huadan* performers, whose names include Hua Wenyi (b. 1941), Zhang Xunpeng (b. 1941), and Zhang Jiqing (b. 1938).

A performer of the young male role, Gu Chuanjie (1910–1965) was noted for his superb artistry and handsome stage presence. His 1930 performance with Mei Lanfang in *A Horse Trader's Tragedy* (*Fanma ji*) was sensational. Gu's life was a drama in itself. In 1931, he experienced difficulties with his colleagues and boldly gave up his performance career. In 1934 he enrolled in Jinling University to study agriculture, and in 1939 he married Zhang Yuanhe (1907–2003), the eldest of the four famous Zhang sisters of kunqu. Gu spent his last years in Taiwan, contributing there to the development of kunqu.

Zheng Chuanjian (1910–1996) specialized in the old man role. He was noted for his rich voice and masculine stage presence. His most celebrated Shanghai student is Ji Zhenhua (b. 1943), one of the most admired performers of the old man role in contemporary kunqu. Zheng also contributed much to the development of Yue opera of Shanghai (*yueju*), teaching Yuan Xuefen (1922–2011) and other top performers of the genre and designing *shenduan* for a number of celebrated shows.[51]

Zhou Chuanying (1912–1988), a specialist in the young male role, is now immortalized by his performances as well as for his leadership in the creation of the *Fifteen Strings of Coins* of 1956.[52] As reported in his memoir, *Kunju shengya liushi nian* (Sixty years of performing kun opera), Zhou brought the character of Judge Kuang Zhong alive on stage. That character was based on historical anecdotes about

---

51. See Ke Jun, ed., *Zheng Chuanjian ji qi biaoyan yishu* (Nanjing: Hehai daxue chubanshe, 1995).
52. Zhou Chuanying, *Kunju shengya liushi nian*, documented by Luo Di (Shanghai: Wenyi chubanshe, 1988).

a late Ming official with the same name. A Suzhou temple now honors the memory of Kuang Zhong, the historical and kunqu figure. Among Zhou's many students, Wang Shiyu (b. 1941) is the most prominent. A winner of the prestigious Plum Blossom Award and a leading performer of the young male role, Wang played seminal roles in the kunqu revival of the 2000s. He was the artistic director of the *Young Lovers* and the kunqu show at the Imperial Granary in Beijing; he groomed many performers' enactments of Liu Mengmei, the male protagonist in the *Peony Pavilion*.

Yao Chuanxiang (1912–1996) played the young female role. His two signature shows were "Searching for the Dream" ("Xunmeng) from the *Peony Pavilion* and "Tihua" ("Writing on the Fan") in the *Peach Blossom Fan*. Formally and informally, he taught many disciples, including Zhang Jiqing of Nanjing and Hua Wenyi and Liang Guyin of Shanghai. Zhang Jiqing reported that her award-winning performance of Du Liniang was based on Yao's teaching.

Visionary Patrons

Besides legitimizing teachers, visionary patrons played seminal roles in developing twentieth- and twenty-first-century kunqu. Four prominent ones can be introduced here. The first one is Zhou Enlai (1898–1976), who was socialist China's beloved foreign minister (1949–1958) and prime minister (1949–1976). An amateur theater performer before he became a political leader, Zhou patronized kunqu for both artistic and nationalist reasons. His presence at post-performance kunqu receptions signified the state's recognition of and support for the genre in mid-twentieth-century China. State endorsement has had a critical impact on kunqu performance and discourse of Chinese culture, history, and personhood.

Commoner patrons have also shaped kunqu developments. A representative example is Mu Ouchu (1876–1943),[53] who studied agriculture and business management in the US. A successful industrialist in twentieth-century China, Mu began to patronize kunqu around 1914, soon after he returned from America. In 1920, he started taking kunqu singing lessons from Yu Zhenfei. In 1922, he organized a charitable three-day performance of kunqu (February 10–12) in Shanghai, raising a substantial sum (more than $8,000 *dayang* dollars of the time) to financially sustain the Academy and its training of the Chuanzibei Masters. The performance took place at the Olympian Theater (Xialingpeike xiyuan). A non-Chinese performance venue in semi-colonial Shanghai,[54] it accommodated Mu's shows only because he was "Westernized" in addition to being a prominent industrialist.

---

53. Zhu Jianming, *Mu Ouchu yu kunqu: Minchu shiyejia yu chuantong wenhua* (Taipei: Xiuwei zixue keji, 2013).
54. Zhu Jianming, *Shenbao Kunju ziliao xuanbian* (Shanghai: Shanghai shi wenhua xitong difangzhi chubanshe, 1992).

Lives, Dreams, Documents, and Character Models 99

Figure 5.3: Prime Minister Zhou Enlai congratulated Han shichang (left 1), Mei Lanfan (left 2), and Bai Yunsheng (left 3), after a performance on June 22, 1957. Source: Wu Xinlei, ed., *Zhongguo kunju dazidian*, front matter.

Mu and a number of socially esteemed amateurs performed in the show. As reported by Yu Zhenfei, Mu's performance was amateurish,[55] but it clearly piqued audience interest: they wanted to hear how a modern Shanghai entrepreneur sang classical kunqu. Performing the popular "Bidding Farewell with Willow Twigs" ("Zheliu yangguan") in the charity show, Mu played the part of Li Yi, a hero, who must survive being despatched to foreign lands, overcome schemes to hurt him, return home victoriously, and be reunited with his wife. The character's story could be a dramatization of Mu's life. In 1909, thirty-three-year-old Mu went to study in the US, leaving behind a family and a career in China. He returned with the latest Western technology and business practices and applied them to build a successful textile enterprise. Mu's decision to enact Li Yi was in all likelihood serendipitous, but dramatic parallels in Mu's biography and Li Yi's story are too obvious for any kunqu audience to ignore.

The historical significance of Mu's patronage of the Academy and the Chuanzibei Masters became crystal clear decades later. Without his generous support, which lasted from 1922 to 1927, the Academy would have collapsed right after its launch and the masters would not have had opportunities to learn kunqu from authoritative mentors. In 1927, Mu's patronage ended with the collapse of his industrial enterprise,

---

55. Mu's musical limitations are clearly documented; see Zhu Jianming, *Mu Ouchu yu kunqu*, 268–269.

but by then it had secured a future for kunqu. The masters had learned kunqu well and were able to sustain and develop the genre as master performers and pedagogues. Mu is now widely admired as a Confucian businessman (*rushang*) and a seminal kunqu patron.

As a visionary kunqu patron, Mu stood unequalled for more than seventy years, until another giant emerged: Bai Xianyong (Kenneth Pai, b. 1937), whose production of the *Young Lovers* (2004) propelled kunqu into the national and international limelight. Strategically, Bai declared that he and his collaborators were staging the 400-year-old *Peony Pavilion* with its "original sauce and taste." Ingeniously, they had their show presented on Chinese university campuses, thus attracting and nurturing a young and educated audience for kunqu. That audience readily identifies with the *qingchun dianya* characters enacted. Bai also gave many kunqu lectures and organized scholarly conferences on the *Young Lovers*, building a cultural and intellectual foundation for the genre as a classical opera and cultural heritage of twenty-first-century China.[56] Since 2011, Bai and his partners have launched a long series of kunqu teaching and learning programs (*chuancheng jihua*) both within and beyond mainland China,[57] creating a web of institutional long-term supports for the genre's development.

Bai could not have achieved his vision had he not been a Chinese gentleman with the right pedigree and international standing. Bai is a *caizi* (talented man) by historical and contemporary Chinese standards; his *shuquanqi* is as forceful as that of Yu Zhengfei. A son of Bai Chongxi (1893–1966), a leading military general in Republican China, Bai grew up in a cultured environment, a child of privilege. He became enamored of kunqu after attending, in 1945, a performance of "Strolling; Dreaming" by Mei Lanfang and Yu Zhenfei. Bai confessed that Mei's singing of the hallowed kunqu aria "Black Silk Robe" affected him profoundly.

In 1963, Bai went to the US to study creative writing at the University of Iowa. After graduating, he began his career as an author and professor of Chinese language and literature at the University of California, Santa Barbara. He produced a series of dramas and novels; all have won praise for their sophisticated presentation of Chinese emotions and experiences. His full-length novel *Niezi* (*Sons of Sin*; 1983), for example, delves into personal desires, father-and-son relationships, and gender identities in mid-twentieth-century Chinese and Taiwanese contexts.[58]

Kunqu inspired Bai to write his 1966 novel *Youyuan jingmeng* (*Strolling in the Garden and Interrupted Dream*). That novel was later transformed into a spoken drama, whose stagings in 1982 and 1988 reinvigorated Bai's enthusiasm for kunqu.

---

56. Bai had academic conferences on kunqu held in Berkeley (2006) and Beijing (2007). Papers presented at the 2007 conference in Beijing have been published as Hua Wei ed. *Kuqun chunsan eryuetian: miandui shiji di kunqu yu Mudanting* (Shanghai: Guji chubanshe, 2009).
57. For an informative report on the teaching and learning program that Bai and Zhou Qin launched at the Suzhou University, see Zhou Qin, "Shengeng yuantou, guben yanggeng" in his *Huawu disheng: Cunxin shuwu kunqu suibi* (Jinan: Shandong chuban jituan youxian gongsi, 2012), 41–58.
58. Bai Xianyong, *Niezi* (1983; reprint, Taipei: Yunchen chubanshe, 1989).

Lives, Dreams, Documents, and Character Models 101

However, what triggered Bai's determination to produce the *Young Lovers* was his negative response to Chen Shizheng's 1999 production of the *Peony Pavilion* at the Lincoln Center. Finding what he saw culturally and historically misrepresentative, he decided to launch his own kunqu productions in order to demonstrate the authentic, beautiful, and classical kunqu/China that he understood and wanted to share with the world.

To produce his show, Bai worked with mainland Chinese and Taiwanese institutions and patrons, securing their artistic, financial, political, and social support. To prepare a textually authentic and dramatically intelligible script for the *Young Lovers*, he collaborated with a group of literary scholars. They streamlined Tang's libretto by purging passages that were narratively dispensable and/or unintelligible to contemporary audiences. Unlike traditional kunqu script writers, they refrained from writing new aria lyrics and speeches for their contemporary production. Bai's claim of authenticity for the *Young Lovers* is textually verifiable.

To produce the *Young Lovers* as he envisioned, Bai wanted young and charming performers to play the protagonists, Du Liniang and Liu Mengmei. His demand was unprecedented; traditionally the characters are played by senior actor-singers who can expressively enact the roles and/or have the seniority to demand that they be cast. Realizing the pragmatic wisdom of Bai's demand, Bai's institutional partner in Suzhou, SuKun, acquiesced. To elevate the junior and chosen actor-singers' performance standards, Bai and SuKun had them personally coached by Zhang Jiqing and Wang Shiyu, two senior kunqu performers and pedagogues. The lessons were intense and rigorous—indeed, they were advertised as "satanic training" (*moguishi xunlian*), which is now a standard term in kunqu parlance, one that highlights kunqu's pursuit of performative excellence through strict teaching and diligent learning. To underscore the seriousness of the training, and also to generate publicity for the *Young Lovers*, the young performers had to go through a public *baishi li*, a ritual during which they bowed to their mentors and requested acceptance as formal disciples. As the ritual concluded, the mentors and disciples sealed an interpersonal relationship that anchored their performance artistry and its reception.

To make the *Young Lovers* achieve the highest level of performance excellence, Bai developed a production team of internationally acclaimed musicians, costume and set designers, and sound and lighting technicians. As a result, the costumes that the *Young Lovers* stars wore were exquisitely tailored and colored. The publicity photographs and audiovisual recordings of the show are works of performance art by themselves. The music the production's composer, Zhou Youliang, arranged or wrote for the show launched the *qingchun dianya* music style of contemporary and symphonic kunqu instrumental music.[59]

---

59. See Zhou Youliang, *Qingchunban Mudangting qupu* (Suzhou: Suzhou daxue, 2015). For further discussion of the music, see Chapter 8.

To share his innovative classical kunqu with global citizens, Bai had the *Young Lovers* performed in California in 2006 and in Athens and London in 2008. By 2020 the production had been performed 400 times within and outside China since its premiere in 2004. Numerous journalists and scholars have written about the show and Bai's kunqu enterprise.

In addition to Mu Ouchu and Bai Xianyong, many other patrons in the present day have promoted kunqu according to their own personal visions. They include Gu Tiehua (b. 1937) of Shanghai and Hong Kong, an industrialist who has created a foundation to financially support kunqu performance and audiovisual documentation. Prominent kunqu patrons in the US include Anna Chen (b. 1941) of the New York Kunqu Society; Tongching Chang of the Wintergreen Kunqu Society of Washington, D.C. Professor Li Fangkuei (1902–1987) of the University of Hawai'i and his wife, Xu Ying; Professor Lindy Li Mark of California State University, Hayward; and Henry Zhang of the Western US Society of Kunqu.

Among kunqu patrons operating in the US, none is more celebrated than Zhang Chonghe (1913–2015), the youngest of the four famous Zhang sisters, who performed kunqu with the Chuanzibei Masters in China in the 1930s.[60] A multitalented artist, Zhang was not only an acclaimed amateur kunqu performer and pedagogue but also an admired calligrapher and painter. She was a real-life example of the artistic, charming, elite Chinese women enacted on kunqu stages. In 1948, Zhang married Dr. Hans Frankel (1916–2003), a sinologist, and moved to the US with him. When Frankel began teaching at Yale University (1961–1987), the couple settled in New Haven, Connecticut; their home subsequently became a US base of kunqu. There Chinese intellectual and kunqu artists gathered to enjoy and discuss kunqu and Chinese arts and culture, as documented in Zhang's *Quren hongzhua benshi* (Traces of kunqu personalities).[61] Featuring exquisite calligraphies, poems, paintings, and photographs exchanged between Zhang and her elite Chinese friends, the volume provides glimpses into artistic elite Chinese lives and dreams.

Many elite kunqu practitioners are actual scholars. In fact, it is their kunqu connoisseurship and scholarship that has lifted the genre to a form of Chinese cultural heritage. The person who spearheaded kunqu scholarship was Wu Mei (1884–1939), a founder of modern Chinese drama studies.[62] Three of his students directly impacted

---

60. For a biography of the Zhang sisters, see Annping Chin, *Four Sisters of Hofei: A History* (New York: Scribner, 2002). For a biography of Zhang Chonghe, see Wang Dao, *Yisheng chonghe* (Beijing: Sanlian shudian, 2017). For Zhang's views on kunqu history and performance practices, see Ch'ung-ho Chang Frankel, "The Practice of K'un-Ch'u Singing from the 1920's to the 1960's," *Chinoperl* 6, no. 1 (1976): 82–92. Zhang's music is notationally preserved in her *Zhang Chonghe shouchao kunqu pu*, comp. Chen Anna (Shanghai: Shanghai cishu chubanshe, 2012).

61. Zhang Chonghe narrated and Sun Kangyi recorded, *Quren hongzhua* (Guilin: Guangxi shifan daxue chubanshe, 2010).

62. Wang Weimin, *Quxue dacheng houshi shibiao: Wu Mei pingzhuan* (Shanghai: Guji chubanshe, 2010). For a current collection of Wu Mei's writings on kunqu, see Wu Mei, *Wu Mei ciqu lunzhuji*, ed. Jie Yufeng (Nanjing: Nanjing daxue chubanshe, 2008).

kunqu scholarship: Ren Erbei (1897–1991), Qian Nanyang (1899–1987), and Wang Jingchang (1913–1985). Ren Erbei, a specialist in Tang dynasty literature and *sanqu* (aria), helped define the core kunqu concept of *qingchang*—performing kunqu arias sans *shenduan*. Qian Nanyang (1899–1987) rediscovered and restored historical scripts of *zaju* and *nanxi*, establishing those genres as kunqu/*chuanqi* models. Qian trained many students at the University of Nanjing, one of them being Wu Xinlei, the dean of twentieth- and twenty-first-century kunqu scholarship. Working with Jiao Chenyu (1902–1996), Xu Yanzhi (1898–1989), and Xian Huanxin, three avocational kunqu masters, Wang Jingchang launched the Taiwanese tradition of kunqu performance and scholarship.

The scholar who established a niche for kunqu in twentieth-century Chinese musicology was Yang Yinliu (1899–1994). A native of Wuxi, Yang studied kunqu under Wu Wanqing (1847–1926) at the local kunqu club, the Tianyun she. Yang made *zaju* and kunqu essential topics in Chinese music history; his *Zhongguo yinyue shigao* (Draft History of Chinese Music) explains kunqu's historical significance and musical complexities; his *Yuyan yu yinyue* (Language and music) provides a musicological methodology for analyzing text and melody interrelationships in kunqu and other Chinese operas.[63] Many Chinese and non-Chinese musicologists have followed Yang's lead to analytically study kunqu, advancing its scholarship and connoisseurship.[64]

Iconic Characters

Kunqu parades many iconic characters on stage; each is a revealing personification of Chinese lives and dreams that kunqu practitioners have either experienced themselves or have learned from their Chinese ancestors, teachers, patrons, and scholars. To illustrate, the following survey of iconic characters in four popular *zhezixi* will suffice. One among many female characters that charm contemporary audiences, especially casual audiences, is Woman Liu, the jealous wife and husband beater in the *Lioness Roars* (*Shihao ji*). Superficially, the drama is a farce; more deeply, it is an intriguing commentary on Chinese marital relationships and gender roles—it is with such a playful blend of fact and fiction that kunqu prompts Chinese to reflect on their lives and dreams. Dramatically, the show presents Woman Liu's wifely dilemma. She wants, on the one hand, to stop her husband, Chen Jichang, from attending parties where he might be tempted by beautiful courtesans; she knows, on the other hand, that he needs to attend such parties to socialize with his male friends and develop career networks. To solve her dilemma, Woman Liu makes her husband promise that he will not attend parties featuring courtesans; if he breaks his promise, he will be punished with a beating at her hands. He agrees, but fails to keep his word.

---

63. Yang Yinliu, *Zhongguo gudai yinyue shigao* (Beijing: Renmin yinyue chubanshe, 1981); and "Yuyan yinyue xue chutan," in *Yuyan yu yinyue*, ed. Anonymous (Beijing: Renmin yinyue chubanshe, 1983), 1–96.
64. For a survey of contemporary kunqu scholarship, see Appendix 1.

Figure 5.4: Woman Liu beats Chen Jichang in a SuKun performance of "Kneeling by the Pond." Photograph by J. Lam, 2014. Courtesy of Weng Yuxian and Zhou Xuefeng.

In the "Kneeling by the Pond" ("Guichi") scene of the drama,[65] a popular *zhezixi*, Woman Liu learns that her husband has broken his promise. She then punishes him with a beating, generating an entertaining and socially transgressive sequence of *shenduan*. The scene reaches its climax when Su Dongbo (1037–1101), a seminal scholar-official of Northern Song China and a beloved figure in Chinese opera, enters the scene and tries to help the humiliated husband restore his masculine dignity. Su and Woman Liu exchange harsh words, which can be paraphrased as follows:[66]

Woman Liu:
> I am a woman, but I know something about the classics and histories. Since ancient times, husbands and wives are told to honor each other like friends. I just found out that my husband is not acting like a man, and not keeping his promise to me. So don't blame me for not acting like a loving wife!

---

65. *Lioness Roars (Shihao ji)*, 2004 performance by Yue Meiti and Zhang Jingxian, accessed May 16, 2021, https://www.youtube.com/watch?v=K7x6hxfB-10&t=5777s. The "Kneeling by the Pond" begins at 51'10."

66. The Chinese texts paraphrased here are taken from Yu Zhenfei, *Zhenfei qupu* (Shanghai: Wenyi chubanshe, 1981), 254 and 256.

Su Dongbo:

> She makes trouble throughout the year, leaving an everlasting and stinking reputation. She leaves the four womanly virtues and three types of obedience behind her head. Speaking with a barbaric voice and projecting a vicious air, she has not a drop of tenderness. Hear how she howls from the room beyond the window, and see how she glares under the drapery in her boudoir. She follows neither rituals nor rules. She grinds her weapons like someone getting ready to avenge a murder. Even ghosts would find her ferocious. Such a woman is a beast that should be skinned.

Many contemporary kunqu audiences laugh heartily at characters in "Kneeling by the Pond," but on their way home, some will reflect on the farce and grasp its poignant commentary on Chinese and gendered lives. Woman Liu's words encapsulate what many traditional Chinese women have experienced and reasoned; Su's diatribe against her is chauvinistic, indeed, misogynist. Womanly jealousy is nothing new in historical or contemporary China; so is Chinese men's making impractical promises to their spouses, getting themselves into avoidable trouble. What Woman Liu, Henpecked Chen, and Scholar Liu enact on kunqu stages rings true for many contemporary Chinese. Should they tell white lies to their spouses? And should they be punished for not keeping impractical promises?

If twenty-first-century Chinese women feel for Woman Liu and her wifely rights, they react differently to Sekong, one of the most alluring female characters on the kunqu stage. As portrayed in "Yearning for the Secular World," Sekong is a young woman who was compelled to enter a nunnery when she was only a child. Growing up, she finds her life unsatisfying, and her daily chores of burning incense and watering plants meaningless and joyless. One day she sees a group of young monks playing outside the nunnery. Instantly she falls in love with a handsome one. Aroused from her torpor, she decides to flee the temple, marry the young monk, have a baby, and enjoy being a wife and mother in the secular world.

Continuously dismissed as a bawdy show by Chinese moralists, "Yearning for the Secular World" nevertheless remains a favorite kunqu *zhezixi*.[67] Sekong is the seductive girl that many Chinese men desire. Many Chinese women find Sekong a titillating model of womanhood—should they pursue their own personal happiness as she does? As acted, danced, and sung on contemporary stages, Sekong's seductiveness is unmistakable. For example, the first aria in the scene features suggestive words, flowing melodies, and tempting *shenduan*. When performed expressively, they bring

---

67. For an English introduction to and translation of the script, see A. C. Scott, *Longing for Worldly Pleasures/Ssu Fan*, in *Traditional Chinese Plays*, Vol. 2 (Madison: University of Wisconsin Press, 1969), 14–39. For two representative performances of "The Yearning for the Secular World," see "Yearning for the Secular World", performance by Liang Guyin, accessed May 15, 2021, https://www.youtube.com/watch?v=hrBAOqDMXnA&t=777s; and "Yearning for the Secular World" ("Sifan"), performance by Shen Shihua, accessed May 15, 2021, https://www.youtube.com/watch?v=MaNfIn4Hvbc&list=RDMaNfIn4Hvbc&start_radio=1.

Figure 5.5: Sekong and her young monk lover in a SuKun performance of "The Young Nun and Monk Leave for the Secular World" in Ann Arbor, Michigan, 2012. Photograph by J. Lam, 2012. Courtesy of Lü Fuhai and Sheng Guofang.

seductive Sekong alive on stage (see Music Example 5). Paraphrased, the lyrics of the aria run as follows:

> A young nun, I am now sixteen years of age. My beautiful and charming hair was shaven off by my teacher, the abbess. Every day, I burn incense, water plants on the altar. The other day, I saw several young monks playing outside the nunnery gate. He stared at me, and I looked at him. He and I, I and he, instantly became connected with desires and worries. Oh, my destined lover, how can we become a couple? For that to happen, I don't mind being taken to hell, and be sent to the king of death. I will let him pound me by hammers, sever my body with saws, crush my bones with a grinding stone, and fry my everything in sizzling oil! Who cares? But if you think of it, has anyone witnessed dead people being punished like that? All we see is the living suffering terribly. So why worry about what would happen? I will only take care of what I see right now. I will only take care of what is burning right now.[68]

---

68. This translation of the lyric is developed from Ben Wang's version; see his *Laughter and Tears: Translation of Selected Kunqu Dramas* (Beijing: Foreign Languages Press, 2009), 225–227.

Lives, Dreams, Documents, and Character Models

Kunqu also parades many male characters who personify all kinds of Chinese and male anxieties and desires. A much-admired hero on the kunqu stage is Lin Chong, from *All Men are Brothers* (*Shuihu zhuan*), a Ming novel about 108 "good men" (*haohan*) banding together to fight evil and injustice. As dramatized in "Flee by Night" ("Yeben"), Lin Chong is a wronged imperial commander being hunted by assassins. Exhausted, frightened, and worried about the safety of his mother and wife, Lin Chong grows emotional as he flees. To project such a Lin Chong, the *zhezixi* has the character dance and sing on stage and by himself for about thirty minutes, generating a spectacular performance of a Chinese man struggling to survive a difficult situation. A superbly enacted Lin Chong will win sympathy from Chinese men who are facing or have experienced difficulties in their lives. It is said that one such man was Mao Zedong, who admired the Lin Chong character and loved to attend "Flee by Night."

The climactic aria of the scene, set to the *qupai* titled "Geese Descending from the Sky" ("Yan'er lou") and "Being Victorious ("Desheng ling") tells of Lin Chong's flight and how he feels as he hurries toward his destination (see Music Example 6).[69] Translated, its lyrics run as follows:

> Looking at the road homewards from afar, and finding it winding further and further away, I ask on whom my mother and wife can now depend? Here, I do not know if I will live or die. There, there is no telling whether they are alive or dead. Oh! Alarmed, I am soaked with sweat that burns my body like a scalding soup; it fries my heart like fire. Where is my young wife? My old mother, I am afraid, has died. I can no longer show my gratitude to her for raising me. I can only sadly and loudly cry. I lament and ask how I can quench this heroic anger in me? How I can quench the heroic anger in me?

As performed nowadays, Lin Chong's male utterances are accented by musical high notes and rhythmic fermatas and kinetically illustrated by virile *shenduan* of high leaps and forceful kicks, virtuoso actions that impress casual and connoisseur audiences alike. As they feel Lin Chong's pain, some would realize that he is crying from the bottom of his heart. The realization even leads some Chinese men to have cathartic experiences—in chauvinistic China, men are not supposed to cry, even though many can hardly hold their tears; when they see Lin Chong cry, they cathartically weep, relieving their penned-up emotions.

As much as kunqu parades heroes and beauties on its stage, it also presents many villains. An especially despicable one is Xian Yuzhi,[70] who appears in the "Dog Exit" ("Goudong") scene from Ruan Dacheng's (1587–1646) celebrated *Swallow Letters*

---

69. For a performance script of the *zhezixi* with English translation, see Wang Hong, Wang Rongbei, and Zhou Qin trans., "The Tale of the Sword," in *Gems of Kunqu Opera* (Suzhou: Suzhou daxue chubanshe, 2006), 136–149.

70. For a contemporary performance script and music of "Goudong," see Shanghai xiju xueyuan fushu xiqu xuexiao, ed., *Kunqu jingbian jumu diancang*, Vol. 4 (Shanghai, Zhongxi shuju, 2011), 18–40. For an audiovisual recording, see "Dog Exit" ("Goudong"), performance by Wang Chuansong, accessed September 20, 2019, https://www.youtube.com/watch?v=GJWNaesxaAE.

(*Yanzi jian*). Ruan is historically known as a talented dramatist and an evil person—program notes on the *zhezixi* regularly refer to him as a negative figure in Chinese and kunqu history. As dramatized, Xian is an ignoramus who has snatched the top candidate honor by passing off a talented scholar's examination paper as his own. As staged nowadays, Xian is locked in a room and ordered to prove his erudition by writing a piece of literary work. Xian cannot produce anything, and thus he has to flee through a dog exit, the only way out of the room. To get the dog out of his way, he has to beg the animal to stop barking and move away; as performed, his begging unfolds with all kinds of ridiculous words and *shenduan*—all created to make him as despicable a man as Chinese people can imagine.

As Xian begs, he sings two melodically simple but verbally revealing arias. Translated, his lyrics tell:

> In actual life, writing essays is not a reliable practice of mine. Today I have to break the vessel and get to the bottom of things. In my heart, I know I have no wings that I can use to fly away [from this room].
>
> I stealthily gaze at the dog exit. Doggie, why do you have to bark on and on like that. Ok. Junior Uncle Doggie, Senior Uncle Doggie, Father Doggie, Grandfather Doggie, please don't bark. I have to squeeze myself in, and go through your exit. Ha! Ha! I have escaped and found a road to freedom. And I will disappear like old Woman Wang's cigarette smoke.

After singing his confession, Xian takes off his formal clothing and sneaks out of the room with nothing but his underwear. Thus dramatized, Xian personifies the fool and pretender that Chinese men want to laugh at, venting their pent-up anger at those who have unfairly acquired fame and wealth at their expense. For some Chinese, seeing Xian fleeing like an animal is a dream come true.

Epilogue

As described in this chapter, kunqu factually references and imaginatively performs Chinese culture, history, and personhood. Its archetypal stories and iconic characters are all modeled after staged ancestors, dramatic forefathers, legitimizing teachers, visionary patrons, and scholarly connoisseurs. All are readily identifiable by Chinese audiences. As the Zhengyici Theater stage couplet reports, kunqu practitioners identify with characters being enacted on stage intellectually and viscerally; they also believe that people sitting beside them in the auditorium feel and think the way they do. Audiences all seem to concur—kunqu reminds them that life is nothing but a dream.

Figure 5.6: Xian Yuzhi, the cheater and ignoramus in the "Dog Exit." Courtesy of ShengKun.

6

Kunqu Operations

Resources, Stakeholders, *Yuescapes*, and Products

Introduction

Viewed broadly, twenty-first-century kunqu has developed as a unified phenomenon productively run by teams of dedicated practitioners. A closer look, however, tells us that it is more complex than this, indeed perhaps more fractured, a conglomerate of regional institutions and competing stakeholders. They make many self-serving claims—for example, Suzhou stages authentic kunqu; Shanghai kunqu fields the best contemporary productions; and Taiwan has the most informed audience.[1] Institutional and individual kunqu stakeholders can hardly be expected to operate uniformly. They all have their own preferences and agendas, and they all operate in and work with specific *yuescapes*, dynamic times and sites that shape the stakeholders' deeds and words, which in turn are shaped by a multitude of interacting variables, such as competition among practitioners, local and national politics, and the availability of material and non-material resources.[2] Thus, to produce artistically and commercially viable shows, kunqu practitioners/stakeholders have to interact with one another as their needs arise.

This chapter presents three accounts of kunqu production. The first describes three distinctive *yuescapes*; two are more local—Suzhou and Taipei respectively, and one is national—mainland China. The second account is a case study of the Nanjing production of the *1699 Peach Blossom Fan* and demonstrates the ways in which dominant practitioners/stakeholders produce kunqu shows that reflect both their ambitions and the realities they face. The third account analyzes selected scenes and arias

---

1. These statements are repeatedly expressed by my kunqu research partners.
2. For further discussion of the *yuescape* concept and its use as an analytical paradigm, see discussion in Chapter 8. The concept is inspired by Arjun Appadurai's *-scapes*, and in particular that of *technoscapes*, fluid and global configurations in which technologies constitute a force that drives their *-scape* and are at the same time a result of the phenomenon generated. See Arjun Appadurai, *Modernity at Large: Cultural Dimensions of Globalization* (Minneapolis: University of Minnesota Press, 1996), 33–37.

Resources, Stakeholders, *Yuescapes*, and Products

in the *1699 Peach Blossom Fan*, demonstrating that kunqu shows are expressions of/from specific *yuescapes*.

Suzhou as a Kunqu *Yuescape*

Many practitioners claim that kunqu matured into a genre of classical Chinese opera in Suzhou in Qing China.[3] Kunqu monuments are scattered throughout the city today. For example, the Zhouzheng yuan (A Humble Administrator's Garden), a UNESCO World Heritage Site and a celebrated venue for kunqu performance, still stands in Suzhou.[4] Suzhou is now a nationally designated center for kunqu performance as well as teaching and learning.

To experience Suzhou as a kunqu *yuescape* where tangible and intangible entities affect local practitioners' engagement with the genre, producing distinctive results, one need only visit the city. Strolling down Pingjiang Road and Shantang Street, one finds many traces of historical kunqu individuals and events. These include Ye Tang's former residence, where he compiled his kunqu scores, and the Shanxi Merchant's Club (Quanjin huiguan), which now serves as a kunqu museum and theater. Visiting the city's Temple of the Old Master Performer (Laolang miao), one finds many old steles registering donations to historical kunqu troupes and their ritual-commercial performances. At the Suzhou Municipal Museum, one finds a rich collection of paintings, ceramics and other *objets d'art* produced or owned by the city's past kunqu patrons. The mansion next door, the former palace of Prince Zhong of the Taiping Rebellion which includes an indoor theatre, is now a kunqu museum and theater. Its *guxitai* has been restored for contemporary performances.

Leaving the municipal museum and the former palace, one can walk over to the neighboring Zhuozheng yuan. Strolling through meandering paths in the natural garden, one comes to the Hall of the Thirty-Six Mandarin Ducks (Sanshiliu yuanyang guan), where Zhang Zidong (1881–1951) and his kunqu teacher, Yu Sulu (1847–1930), sang kunqu, entertaining themselves and their exclusive guests.[5] Visitors will note that the hall is split into two halves: men of the Zhang family and their male guests enjoyed kunqu in the front half, women in the back. At the left and right corners of the front hall, one finds two small rooms where performers awaited

---

3. This account of Suzhou as a kunqu site is based on my own observations, interactions with local citizens, and reading of published studies. For representative studies on Suzhou and kunqu, see Gu Lingsen, *Kunqu yu renwen Suzhou* (Shenyang: Chunfeng wenyi cubanshe, 2005); Zhu Lin, *Kunqu yu jiangnan shehui shenghuo* (Guilin: Guangxi shifan daxue chubanshe, 2007) and Luo Qin, "Chengshi yinyue de lishi jidian, shengtai jiegou ji qi yanjiu de jizhixing yinsu—lun Mingmo zhi minguo Suzhou yinyue wenhua de lishi fazhan ji qi tezheng," *Yinyue yishu* 2 (2020): 68–84.
4. For an account of kunqu activities at famous Suzhou sites, see Liu Jianchun and Jiang Haofeng, eds., *Zhongguo kunqu ditu* (Shanghai: Wenhua chubanshe, 2009), 15–59. See also Li Yi, "Suzhou yuanlin yu kunqu wutai," MA thesis, Shanghai xiqu xueyuan, 2012.
5. For Zhang Zidong's kunqu activities in Zhuozheng yuan, see Zhang Xiuyun, *Buyuan jiushi* (Suzhou: Guwuxuan chubanshe, 2005); see esp. 91–93, 97–103, 113–125, 153–178.

Figure 6.1: The Qianrenshi in Huqiu, Suzhou, China. Photography by J. Lam, 2016.

their turns to perform. The colored glass panes of the windows in the front hall are said to have been designed to enhance the sounds and sights of the performances.

Leaving Suzhou, one comes to Huqiu, four and a half miles from the city's downtown. Climbing its gentle hill, one encounters the imposing Qianren shi (Stone terrace for thousands of people), a natural performance site where Ming and Qing kunqu masters once sang their kunqu arias to discriminating audiences. Tourists who visit Huqiu today during Mid-Autumn Festival may encounter historically inspired kunqu singing activities there.[6]

Suzhou city officials and kunqu practitioners work closely together to promote kunqu itself as well as Suzhou as the genre's current home. In 2005, they persuaded national authorities to declare Suzhou the national nexus for the genre's revival. This was quite a coup for them, given that Beijing, Shanghai, Kunshan, Qiandeng, and other Chinese cities also played critical roles in the development of kunqu and are actively claiming kunqu as their local expressions.[7] Suzhou won because the city's historical connections with kunqu are indisputable and because its municipal leaders formulated a strategy to transform Suzhou's historical kunqu *yuescape* into a site of cultural tourism. They grasp that kunqu fans and other tourists want to trace the steps of historical kunqu figures, such as Li Yu (1591–1671?), the leader of a group

---

6. For two reports on twenty-first-century kunqu singing activities at Huqiu, see Bret Sutcliffe, "Kunqu Concert at Lion Hill and Kunqu Amateur Convention at Suzhou, November 2001," *Chinoperl* 24 (2002): 133–136; and Min Yen Ong, "A Report on the 2010 Tiger Hill Amateur Kunqu Fesitval," *Chinoperl* 30 (2011): 259–264.
7. Each has its own kunqu and tourism promotion programs; for further details, check the cities' websites.

of seventeenth-century Suzhou dramatists,[8] and Zhang Zidong, who compiled an important collection of kunqu *gongche* notated scores and bequeathed it to the Suzhou Municipal Museum.[9] Many prominent Suzhou men and women of the past, such as Kuang Zhong (1383–1442), have been staged as kunqu characters.[10]

Many active and influential kunqu practitioners still live in Suzhou. With their local pride and their intimate knowledge of local resources, they work together to sustain and develop Suzhou as a kunqu center. Indeed, Suzhou officials, performers, and scholars had begun to revive the genre long before UNESCO honored it in 2001. As early as 1959, Suzhou established a municipal research center for salvaging the genre, collecting documents and conducting research that now serves as a foundation for current efforts. In 1986 the city founded the Suzhou Kunqu Museum.[11] Since 2000, Suzhou has been hosting a national festival and conference celebrating the genre; since 2003, the city has become the permanent host of the national event.

Suzhou's success as a "kunqu city" is the result of local practitioners' strategic maneuvers. For example, Cai Shaohua, who directed SuKun between 2002 and 2020, pragmatically chose to work with well-heeled external patrons.[12] To overcome the lack of funds for mounting new productions, and to develop a market share beyond Suzhou, Cai worked with Taiwanese patrons to produce the 2004 version of the *Palace of Everlasting Life*. Directed by Gu Duhuang (1933–2022),[13] a conservative Suzhou kunqu artist and scholar, the show featured Wang Fang and Zhao Wenlin, two local stars, as its lead performers. Showcasing traditional singing, instrumental music, *shenduan*, and staging practices, the show was strategically promoted as authentic kunqu from Suzhou.[14] At the same time, Cai Shaohua collaborated with Bai Xianyong to produce the *Young Lovers*, which established the *qingchun* and "original sauce and taste" aesthetics and practices of contemporary kunqu. SuKun, a struggling troupe in the late 1990s, was thus transformed into a leading twenty-first-century kunqu troupe.

---

8. For a study on Suzhou dramatists, see Gu Lingsen, *Li Yu yu kunqu Suzhou pai* (Yangzhou: Guangling shushe, 2011).
9. Zhang Zidong, *Kunju shouchao quben yibaice*, comp. Zhongguo kunqu bowuguan (Yangzhou: guangling gujie keyinshe, 2009). For two other seminal collections of kunqu documents compiled by Suzhou practitioners, see Suzhou kunju chuanxisuo, ed., *Kunju chuanshi yanchu zhenben quanbian*, 5 vols. (Shanghai: Renmin chubanshe, 2011), and Zhou Qin, comp., *Kunxi jicun*, 12 vols. (Hefei: Huangshan shushe, 2016).
10. For brief biographical accounts of Suzhou kunqu personalities, see Wu Xinlei, *Zhongguo kunqu dacidan* and Hong Weizhu, *Kunqu cidian*.
11. For more information about the museum, see its website: https//: www.kunopera.com.cn.
12. For an autobiographical account, see Pan Xinghua, "Qianzai nanfeng di jihui—Cai Shaohua fangtanlu," in *Chunse ruxu: Qingchunban mudanting renwu fangtan lu* (Singapore: Bafang wenhua chuangzuoshi, 2007), 15–23.
13. For a description of Gu Duhuang's kunqu career, see "Qujia ji xuezhe: Gu Duhuang," in *Kunqu yanyijia, qujia, ji xuezhe fangwen*, ed. Hong Weizhu (Taipei: Guojia chubanshe, 2002), 571–576.
14. *The Palace of Everlasting Life* (*Changsheng dian*), 2004 performance by SuKun, accessed May 16, 2021, https://www.bilibili.com/video/av12636683.

114   *Kunqu*

In addition to Cai, Gu, Wang, and Zhao, many other Suzhou kunqu stakeholders contributed to the rise of Suzhou as a contemporary kunqu *yuescape*. One Suzhou resident who contributed greatly to the intellectual and musical foundations for this rise is Zhou Qin (b. 1949) of Suzhou University. Since the 1990s, he has been composing, singing, playing, and teaching kunqu music. He continues to lecture on the genre's aesthetics, history, theory, and performance at national and international venues.[15] Until his retirement in 2016, he directed a kunqu teaching and research center at Suzhou University, where he trained many students. Some have become amateur or professional kunqu practitioners; many have become patrons and fans of the genre. They regularly gather to hold kunqu singing and appreciation activities, thus sustaining and transforming Suzhou's kunqu *yuescape*.

Taipei as a Kunqu *Yuescape*

Compared to Suzhou, Taipei is a new kunqu *yuescape*, one that local patrons, pedagogues, scholars, and audiences have collaboratively built in a relatively short time.[16] Today the city offers regular kunqu performances and boastfully claims that it has the most informed and appreciative audience for the genre. Most Taiwanese audiences attend kunqu shows with contemporary etiquette: they pay attention to what is being enacted and sung on stage, and during the performance, they refrain from talking with friends sitting next to them.

The kunqu *yuescape* in contemporary Taipei has some historical roots. Beginning in the 1700s, mainland kunqu performers occasionally toured Taiwan, entertaining local elites and contributing to the development of *beiguan*, a genre of Taiwanese opera. Some nineteenth-century Taiwanese kunqu patrons supported Suzhou kunqu; an acknowledgement of their donation to the Suzhou Club of Professional Theatrical Performers (Suzhou liyuan gongsuo) is carved on a stone stele preserved in the Suzhou Temple of the Old Master Performer.

Since 1949, Taiwan has practiced kunqu as a classical opera of China. In that year the Kuomintang government moved to the island, bringing with it a number of kunqu patrons and performers. Those patrons included Zheng Qian (1905–1992) of Taiwan National University and Jiang Fucong (1898–1990) of the Palace Museum. Names of kunqu artists included Xia Huanxin (1905–1988), Jiao Chengyun (1902–1996), and Xu Yanzhi (1898–1989).[17] Exercising their leadership roles on the island, they nurtured local interest in kunqu, creating opportunities for young Taiwanese to learn

---

15. Zhou Qin has authored/edited many kunqu publications; for autobiographical reports, see his *Huawu disheng: Cunxin shuwu kunqu suibi* (Jinan: Shandong chuban jituan youxian gongsi, 2012).
16. This account of kunqu in Taiwan is based on my fieldwork observations and information culled from Li Bin, "Shilun Taiwan kunqu chuanbo," *Zhong guo xiqu xueyuan xuebao* 30, no. 1 (February 2009): 32–37; and Cai Xinxin, "Kunqu zai Taiwan fazhan zhi lishi jingguan," *Zhonghua xiqu* 38 (2008): 184–230.
17. See biographical entries of these Taiwanese kunqu figures in Hong Weizhu, *Kunqu cidian.*

its performance practices. In the late 1970s, talented performers like Guo Xiaozhuang began to win recognition for their kunqu performances. By the late 1980s, Taiwan was home to a number of noncommercial kunqu institutions, such as Taida kunqushe (Kunqu Club of National Taiwan University) and the Shuimo quji (Kunqu club of water-polished melodies).[18]

In the 1990s, Taiwanese interest in kunqu began to blossom, propelled by gradual changes in local, national, and international politics and cultural-social needs. In 1987, the Taiwanese government began to lift its ban on cultural exchanges between mainland China and the island. In 1981, the island government launched the Wenjian hui (Council for Cultural Planning and Development) to oversee local cultural development. In 1991, the council formulated policies to encourage Taiwanese performance troupes to develop programs that would make a name for Taiwan. Successful results soon emerged, and performance troupes like Lin Huaimin's Yunmen wuji (Cloud Gate Dance Theatre) and Chen Mei-e's Hantan yuefu (Song and Dances from Han and Tang China) became internationally renowned. In 1993, the Taiwanese government formulated policies to allow senior mainland Chinese artists to visit, teach, and perform in Taiwan. Over the following decade, a number of senior mainland kunqu masters taught in Taipei under the auspices of the Kunqu chuanxi jihua (Kunqu Transmission and Learning Project). Some of the 400-plus graduates of that program, including Yang Hanyu and Lin Zucheng, are now leading kunqu practitioners in Taiwan.

To research kunqu in its original *yuescape*, many Taiwanese kunqu practitioners visited mainland China in the 1990s. A series of formal visits (1992–1996) produced results that affected the development of kunqu on both sides of the Taiwan Strait. Led by Zeng Yongyi (b. 1941) and Hong Weizhu (b. 1943), these visits allowed influential Taiwanese kunqu scholars and connoisseurs to closely examine kunqu as a classical performing art as well as observe the genre's precarious condition in mainland China.[19] They realized that unless drastic action was taken, the genre would soon vanish. As self-appointed guardians and transmitters of classical Chinese culture, they set out to save kunqu, making effective use of the financial and technological resources at their command.

They launched an ambitious program of video-recording kunqu performances by mainland master performers. All were getting old and suffered from a dire lack of financial and moral support. With funding provided by the Chuanyi zhongxin (Council for Cultural Planning and Development and the Center for Transmission of Traditional Arts), Zeng and Hong led a team of scholars and technicians to mainland China and recorded performances of a critical repertory of *zhezixi* by celebrated performers in Shanghai, Suzhou, Beijing, and Nanjing.

---

18. For information on these Taiwanese kunqu organizations, visit their websites or blogs.

19. Zeng Yongyi and Hong Weizhu are two leading kunqu scholars of Taiwan. For a representative sample of Zeng's kunqu publications, see his *Cong qiangdiao shuodao kunju* (Taipei: Guojia chubanshe, 2002). Hong is celebrated for his *Kunqu cidian*.

At the time, these seventy-plus hours of videotape constituted the largest and most representative recorded collection of kunqu performances.[20] The first series preserves sixty-nine *zhezixi* from twenty-nine *chuanqi* dramas. The second series preserves seventy-two scenes from forty-five plays. Once the project was completed, one hundred copies of the two sets of videotapes were sent to representative institutions and leading scholars of Chinese studies around the world. Those videotapes serve as monuments not only to Taiwanese kunqu efforts of the 1990s but also to the island's geopolitical position as a guardian of Chinese cultural heritage. The videotapes stimulated international interest in kunqu. Viewing them, many overseas Chinese scholars were able to "see," for the first time, realizations of *chuanqi* dramas they had been able to study only as texts.[21]

Thus, the kunqu *yuescape* in today's Taiwan extends well beyond the island. Indeed, it has strongly impacted kunqu in mainland China. While teaching and performing kunqu in Taiwan in the 1990s, many mainland master performers were delighted to find an appreciative audience and thrilled to see their artistry respected and valued. Some masters reaped material rewards that they deserved but had not received in mainland China.

Taipei is now a prominent *yuescape* of kunqu production and consumption. Many mainland kunqu masters, such as Zhang Jun of Shanghai, work with Taiwanese artists to produce their contemporary shows. Zhang's *Spring River* (*A Night of Moonlit Flowers in Spring and by the River*; *Chunjiang huayueye*; 2015), for example, was produced with a team of Taiwanese artists. In addition, Taiwanese kunqu performers have secured their rightful place in the national and global world of kunqu. A number of them play leading roles in contemporary productions. For example, Wang Jiaming (b. 1971), a celebrated Taiwanese performance director, helmed ShengKun's *The Story of the Western Mansion* (*Xilou ji*; 2019). Taiwanese are also involved in preservation efforts. In December 2017, Taiwan's kunqu museum at the National Central University (Zhongyang daxue) opened as a permanent home for the resources, scholarship, and expertise gathered by Taiwan's kunqu practitioners. Clearly, Taipei's kunqu *yuescape* is thriving and becoming more and more influential.

Mainland China as a Kunqu *Yuescape*

Taiwan's kunqu *yuescape* is in poignant contrast to the one in mainland China, which is controlled by state officials, bureaucratically appointed troupe administrators, award-winning master performers, and authoritative scholars and scholar-officials. In other words, the mainland Chinese kunqu *yuescape* is historically and politically grounded. In 1956, kunqu was "salvaged" by state promotion of the *Fifteen Strings*

---

20. For a catalog of titles in the videotape series, see "Taiwan zhizuo zhi kunqu luyingdai mulu," Appendix 9, in *Kunqu cidian*, 1322–1328.

21. My mentor, Professor Rulan Chao Pian, loaned me her copy of the videotapes for two years. Repeated viewing of them shaped my understanding of kunqu sounds and sights.

of Coins and the launching of seven professional kunqu troopes-academies. In 1978, the central government gathered a group of kunqu troupe administrators and senior artists and scholars to explore ways to reinvigorate kunqu, performances of which had been banned during the Cultural Revolution. In 1981, a kunqu performance festival (*huiyan*) was held in Suzhou, celebrating the sixtieth anniversary of the Academy and the Chuanzibei Masters. There and then, the leaders agreed to have kunqu masters train students within and outside their own schools and to hold more performance conferences. All of this reflected socialist China's top-down approach to safeguarding and developing kunqu.

In 1985 the Ministry of Culture organized a meeting of kunqu troupe directors in Kunshan. By the end of the meeting, they had agreed on three actions: traditional performances by senior artists would be video-recorded; master performers would be assigned to teach young students; and kunqu would be rescued by staging exhibitions as well as educational performances of classical shows. In 1987 a performance conference was held in Beijing, where twenty-eight out of 133 "salvaged" scenes were presented.

In 1992, another performance conference was organized in Kunshan to celebrate the seventieth anniversary of the Academy. Three years later, in 1995, a second kunqu advisory committee was organized, which formulated a comprehensive policy for preserving and developing the genre. Encapsulated with four bisyllabic Chinese words, it prescribed actions of "*baohu, chengji, chuangxin, fazhan*," which literally mean "preserving and protecting, inheriting and continuing, creating and innovating, and expanding and developing." Concrete guidelines were not publicly announced, however, nor were funds for implementing the national policy. Whatever concrete results the policy generated, they did not significantly improve conditions for kunqu in the mid- and late 1990s. To survive, many performers left the stage, and a few emigrated to the US, abandoning their careers as kunqu artists.

In 2000 the Ministry of Culture, the Jiangsu provincial government, and the Suzhou municipal government together launched a large performance conference in Suzhou. Top kunqu performers gathered and delivered grand performances of thirteen dramas and nine selected *zhezixi*, demonstrating their determination to preserve and develop the genre. In 2003 the Ministry of Culture designated Suzhou the permanent base for safeguarding and promoting kunqu; to that end, a national performance and scholarship conference would be held there every three years. The decision was clearly a direct response to the 2001 UNESCO declaration of kunqu as a Masterpiece of the Oral and Intangible Heritages of Humanity.

In 2005, the China government announced that it would earmark RMB1,000,000 to support the seven state-sponsored kunqu troupes that year and in each of the next four years. This indicated that an increasingly prosperous China was determined to promote kunqu with generous funds. In addition to this, state, provincial, and municipal resources were directed toward building an extensive infrastructure for promoting kunqu in Beijing, Nanjing, Shanghai, Suzhou, and other major Chinese cities. The infrastructure would feature regular performances by professionals, support research by scholars, and generate TV shows and other media and promotion programs. By 2011, many substantive results had emerged. Suzhou, for example, had founded the Suzhou Kunju Museum, relaunched the Academy, built up SuKun, launched the Kunju Research Center at the Suzhou University, established a number of formal venues for regular performances in the city, and begun producing kunqu programs on Suzhou and Kunshan TV.

In addition to all this, mainland China supports kunqu through various institutional measures. The following four have critically shaped the kunqu *yuescape* in mainland China and allowed its influence to reach beyond national boundaries. The first is a system of ranking performers into three classes of national artists. All senior and nationally celebrated performers are designated Class I performers. They are given prizes, honors, national stipends, and licences to perform and teach. Many kunqu artists have earned Class I status. Active and professionally recognized performers are ranked as Class II performers. Young and promising performers are ranked as Class III.

The second institution is a variety of local and national performance competitions that allow talented performers to win recognition. For kunqu and other traditional opera performers, the most important competition is the Plum Blossom Prize (Meihua jiang).[22] Founded in 1983 by the Association of Chinese Dramatists (Zhongguo xijujia xiehui) and the *Drama Daily* (*Xiju bao*), the Plum Blossom Prize honors individual performers in four categories of performing arts: traditional Chinese opera, spoken drama, musical theater, and dance. Between 1983 and 2005, the competition was an annual event; since 2005, it has been held in alternate years.

The competition has four requirements. First, competitors for the prize must be under forty-five years of age when they formally enter the competition, and they must perform a number of required feature presentations (*zhuanchang*). Second, some of the presentations must be staged in Beijing in the year before competition decisions are made. Third, the presentations must include both traditional and modern works. Fourth, judges appointed by cultural and governmental authorities will assess the presentations. In other words, competing for the Plum Blossom Prize is a complex and high-stakes process, one that demands great efforts and resources on the part of the competitors and the institutions that support them. Significantly, competitors are nominated by local theatrical troupes and institutions. And only after the nominations are accepted can production of the feature presentations in Beijing begin. Clearly, this process is complicated. For example, booking Beijing performance venues, developing new shows, and organizing casts all demand meticulous planning and tactical maneuvers. Many of the shows staged for the Plum Blossom Prize are created specifically to impress judges and to showcase the competitors' talents. Some have become hit shows.

---

22. For a description of the competition, see "Meihua jiang," accessed May 20, 2016, http://www.xijucn.com/html/jingju/20081208/6427.html.

Kunqu performers do well in the Plum Blossom Prize. The first kunqu winner of the prize was Zhang Jiqing, whose enactment of Du Liniang in the *Peony Pavilion* won universal acclaim. By 2020, more than thirty kunqu master performers had won the Plum Blossom Prize. Several of them, such as Wang Fang and Lin Weilin, have even won twice. All winners of the Plum Blossom Prize are now celebrated kunqu stars.[23]

The third means by which Chinese national authorities directly and indirectly influence kunqu operations is through the media, in particular state-controlled TV stations. For example, CCTV 10, the national channel for theatrical arts (*xiqu pindao*), offers regular programs of kunqu, alongside those of Peking opera and other local genres. One prominent and influential kunqu program on CCTV is the documentary *600 Years of Kunqu*. Kunqu institutions and performers compete for opportunities to appear on national TV programs; exposure through mass media promotes their stardom.

The fourth means for the Chinese state to influence the nation's kunqu *yuescape* involves the genre's scholars. Theoretically they conduct their research individually and according to their interests. In practice, their scholarship is affected by national education and research policies, faculty appointments at universities and colleges, and guidelines for the publication of scholarly results. Scholars supported by local and central authorities have ready access to governmental grants and publication venues as well as to officials who supervise kunqu productions in mainland China.

Collaboration between officials and scholars is a centuries-old Chinese tradition. Culturally and historically, many officials are scholarly, and many scholars serve as officials at some point in their careers. Officials, needless to say, hold the political power as well as the purse strings, a fact that kunqu performances and conference events in mainland China rather poignantly indicate. Note, for example, that it is officials who give the welcoming greetings at opening ceremonies of kunqu festivals or conferences, events they support financially and politically. Many performances cannot begin until official sponsors have arrived and are ushered to their reserved seats.

The extent to which China's national policies and institutions shape the mainland's kunqu *yuescape*, the principal stage of the genre's current development, awaits thorough investigation. For now, it is reasonable to say that the *yuescape* is steered collaboratively by government-appointed officials, troupe administrators, and master performers, whose actions are, however, "constrained" by forces that constitute the *yuescape*, including actions by kunqu amateur performers and audiences. Many professional kunqu performers lament that "outsiders" (*waihang*) now control the genre's institutions, resources, and performances to such an extent that they are suffocating the genre.[24] That lament is somewhat valid. Regional and cultural officials like

---

23. For a list of kunqu winners of the Plum Blossom Prize, see "Zhongguo xiju meihuajiang ji lijie huo-jiang mingdan", accessed January 10, 2019, http://www.xijucn.com/html/jingju/20081208/6427.html.

24. See Zhang Weidong, "Zhengzong kunqu daxia jiangqing," in *Shanghua you shi duqu you dao—Zhang Weidong lun kunqu* (Beijing: Shuangwu chubanse, 2013), 1–7.

120 *Kunqu*

to spend their resources on grand productions of new operas, which serve as visible and quantifiable results of their policies. These grand operas may or may not have artistic worth. Many kunqu shows produced according to political guidelines and/or powerful officials' visions are forgotten soon after their premieres. Some have, however, become contemporary classics. It all depends on how individual performers, institutions, and other stakeholders operate and interact with one another in their *yuescape*.

A Strategic Kunqu Operation in Nanjing

To illustrate the ways contemporary kunqu operations unfold in specific *yuescapes*, a case study of ShengKun's production of the *1699 Peach Blossom Fan* will suffice.[25] Based in Nangjing, ShengKun is institutionally unique among the eight national and professional kunqu troupes in mainland China. It operates like a commercial corporation, a result of economic transformations in twenty-first-century China. In 2001 the Jiangsu provincial government reorganized the performing arts troupes under its control and established the commercial and independent institution named Jiangsu yanyi jituan (Jiangsu Province Arts Group Co., Ltd.), a conglomerate that includes Shengkun. This unprecedented action simultaneously inspired Nanjing kunqu artists and presented them with urgent challenges. If troupe members were no longer to receive fixed, guaranteed salaries, what kind of income would they get? Would, or should, performers be paid according to the frequency and success of their shows? Who would get to perform what? Who would decide whether a show was successful, and by what criteria?

These problems were both created and solved by Gu Xin (b. 1956), the new director of the restructured ShengKun, who steered the production of the *1699 Peach Blossom Fan*. Gu was an administrator with a mission: he knew what he wanted and had the means to get it. Gu knew China's arts world and its games. He had been an award-winning opera singer himself. In 1986, he had won a special prize at the sixteenth Paris International Singing competition; in 1992, he had received a Plum Blossom Award; in 1999, he had won a Wenhua Prize (Cultural Achievement Prize). He was no stranger to traditional Chinese operas. To prepare for his 1986 performance as Scholar Zhang in the newly composed Chinese opera the *Story of the Western Wing* (*Xixiang ji*), he had studied the performance practices of the young male role (*xiaosheng*) in Shanghai opera (*yueju*), a genre that borrowed much from kunqu.

In tandem with his singing career, Gu worked as an arts administrator. In 1991 he took over as director of the Jiangsu sheng gewu yuan (Song and Dance Theater of Jiangsu Province), which at the time was on the verge of bankruptcy. Gu promptly restructured that institution, aligning individual members' salaries and rights with the

---

25. For an anthology of essays on the show, see Jiangsusheng yanyi jituan ed., *1699 Taohuashan, Zhongguo chuanqi dianfeng* (Nanjing: Fenghuang chubanshe, 2007). For an audiovisual recording of the show see *1699 Peach Blossom Fan*, 2006 performance by ShengKun, accessed May 16, 2021, https://www.youtube.com/watch?v=CUPkUkLT69Y&t=7984s.

Resources, Stakeholders, *Yuescapes*, and Products

frequency and sales of their performances. By 1993, he had turned the troupe's fortunes around with new, popular, profitable shows. In 1995, Gu was appointed a vice-director of the Cultural Bureau of Jiangsu Province. In October 2001, he became the director of the Jiangsu yishu juyuan (Jiangsu Operatic Theater). In 2005, he became the CEO of the newly established Jiangsu yanyi jituan.

As an experienced artist and arts administrator, Gu had developed proactive theories for marketing performing arts in socialist China. Boldly yet tactfully, he applied his ideas to manage ShengKun, generating a distinctive *yuescape* for himself and his colleagues. As reported in various newspaper articles and interviews and in his own writings, he saw opportunities for growth in China's performing arts market.[26] He declared that there were no declining arts markets in China, only declining performance troupes: as long as Chinese people lived, they would demand artistic products, and thus there would always be a market for the performing arts in China. He found socialist China's support system for performing arts troupes ineffective, and its control of performance content and style stifling. As long as troupes relied on state-controlled financial and political supports, Gu surmised, they would only produce shows the state authorities wanted, and no actions would be taken until government money showed up in the troupes' coffers.

Insightfully, Gu pointed to the vicious circles that government money generated. If performers were paid with salaries pegged to their official ranking, senior ones had neither the incentive to advance their artistry nor the motivation to nurture young performers, for the latter would eventually become competitors. ShengKun of the early 2000s had more senior performers than young and promising ones, Gu noted. In other words, senior masters might have plenty of performance skills, but they lacked *qingchun* attributes that appealed to young audiences. By contrast, young performers who had plenty of physical charms lacked the virtuoso skills that would mesmerize audiences. Unavoidably, the imbalance created difficulties in staging artistically meritorious and economically marketable shows.

To address these issues, Gu argued, the troupe needed to tap into all kinds of talent available within and outside of Nanjing, ShengKun's home base. Only through tactical use of local, national, and even international talents could the troupe produce shows that audiences would pay to see. Gu suggested that China could then export these productions to win its share of the global entertainment and leisure market.

For kunqu to become locally and globally marketable, Gu declared, it had to be stylistically fashionable (*shishang hua*), flow along national and international mainstreams of arts and commerce (*zhuliu hua*), and be marketed with a trusted "brand" or selling point (*pinpai*). In other words, for ShengKun to produce hit shows, it would have to develop a sustainable strategy for establishing its artistic and commercial trademark. To sustain its operations in the long term, ShengKun would have to generate

---

26. A summary of Gu's theories appears in his essay: "1699 Taohuashan de zhanlüe gouxi jiqi shisi," in *1699 Tao huashan: Zhongguo chuanqi dianfeng*, 44–55.

not only financial profit in terms of ticket sales but also material and intangible goods for society as a whole. That would entail staging artistically and culturally meritorious works and grooming new generations of performers. And to ensure long-term success, ShengKun would have to overcome the roadblocks that were negatively affecting its operations.

A strong-willed administrator and shrewd stakeholder, Gu had ShengKun ride the wave of Chinese fascination with *qingchun dianya* kunqu that Bai Xianyong's *Young Lovers* of 2004 had launched. To quickly produce a hit show, Gu invited Tian Qinxin as a guest dramatist and director.[27] Tian was a shining star of Chinese theater at the time. Her 1999 production of the *Field of Life and Death* (*Shengsi chang*) had rocketed her to fame; since then, she had won a number of prestigious prizes, including the 2000 Cultural Achievement Prize. She was noted for her dramatic use of actors' body movements and her modern interpretations of classical and dramatic texts. Gu decided she would be the "right" librettist and director for his innovative *qingchun* production.

Tian brought in her own collaborators, Lao Xiang and Li Dong, who shared her artistic experiences and international vision. Lao Xiang had studied in Japan for almost a decade. In 2004 he began producing his own spoken dramas. In 2007 he launched his Fan-theater, the romanized nomenclature of which underscores his aesthetics and sensitivity. The Chinese word *fan* sonically echoes the English word "fan," namely people who chase after stars. In Chinese, depending on the linguistic tone applied to it, *fan* can mean rice/food, reversal, annoyance, resistance, or selling. Lao was a successful entrepreneur.[28] All his shows succeeded, because their staging was supported by hard data: before they began production, Lao and Li would do market research on their target audience and market trends.

Under the ideological and entrepreneurial guidance of Gu Xin, and bolstered by the creativity and pragmaticism of Tian, Lao, and Li, ShengKun wisely chose to stage a new version of the *Peach Blossom Fan* (*Taohua shan*) by Kong Shangren (1648–1718). Strategically, they named it the *1699 Peach Blossom Fan* to underscore its traditional, innovative, and fashionable features. The reference to the year 1699 was culturally and historically meaningful, for that was the year Kong Shangren completed his masterpiece, *Peach Blossom Fan*, an operatic political-romantic story set in Nanjing in the 1640s and 1650s; by the end of the seventeenth century it had become legendary. The year 1699 was also a watershed in kunqu history—conventional wisdom declares that no *chuanqi* libretti written after 1699 could rise higher than the dramatic-literary excellence that Kong's work and Hong Sheng's *Palace of Everlasting Life* of 1688 had achieved. Thus, by attaching the chronological year 1699 to the title of their *qingchun*

---

27. For a biosketch of the director, see Anonymous, "Tian Qinxin," accessed September 15, 2020, https://baike.baidu.com/item/%E7%94%B0%E6%B2%81%E9%91%AB/10366199

28. The website of the Fan-theatre is www.fan-theatre.com.

dianya opera, Gu branded his production as a significant and historically informed production.

While tapping outside talents to produce his new show, Gu did not ignore his own artists and resources. He realized that ShengKun had already staged modern realizations of Hong's libretto and that a number of senior performers in the troupe, such as Shi Xiaomei, Ke Jun, and Wang Xiaowu, had performed core and popular *zhezixi* from the famed drama. Shi Xiaomei, for example, was renowned for her performance of the "Writing on the Fan" ("Tihua") scene. [29] Ke Jun, a celebrated performer of the martial male role, had successfully played the tragic hero in the *zhezixi* known as "The General Drowns Himself" ("Chenjiang").[30] Gu, however, did not cast the masters to play leading roles in his *qingchun* opera, and instead asked them to coach the troupe's young performers who had been chosen to appear in the innovative production. Their youthful physicality was needed to make it a *qingchun dianya* entertainment. Some masters were nevertheless given minor roles; for example, Ke was asked to play Shi Kefa (1601–1645), a tragic hero in the story.

ShengKun had talented composers and instrumentalists on its staff, and Gu asked them to compose or arrange all the vocal and instrumental music. Composer and instrumentalist Sun Jian'an arranged new vocal melodies for the arias.[31] Similarly, senior instrumental music master Dai Peide designed *luogu* music that articulated dramatic *shenduan*. A young orchestrator, Jiang Jinghong, provided symphonic and programmatic incidental music to drive the 186-minute production.

To provide the show with an international gloss, Gu sought input from international masters such as Nagaoka Seikou of Japan (music), Son Jin Chaek of Korea (theater), and Yu Guangzhong of Taiwan (literature). And to market the show internationally, foreign venues, such as the BeSeTo Festival of Korea, were booked.

The production time of the *1699 Peach Blossom Fan* was atypically short. In January 2005, Gu invited Tian, Lao, and Li to produce a kunqu show. Four months later, on May 18, they announced the production. That announcement date was strategic: May 18 marked the fifth anniversary of the UNESCO declaration of kunqu as a Masterpiece of the Oral and Intangible Cultural Heritage of Humanity. On March 17, 2006, the show premiered at the Poly Theater (Baoli juchang) in Beijing, at the heart of the nation's performing arts world.

---

29. For an audiovisual recording of Shi Xiaomei's 1985 performance of "Tihua," see *The Peach Blossom Fan (Taohuashan)*: "Writing on the Fan" (Tihua), performance by Shi Xiaomei, accessed March 15, 2018, https://www.youtube.com/watch?v=-4QEWMcLgZo.

30. For a biography of Ke Jun, see Gu Lingshen, *Yeben xiang liming: Ke Ju pingchuan*; see esp. 42–50 for his involvement with *1699 Peach Blossom Fan*.

31. For a study on Sun Nai'an's kunqu music, see Juliane Jones, "Contemporary Kunqu Composition," Dissertation, University of British Columbia, Canada, 2014.

The *1699 Peach Blossom Fan*: A Sensational Product

The show was well-received. Gu Xin's strategy for producing a *qingchun dianya* show hit its target. The political-romantic story appeals to local and national audiences. Tian's script condensed Kong's historical but abstruse libretto of forty-four scenes into a dramatically tight story of six acts.[32] Act I covers the meeting and wedding of Hou Fangyu (1618–1655)and Li Xiangjun (1624–1654), the historical lovers. Act II introduces the evil character Ruan Dacheng (1587–1646), who wants to buy Hou's friendship by paying for Li's trousseau; she rejects it and incites Ruan's anger; as revenge, he schemes to hurt the lovers. To avoid being trapped by Ruan, Hou has to flee from Nanjing, leaving his lover behind. Act III packs in a lot of dramatic action, ranging from military battles to preserve the collapsing Ming empire to Li's rejection of a marriage proposal cooked up by Ruan. Act IV develops the drama along two themes: political corruption that led to the demise of the Southern Ming court, and Hou's return and failed attempt to reunite with Li. Act V relates the demise of the Southern Ming and the death of two heroic generals, Zuo Liangyu (1599–1645) and Shi Kefa. Act VI has the separated lovers accidentally meet by a Daoist shrine. As they try to reunite, a monk scolds them for indulging themselves in selfish love and ignoring the ethnic and political crisis their nation is facing. The drama ends with the lovers permanently separated.

Besides telling a historical drama, the *1699 Peach Blossom Fan* sensually entertains. The young and handsome actor-singers and their gorgeous costumes charmed audiences who themselves were or wanted to be young, glamorous, and prosperous. The movable stage-within-a-stage rendered rapidly changing dramatic times and sites performatively intelligible. The innovative backdrop, which enclosed the stage almost entirely on three sides, presented a panoramic view of mid-seventeenth-century Nanjing, a cultural and political center of Ming China. The backdrop is a gigantic copy of a celebrated historical painting, the *Nandu fanhui jingwu tu* (A view of busy and prosperous Nanjing, the southern capital).[33]

The production was the hit that Gu Xin had set out to create, which raised ShengKun's profile and contributed to the local Nanjing society and economy. In terms of kunqu performance and marketing, the *1699 Peach Blossom Fan* was a commercial hit: it is aesthetically *qingchun dianya* and operatically entertaining. It attracted, and still charms, young Chinese and international audiences. In terms of kunqu history, the show marked a turning point for ShengKun: it helped brand the troupe as artistically forward-looking and financially successful. By presenting Nanjing as a historical and

---

32. For the original Chinese text of the drama, see Kong Shangren, *Taohua shan* (Reprint, Beijing: Renmin wenxue chubanshe, 1980). For its English translation, see Chen Shih-hsiang and Harold Acton, trans., *Peach Blossom Fan* by Kong Shangren, with the collaboration of Cyril Birch (Berkeley: University of California Press, 1976).

33. For an online description and image of the historical painting, see "*Nandu fanhui jingwu tujuan*," accessed May 16, 2021, http://www.chnmuseum.cn/enlarge.html?path=/tilegenerator/aggregate/004/069/069.xml.

Figure 6.2: A parade of beauties, a historical painting as stage backdrop, and a movable stage-in-stage in the *1699 Peach Blossom Fan*. Courtesy of ShengKun.

romantic site, the show promoted the city's cultural tourism and clothing industries. The city's Qinhuai area, a historical entertainment district where Hou Fangyu and Li Xiangju first met, has become more popular as a tourist destination. The show's glamorous costumes have prompted audiences and tourists to purchase, as souvenirs, Nanjing-made clothing and other silk products. Traditionally, Nanjing is a center of Chinese clothing and fabric trades.

By all accounts, the *1699 Peach Blossom Fan* met the expectations of all its stakeholders, save those of critical connoisseurs. Some declared that the show had "no game" or "no show" (*meixi*), meaning that its telling of stories was dramatically flat and that its music and dance acts were adequate but not mesmerizing. The criticisms have some merit: the best the young and inexperienced performers could do on the stage of the *1699 Peach Blossom Fan* was professional acting, singing, and dancing. Their performative expressions were handicapped by the relative brevity of the show—it does not afford the performers adequate time and space to showcase their talents. This inadequacy becomes apparent with a comparison of the "Writing on the Fan" scene in Hong's libretto and Tian's summary of it in her abridged rendition. As written by Kong Shengren, and as traditionally performed, the scene has eleven arias and a performance time of thirty-two minutes or so. As such, the scene affords performers a dramatically extended space and time to sing Kong's literary lyrics with flowing tunes, enact realistic *shenduan*, and project the lovesick Hou's rapidly changing emotions— the *zhezixi* begins with the character anticipating a reunion with his beloved and ends with his collapsing into a heartbroken wreck who finds his lover gone.

As scripted in the *1699 Peach Blossom Fan*, and as performed by Shi's student, Xia Shiming (born 1985), the episode of Hou's return to his former love nest where he finds Li gone gets only six and a half minutes of stage time; that is barely long enough for the talented and handsome young performer to sing out what is happening then and there on stage (2:9′13″ to 2:15′43″). It is also barely enough time for connoisseurs who want to feel and savour Hou's feelings of expectation, shock, and disappointment.

The verdict of "no game" or "no show" also finds fault with Tian's dense script. Its packing together of numerous dramatic actions and characters taxes the audience's attention, besides raising questions of what the show is about. As scripted and staged by Tian, the 1699 Peach Blossom Fan fails to operatically present serious questions that Kong Shangren, the original dramatist, asked. He had written a complex drama about the dilemmas of love, duty, and sacrifice that Chinese must face during turbulent times of dynastic change; he did not merely dramatize a historical story to showcase a romantic affair. The 1699 Peach Blossom Fan is an entertaining opera, but it fails to bring Kong's thesis to life on stage; it is no longer a thought-provoking dramatization of late Ming culture, history, and personhood. It is no accident that some critics harshly, and perhaps unfairly, dismissed the show as a mere "knock-off" of the Young Lovers. Unmistakably, the criticism missed the show's particular agenda; the 1699 Peach Blossom Fan was a qingchun dianya kunqu show staged for national and international audiences newly introduced to kunqu, the six-century-old classical opera of twenty-first-century China.

Epilogue: Localized Operations and Individualistic Shows

If the 1699 Peach Blossom Fan is not representative of the historical-fictional chuanqi that Kong Shengren wrote, it nevertheless vividly illustrates the Nanjing yuescape of the early 2000s, which framed ShengKun's production of the show and was in turn transformed by it. This becomes apparent with any comparison of the show with the Young Lovers and its yuescape. The latter has a focused goal of promoting kunqu as Chinese cultural heritage and showcasing what Bai Xianyong envisions as Chinese beauty and classicism. Bai's agenda comes across vividly because his production deliberately highlights its "authentic" expressions at the expense of its contemporary elements.

For ideological and practical reasons, the Young Lovers does not make unnecessary compromises; it demands that the audience rise to its aesthetic and performance excellence. The total performance time of the Young Lovers, a series of three formal shows, is more than seven hours. That performance structure/length ignores the practical needs of contemporary Chinese audiences who are unused to cultural presentations lasting longer than two hours. With ample operatic time and space, however, the Young Lovers affords its young and beautiful performers an expansive stage to act out the beauty, youth, and performance artistry they have mastered. In addition, the show unfolds with creatively crafted contemporary kunqu instrumental music, sounds that contemporary audience understand and can use as a key to open the door to worlds they want to inhabit.[34] In short, notwithstanding their superficial similarities, the *1699 Peach Blossom Fan* and the *Young Lovers* are contrasting statements from two contemporary and competing kunqu *yuescapes*. Each is a particularized combination of kunqu institutions, stakeholders, aesthetics, agendas, and other variable elements. Each is heavenly and earthly in its own right.

---

34. For further discussion of the music, see Chapter 8.

7

Contemporary Kunqu

Creative Performers and Evolving Shows

Introduction

Contemporary kunqu performances are produced by creative professionals, who work in specific *yuescapes* as scriptwriters, directors, producers, composers, choreographers, actor-singers, instrumentalists, costume designers, stage designers, publicists, and others with specified or unspecified tasks. Each creatively exercises his/her personal talents and skills, expressing their own artistic selves while contributing to the greater production. All of them work closely together to ensure that their results abide with the genre's established aesthetics, compositional and performance practices, operational needs, audience demands, and other features specific to the *yuescape* in which they operate. Only by being simultaneously individualistic, collaborative, convention-abiding, and innovative can kunqu performers as well as stakeholders produce continuously appealing, evolving, and profitable shows.

To discuss contemporary kunqu as creative and re-creative performance and discourse by kunqu practitioners, this chapter presents three accounts. The first surveys the genre's creative and re-creative processes, demonstrating their cumulative and collaborative results. The second presents a case study of Gao Lian's *Jade Hairpin* (*Yuzan ji*) as an opera created and re-created in changing times and sites. To illustrate the opera's evolving performance and expressions, a case study of three different realizations of "Zither Seduction" ("Qintiao") from the *Jade Hairpin* will be analyzed.

Kunqu Creativity and Re-creativity

Contemporary kunqu performers stage both original works and pre-existing ones in which some of the elements are composed/fixed and others are adjusted or newly created.[1] In theoretical terms, creative kunqu shows are original works with distinctive

---

1. For current studies on kunqu scriptwriting, see Ding Sheng, *Dangdai kunqu chuangzuo yanjiu* (Shanghai: Guji chuanshe, 2017), and Wang Ankui and He Yuren, *Kunqu chuangzuo yu lilun* (Shenyang: Chunfeng wenyi chubanshe, 2005).

structural and performative attributes, whereas re-creative ones are derived from pre-existing expressions and known materials. In practical terms, the creative and the re-creative in kunqu are hardly separable. For instance, while kunqu *zhezixi* shows realize canonized performance scripts with codified performance practices, what is actually performed on stage and witnessed by audiences is continuously filled with features unique to specific performers and performances. Indeed, the more kunqu *zhezixi* are examined as performance and discourse, the more their expressive and performative particulars become clear. Even shows of a same *zhezixi* performed by same cast in back-to-back seasons may have subtle or not so subtle differences. "Routinely" performed kunqu would only appear on amateur stages.

For discussion convenience here, the terms creativity and re-creativity are defined as follows. *Creativity* in contemporary kunqu refers to the inventive production of original scripts, music, *shenduan*, and other dramatic features, communicating expressions that strike critics and audiences as new or unexpected. *Re-creativity* involves adjusting pre-existing lyrics, music, *shenduan*, and other dramatic features, subtly changing their established structures and meanings. Since the line separating creativity and re-creativity in kunqu is thin and permeable, and since artistic faculties and results are inseparable, the former term will be used to broadly address creative and re-creative processes and expressions; only when they are clearly re-creative, or derivative, will they be discussed as such.

The creative processes that produce kunqu shows are complex and fluid. For convenience's sake, however, here they can be heuristically conceptualized as a linear progression of developmental actions. It begins with an idea for a dramatic story, then proceeds to the writing of the performance script, the composition of music, the choreographing of *shenduan*, the fine-tuning of costumes and makeup, and the construction of backdrops, props, and lighting and sound effects, all of which will be integrated into an intelligible multimedia show.[2] In short, when a kunqu show is staged as an opera, it is very much a collaborative project.[3] And whenever it is performed again in the years to follow, it will be collaboratively adjusted as needed. A kunqu show that substantively deviates from earlier productions is declared a new edition (*xinban*, *xinbian*) of the show being presented.

---

2. For a recent study on the process, see Joseph S. C. Lam, "The *Southern Story of the Western Wing* (*Nan xixiang*): Traditional Kunqu Composition, Interpretation and Performance," in *How to Read Chinese Drama*, ed. Patricia Sieber and Regina S. Llamas (New York: Columbia University Press, 2022), 191–211.

3. Kunqu directors (*daoyan*) are playing more and more leadership roles in the process. For a revealing account, see Shen Bin, *Pinlan tanyou: Kunju daoyan zhi lu* (Shanghai: Dongfang chuban zhongxin, 2018).

A vivid example of all this is ZheKun's *Story of General Gongsun Zidu* (*Gongsun zidu*), a contemporary kunqu show about a hero/villain from the distant past.[4] Conceptualized in 1997, the show premiered in 2003, but its award-winning version was finalized in 2008 after several rounds of revisions. The opera is deemed creative because of its original script and sharp breaks from traditional kunqu practices. The script dramatizes a historical figure named Gongsun Zidu (fl. ca. 700 BC?) as a cowardly murderer and a repenting hero, a Janus-faced character of the sort that rarely appears in traditional kunqu. Dramatically structured as a martial play (*wuxi*), the opera presents an innovative dream scene in which the hero/villain learns of his mistakes and develops intense guilt and a need to atone. The opera ends with a scene that is both tragic and atypical: the protagonist jumps to his death from a tower (most traditional kunqu operas have happy endings). The opera narratively revolves around the hero/villain, showcasing the traditional performance artistry of the kunqu martial role. The actor-singer featured in the opera is Lin Weilin (b. 1964), a celebrated ZheKun performer of the martial male role, a two-time winner of the Plum Blossom Prize, and the troupe's director.[5]

Most contemporary kunqu shows present historical/traditional *chuanqi* dramas/*zhezixi* with rewritten scripts, newly composed and arranged music, and choreographed *shenduan*. To render traditional scripts/stories intelligible to contemporary audiences, pre-existing lyrics and speeches are adjusted; antiquated or opaque words in the script are changed to more modern ones; aria melodies and/or *shenduan* are adjusted for similar reasons. In other words, much that appears on the kunqu stage has been customized to match the performers' talents, the audience's needs, and staging "fashions."

An example of a thoroughly customized kunqu show is ShangKun's 2005 production of the *Butterfly Dream* (*Hudie meng*),[6] a tragicomedy about a young widow trying to cure her new lover, who has taken ill. Dramatically, the medicine needed for the cure happens to be the brain of her newly deceased husband; to get the brain, the widow has to crack open the husband's coffin. As performed in late Qing and early twentieth-century China, the *Butterfly Dream* featured fiendishly entertaining but morally transgressive actions—the play was repeatedly banned in both historical and socialist China. To make the story palatable to twenty-first-century critics and audiences, its dark elements have been suppressed and its comic and erotic inflections

---

4. For information on the opera, see Zhao Heping and Zhou Yude, *Linghun de jiushu: Kunju "Gongsunzidu" chuangzuo pinglunji* (Beijing: Zhongguo xiju chubanshe, 2010). An audiovisual recording of the show is accessible as *The Story of General Gongsun Zidu* (*Gongsun Zidu*), performance by ZheKun, accessed April 23, 2018, www.youtube.com/watch?v=D5kia8H5NKY. The dream scene begins at 1:24.'

5. For Lin Weilin's biography, see Wu Xinlei, *Zhongguo kunqu dacidian.*

6. See Lei Jingxuan, ed. *Kunju hudiemeng—yibu chuantongxi de zaixian* (Hong Kong: Oxford University Press, 2005.) Many audiovisual recordings of the show are accessible online; see for example, "Marriage Proposal" ("Shuoqin") from the *Butterfly Dream*, performance by Liu Yilong and Xing Jingsha, accessed May 16, 2021, https://www.youtube.com/watch?v=pBpkKWMlDY4.

have been highlighted. Furthermore, to render the opera practical for touring performances, its cast has been reduced to six characters enacted by four actor-singers.

Most contemporary kunqu stagings of traditional works look and sound as they did in the past or as what casual audiences expect to see and hear. This "traditionality" can be misleading; critical viewing brings innovations to light. For example, a kunqu performer of the martial role enacting Lu Zhishen in "The Drunken Monk Shatters the Gateway" ("Shanmen") always appears with his shirt open, a standardized image for the character. That image can, however, be re-creatively individualized; a performer of the role can adjust the degree to which his shirt is open, revealing a more or less bare chest. The costumes that actor-singers don on stage indicate how traditional their shows are, or how contemporary or experimental. Kunqu makeup and costumes are noticeably innovative in grand productions of contemporary shows like the *Young Lovers* and the *1699 Peach Blossom Fan*.[7] Also, expressive and performative nuances in kunqu singing and dancing sonically and kinetically demonstrate individual actor-singers' talents and artistic goals.

Contemporary kunqu abounds with tactical mixtures of old and new elements, thus generating unexpected meanings with familiar materials. One impressive example is the stage design for XiangKun's 2013 production of the *Story of the White Rabbit* (*Baitu ji*), which featured a series of tall panels that looked like pages taken from old Chinese books.[8] Semantically and visually, the panels underscored the historicity of the drama and affirmed XiangKun's claim that the presentation was historically significant. The *Story of the White Rabbit* has its roots in fourteenth-century China. Kunqu reached Hunan Province in late Ming or early Qing China, a historical claim that XiangKun made to legitimize its institutional voice.[9] The troupe's use of book panels as props was unprecedented; yet using books as props in kunqu shows is in fact an old tradition.

Kunqu creativity and re-creativity seamlessly integrates kunqu singing and *shenduan* performance.[10] In theory, *shenduan* are codified expressions; as performed by master performers, however, *shenduan* are more re-creative than formulaic, as indicated by any detailed comparison of what performers do at identical points of

---

7. For colorful high-definition pictures from the performance, see Anonymous, "1699 Taohuashan juzhao," accessed September 25, 2020, http://image.haosou.com/i?src=rel&q=%E6%98%86%E6%9B%B2%E6%A1%83%E8%8A%B1%E6%89%871699%E5%89%A7%E7%85%A7.
8. See *The Story of the White Rabbit* (*Baitu ji*), performance by XiangKun, accessed May 16, 2021, https://www.bilibili.com/video/av4637119.
9. For historical notes on XiangKun, see Li Liqing, *Xiangkun wangshi* (Zhenzhou: Hunan renmin chubanshe, 2014), 1–64.
10. For two recent studies on kunqu creative and performance practices, see Dongshin Chang, "Borrowing the Fan: An Example of Actable Plays (Zhezixi) for the Kunqu Stage," *Asian Theatre Journal* 34, no. 2 (2017): 259–283; see also Ming Yang, "Return of the Soul: In Heritance and Innovation in the Process of Artistic Creation in Major Kunqu Productions in the People's Republic of China, 2001–2015" (PhD diss., University of Hawai'i, 2019). For a study of Chinese opera actors and their artistry, see Jo Riley, *Chinese theatre and the Actor in Performance* (Cambridge, UK: Cambridge University Press, 1997).

Figure 7.1: A kunqu stage with panels of Chinese books in traditional binding. Photograph by J. Lam, 2014.

performances of the same kunqu drama. The paradox between formulism and flexibility dissolves when codified *shenduan* gestures are understood as fixed words in verbal communications and when dramatic sequences of *shenduan* acts are understood as distinct sentences constructed with common words. The same can be said about contemporary kunqu instrumental and vocal music, which theoretically are composed and performed according to preexisting *qupai* and *luogu* patterns and are generally heard as recognizable tunes/sounds. In practice, kunqu instrumental and vocal music is flexibly structured and is played to serve specific dramatic situations.[11]

Many kunqu arias are composed and sung according to the same familiar *qupai*; and yet few of the arias would unfold with identical melodies and rhythms. They only share common features, such musical modes and scales, melodic motives, and specific rhythms.[12] To identify different tunes derived from a same *qupai*, kunqu practitioners

---

11. Zhongyang yinyue xueyuan minzu yinyue yanjiusuo, ed., *Zhongguo kunju chuida qupai* (Beijing: Yinyue chubanshe, 1956); and Wu Jinya, *Kunqu luogu* (Suzhou: Guwuxuan chubanshe, 2009).

12. For representative discussions on kunqu aria compositions, see Lindy Li Mark, "From Page to Stage: Exploring Some Mysteries of Kunqu Music and Its Melodic Characteristics," *Chinoperl Papers* 32 (July 2013): 1–29; Tian Shaodong, *Kunqu yanchang yishu yanjiu* (Hangzhou: Zhejiang daxue chubanshe, 2013); Wang Jilie, *Yinlu qutan* (Shanghai: Shangwu yinshuguan, 1934); Wang Shoutai,

Creative Performers and Evolving Shows

specify them with titles of the *zhezixi* in which they appear, such as the "Dark Silk Robe" of "Strolling; Dreaming." And to further specify distinguished renditions by specific actor-singers, they would, for example, say the "Dark Silk Robe" of "Strolling; Dreaming" of Zhang Jiqing's 1984 performance.

Any critical listening to kunqu singing would identify a master performer's unique grain of voice and re-creative expressions. A prime example is Cai Zhengren's musical enactments of Tang Minghuang in his many performances of the *Palace of Everlasting Life*. He sings the character's arias with his uniquely resonant voice and occasional bursts of energetic tones (*baoyin*). Each time he performs the role, he may, however, deliver nuanced sonic and non-sonic expressions of a Chinese and romantic emperor.[13] As a result, Cai's Tang Minghuang voice/singing is always uniquely expressive. It does not mimic his mentor, Yu Zhenfei, nor does it present something his colleagues or disciples can mechanically copy. No kunqu connoisseur would confuse Cai's voice with those of his students who strive to sound like him. And any critical audience would hear that Cai's singing is performatively and sonically different from that of Zhao Shanlin, a SuKun master who performed the Tang Minghuang role in the 2004 SuKun version of the *Palace of Everlasting Life*.[14]

Master kunqu performers' creative and re-creative artistry is the result of extensive training and the cultivation of natural talents.[15] For example, Liu Yilong did not accidentally become the most celebrated clown in contemporary kunqu. He is jovial by nature, and he trained hard under Wang Chuansong, a Chuanzibei Master. Another kunqu master who has made kunqu fresh and meaningful to contemporary audiences is Zhang Jiqing (1938–2022), who brought her *huadan* characters to life on stage with her transcendental singing and *shenduan* acting.[16] As noted by Zhang Geng (1911–2003), a socialist opera historian and critic, Zhang's performances are

---

Kunqu gelü (Yangzhou: Jiangsu renmin chubanshe, 1982); Wu Junda, *Kunqu changqiang yanjiu* (Beijing: Renmin yinyue chubanshe, 1993); and Yu Zhenfei, *Zhenfei qupu* (Shanghai: Shanghai wenyi chubanshe, 1982).

13. Many audiovisual clips of Cai's performance as Tang Minghuang are online: to access them, Google "Cai Zhengren" and "Changshengdian." For his biography, see Xie Boliang and Niu Junyi, *Yabu zhengyin guansheng huishou: Cai Zhenren chuan* (Shanghai: Guji chubanshe, 2012).

14. For an audiovisual clip of Zhao Shanlin's performance, see *The Palace of Everlasting Life (Changsheng dian)*, 2004 performance by SuKun, accessed May 16, 2021, https://www.bilibili.com/video/av12636683.

15. For a report on a performer's learning and creative experiences, see Josh Stenberg, "An Annotated Translation of Zhang Jiqing's Lecture on Playing Cui-shi in Chimeng (The Mad Dream): A Sample Lecture from *Kunqu Baizhong, Dashi Shuoxi* (One Hundred Pieces of Kunqu, Master Performers Talk about Their Scenes)," *Chinoperl* 35, no. 2 (2016): 153–175. See also Kim Hunter Gordon, "Contesting Traditional Luzi ('Choreographic Paths'): A Performance-Based Study of Kunqu" (PhD diss., Royal Holloway, University of London, 2016).

16. For an informative biography on Zhang's artistry and stardom, see Zhu Xi and Yao Jikun, eds., *Qing chu yu lan: Zhang Jiqing kunqu 55 nian* (Beijing Wenhua yishu chubanshe, 2009).

134   *Kunqu*

singularly expressive: she performs as she understands her characters while displaying her virtuoso performance skills.[17]

The "Zither Seduction": A Case Study of Kunqu Creativities

Cumulative and collaborative creativity permeates all kunqu shows and their evolving expressions. To illustrate, a detailed case analysis of the "Zither Seduction" scene from the *Jade Hairpin* (*Yuzan ji*) by Gao Lian (1527–1603?) will suffice. The drama was inspired by a historical anecdote popularly told in traditional China about Zhang Xiaoxiang (1132–1170), a much admired top candidate (*zhuangyuan*) of Southern Song China; supposedly, he once flirted with a beautiful nun whom he encountered in a nunnery. Fact or fiction, the anecdote promptly appeared in Yuan and Ming dramatic and fictive writings. Thus, Gao's writing of his *Jade Hairpin* is as creative as it is re-creative.[18]

As a drama of thirty-three scenes,[19] Gao's *chuanqi* presents many literarily elegant lyrics and dramatically effective speeches. This is why several scenes of the *Jade Hairpin* have been popularly realized as *zhezixi*. As a performance script, however, Gao's text is incomplete; for instance, it includes no notated music and indicates very few stage directions. To realize Gao's drama, kunqu performers must collaboratively create or amend many dramatic interpolations.

Since the 1980s, the *Jade Hairpin* has been popularly performed as a contemporary show of six to eight scenes, telling a love story that can be synopsized as follows. Pan Bizheng, the male protagonist, is a commoner scholar temporarily staying at a nunnery where his aunt is the abbess. He is staying there because he has just failed his examinations in the capital and is too ashamed to go home; he plans to study hard and then retake the examinations. Chen Miaochang, a beautiful lady, also lives at the nunnery; she has recently been separated from her elite family and must survive, reluctantly, as a Buddhist nun. Pan and Chen meet by chance inside the nunnery and promptly begin a passionate affair. When Pan's aunt gets wind of it, she sees a scandal brewing. To end it, she orders the young man to immediately return to the capital to take the examinations again. He goes, passes the examinations as the top candidate, and returns to claim Chen as his wife. As convention dictates, the story ends happily.

---

17. See Zhang Geng, "Cong Zhang Jiqing di biaoyan kan xiqu biaoyan yishu di jiben yuanli," in *Qing chu yu lan: Zhang Jiqing kunqu 55 nian* (Beijing: Wenhua yishu chubanshe, 2009), 150; Bai Xianyong, "Wodi kunqu zhilü," in *Kunqu 600 nian*, ed. Zhou Bing and Jiang Wenbo (Beijing: Zhongguo qingnian chubanshe, 2009), 183.

18. For a historical account of Gao Lian's dramatic text, see Li Zhongyao, "*Yuzangji* di zuozhe, gushi yanbian ji banben liuchuan," *Xinjiang daxue xuebao zhexue shehuigexuebao* 19, no. 3 (1991): 85–91; see also Andrew Lo, "Textual Representations of the Sixteenth-Century Chinese Drama *Yuzan ji* (*The Jade Hairpin*)," *Oral Tradition* 20, no. 2 (2005): 335–361. See also Xu Huaizhi, "Gao Lian *Yuzanji* yanjiu—cong wenxue juben dao kunqu yanchu" (MA thesis, Guoli Zhongyang daxue, 2010).

19. Gao Lian, *Yuzanji*, in *Liushi zhongqu*, ed. Mao Jin, Vol. 4 (Reprint, Beijing: Zhonghua shuju, 2007).

The most popular scene in contemporary productions of the *Jade Hairpin* is the "Zither Seduction," derived from scene sixteen in Gao Lian's dramatic text. Currently, the best known and most widely available performance script of the *zhezixi* is the version that appears in the authoritative *Zhenfei qupu*.[20] Many audiovisual recordings of the *zhezixi* staged since the 1960s are available online. For the convenience of analysis here, Yu Zhenfei's performance script and the 2004 recording of the ShangKun performance by Yue Meiti (b. 1941) and Zhang Jingxian (b. 1947) will be examined as the standard text of the *zhezixi*.[21]

All renditions stage a mix of scripted and unscripted expressions; except for the lyrics and words that Gao Lian wrote, much of what actor-singers sing and dance on stage is not scripted/created by him. To illustrate, "Zither Seduction" needs to be analyzed in three stages. The first discusses how scripted words verbally relate the lovers' rendezvous in the moonlight garden and how *shenduan* are performed to somatically complement the scripted expressions.[22] The second stage analyzes how Gao Lian created his dramatic text and how subsequent performers re-creatively fine-tuned it with music and *shenduan*. The third stage analyzes the scene's vocal and instrumental music, sonic interpolations that contemporary musicians have created to articulate and to comment on the actor-singers' verbal, musical, and choreographic expressions.

As scripted in the *Zhenfei qupu*, the "Zither Seduction" scene unfolds in three episodes and ten units of arias and speeches.[23] Episode 1, which goes up to Aria 4, presents Pan Bizheng and Chen Miaochang coming into the garden, telling the audience how they feel lonely and restless; the two then meet. Episode 2, which is structurally flanked by Arias 5 and 8, begins with Chen's inviting Pan to play *qin* music and ends with his leaving the garden as a rejected lover; this episode is where the lovers flirt with each other while playing *qin* music. Episode 3, which features Arias 9 and 10, shows Chen confessing her true feelings about Pan while he eavesdrops nearby—he has just excused himself and walked away from her. This episode concludes with Pan singing as a man who has found love.

As Episode 1 begins, Pan, as enacted by Yue Meiti,[24] a male impersonator, appears on the stage, which is decorated as a moonlit garden on an autumn night. Revealing his loneliness and ennui, he sings Aria 1 (0.00"–3'27"), describing the scenery he sees and what he feels in his heart. The lyrics of Aria 1 suggest that Pan is a handsome

---

20. Yu Zhenfei, "Yuzanji qintiao," in *Zhenfei qupu* (Shanghai: Wenyi chubanshe, 1982), 208–218.

21. An audiovisual recording of the performance is accessible online, see *The Jade Hairpin*, 2004 performance by Yue Meiti and Zhang Jingxian, accessed May 16, 2021, www.youtube.com/watch?v=-flPnhK3hyM.

22. For a historical description of *shenduan* performance in "Zither Seduction," see Zhou Chuanying, "Nongqin jiyi wen ziyin," in *Kunju shengya liushi nian* (Shanghai: Wenyi chubanshe, 1988), 172–195.

23. For an English translation of the script, see Ben Wang, *Laughter and Tears: Translation of Selected Kunqu Dramas* (Beijing: Foreign Languages Press, 2009), 2–15.

24. In this discussion, actor-singers' performance will be described as what characters do on stage, such as "Pan Bizheng sings aria 1." How performers create and/or learn specific arias tunes and *shenduan* are historical and theoretical questions beyond the scope of the current analysis.

commoner scholar; it does not, however, prescribe how Pan should look or act on stage. As re-created by Yue Meiti,[25] who learned the role from Yu Zhenfei, Pan presents himself as a young commoner in a plain gown, a codified costume practice on the kunqu stage.

Pan comes onto the stage like a gentleman, comporting himself like a *xiaosheng*. Thus Pan walks toward the center of the stage with his torso held upright. To underscore the *mis-en-scène* as a moonlit garden, he tilts his head slightly to look up at the moon, and to mark his manhood, he takes out his folding fan, a scholar's accessory in traditional China. He then advances to the center of the stage, stylishly waving his arms and hands, opening and closing his folding fan, as if he is bored and hoping for something to happen. Before he sings the last phrase of Aria 1, he delivers a scripted monologue (3'36"–4'24"), introducing himself and reporting on his earlier meeting with Chen. This self-introduction of Pan's is scripted and is a kunqu performance convention. After the speech, he finishes Aria 1 and exits the stage. Delivering the monologue before the last phrase of Aria 1 is a dramatic and elocutionary device, one that is not specified in historical prints of the *Jade Hairpin*. Reportedly, the act reflects a staging adjustment that performers made some years ago, one that was orally transmitted until it became "fixed" in Yu Zhenfei's score.

As soon as Pan exits the stage, Chen, as enacted by Zhang Jingxian, comes onto the stage, singing Aria 2 (4'54"–8'14"), in which she describes what she sees and feels while enacting a number of feminine poses. Dressed in a nun's costume, Chen walks onto the stage holding a small, stage-sized *qin* in her left arm and waving a *fo* (hair whip) in her right hand. Her poses and *shenduan* project her as an elegant, intelligent, and somewhat melancholy woman, a traditional image of the character that many kunqu performers have realized.

Before Chen sings the last phrase of Aria 2, she chants a monologue (6'58"–7'46") to relate her name, feelings, and reasons why she has come to the garden. She wants a break from her daily chores, and she has love in her heart-mind, she confesses. To calm her nerves, she wants to practice *qin* music in the garden, playing a composition titled the "Mist and Clouds over Rivers Xiao and Xiang" ("Xiaoxiang shuiyun"). Then Pan reappears on stage, walking along a path in the garden, and singing Aria 3 (8'17"–10'08"), in which he asks what the heavenly music is that he hears and whence it comes.

Singing the aria, Pan does many *shenduan* to clarify the developing story. None of these, though, are detailed in the *Zhenfei qupu* or other commonly available performance scripts of the scene. As performed in the 2004 ShangKun production, Pan explores the garden, is surprised by the sound of *qin* music, and is curious about what he hears. To dramatize his act of hearing, he pauses and tilts his head as if he wants to listen closely. Having identified the direction where the sound is coming from, he

---

25. For Yue's descriptions of her performance of the *zhezixi*, see her *Linfeng duqu: Yue Meiti Kunju jinsheng biaoyan yishu* (Taipei: Shitou chubanshe, 2006), 1–104.

Creative Performers and Evolving Shows

walks toward it, wondering who would be playing it and why. Walking, he makes gestures with his arms, *shuixiu*, fan, torso, face, and eyes, none of which are scripted in traditional scores—all were/are created by actor-singers according to what they have learned from their mentors and experienced in their daily lives. For example, when Pan ponders the music he has heard, he opens his arms, an everyday gesture of asking questions and demanding answers. Some of Pan's *shenduan* in this sequence have no semantically specific meanings, but collectively they project him as a playful young man.

As Pan realizes that Chen is playing the *qin*, he approaches her, performing a long, unscripted, but dramatically clarifying sequence of *shenduan*. Gingerly he approaches Chen, his love interest; as he gets closer and closer to her, he examines her stealthily again and again. He finally gathers the courage to appear right in front of her, announcing his uninvited presence by putting his hands on her string-plucking hands and fingers, saying "Bravo! Excellent playing!" Surprised, she utters a womanly "oh" (*ya*), and then asks where he has come from and how he can just show up like that—singing the third and fourth phrases of her Aria 4. Once she settles down, the couple greet each other and then engage in their scripted dialogue. She explains why she is practicing music in the garden and flirtatiously declares that he would not show up in the garden just to listen to music. As they talk, they grasp the erotically charged situation they are in. They look at each other as if they are saying, "How dare you approach me like this?," while asking themselves "How do I respond to his/her teasing?" Their revealing *shenduan* (13'14") are not scripted in the *Zhenfei qupu*.

To cover up her awkwardness and to probe his intentions, she invites him to play the *qin*, and so begins Episode 2. Responding to her invitation, Pan briefly declines and then agrees to play, evoking what traditional *qin* musicians would ritually do in their musical gatherings, rendering the cultural and social meanings of their acts readily decipherable. The couple's intentions become unmistakable when they theatrically utter their invitations to play music. Both utter the word of "pleeease" (*qing*) with long and suggestive tones, none of which would be heard in daily conversation. The word is scripted, but its exaggerated delivery is not. How long the "pleeease" should be vocalized depends on the individual performers and the particular stage. How entertaining (or not) the affected utterances are will be meticulously critiqued by connoisseurs.

As Pan accepts her invitation, he moves to the performance side of the *qin* table and Chen goes to the audience side. As they walk past each other, they swing their arms and the flowing sleeves of their costumes. In doing so, they appear to accidentally or deliberately touch each other, a theatrical and kinetic illusion that is not scripted. As performed on the stage, the *shenduan* is articulated by *luogu* music, the playing of which is neither scripted nor notated. Finishing the walk, the characters turn to face the audience, telling them what has just happened—a non-traditional and rather Brechtian effect of puncturing dramatic reality to reaching out to the audience. Then Pan settles into the chair by the *qin* table and plays the zither while singing Aria 5 (14'38"), which describes a male bird flying alone and lamenting its lonely life.

Instantly Chen grasps Pan's thinly disguised tease. Now she turns away from watching him playing, looks at the audience, and performs a *shenduan* of trying to think of a response. Then she turns to him and asks why he plays such a sad song about single men. He answers by declaring that he has no wife, which leads her to spit out: "That's none of my business!" Read literally, Chen's scripted utterance is logical and factual; heard as an affected expression of virtuosity, the double entendre is unmistakable, and operatically entertaining.

Chen's utterance surprises Pan because it ironically reveals what she is thinking and feeling. Pan becomes dumbfounded and can do nothing but invite her to play *qin* music, continuing their musical flirting game. She ritually declines and then agrees. Now she walks toward the performer's side, and he to the audience's side. As they walk past each other, their swinging arms and flowing sleeves touch each other again. Immediately after that *shenduan*, they smile at each other. They then turn their faces and torsos toward the audience, revealing their joy of discovering what their partners have in mind. Finally, Chen sits down at the *qin* table, plays, and sings her zither song, which is Aria 6 (17'14"), in which she describes herself as an angel with no earthly desires.

As she plays, Pan acts out his impulsive manhood—actions that are not scripted in the *Zhenfei qupu*. He stands up, compliments her excellent playing, and extends his hands to touch hers. She asks him to sit down and continues playing and singing. To rebuke what she says, he declares that only angels residing on the moon could live without desires. To kinetically articulate his words, he lightly beats his left hand palm with his fan. He then asks her a pointed question: how can a nun endure a life devoid of entertainment? She answers by declaring that nuns have no need for pleasure. The couple continue to flirt, sitting on opposite sides of the *qin* table, facing each other. Finally, he challenges her by waving his fan left and right to show his disbelief at what she says. He knows he has cornered her, and thus he strikes a cocky pose: to kinetically show his confidence, he stretches and crosses his legs, then slightly raises his right foot up and down a few times, an everyday gesture but one that is not scripted.

To further declare that she is indifferent to earthly pleasures, Chen sings Aria 7 (18'54" to 23'46"), in which she describes herself as a detached woman who cares nothing for what people say about what she plays, feels, and thinks. As Chen sings and Pan listens, they begin a series of *shenduan*, illustrating their interactive thoughts and feelings. To do the *shenduan*, they stand up and walk side by side, facing the audience, performing circular hand gestures and swinging their *shuixiu* to visually suggest feelings in their excited hearts. Before they return to their seats, they perform more gendered and mirroring *shenduan*, such as her waving her nun's *fo* and his playing with his fan. The mirroring of his and her gestures underscores the ways they romantically challenge and support each other.

At the end of their choreographed conversation, Pan responds to Chen by singing the first part of Aria 8, asking how nuns can endure life with no love (23'46"). As Pan sings, he performs a sequence of bold, flirtatious actions. For example, he strikes the

Creative Performers and Evolving Shows 139

Figure 7.2: Pan Bizheng flirts with Chen Miaochang in a ShangKun performance of "Zither Seduction" in New York. Photography by J. Lam, 2011. Courtesy of New York Kunqu Society.

table with his fan to emphasize the word "lonely" (24'05"); pushes the table toward her as if he wants to forcefully crack her facade (25'09"); seductively flicks his fan at her chin (25'34"); bawdily waves his fan at her as if he is caressing her body (25'58"); and finally taps the table with his fan several times at the end of his singing, kinetically and sonically marking his challenge to her (26'33"). Responding to his transgressive acts, Chen makes facial and bodily gestures to show her discomfort. She then stands up to protest, declaring her intention to report his insulting words and behavior to his aunt. Realizing that he has acted inappropriately, he apologizes, making a deep bow to her; then he sings the second part of Aria 8 (27'08"), which begs her forgiveness.

Listening to Pan's words of apology, Chen stands up again and turns her head to avoid seeing him face to face, demonstrating her conflicted feelings—her sad face and *shenduan* of escaping from him simultaneously suggest rejection and forgiveness. Then, as he is leaving, she admits that she has rebutted him with strong words and advises him to walk carefully on the garden's slippery, winding paths. Responding to her kind words, and grasping her conflicted emotions, he asks if he can borrow a lantern, making a gesture to reach her. She rejects him by uttering a long and suggestive "*cui*," a vocable that a young Chinese woman in love would use to playfully rebuke her lover—the word is scripted, but its unscripted delivery needs to be suggestively performed by individual performers.[26] Pan leaves perplexed, softly asking why she would get angry at his flirting when she is obviously interested in him. He decides to hide in the garden—he walks away with his right arm raised to "hide" his face while trying to catch what she is saying to herself.

What follows is Episode 3 of the *zhezixi*. Chen looks into the garden to see if Pan has left. Finding no sign of him, she sings Aria 9 (31'04"), confessing that while she finds him a handsome and desirable man, she is a modest woman and so has to reject his advances. As she sings, Chen performs a sequence of *shenduan* revealing a young and enamored woman's rapidly changing emotions. She smiles when she thinks of him and makes a sad face when she remembers she is alone and tormented with yearnings for him. She calls out his name, but as she does so, she raises her hands to cover her mouth and stop herself from saying his full name (30'49")—being a shy nun, she cannot declare her desires; above all, she cannot afford to have her words overheard. As she confesses, Pan gradually comes out of "hiding," getting closer and closer to her moment by moment. Without noticing him, she collects her *qin* and gets ready to leave. At that moment, he softly utters "*ha*" (hey), letting her know he has been near and has heard every word of her confession. She responds by uttering the multivalent "*cui*," communicating her surprise and delight. They now acknowledge each other's presence and love intentions with another round of long and erotically charged vocables (34'30"). Finally, she utters a long and suggestive "*cui*" while leaving the stage. Responding to her feminine exclamation of love, Pan laughs heartily, feeling confident that they are now connected. Singing the scene's coda, Aria 10, Pan declares his wish to marry Chen. As he sings, Pan performs a series of *shenduan* that kinetically express a young man's happiness at having found love. His use of energetic *shuixiu* movements attests to his invigorated male heart. Then as he realizes he is alone in the garden, he feels the night chill, does a *shenduan* of shivering, and exits the stage, concluding the *zhezixi* of the "Zither Seduction."

As described here, the words and *shenduan* in the "Zither Seduction" weave into a verbal and kinetic counterpoint of dramatic expressions. The author, Gao Lian, in his script indicates how the lovers are to interact with each other, but he has specified their *shenduan* only in the most general terms, for example, "she does the *shenduan* of surprise." Prescribed or not, most of the *shenduan* kunqu actor-singers perform on stage are both creative and re-creative: some elements of their actions are taken from daily life; some are learned from teachers; and some have been designed for specific performers and their target audiences.

Given that Gao Lian created the *Jade Hairpin* more than four hundred years ago, given that generations of actor-performers have created and re-created *shenduan* to kinetically realize Gao's telling of the love story, and given that history has not comprehensively recorded what they have enacted on stage, it is a challenge to trace what

---

26. See Yu Zhenfei's insightful comments on the "*cui*" expression in his "Qintiao: Cong 'ya' dao 'cui'," in *Yu Zhenfei yishu lunji* (Shanghai: Wenyi chubanshe, 1985), 112–117.

Creative Performers and Evolving Shows   141

has been individually or collaboratively created or re-created as well as to explain how the performers' actions have accumulated over the years since this *zhezixi* has been performed.

Even so, some creative and re-creative efforts and expressions can be heuristically identified for discussion. Some aspects of Gao Lian's literary-musical creativity and expressions are, for example, theoretically traceable. His lyrics are creatively and poetically expressive of cultural and historical memories. Pan's Aria 1 alludes to Song Yu (298 BCE? to 222 BCE?), a man long deemed to have been handsome, talented, and romantic. This suggests that Pan charms women like Song Yu did. Similarly, Gao casts Chen as a romantic by having her name the *qin* composition she plays: "Mist and Clouds over Rivers Xiao and Xiang." The title is not only the name of a celebrated Chinese *qin* composition but also a trope in Chinese and romantic discourse. It alludes to the myth of an ancient king rendezvousing with an angelic woman by a river flowing through a mountainous and mist-covered land. In addition to literary allusions, Gao also uses plain language, such as Chen's "It is none of my business!," and "*cui*," thus transforming quotidian words and exclamations into suggestive utterances.

Gao's use of three different *qupai* to structure the "Zither Seduction" is musically astute.[27] The first *qupai*, the "Lazy Bird" ("Lanhuamei"), is a southern aria tune pattern with well-defined musical attributes. It has five phrases of differing lengths, an overall rhythmic structure of thirteen *ban* strokes that should be played with a relatively slow tempo, and a pentatonic musical mode that requires the phrases to end on low tones/cadences. Repeated four times, the *qupai* generates a set of four aria variations, Arias 1 to 4 of the scene, that constitute a calm soundscape for the protagonists to sing in turn, expressing their rapidly developing feelings and thoughts.[28]

The second *qupai* in the "Zither Seduction" is the "Zither Tune" ("Qinge"), a simple tune that Gao sets to two lyrics of four phrases written in a classical literary style. It calls for the words in each phrase of the lyrics to be structurally split into semantic units of 3+1+2 words. With this rhetorical structure, the simple lyrics of Arias 5 and 6 demand a vocal delivery that is relatively slow and free of elaborate melodic ornaments—Ming musicians believed that ancient songs were to be sung syllabically and/or with simple melodies. As notated and performed, the melodies of Arias 5 and 6 are simple but expressive of the protagonists' romantic intentions and

---

27. For two studies on the "Zither Seduction" and its music composition and performance, see Lindy Li Mark, "Tone and Tune in Kunqu," *Chinoperl Papers* 12 (1983): 9–60; and "From Page to Stage: Exploring Some Mysteries of Kunqu Music and Its Melodic Characteristics," *Chinoperl: Journal of Chinese Oral and Performing Literature* 32, no. 1 (July 2013): 1–29.

28. For two English descriptions of the relationships between text and *qupai* melodies, see Luo Qin, "Linguistic Features" and "Musical Construction, in "Kunju, Chinese Classical Theater and Its Revival in Social, Political, Economic, and Cultural Contexts" (PhD diss., Kent State University, 1997), 53–110; and François Picard and Kar Lun Alan Lau, "Qupai in Kunqu: Text-Music Issues," in *Qupai in Chinese Music: Melodic Models in Form and Practice*, ed. Alan Thrasher (New York: Routledge, 2016), 119–154.

elite status—in Ming or contemporary China, only elite people would use classical rhetorical devices to express themselves in conversation.

The third *qupai*, which Gao uses to construct the last four arias of the scene (Arias 7 through 10), a set of four variations, is the "Attending a Court Audition" ("Chaoyuange"). A complex literary-musical structure, it features fourteen irregular phrases, a rhythmic structure of twenty-eight ban strokes, and flexible melodic progressions and cadences. Arias 7, 8, 9, and 10 in the "Zither Seduction" scene are melodically more different than similar, generating a sonic effect that parallels dramatic developments in the scene. Particularly noteworthy is that Aria 8 breaks into two parts, the latter of which sounds like a new aria. At the point the aria breaks, Pan stops singing and utters an apology to Chen for being too forward with her. Thus, Gao's "breaking" of Aria 8 is a dramatically logical and effective device, one that vividly underscores Gao's, or some actor-singers', dramatic manipulation of singing and speaking in kunqu.

Gao Lian's dramatic musical maneuvers in the "Zither Seduction" are not without *re-creative* elements. He was not the first Chinese author to dramatize the love story of Pan Bizheng and Chen Miaochang. His dramatization of *qin* music as romantic communication echoes at least two celebrated precedents that educated Ming knew well, as do Chinese today. The first is the ancient story of SiMa Xiangru's (179 BCE–117 BCE) playing *qin* music to seduce the newly widowed Zhuo Wenjun. The second is the *qin* music-playing scene in the *Story of the Western Wing* (*Xixiang ji*), a popular love story that has been told many times and with different words and performance practices since the Tang dynasty. Gao's use of the "Lazy Bird" *qupai* to organize arias follows well-known models, such as Gao Ming's *Lute*, an early and exemplary *chuanqi* drama. The "Viewing Lotus Blossom Flowers" ("Shanghe") scene in the *Lute* features the "Lazy Bird" *qupai* as a musical device for developing a dramatic conversation between a questioning wife and her emotionally fraught husband.[29]

Gao Lian could not on his own have created the music for his lyrics for the "Zither Seduction," a fact that becomes clear with the following notes on kunqu *qupai* music composition. In theory, kunqu dramatists write original lyrics according to preexisting *qupai*, matching the linguistic tones of individual words in their newly composed texts with melodic tones and rhythms of preexisting *qupai*, linguistic-literary-musical models they have chosen for the lyrics they are writing.[30] The process is traditionally called "*tianci*," literally, "putting words into structural slots of preexisting tunes to make arias." The literary-musical compositions thus produced are, however, merely sketch-arias: they do not make the flowing tunes that kunqu singing is celebrated for. For the sketch-arias to become musically expressive and performable compositions,

---

29. For a representative performance script of the "Shanghe," see Yu Sulu, *Sulu qupu* (Reprint, Taipei: n.p., n.d.), 31–46.

30. For a contemporary manual on kunqu linguistics, see Han Jia'ao, *Kunqu ziyin* (Hong Kong: Hong Kong Zhonghua wenhua cujin zhongxin, 2001.)

their melodic and rhythmic details must be adjusted or elaborated by music masters (*qushi*).

To demonstrate the incomplete nature of the sketch-arias composed by kunqu dramatists, and to demonstrate how they can be musically "completed" by *qushi*, an analysis of Aria 1 in the "Zither Seduction" will suffice. As kunqu connoisseurs have noted, verbal and sonic elements of the aria composed after the "Lazy Bird" *qupai* are seamlessly coordinated (see Music Example 7). The effect, which is neither natural nor routine; can only be achieved through the creative and re-creative matching of linguistic tones and melodic pitches. For example, the first word, "*yue*"(moon), is a *rusheng zi* (entering tone), and thus its musical setting has to be either melodically short or rhythmically syncopated; however, the pitch for singing the word does not need to be low like it is in Aria 1. The fourth word, "*dan*"(pale), is a *qusheng zi* (falling tone), and thus its musical setting has to involve some relatively high pitches so that a cascading effect can be produced.[31] As it is sung in Aria 1, the melodic setting for the word goes up before it goes down, making a melodic arch. To musically articulate the literary-musical structure of Aria 1, the rhymed words at phrase endings have to fall on pillar tones ("a" and "d") of the musical mode in which the "Lazy Bird" is modally cast, generating strong musical cadences. Melodic progressions toward the cadences flow freely, and this balance of musical structure and freedom is what renders Aria 1 an expressive and through-composed composition.

How Gao Lian and his collaborating *qushi*/actor-singers actually sang the arias of the "Zither Seduction" has not been documented. At this time, the earliest known and available notated music of the *zhezixi* is what the *Jiugong dacheng nanbeici gongpu* (A comprehensive and notated formulary of northern and southern arias in nine musical modes) of 1746 has preserved. Any comparison of that historical score with contemporary ones would show that the former is melodically and rhythmically much simpler than the latter, even though the latter is clearly derived from the former. In other words, it is reasonable to posit that generations of *qushi*/actor-singers have adjusted and/or re-created their singing of the arias that Gao and his *qushi* have sketched or sung.

They have adjusted the arias to express themselves musically. To sing expressively, they must match the composed or transmitted music with their singing artistry, highlighting their vocal strengths and glossing over their weaknesses. Otherwise, they could neither bring their enacted characters to life on the stage nor entertain their audiences. It is no accident that as master actor-singers "refresh" their singing of canonic arias like those found in the "Zither Seduction," they introduce creative and/or re-creative touches: melodic fermatas and melismas, use of particularly high or low

---

31. For a musicological discussion of relationships between linguistic tones and Chinese melodic progression, see Yang Yinliu, "Yuyan yinyue xue chutan," in *Yuyan yu yinyue*, ed. Anonymous (Beijing: Renmin yinyue chubanshe, 1983), 1–96.

notes, rubato treatment of specific words/tones/rhythms/tempi, and other musically affective and intelligible expressions.

Actor-singers also perform their oral deliveries with utmost care and ingenuity. This is particular clear with their affective and re-creative utterances of scripted vocables such "*ya*," "*ha*," and "*cui*," which communicate more emotions than semantic messages. Unless the vocables are uttered in ways that are "right" for specific performances and target audiences, they cannot accurately communicate dramatic emotions and meanings.

Unless we uncover new information, we will never know for certain how Gao Lian and historical musicians composed and played instrumental music for performances of the "Zither Seduction." That the music must be performed creatively is a certainty. Whether that music is historical, traditional, or newly composed, instrumental tunes played for any staging of the "Zither Seduction" need to coordinate with performers' singing and acting-dancing. *Luogu* musicians must coordinate their playing with actor-performers' *shenduan*, which take place in humanly dynamic times and places. Kunqu performers sing arias and perform *shenduan* with their physical bodies, taking into account the size and proportions of the stages on which they perform. For example, when Pan walks in the moonlit garden, he has to adjust the number of steps and the speed of his walking to the size of the stage where the garden is being presented. And consequently, the *luogu* musicians have to strike their drums and gongs differently.

Evolving Shows

When actor-singers and instrumentalists seamlessly coordinate with one another, they create/re-create transcendental shows out of popular *zhezixi*, entertaining the audience with something original/unexpected and/or something expected but nuanced. Kunqu is a living art, as the following comparison of five representative and recorded performances of the "Zither Seduction" will attest. The performances are: a 1957 show by Yu Zhenfei and Yan Huizhu (1919–1966); a 1981 rendition by Yu Zhenfei and Zhang Xian (1915–2006); a 1985 presentation by Hua Wenyi and Yue Meiti; a 1988 version by Wang Shiyu and Wang Fengmei; and a 2008 production by Yu Jiulin and Shen Fengying.

The 1957 performance by Yu Zhenfei and Yan Huizhu exemplifies traditional kunqu as it is now known.[32] As preserved in its audio recording, the performance demonstrates the ways Yu projected his *shujuanqi* with his characteristic grain of voice, which often shifted between falsetto and natural registers. Yu's low tones were richly resonant; his high tones, focused and clear. He enunciated every word of the lyrics clearly, taking care to articulate the beginning, middle, and end consonants or

---

32. A historical audio-recording of the 1957 performance is accessible as *The Jade Hairpin* (*Yuzanji*), 1957 performance by Yu Zhenfei and Yan Weizhu, accessed January 18, 2016, www.youtube.com/watch?v=O9mEo0muk-o.

vowels of the uttered words. His melodies flowed with controlled breathing, shaped ornaments, immaculate phrasing, and nuanced dynamics.

The same audio recording shows Yan Huizhu, a master performer of Peking Opera and kunqu, singing with her natural voice, featuring a low register that was atypically resonant for a female performer. Yan chanted exclamatory words and vocables elegantly. Her "*cui*" were long enough to be noticed but not so long that they would sound affected and be dismissed as vulgar.

The instrumental music accompanying the speaking and singing by Yu and Yan matched traditional ideals. The *dizi* playing supported the masters' singing seamlessly, generating a *pas de deux* of melodies. The lute (*xianzi*) played repeated notes to give the sung music a rhythmic push. The other instrumental parts had their own distinctive sounds; they played, however, neither a harmonic bass line nor the *om-pah* rhythmic and textual fillers that have become commonplace since the 1980s.

Yu Zhenfei gave a stylistically similar but expressively different performance of "Zither Seduction" in 1981, partnering with Zhang Xian.[33] As the audiovisual recording shows, Yu and Zhang performed like the kunqu masters they were. Their aging bodies, however, affected their performance and the audience's reception. Yu appeared to be physically weak—he looked like the eighty-year-old man he was. He sang artistically and tried to ooze his trademark *shujuanqi*, but he projected no youthful, impulsive scholar, and his *shenduan* acts were restrained. For example, he did not even make that dramatic fan strike on the *qin* table as he did in his 1957 show. Singing Aria 8, he performed the *shenduan* of fanning Chen Miaochang casually, but he failed to evoke any illusion of a young man teasing his lover. Yu's performance in this 1981 lacked the erotic *frisson* that "Zither Seduction" should provide.[34]

Zhang Xian, Yu's partner in this recording, performed like a mature woman. Dressed in the prescribed nun's costume and holding the required *fo*, she looked elegant, but her physical presence and movements betrayed that she was in her sixties. Zhang sang with a clear voice. Its low register, however, did not have the rich tones that Yan Huizhu had. Zhang's chanting of the vocables was effectively accompanied by her orchid-like finger gestures. All in all, the 1981 performance by Yu and Zhang made for a historical presentation, one that documented their celebrated artistry.

Poignantly, the Yu and Zhang recording underscores that much of kunqu's earthly appeal depends on individual performers' artistic creativity, performance skills, and personal or physical presence. All must converge seamlessly to make a kunqu show heavenly. An example of a legendary kunqu performance is the *Jade Hairpin* of

---

33. An audiovisual recording of the performance is accessible online as : *The Jade Hairpin* (*Yuzanji*), 1981 performance by Yu Zhenfei and Zhang Xian, accessed January 18, 2016, http://v.youku.com/v_show/id_XMzc4NjQ2MjQ4.html.
34. For an analysis of the drama as a representation of erotic desire, see Joseph S. C. Lam, "Impulsive Scholars and Sentimental Heroes: Contemporary Kunqu Discourse of Traditional Chinese Masculinities," in *Gender in Chinese Music*, ed. Rowan Pease, Rachel Harris, and Shzr EeTan (Rochester, NY: Rochester University Press, 2013), 140–167.

1985 by Hua Wenyi and Yue Meiti.[35] Produced with basic cameras and microphones, the audiovisual recording is visually and sonically fuzzy, but it still shows how the stars shone as experienced but still young and charming artists. Hua had what kunqu connoisseurs consider an ideal classical physique and voice. She sang what she had learned from her mentors even while performing with a tonality that was uniquely musical and uniquely her own. To her fans' ears, she performed the suggestive vocables with perfect timing and intensity. Her *"cui"* in Episode 3 sounded more "girlish" and "playful" than those by her peers, Hua's fans claim.

In this recorded performance, Yue Meiti, a male impersonator, acted and sang like a young man in love. Compared to the Pan Bizheng played by the aged Yu Zhenfei, Yue's Pan oozes *shujuanqi*. Having learned well from Yu Zhenfei, Yue sang expressively and superbly. As a woman, she could sing many high notes with her natural voice—she did not need to make frequent shifts between falsetto and natural registers. Her low tones, however, were not rich and resonant like those of her mentor or other celebrated male actor-singers. Yue's performance of a *qingchun dianya* Pan appeals to male and female audiences alike.

The 1985 performance by Hua and Yue highlighted many contemporary kunqu performance practices. Two are particularly obvious. First, their stage had a backdrop with realistic paintings of trees and shrubbery that visually defined the setting, namely a moonlit garden in autumn. Second, the instrumental music that accompanied their singing and *shenduan* sounded like post–Cultural Revolution Chinese instrumental music (*minyue*).[36] The musicians played traditional tunes, but their timbres, textures, and practices had been modernized. For instance, while *dizi* and *erhu* played melodies, *pipa* and *yangqin* produced *om-pah* rhythmic and harmonic fillers, and bass fiddles and lutes generated a walking bass line.

The performance by Hua and Yue was not the only production of the "Zither Seduction" in late twentieth-century China. A very different contemporary production was a 1988 performance by Wang Shiyu (b. 1941) and Wang Fengmei (b. 1945), stars of ZheKun and direct disciples of Quanzhibei Masters.[37] In terms of scripted lyrics, prescribed *shenduan*, and notated melodies, the Wang/Wang performance was not significantly different from that of Hua and Yue. Nevertheless, in terms of expressive details, the Wang and Wang presented a performance apart.

In 1988, Wang was forty-seven years old, with a rather square face and a well-defined physique. He showed none of the androgynous charm that Yue Meiti and many other young *xiaosheng* characters/performers would project and that their fans

---

35. An audiovisual recording of the performance is accessible online as: *The Jade Hairpin* (*Yuzanji*), 1985 performance by Hua Wenyi and Yue Meiti, accessed May 16, 2021, www.youtube.com/watch?v=pqLYPefnV3g.

36. See discussion of *minyue*-ized kunqu instrumental music in Chapter 8.

37. An audiovisual recording of the performance is available online: *The Jade Hairpin*, 1988 performance by Wang Shiyu and Wang Fengmei, accessed May 16, 2021, https://www.bilibili.com/video/av56425644.

cherish. Compared to those performed by Yue, Wang Shiyu's *shenduan* were more masculine. His walk covered more stage space; his head, torso, and limb movements were more pronounced. Even his smiles looked broader. Wang enacted many typical male gestures in his show. For example, singing Aria 6, he stretched his left leg far out while sitting on the chair, a demeanor that is physically expansive if not manfully aggressive. Wang's enunciation was expressive, as to be expected from a master performer. It is, however, noteworthy that Wang sang traditionally, that is, with a clear but rather thin voice, echoing those preserved in early twentieth-century audio recordings. Given the physical command the young scholar projected on stage, his voice lacked what contemporary audience hear as "male timbres." Some casual and uniformed audiences felt that Wang's singing was "unnatural," a verdict that attests to changing kunqu sounds and singing practices as well as to evolving paradigms for kunqu appreciation.

Wang's partner, Wang Fengmei, performed Chen Miaocheng professionally. She wore fancifully bejeweled headgear, which some critics found too ornate and expensive for a young nun. Also, she performed specific facial expressions to match the words she sang. As she sang Aria 2, she transformed a calm facial expression to one of sadness. To some audiences, her facial expressions seemed affected, if not exaggerated.

The instrumental music for the Wang/Wang production sounded like typical *minyue* from 1980s China. Clearly audible was how the *erhu* competed with *dizi* to lead the ensemble. Rhythmic and textual *om-pahs* were played loudly and incessantly between the solo melodies and the supporting harmonic bass. The instrumental music featured in this Wang/Wang production was not, however, identical with the music performed for the Hua/Yue production. The differences attest that even if contemporaneous kunqu performers and institutions share the same scripts and performance practices and materials, they still make creative and personalized decisions about sounds and sights.

Such sounds and sights render SuKun's *Jade Hairpin* (2008) distinctive. While its performance script featured canonized lyrics and dialogues, and while its stars, Yu Jiulin and Shen Fengying, performed *shenduan* learned from Zhang Ziqing and Wang Shiyu, the production pursued *qingchun dianya* goals, which Bai Xianyong, the show's artistic director, and his SuKun collaborators worked hard to achieve.[38] And to enrich the show's cultural and intellectual import, they intensified an underlying theme of the drama, namely the moral-religious conflict between secular pursuit of sexual love and its suppression by Buddhist moralists.[39] The show prominently displayed backdrops with lotus flowers and other pictorial/calligraphic representations of Buddhist teachings, as well as gong sounds that rang like temple bells.

---

38. For audiovisual excerpts of the show, see *The Jade Hairpin*, 2009 performance by Shen Fengying and Yu Jiulin, accessed May 16, 2021, www.youtube.com/watch?v=URmZI1YaT6Q.

39. For further details on the show, see Bai Xianyong, ed., *Sedan baotian Yuzanji—qinqu shuhua kunqu xinmeixue* (Taipei: Tianxia yuanjian chuban gufen youxian gongsi, 2009); and Bai Xianyong, ed., *Yunxin shuixin yuzanji* (Beijing: Renmin wenxue chubanshe, 2011).

To highlight kunqu elitism and historicism, and to showcase the dramatic role that *qin* (seven-string zither) played in the "Zither Seduction" scene, the *Jade Hairpin* of 2008 featured *qin* music that Li Xiangting (b. 1940), one of contemporary China's top *qin* performer, played on an authenticated Tang dynasty *qin* zither. A deliberate effort to link the sounds of a thousand-year-old musical instrument with those of six-century-old kunqu, the feature drew many positive and negative responses.

And to materially and visually underscore kunqu *dianya* as Bai and his SuKun collaborators envisioned, their *Jade Hairpin* had actor-singers wear costumes made with atypically soft silk in ascetically bland colors. The garments critically affected the performers' *shenduan*: some connoisseurs commented that the performers could not make their *shuixiu* flow the way they should—the *shuixiu* made with atypically soft silk could neither flow straight nor visually project dramatic tension.

Yu Jiulin, who played Pan Bizheng in the production, sang with a voice that some critics found less polished than the *shenduan* he performed and had learned from Wang Shiyu. Shen Fengying, who played Chen Miaochang, performed as a kunqu star cherished for her personal charms and for having learned well from Zhang Ziqing. Her singing, chanting, and *shenduan* were all favorably received by audiences. Her exclamatory "*cui*" were praised as exquisitely communicative.

The instrumental music played in the 2008 *Jade Hairpin* was programmatic and symphonic. It played many string tremolos to warn audiences when something dramatic was about to happen. It also featured heptatonic and chromatic counter-melodies, generating *qingchun* sounds that conservative connoisseurs found too Western for their tastes. Some critics have dismissed the show as nothing but a Broadway musical camouflaged as kunqu. Their harsh words would not, however, convince anyone familiar with the American genre. They do, nevertheless, underscore the ways contemporary kunqu practitioners are boldly exploring and incorporating new ways to make their genre continuously expressive and marketable. It is why classical kunqu is a living opera and why its shows continuously evolve.

Epilogue: A Diversity of Creativities, Expressions, and Selves

Clearly, different productions of the "Zither Seduction"/*Jade Hairpin* are creative and expressive in their own ways. Each constitutes a unique performance and discourse with something old and something new. And each elicits positive or negative criticisms from diverse audiences. Kunqu fans always favor one version of their favorite shows over others, claiming that it is more authentic, more creative, more dramatic, or more realistic in one way or another. Subjective and objective verdicts are integral components of kunqu performance and reception.

Subjective verdicts are most meaningful when they are pragmatically interpreted. For instance, when a critic declares that Yu Zhenfei's performance exuded *shuquanqi*, she is not merely describing what she sees and hears; she is also asserting an aesthetic ideal and cultural image that she believes is authentic and relevant to her appreciation

Creative Performers and Evolving Shows

of kunqu and understanding of an elite Chinese gentleman. By contrast, when an uninformed audience declares that Yu Zhenfei's 1981 performance was performatively lacking, the commentator reveals himself to be an outsider to the kunqu world. His criticism imposes a set of contemporary values that ignores Yu's stature as the leading performer and pedagogue of twentieth-century kunqu.

Novice or informed, kunqu audiences react to evolving kunqu shows from their personal positions and through their own cultural-social values. Most traditional and scholarly connoisseurs of kunqu, for example, focus their attention on whether performers are accurately enunciating the lyrics of the arias they are singing and whether the characters have been performed as they have understood or imagined. In contrast, many young, twenty-first-century young kunqu fans are more concerned about how beautiful or handsome their idols appear on or off stage. Some causal audiences are simply mesmerized by the fanciful costumes. To express themselves, and to satisfy their audiences/discursive partners, and to sustain the genre, kunqu practitioners must continuously fine-tune and even transform their shows so that they evolve with Chinese lives and dreams.

8
Kunqu as *Yue* Performance and Discourse

A Case Study of Kunqu Instrumental Music

Introduction

Kunqu practitioners praise or dismiss performances that they consider meritorious or defective, generating diverse comments. Heard as isolated utterances, most comments are nothing more than personal opinions. Heard collectively and in their *yuescapes*, the opinions nevertheless constitute cultural and historical debates, and even controversies. In twentieth- and twenty-first-century China, two kunqu shows stand out as discursive foci. The first one is the *Fifteen Strings of Coins* of 1956,[1] an innovative opera and opera-film that invigorated kunqu in mid-twentieth-century China and provided a model for making traditional operas serve contemporary and national needs. The opera is still being performed regularly and discussed passionately. The second one is the *Young Lovers* of 2004, a production that claims to have presented kunqu in its "original sauce and taste." By 2020, the show had been staged more than 400 times, and its audiovisual recordings are popular online viewing.[2] Its *qingchun dianya* aesthetics and practices are now core issues in contemporary kunqu debates.

This chapter examines kunqu as a case study of *yue* performance and discourse; the discussion will focus, however, on kunqu instrumental music, a controversial topic in contemporary debates about the genre. This chapter unfolds in three stages: an introduction to theories and methods for analyzing kunqu as a *yue* discourse; a report on the kunqu instrumental music controversy the *Young Lovers* has generated; and an

---

1. For two English studies on the opera, see Ann Rebull, "Locating Theatricality on State and Screen: Rescuing Performance Practice and the Phenomenon of *Fifteen Strings of Cash*" (*Shiwu guan*; 1956), *Chinoperl* 36, no. 1 (2017): 46–71, and A. C. Scott, *Traditional Chinese Plays*, Vol. 2 (Madison: University of Wisconsin Press, 1969), 61–153. For two representative Chinese studies on the opera, see Wang Shide, *Shiwuguan yanjiu* (Shanghai: Wenhua chubanshe, 1981); and Fu Jin, "Kunqu Shiwugu xinlun," in *Xinhuo xiangchuan: feiwuzhi wenhua yizan baohu di lilun yu shijian* (Beijing: Zhongguo shehui kexue chubanshe, 2008), 266–289.
2. On average, each performance of the *Young Lovers* would attract a 1,000-plus audience. Many audio-visual clips of the opera have been posted online. On average, each of the popular clips would attract 30,000-plus viewers.

analytical survey of five renditions of the instrumental music for the "Dark Silk Robe" aria in the "Strolling; Dreaming" *zhezixi*.

Kunqu as *Yue* Performance and Discourse

As kunqu practitioners perform their operatic works, they communicate with their audiences, generating a series of performance and discourse events that but overlap with and differ from one another, communicating evolving meanings as times and sites change. The events can be broadly and/or thematically analyzed as artistic, cultural, historical, social, and/or political phenomena that take place over short or long periods of time. Such analyses, however, cannot clarify how and why repeated performances of a same kunqu play generate different audience reactions. Is there anything new or changed in each of the events and/or performances? If so, what is new or changed? Analyses that focus on particular theoretical and/or practical concerns gloss over performance and discursive details that lie outside those analytical bounds, generating meaningful but limited observations. In other words, what kunqu practitioners similarly and/or dissimilarly communicate or achieve in specific rounds of performance and discourse, and why and how, are questions that cannot be answered with either broad generalizations or focused interpretations. To comprehensively understand kunqu performance and discourse, the practitioners/stakeholders, the performance practices and materials, and the results all need to be examined both one at a time and collectively. And all analytics need to be pragmatically interpreted from insider and outsider perspectives. To achieve such an understanding of kunqu, the analytical method of Chinese *yue* performance and discourse is proposed and applied here.[3]

This method has been formulated with what this author has learned from international theories and Chinese music history.[4] Four international scholars' theories of music, ritual, and/or performance are especially seminal, so I will briefly review them here. The first is Christopher Small's musicking thesis:[5] "music is not a thing at all but an activity, something that people do" to activate mythologized, idealized, and/or experienced social relations they subscribe to and that they use to affirm and celebrate their selves/lives. For Small, to musick is to "take part, in any capacity, in a musical

---

3. I have been developing this *yue* hypothesis since 2008; for a recent application, see Joseph S. C. Lam, "Eavesdropping on Zhang Xiaoxiang's Musical World in Early Southern Song China," in *Senses of the City: Perceptions of Hangzhou and Southern Song China, 1127–1279*, ed. Joseph Lam, Shuen-fu Lin, Christian de Pee, and Martin Powers (Hong Kong: Chinese University of Hong Kong Press, 2017), 25–54.
4. There are numerous studies on Chinese and Western operas as a cultural, historical, social, and political discourse. For a current study on Chinese opera as a social-political phenomenon, see Li Hsiao-T'i, *Opera, Society, and Politics in Modern China* (Cambridge, MA: Harvard University Asia Center, 2019).
5. Christopher Small, *Musicking: The Meanings of Performing and Listening* (Middletown: Wesleyan University Press, 1998). Small's words cited and or paraphrased in this paragraph are culled from pages 2, 9, and 147.

performance, whether by performing, by listening, by rehearsing, or practice, by providing material for performance." Small posits that music/musicking is meaningful because its sonic signs and gestures have their origins in ritual and musical theater. It was Monteverdi, Caccini, and other operatic composers who developed a systematic vocabulary of musical signs and gestures that Westerners employ to represent not only their human relationships and emotions but also their personal characteristics; so Small surmises.

Small offers an inspiring thesis but provides no analytical procedures that can be fruitfully employed to examine kunqu works, performances, and debates. In addition, his prioritizing music as performance/process over its being as objects/works makes it difficult to identify how specific kunqu expressions are creatively/re-creatively composed, performed, heard, and interpreted. For example, while Small cites Beethoven's Fifth Symphony as an archetype of Western heroic symphonies, he does not tell how that masterpiece culturally and sonically communicates Western heroism.

When Small confesses that he "cannot imagine what could be the point of listening to the performance of a symphony—or of performing or composing one," if it is not a narrative that tells "of the development of human relationships and in telling their stories they explore, affirm, and celebrate concepts of what those relationships are and what they ought to be," he exposes the limitations of his understanding of music in broad, humanist terms.[6] Would music lovers listen to music for its entertaining sounds? And when Small concludes his monograph with the metaphor of a solitary African herdsman playing flute music to himself while guarding his flock, thus declaring "here I am, and this is who I am," the author is making a poetic statement. If it evokes humanist understandings of music as a performance and discourse of the human self, it offers no concrete clues for musical analyses and interpretations. And when Small lodges the caveat that "we cannot, of course, know what he [the African herdsman] is thinking as he plays or what he imagines he is doing," the author makes it clear that he is not concerned with interpreting music as expressions with identifiable and evolving meanings. Thus his musiking thesis cannot be applied to analyzing kunqu as a performance of Chinese culture, history, and personhood. Unlike the African herdsman, kunqu practitioners meticulously articulate and document their deeds and words about kunqu as a microcosm of their *qingchun dianya* lives and dreams.

Kunqu practitioners purposefully stage and negotiate performances, generating artistic, communicative, and social-political realities that Howard Becker calls "art worlds"—networks of artists who create/perform not only with established conventions, available resources, and specialized knowledge/skills but also through contextualized and personal choices, which they either routinely make or tactically improvise at various points in the process.[7] Insightfully, Becker offers an inclusive, dynamic, and

---

6. Small, *Musicking*, 173 and 203.

7. Howard S. Becker, *Art Worlds*, 25th anniversary updated and expanded edition (Berkeley: University

practical approach to art as an activity of aesthetic and social performance and discourse. His approach can be fruitfully applied to kunqu studies for obvious reasons. He not only gives agency to people who make and consume art for a variety of idealistic and practical reasons but also offers guides for analyzing their acts of creating and consuming. Artists create in order to produce results worthy of their talents and efforts, so as to, for example, enhance their artistic reputation or allow them to make a living. Patrons use art to achieve their personal and communal authority/agendas. Dealers promote and distribute artworks for cultural and/or financial profit. Audiences consume art for expressive and personal needs. However art world citizens produce and consume art works, Howard notes, they dynamically operate through aesthetic principles and systems that both influence and are influenced by their established conventions, training, available resources, and operative modes of distribution and presentation. In other words, artists in Becker's art worlds are free to follow or break conventions, innovate, make aesthetic judgements, compete with fellow artists, and make use of chances that come and go. As a result, what artists meticulously produce and/or fine-tune is dynamic and meaningful by itself. And by virtue of its subtle or unmistakable particulars, creative/re-creative art teaches its audiences something new: a new symbol, a new form, a new mode of representation. And in return, audiences respond critically, interacting "with the [new] work, and frequently with other people in relation to the work. They see and hear the new elements in a variety of contexts."

Becker's art worlds thesis serves as a practical guide for objectively analyzing and interpreting kunqu works, performances, and debates; however, it offers no tools for probing subjective claims and/or competing interpretations—as Becker admits, he is not concerned with aesthetic evaluations of art works and processes. This lacuna renders Becker's theory an incomplete method for studying kunqu performance and discourse. Evaluative statements on kunqu acts, objects, and communications are fundamental components of kunqu discourse. However personal and unverifiable the statements are, they anchor and/or define the ways kunqu practitioners perform and negotiate. What renders specific kunqu shows performatively meaningful and discursively persuasive involves not only created and performed expressions but also feeling, thinking, and action-taking Chinese selves.

A useful tool for probing multivalent kunqu performance and discourse is Jeffry Alexander's theory of cultural pragmatics.[8] Drawing from an abundance of historical data and a series of developmental arguments about Western rituals and social performances, he posits that in simple hierarchical societies, rituals and cultural performances are authoritatively staged and consensually understood because their

---

of California Press, 2008). Becker's key ideas cited in this discussion appear on pages 69–78, 87, 99–126, 131–134, and 376.

8. Jeffry C. Alexander, "Cultural Pragmatics: Social Performance between Ritual and Strategy," *Sociological Theory* 22, no. 4 (December 2004): 527–573; see also Yan Huang, *Pragmatics* (New York: Oxford University Press, 2007).

performance materials and practices directly reflect participants' daily experiences. In other words, when performance features and meanings are fused, or dynamically linked, they communicate what performers want to tell and what audiences want to hear.

However, in complex, fragmented, modern societies, rituals and cultural performances may not be consensually staged and understood; their performance practices and materials may be detached from the participants' daily realities. In other words, the performances and their meanings are "de-fused" and thus can be rejected or resisted by participants who want the performances and their lives "fused." To make effective performances, Alexander argues, performers must skillfully "re-fuse" known performance practices and materials in strategically constructed or identified mise-en-scènes that afford performers and audiences times and sites to intellectually and emotionally interpret what that is being staged and how their features and meanings are fused.

Alexander's thesis offers a pragmatic methodology for analyzing kunqu, if the genre's complex and fragmented art world in historical and contemporary China can be heuristically defined and its coordinated and uncoordinated elements can be meaningfully identified. Toward that goal, Arjun Appadurai's theory of "scapes" proves to be most instrumental.[9] Contemporary kunqu performances and discourses take place in an art world that is fluid and multifaceted. What individualistic and pragmatic kunqu practitioners perform and critique concerns not only cultural-historical experiences and ideologies but also the structural details of operatic works, the performance skills of individual performers, and the discursive goals and styles of audiences. All continually transform one another, and thus they demand to be discussed in both broad and specific terms. In other words, kunqu performance and discourse operate like Appadurai's "scapes," which are "deeply perspectival constructs, inflected by the historical, linguistic, and political situatedness of different sorts of actors: nation-states, multinational, diasporic communities and as well as subnational groupings and movements (whether religious, political, or economic), and even intimate face-to-face groups, such as villages, neighborhoods, and families. Indeed, the individual actor is the last locus of this perspectival set of landscapes, for these landscapes are eventually navigated by agents who both experience and constitute larger formations in part from their own sense of what these landscapes offer."[10]

With his "scape" theory, Appadurai offers a practical means to define and describe the complex, fluid, fragmented realities in the art world of kunqu, in which historical and contemporary performance and discourse practices and materials are continuously being de-fused, fused, and re-fused by feeling, thinking, and action-taking kunqu practitioners. Coordinating the theories by Alexander, Appadurai, Becker, and Small,

---

9. See Arjun Appadurai, *Modernity at Large: Cultural Dimensions of Globalization* (Minneapolis: University of Minnesota Press, 1996), 32–37.

10. Appadurai, *Modernity at Large*, 33.

and customizing their analytical paradigms with kunqu particulars, turns out to be an effective method for analyzing kunqu performance and discourse as a microcosm of Chinese lives and dreams.

Such customizing is necessary because kunqu has a long history; its performance and discourse practices and materials have been evolving for centuries. When examined in detail, and with reference to insider tropes and keywords, kunqu is dissimilar to what Westerners theorize and practice as music/opera. Since the 1600s, Westerners have been approaching music more and more as autonomous, composed, and notated works by individual composers that performers faithfully perform/realize for themselves and their audiences. Indicative of such an approach is the fact that Western composers and musicologists study operas mostly in terms of story-telling libretti and composed/notated music—not unlike kunqu fans, many Western opera afficionados would, however, choose to focus their attention on the performers and the human emotions they project.

This Western, positivist approach to opera cannot be applied literally to kunqu. In traditional China, kunqu is performed and discussed as *xiqu* (theater and songs) in particular, and as *yue* in general. Technically, *xiqu* is defined as telling dramatic stories with words, music, and dance, a definition that underscores its multimedia nature; as central as music/sound is in kunqu, it does not in itself constitute the genre. *Yue* is often translated as "music" in Western scholarship, even though *yue* and music display critical differences. As performed, witnessed, and debated, an item of Chinese *yue* is an elastic entity of words, sounds, dances, and visuals, all of which can be adjusted as needed. Even if a piece of *yue* is attributed to a known artist and can be defined by its essential features (*shenyun*), it is hardly an autonomous composition/performance with fixed features and meanings.[11] As discussed in previous chapters, a kunqu work/performance is a collaborative and evolving expression, one that can be adjusted, re-created, and/or reinterpreted as necessary by practitioners working in contemporaneous or noncontemporaneous times and operatively dissimilar or similar sites. Kunqu performance scripts are written and rewritten by dramatists/scriptwriters. Kunqu arias' melodies and rhythms are creatively and re-creatively composed, notated, and taught by music masters; what is actually performed and heard inside and outside theaters, however, depends on individual actor-singers; what the music signifies is interpreted by audiences. In other words, kunqu as performance and discourse not only turns on dramatic scripts, notated music, and performance venues but also changes with the various agencies of performers and audiences. Each kunqu event and discourse involves a fusing, de-fusing, and re-fusing of diverse elements.

And each is a process through which practitioners/stakeholders both creatively and pragmatically maneuver the genre's codified performance practices and materials, re-fusing them with selected facts and claims, each of which may or may not be

---

11. For a representative study on Chinese music aesthetics, see Cai Zhongde, *Zhongguo yinyue meixue shi* (Beijing: Renmin yinyue chubanshe, 2004).

intrinsically connected to the structural, performative, and/or stylistic features of the kunqu works being produced, staged, and consumed. Kunqu criticism is often more concerned about moralistic ideals and cultural-historical associations and less about the objective and performative features of the productions being critiqued. For example, kunqu is often discussed as a *ya* (cultivated, cultivating, elitist, refined) opera. This sharply contrasts with *su* (vernacular, vulgar) performing arts, which are ideologically dismissed, if not socially and politically banned.

To approach kunqu as *ya* performance and discourse of *yue*, the phenomenon's cultural and historical provenance needs to be traced, and paradigms for analysis must be defined. Kunqu as *ya* performance and discourse is a tradition propelled by the centuries-old Confucian ideology of *yue*, and its corollaries of *yayue* and *suyue*. The tradition's core aesthetics and practices have been ideologically prescribed by Confucius himself. For instance, the sage once asked his disciples if *yue* meant merely the striking of gongs and drums. In asking the question, the sage was making it clear that moral-social-political concerns are integral elements of *yue* composition, performance, and reception. Another time, Confucius declared that a performance of Wan dance (*wanwu*) that he once witnessed at Lord Ji's court was socially and politically transgressive, and thus not *ya*—the lord had usurped the emperor's rights by staging the dance as an imperial expression—as defined by the choreographic practice of having sixty-four dancers performing in a formation of eight lines of eight performers each. With the statement, Confucius prescribed that the *ya* of a *yue* item depended not only on its structural and stylistic features but also on the identities of its performers and audiences and the particulars of performance and discourse intentions, times, and sites. Applying Confucius's *ya* and *yue* teachings, scholar-officials in historical and imperial China strongly promoted their own *yue* as refined and civilizing, while dismissing those of their rivals as vulgar and corrupting.

Since mid-Qing China, elite Chinese kunqu practitioners have continuously promoted kunqu as *ya* opera, substantiating their efforts with a wealth of historical facts, associative arguments, and unverifiable claims.[12] Having inherited this tradition, contemporary kunqu practitioners stage and discuss their shows as utterances of their *dianya* selves, demonstrating social-political relationships that Small has poetically noted, constructing dynamic art worlds that Becker has insightfully dissected, and de-fusing and re-fusing performance practices and materials as Alexander theorized. Since they live in a complex, contemporary China that is being pulled in various directions by regional, national, and international forces, kunqu practitioners do not always agree on what is or is not re-fused/re-fusable. Diversely and revealingly, they stage and discuss similar and/or dissimilar kunqu shows with complementary and/or conflicting words.

---

12. For a historical discussion of *ya* and *su* in Chinese opera, see Liu Zhen, *Xiqu lishi yu shenmei bianqian* (Beijing: Zhongguo wenlian chubanshe, 2015); see esp. 9–65. See also Joseph S. C. Lam, "*Ya* kunqu in Late Ming and Early Qing China," *China Arts Quarterly* 6 (September 2019): 68–94.

As *Yue* Performance and Discourse

To analyze meaningfully kunqu as discursive performances and debates, its phenomena can be heuristically defined and analyzed as follows. Kunqu performance and discourse unfolds dynamically with fluid components, which can be identified as *yue*-items, *yue*-stakeholders with particularized agendas, *yue*-events, and *yuescapes*. When Chinese perform and negotiate kunqu performances at specific times and sites to advance particularized agendas with specific materials and strategies, they generate distinctive and identifiable *yue* phenomena/processes of performance and discourse. Each involves particularized and meaning-generating fusion, de-fusion, and re-fusion of all kinds of kunqu elements.

Kunqu *yue*-items exist in multiple material and nonmaterial forms, ranging from preserved scripts and notated scores of dramatic works to their realizations as musical arias and choreographed *shenduan* and the audience responses they elicit. All kunqu *yue*-items can be pragmatically de-fused, fused, and re-fused as needed. Newly created/re-created, performed, and critiqued *yue*-items may or may not replace old ones. Forgotten or ignored *yue*-items can be recalled/reconstructed as needed. As a result, old and new kunqu *yue*-items and their meanings coexist and continually evolve. To identify and discuss old, new, and changing *yue*-items, they will be chronologically, topically, and numerically labeled in the following analysis, such as *yue*-item 6 of kunqu instrumental music, which is what kunqu practitioners played and discussed as the genre's traditional instrumental music from the 1960s through to the 1980s.

Kunqu *yue*-items are not autonomous objects with fixed meanings; their features and meanings are constructed and/or defined during kunqu *yue*-events, namely activities that kunqu *yue*-stakeholders deliberately organize and participate in to advance their agendas. In the process, they exercise their kunqu knowledge and performance and discursive skills, while maneuvering material and nonmaterial resources to which they have access. In the same process, they interactively and tactically negotiate with fellow practitioners/stakeholders, making routine or improvised choices as needed, advancing their agendas and selves with or against those of others. Given that all kinds of creative decisions are made to fuse/re-fuse *yue*-items, *yue*-events are transforming activities. In other words, even if a *yue*-event involves the same *yue*-items of stories, arias, and *shenduan*, it can generate contrasting understandings and communications. To trace and discuss specific rounds of *yue*-events, in this chapter they will be chronologically and topically defined and numerically labeled. For example, *yue*-event 2 of *c-yue* in Table 8.2 refers to the performance and discourse events the *Young Lovers* generated. And to highlight stakeholders who have effectively negotiated and fruitfully produced desired results in specific *yue*-events, they will be addressed as *dominant stakeholders*; their names will be used to identify their individualized operations and agendas.

To produce their desired results, dominant stakeholders need to act effectively in fluid *yuescapes*. Then and there, they need to make maximum use of not only *yue*-items that are available/accessible but also all kinds of relatable associations. They also need to somehow overcome challenges and restraints that competing stakeholders and performance conditions might introduce. Otherwise, they cannot productively de-fuse, fuse, or re-fuse kunqu *yue*-items in their *yue*-events. As performance and discursive times and sites, *yuescapes* make dynamic *mis-en-scénes* of the sort that Alexander theorizes. They contextualize specific kunqu performance and discourse and at the same time are themselves contextualized by kunqu stakeholders, along with all the *yue*-items they activate or reference. Conceptually, *yuescapes* are most comparable to Appadurai's *technoscapes*, which define and are defined by rapidly transforming technologies. Broadly speaking, kunqu is not unlike a technology that people create and use to express themselves and to achieve their goals; people and their lives are, however, transformed by their technologies.

This is to say that kunqu *yuescapes* are not merely contexts of performance and discourse; they themselves are performative and discursive phenomena that are temporally and/or physically fluid. Temporally, kunqu *yuescapes* can flexibly stretch from the limited duration of a production to expansive periods of decades or even centuries, during which stakeholders perform and negotiate what they reify as kunqu. Indeed, kunqu *yuescapes* crisscross dynastic boundaries in Chinese culture and history, over the course of which stakeholders historically recall facts and memories from the genre's past. Spatially, *yuescapes* span from the studio where the *yue*-item of a kunqu aria is being composed, to the stage where it is performed, to any venue where it is heard and critiqued. As *yuescapes* are spatially expanded or shrunk, arias acquire different meanings as they are constructed by changing stakeholders and evolving *yue*-events. Being fluid and situational, *yuescapes* clarify or obfuscate kunqu expressions and meanings with their stable and/or flexible attributes. For example, the *yuescape* of a stage might clarify the meanings of a performance as a reflection of the performance venue's physical measurements and/or its established uses as a ritual or secular site. By the same token, the *yuescape* that actor-singers and audiences define through their personal presence, aesthetics, and social-political agendas and other *yue*-items and/or *yue*-events may confuse or complicate the issues being negotiated. For analytical convenience here, *yuescapes* will be chronologically and topically demarcated and numerically labeled, such as the *yuescape* 4 in Table 8.1, which unfolded in early twentieth-century war-torn China when and where imported Western music challenged kunqu and other traditional Chinese performing arts.

Kunqu Instrumental Music: A *Yue* Discourse of Contemporary China and *Qingchun* Selves

The *Young Lovers* of 2004 is a controversial kunqu work.[13] In particular, its instrumental music has provoked heated debate over what authentic kunqu music was, is,

---

13. There are numerous comments on the opera. For a report on its production and stakeholders, see Pan Xinghua, comp., *Chunse ruxu: Qingchunban kunqu Mudanting renwu fangtanlu* (Singapore: Global Publishing, 2007).

and should be. Initially, debates about the instrumental music in the *Young Lovers* focused on the structured and stylized sounds of the production; after which, technical arguments about the sounds promptly led to competing understandings of kunqu sounds and the ways they sonically and symbolically indexed Chinese culture, history, and personhood.[14]

Kunqu practitioners debate the genre's instrumental music in terms of culturally and historically established notions; that the music evolves and may not align with established notions is typically glossed over. Traditionally, kunqu instrumental music was composed and played to complement performers' acting, dancing, and singing and/or to enhance the telling of stories. As performed and heard, traditional kunqu instrumental music unfolds either as heterophonic counterparts to sung melodies or as nondiegetic music that articulates the dramatic and narrative structures of acts, arias, and *shenduan*. In terms of structured and stylized sounds, traditional kunqu instrumental music is played to achieve idealized sounds and dramatic effects. *Dizi*, *erhu*, and other kunqu melodic instruments play tunes that are essentially the same as what actor-singers sing, facilitating the performers' execution of vocal expressions, clarifying their dramatic meanings, and enriching their sensual or entertainment appeal. Drums, gongs, and other rhythmic and percussion instruments are played to generate sounds/sonic expressions that articulate performers' execution of *shenduan*, clarifying its structural and semantic meanings, and affectively and sonically help propel dramatic developments.

Until recently, vocal music in kunqu was inseparable from instrumental music, and even today, neither can be meaningfully discussed without reference to the other.[15] Since the 1990s, however, kunqu instrumental music has become more and more "independent" of its vocal counterpart. As a result, evolving compositions and performance styles of kunqu instrumental music have been dichotomized into traditional and contemporary camps. For convenience of discussion, the former will here be labeled traditional kunqu instrumental *yue*, or *t-yue*, and the latter as contemporary kunqu instrumental *yue*, or *c-yue*; their supporters will be respectively called *t-stakeholders* and *c-stakeholders*.

---

14. Controversies on kunqu instrumental music are less documented than debates on dramatic story-telling, character enactment, cultural and historical developments, and other issues that can effectively be examined as text. For three recent publications on kunqu instrumental music, see Lin Cuiqing, "Shijie yinyue wenhua quanqiuhua duihua zhong de kunqu yinse yu yinxiang tizhi," in *Kunqu·Chunsan eryue tian: Miandui shijie de kunqu yu Mudanting*, ed. Hua Wei (Shanghai: Shanghai guji chubanshe, 2009), 152–164; Yu Siuwah, "Cong Zhu Maichen xiuqi kan kunqu di yinyue banzou," in *Kunju Zhu Maichen xiuqi—Zhang Jiqing Yao Jikun yanchu banben*, ed. Lie Jingxuan (Hong Kong: Oxford University Press, 2007), 179–195; and Zhou Youliang's essays in *Qingchunban Mudanting quanpu* (Suzhou: Suzhou daxu chubanshe, 2015), 223 and 229–239.

15. For two anthologies of *t-yue qupai*, see Zhongyang yinyue xueyuan minzu yinyue yanjiusuo, ed., *Kunju chuida qupai* (Beijing: Yinyue chubanshe, 1956); and Gao Jingchi, *Kunqu chuantong qupai xuan* (Beijing: Renmin yinyue chubanshe, 1981). For a historical account of Chinese instrumental music and its use in multimedia performance arts, see Yang Yinliu, *Zhongguo yinyue shigao* (Beijing: Renmin yinyue chubanshe, 1980); see esp. 212–220, 367–379, 725–736, and 987–1003.

T-yue is composed according to established instrumental *qupai* and played with idiomatic performance practices.[16] *T-yue* pieces are recognized as singular *yue*-items, but they are neither performed as dramatically autonomous expressions nor discussed as expressively independent works. Indicative of such practices is the fact that names of composers and arrangers of *t-yue* are hardly known; also, structural features of *t-yue* items are sketchily documented and discussed. To *t-*stakeholders, most of whom have learned kunqu instrumental music from traditional teachers, *t-yue* is authentic, native Chinese music. Its stylized sounds embody culturally and historically established Chinese aesthetics, tuning, orchestration, and other traditional performance practices and materials, so history tells us. As performed and heard nowadays, *t-yue* sounds different from the modernized, Westernized, and/or popular musics that have permeated contemporary China. A prime example of such *t-yue* is the "Pipa Tune" played in the "An Audience with the Censor" ("Jiandu") scene in the *Fifteen Strings of Coins* (see Music Example 8). This simple tune is played repeatedly with accelerating tempi but no structural or timbral changes. It enhances the scene's dramatic portrayal of a judge growing more and more agitated while waiting for a tardy high official.[17]

C-yue compositions/passages may or may not be composed according to kunqu instrumental *qupai* and other traditional kunqu conventions. All are, however, composed to serve dramatic needs; their structural and stylistic features are created as needed or as deemed dramatically effective. *C-yue* is played with a mixture of traditional Chinese and Western/Westernized musical instruments, which include, to cite but a few, keyed and enlarged mouth organs (*sheng*), dulcimers (*yangqin*), lutes (*pipa*), chime-bells, Western cello, and even synthesizers. All of the instruments are tuned according to international pitch standards. As performed and heard, *c-yue* compositions display characteristic features, including recurring *zhu xuanlü* (main motives or themes), melodies/sounds with programmatic references/associations, triadic and modal harmonies outlined by walking bass lines, and continuously ebbing and flowing dynamics, textures, and timbres. Many *c-yue* passages/items make nondiegetic comments on the dramas being staged, and thus they draw attention to kunqu instrumental music as an independent dramatic voice. Appropriate to their elevated roles in contemporary kunqu productions, *c-yue* items are discussed as creative compositions, and the artistry of their composers and orchestrators is increasingly being discussed. For example, the *c-yue* played in the *Young Lovers* are known and discussed as compositions and musical arrangements by Zhou Youliang, the SuKun composer appointed to the production.[18]

---

16. For brief descriptions of the instruments, see the discussion in Chapter 2. For a practical introduction to Chinese instrumental music, see Gao Houyong, *Minzu qiyue gailun* (Reprint, Taipei: Danqing tushu youxian gongsi, 1988).

17. For an online audiovisual recording of the scene, see *Shiwuguan*, a 1956 opera-movie by Zhou Chuanying and others, accessed April 23, 2021; https://www.youtube.com/watch?v=2jjNDkbCVTk&t=4134s; the playing of the "Pipa Tune" begins at 58'00.

18. For Zhou Youliang's views on his *c-yue*, see his essays in *Qingchunban Mudanting quanpu*, 223 and 229–239.

As *Yue* Performance and Discourse

Most *c-yue* musicians are young, forward-looking professionals and graduates of Chinese music conservatories or performing arts academies. Generally, they aspire to "improve" *t-yue* by purging its use of "intrusively loud and percussive" *luogu* music and by making its "bland, antiquated" sounds more "musically expressive and intelligible" to contemporary audiences.

Kunqu practitioners perform and discourse on their *t-yue* and *c-yue* with a wealth of associatively or logically referenced facts and claims about twentieth- and twenty-first-century Chinese music aesthetics and *minyue* (Chinese and ethnic instrumental music).[19] For convenience of discussion, the *yue*-items, *yue*-events, stakeholders, *yuescapes*, and agendas the practitioners freely evoke in their debates are summarized here in Tables 8.1 and 8.2.

As is clear from Tables 8.1 and 8.2, kunqu practitioners evoke a diversity of *t-* and *c-yue* items, *yue*-events, and *yuescapes* in their debates about the kunqu instrumental music played in the *Young Lovers*. The actual sounds of the performance are less a singular and core concern and more a springboard to a plethora of related issues. Indeed, the controversy over the music amounts to a discourse on contemporary Chinese instrumental music aesthetics, performance practices and materials, their historical and current developments, and their cultural and ideological meanings for twenty-first-century kunqu practitioners. The crux of these issues is that for kunqu to survive as a genre of Chinese opera, its instrumental music and other expressive features have been undergoing transformation since late-Qing China. And as these transformations have happened, kunqu instrumental music has become entangled with twentieth- and twenty-first-century Chinese *minyue* practices, theories, and historical developments.

Minyue is itself a complex and evolving *yue* phenomenon. Theoretically, *minyue* aesthetics, practices, and repertory are clearly defined; as performed and heard sounds, however, *minyue* is a fluid phenomenon that resists rigid categorization. Historically speaking, *minyue* is the product of a century-long Chinese effort to modernize its historical musical practices and materials. Early examples of *minyue* began to emerge by the 1920s. In 1923, Zheng Jinwen (1872–1935) launched the Great Unity Music Association (Datong yuehui) and spearheaded the institution of playing Chinese music with large ensembles/orchestras of native and modernized musical instruments. In the same period, Liu Tianhua (1895–1932), a seminal figure in twentieth-century Chinese instrumental music, transformed the *erhu* from a folk fiddle into a concert instrument emulating the Western violin. The *erhu* is now a prominent melodic instrument in kunqu performance.

Between the 1930s and the early 1950s, Chinese instrumental music developed rapidly by learning from Western music and by blending native and regional sounds. For example, in 1935, Radio China in Nanjing launched its Chinese music ensemble

---

19. For a recent study of *minyue* with reference to Chinese opera, see Fu Jin, "Yinyue yu minyue," in *Xi zai shuwai: Xiju wenhua suibi* (Beijing: Beijing daxue chubanshe, 2014), 147–153. For notes on early and mid-twentieth-century *minyue* artists, compositions, and institutions, see Miao Tianrui, Ji Liankang, and Guo Nai'an, *Zhongguo yinyue cidan* (Beijing: Renmin yinyue chubanshe, 1985).

Table 8.1: Six types of *T-yue* commonly referenced in contemporary kunqu debates

T-yue Items	Events	Dominant stakeholders	*Yuescapes*	Claims/agendas
T-yue item 1: vocal and instrumental kunqu music (*shuimo qiang*) of late imperial China	*T-yue* event 1: late Ming and early Qing kunqu activities that developed kunqu vocal and instrumental music	Wei Liangfu, his collaborators; early Qing kunqu practitioners	*T-yue* yuescape 1: late Ming and early Qing China, a culturally and socially developing time and site	Kunqu as a distinctive genre of vocal/operatic music, one that closely affiliated with Wu culture, locale, and personages
T-yue item 2: kunqu music notated between 1740 and 1850	*T-yue* event 2: Mid- and late Qing activities that reified kunqu with notated scores and theoretical writings	Elite and scholarly late Qing kunqu music masters, such as Prince Yun Lu, and Ye Tang	*T-yue* yuescape 2: elite kunqu masters' private studios and social venues	Kunqu as *yayue*, one that elite and erudite practitioners strived to codify and promote
T-yue item 3: Kunqu music practiced and notated between 1850 and 1911	*T-yue* event 3: Performance and discourse by avocational and vocational kunqu practitioners	Elite and avocational practitioners like Yu Shulu and Wang Jilie; commercial and commoner professionals like Yin Guishen	*T-yue* yuescape 3: a late imperial China torn by wars and social divisions, where and when kunqu continually declined	As kunqu declined, it was sustained by nationalistic elitists; artistic and social boundaries between elite and commoner practitioners became more and more a concern
T-yue item 4: Kunqu music as practiced between 1911 through 1949	*T-yue* event 4: private and public kunqu performances and debates organized and attended by early twentieth century and elite Chinese	Conservative, traditional, nationalist, and elite practitioners of kunqu	*T-yue* yuescape 4: A cultural China when and where imported Western music challenged domestic genres	Kunqu practitioners promoted the genre as an authentic and traditional expression, and as a symbol of classical and historical China
T-yue item 5: traditional kunqu instrumental music, 1950 through 1966	*T-yue* event 5: efforts to define and adjust traditional kunqu into something that contemporary and national audiences would understand and support	Cultural officials and leaders, and professional performers	*T-yue* yuescape 5: A socialist China that strived to "update" the nation's traditional performing arts	Kunqu should be updated so that it would better represent and serve the nation
T-yue item 6: kunqu music that is considered traditional, since 1976	*T-yue* event 6: Contemporary and professional performances and discussions of kunqu music	Professional kunqu composers and instrumentalists	*T-yue* yuescape 6: A musical China when and where *minyue* has become a national standard	*Minyue-ized* kunqu music is performed and negotiated as authentic and traditional music of contemporary China

Table 8.2: Four types of C-*yue* referenced in contemporary kunqu debates

C-yue items	Events	Dominant stakeholders	Yuescapes	Idealistic claims/agendas
C-*yue* item 1: Kunqu music that emulates *minyue*, and Western music; since the late 1970s	Event 1: commercial and public kunqu shows staged by professional troupes	Conservatory-trained kunqu professionals	C-*yue yuescape* 1: Prospering late twentieth-century China that *minyue* has permeated	To survive, kunqu needs to be contemporized by emulating *minyue*, Western art music, and other popular genres
C-*yue* Item 2: Programmatic and symphonic kunqu music, as popularized by the *Young Lovers*, since 2004	Event 2: *qingchun dianya* kunqu shows since 2004	Kunqu practitioners who strive to contemporize and popularize kunqu	C-*yue yuescape* 2: the kunqu world of young, forward-looking Chinese	Kunqu can be simultaneously classical and fashionable
C-*yue* item 3: kunqu music hybridized with various elements culled from Chinese and international musics	Events 3: Contemporary and popular kunqu shows	Contemporary kunqu composers, such as Sun Jian'an of ShengKun, Zhou Xuehua of ShangKun, and Zhou Youliang of SuKun	C-*yue yuescape* 3: the Chinese musical world where traditional, contemporary, and foreign genres of music overlap	Kunqu is, and can be, anything that its artists create and perform, and that its audiences embrace
c-*yue* Item 4: experimental kunqu music featuring innovative sonorities that have little or no connections with the genre's historical sounds	Events 4: performances of experimental kunqu	Progressive kunqu practitioners, such as Tan Dun, Danny Yung, and Zhang Jun	C-*yue yuescape* 4: the cosmopolitan and forward-looking segment of the world of twenty-first-century kunqu	To safeguard and develop kunqu with new and/or old aesthetics of the genre and of the globalized world

with musicians recruited from various regions of the country; their mission was to modernize Chinese instrumental music. In 1942, Mao Zedong proclaimed the need to make music intelligible to commoners with his "Yan'an Forum on Literature and Art." In 1953, the Central Broadcasting Corporation organized its Chinese orchestra with twenty-plus musicians from a variety of regional Chinese ensemble music traditions. Composing and performing together, they created a new type of Chinese instrumental music, one that blends traditional, neotraditional, transplanted, hybridized, and newly formulated performance practices and materials. It is a bona fide fountainhead of *minyue* as it is now known and practiced.

The rise of *minyue* as a model of Chinese instrumental music was culturally and politically inevitable, a development that was propelled by educational and social changes in socialist China. In the 1950s the nation launched a number of new/ reconstituted Chinese music conservatories, opera troupes, and institutes of music training and transmission. The institutes promoted contemporary repertories and performance practices at the expense of traditional ones.[20] By the early 1960s, a new generation of conservatory-trained composers and instrumentalists had emerged and a new repertory of *minyue* compositions had entered the canon. Most of the compositions have programmatic titles, such as "The Golden Snake's Dance" ("Jinshe kuangwu") for small ensembles and the "Fighting Typhoon" ("Zhan taifeng") for *guzheng* (zither). Also, many *minyue* compositions feature tunes and rhythms derived from Chinese folk songs and operatic tunes, which are performed and heard as musical indices to cultural, historical, and nationalistic memories and ideals. Nationally promoted and repeatedly performed, *minyue* compositions have permeated the Chinese music scene and critically informed kunqu instrumental music composition, performance, and discourse.

Since the late 1970s, distinct *minyue* sounds with somewhat definable/refusable meanings and associations have developed. They include *erhu* melodies that slide down or soar high to project Chinese people's suffering and resilience; lofty *guqin* sounds that sonically represent China's classical and timeless past; *guzheng* glissandos that mark the passing of historical time and change of place; fast and percussive strumming on the *pipa* and other lutes that depicts battle scenes and/or heroic struggles; loud and resonant drum and gong music that sonically constitutes farmers' harvest celebrations and happy lives; and the metallic resonances of chime-bells that project ancient and imperial China. By the mid-1980s, *minyue* theories and practices had infiltrated all kinds of Chinese music composition, performance, and scholarship. By the mid-1990s, many *minyue* concertos, overtures, and symphonies had been composed and performed, a development that spurred kunqu instrumental

---

20. These musical institutions include, for example, the Shanghai Conservatory of Music, which was first established in 1927, the Central Conservatory of Music, launched in Tianjin in 1950, and the Shanghai National Music Orchestra (Shanghai minzu yuetuan), launched in 1952.

As *Yue* Performance and Discourse   165

music to sound more and more programmatic and symphonic. Symphonic kunqu instrumental music has become fashionable.

Minyue-ized kunqu instrumental music draws both positive and negative responses from audiences and critics. As they classify it as either *t-yue* or *c-yue*, and reference it against *yue*-items, *yue*-events and *yuescapes* to which they are accustomed, they make dynamic and fluid arguments—some of which are, needless to say, more associatively than logically developed. For example, the instrumental music featured in the 1998–1999 Lincoln Center production of the *Peony Pavilion* was promoted as historical and authentic because it played *t-yue*-item 2 that Ye Tang notated in late eighteenth-century China. Similarly, the music featured in Zhang Jiqing's opera-film of 1987 is heard by her fans as *t-yue* because it does not sound like *c-yue* performed in the 2000s. In other words, verdicts on kunqu instrumental music as *t-yue* or *c-yue* are as subjective as they are objective. Viewed through the prism of kunqu as *yue* performance and discourse, the verdicts are less facts about kunqu sounds per se and more tools for and results of negotiating kunqu by stakeholders operating in particularized *yuescapes* and advancing individualistic agendas.

The *C-yue* of the *Young Lovers*

To illustrate kunqu as *yue* performance and discourse, an analysis of the vocal and instrumental music performed as the "Dark Silk Robe" aria in the "Strolling; Dreaming" scene in the opera will suffice (see Music Example 9). As notated, performed, and heard, the "Dark Silk Robe" is derived from a clearly defined *qupai*: it is a sequence of ten textual-melodic phrases that unfold against a rhythmic structure of twenty-five *ban* cycles/measures. As performed nowadays, and in structural terms of pitches and rhythms, the vocal melodies of the "Dark Silk Robe" aria performed in various shows are essentially identical; the instrumental accompaniments played before, after, and along with the sung melody, however, vary widely. It is these instrumental variations/ nuances that trigger all kinds of debates about kunqu *t*- and *c-yue*.

As heard in live performances or as recorded music,[21] the symphonic renditions of the "Dark Silk Robe" and the flower angels' dance music in the "Strolling; Dreaming" scene in the *Young Lovers* are distinctive *yue*-items (see Music Example 10). In addition to playing a heterophonic counterpart to the vocal melody, the *yue*-item features readily recognizable melodic motifs, a rich texture of sonic colors/timbres, structurally positioned transitions, and frequent changes in dynamics and intensity. Connoisseurs

---

21. A complete audiovisual recording of the *Young Lovers* is accessible online as *Peony Pavilion*, 2004 performance by SuKun, accessed May 16, 2021,
    Book 1: https://www.youtube.com/watch?v=kn1du7m-vj8&t=3637s;
    Book 2: https://www.youtube.com/watch?v=rcYkExD7Szc&t=50s;
    Book 3: https://www.youtube.com/watch?v=MwFUbkkbuDQ&t=106s.
    For a clip of the "Dark Silk Robe" with English subtitles, see "Peony Pavilion with English Subtitle," performance by SuKun, accessed November 23, 2021, www.youtube.com/watch?v=AV1JMA1CwrI.

will find, for example, short, distinctive melodic motifs played by *gaohu* (high fiddle), chime-bells, and mouth organs, expressive sounds that contrast with the strumming of *pipa* and dulcimer and with the pizzicato plucking of bass string instruments. Singularly and collectively, these musical and instrumental features render the "Dark Silk Robe" in the *Young Lovers* an unmistakable item of *c-yue*.

When dissected as structured and stylized sounds, the "Dark Silk Robe" in the *Young Lovers* displays many contemporary *minyue* features and aligns with its aesthetics. This is why the piece appeals to young Chinese audiences, many of whom grew up with *minyue* as Chinese music. They welcome it as a type of "authentic" kunqu or Chinese instrumental music, even though they realize it is sonically different from what was practiced as *t-yue* of the 1970s and in earlier times. By contrast, conservative kunqu connoisseurs find Zhou's instrumental *c-yue* too "modern," too "symphonic," and/or too "Westernized." They essentially define *t-yue* as *yue*-items 4 as listed in Table 8.1 and hesitate to accept items 5 and 6 as *t-yue*.

Zhou's *c-yue* elicited negative reactions in part because it drew attention to his creative compositions and arrangements. Unlike the instrumental music played in most traditional and contemporary kunqu performances, Zhou's *c-yue* presents an unignorable musical voice. It projects that the composer is a prolific and award-winning composer of contemporary kunqu music, popular songs, and Jiangnan silk and wind music. Unlike nameless and faceless kunqu composers of the past, Zhou has a powerfully contemporary musical self—he wants to be known as the composer of the music played in the *Young Lovers*. Unapologetically, he has declared not only that his kunqu instrumental music is authentic but also that it is a fundamental reason why the *Young Lovers* was successful—and this author agrees. As a dominant stakeholder, he negotiated successfully with the production's other artistic directors/producers/stakeholders and got their approval to make the *Young Lovers* sound the way it is now heard—it is now celebrated as the sound of *qinchun dianya* kunqu.

When Zhou's *c-yue* is heard and interpreted simply as a fresh, or individualistic, version of kunqu instrumental music, it is hardly controversial. As a piece of *c-yue*, it is innovative but not as "excessively Westernized" as some critics have maintained. However, when Zhou's *c-yue* is heard and critiqued in a Chinese *yuescape* where streams of kunqu agendas, facts, and claims merge, it elicits contrasting personal responses, which lead to positive and negative verdicts, as well as heated debates.

That *yuescape* defines, and is defined, by historical memories and nationalistic feelings of today's prosperous China. In 2001, kunqu was declared a UNESCO Masterpiece of the Oral and Intangible Heritage of Humanity. That declaration anchored the making of the *Young Lovers*, which premiered in 2004; in turn, the tremendously successful opera made the UNESCO declaration socially and politically relevant. Only because the *Young Lovers* generated a wave of Chinese interest in kunqu, the UNESCO declaration became a force that prompted the Chinese central government to recognize the genre as a classical opera/ICH of China and to employ it as a form of soft power. Government support expedited kunqu's rise as a classical opera of twenty-first-century China. Audience enthusiasm for the *Young Lovers* then transformed it into a model of contemporary *qingchun dianya* kunqu that embodied the genre's "original sauce and taste." Whatever the catchphrase actually signifies for kunqu performance and discourse, it has effectively promoted the *Young Lovers* and its aesthetics, even while antagonizing diehard conservatives who have their own notions of "authentic" kunqu.

Given that the *Young Lovers* realizes Tang Xianzu's original script literally, and given that the show's contemporized costumes, makeup, and *shenduan* acting-dancing only subtly deviate from traditional practices, there is little that conservative critics can find fault with. The production's kunqu instrumentation, which is temporal, non-verbal, and "Westernized," however, makes an obvious target by itself. As such, it provides an entry point to find faults with the show's claims to authenticity. Thus, Zhou's *c-yue* has become controversial, generating a *yue* discourse that continually expands, crisscrossing all segments of China's twenty-first-century musical scene, thereby generating harmonies and dissonances. If some practitioners praise the *c-yue* of the *Young Lovers* as what contemporary kunqu music should be, others dismiss it as a rupture from the authentic kunqu that Wei Liangfu, or Ye Tang, or Mei Lanfang, namely *t-yue* items 1, 3, and 4, sang/played in the past. Focusing on the Westernized features of Zhou's *c-yue*, some critics have even dismissed it as a colonial or postcolonial emulation of Western concert music or Broadway musicals.

More *Yue* Discourses of the "Dark Silk Robe"

Verdicts on *t-* and *c-yue* are multivalent and partial. They report on similar or dissimilar *yue* phenomena, each of which unfolds with distinctive combinations of *yue*-items, events, stakeholders, *yuescapes*, and agendas. To further illustrate this nature of kunqu as *yue* performance and discourse, a comparative analysis of four historically significant realizations of the "Black Silk Robe" aria would be useful. In 1960, Mei Lanfang made a kunqu opera-film titled "Strolling in the Garden and an Interrupted Dream,"[22] in which he and Yan Weizhu sang the "Black Silk Robe." As recorded, a soft passage of *dizi* music with articulatory gong-strikes is played to introduce the aria/ episode (14'50"). Then as the performers sing, the *dizi* and other melodic instruments in the ensemble play heterophonic counterparts. At the end of the performers' singing (18'42"), an instrumental postlude plays melodic echoes of the aria, accompanying the female character's continued strolling in the garden. Neither the instrumental prelude nor the postlude draws undue attention to itself, though both feature subtle shifts in tone colors, textures, and timbres. Both are now heard as representative samples of *t-yue*-item 4, a verdict that kunqu connoisseurs and Mei's fans have promoted. The

---

22. The 1960 movie is accessible online: the *Peony Pavilion* (*Mudanting*), 1960 performance by Mei Lanfang, Yan Huizhu, and Yu Zhenfei, accessed May 16, 2021, https://www.youtube.com/watch?v=nNydt77MhzQ&t=2759s.

verdict is, however, not unchallenged. Some critics would argue that the music is not totally traditional, or representative of early twentieth-century kunqu instrumental music. Indeed, it does reveal some unmistakable *minyue*-ized adjustments to accommodate cinematographic needs. Mei was a creative artist who made effective adjustments in his stage performances and opera-films.[23] For the time being, and for the lack of sonic data, there can be no definitive conclusion as to the authenticity and traditionality of Mei's kunqu singing and instrumental music. Debates will continue until the need to argue one way or the other dissipates.

In 1964, Li Shujun (d. 2011), a kunqu star of mid-twentieth-century China, performed the same aria/episode in a Beikun production of the *Peony Pavilion*. A sound recording of the production was released in the late 2000s, reviving interest in Li's kunqu artistry and legacy.[24] As recorded, the *t-yue* played in that performance is distinctive: it features active ornamental drum strokes, sounds that rhythmically energize Li's distinctive singing. Some critics have interpreted those drum strokes as evidence that Beikun's *t-yue* has either been "northernized"—that is, has adopted techniques from Beijing opera—or *minyue*-ized. Both interpretations are informative. If the drum strokes and their rhythmic effects render Li's instrumental music a sample of *t-yue* item 5, it not only indexes northern kunqu of the mid-1960s but also serves as a monument to Li's singing. Li's fans would describe Li's voice as "sweet" (*tianrun*) and view it as a reminder of the actress-singer's personal tragedy: her kunqu career/stardom was cut short by the Cultural Revolution.

In 1987, Zhang Jiqing, one of the most admired female kunqu performers in late twentieth-century China, performed the aria/episode of "Dark Silk Robe" in an opera-film titled "Strolling; Dreaming."[25] Produced by Nanjing Cinema, the film is now treasured as a document of Zhang's performance artistry at its peak. She won the Plum Blossom Award in 1984, the first time the award was given in China.

The instrumental music that accompanies Zhang's singing and dancing in that episode is *c-yue*-item 1 par excellence, this author argues. As recorded, it begins (11'30") with a short, programmatic prelude featuring dramatic tremolo playing of *erhu*, recorded sounds of birds chirping, and the characteristic *minyue* "sonic fillers" played by the *yangqin* and *pipa*. As performed and heard, the *c-yue* that unfolds with Zhang's singing of the first stanza of the "Dark Silk Robe" aria is filled with *minyue*-ized kunqu sounds, which include short but idiomatic transitory *dizi* and fiddle-playing, a rhythmic bass line, and counter-melodies and transitions that articulate structural divisions of the aria Zhang sings. The music that accompanies Zhang's singing of

---

23. For an insightful study of Mei Lanfang's operatic creativity, see Zou Yuanjiang, *Mei Lanfang biaoyan meixue tixi yanjiu* (Beijing: Renmin chubanshe, 2018); see in particular 371–426.

24. Track 9, "Beifang kunqu juyuan mingjia yanchang xilie—Li Shujun," ISRC CN—A05-aa-306-00/A. JB. For Li's biography, see Chen Jun, *Xianyue piaomiao: Li Shujun pingchuan* (Shanghai: Guji chubanshe, 2011).

25. Zhang Jiqinq's 1987 performance/movie rendition is accessible online: the *Peony Pavilion*, 1987 performance by Zhang Jiqing, accessed May 16, 2021, www.youtube.com/watch?v=VWuEZkjK7ak.

the second stanza (14′10″) of the aria presents soaring *erhu* melodies and repeated notes played by *yangqin* and *pipa*, sounds that are played to sonically evoke the floating clouds, blowing breezes, and falling raindrops the lyrics describe. Interestingly, this *c-yue* features one of the earliest uses of xylophone in a kunqu orchestra, generating a distinctive metallic sonority. Intentional or not, it sonically reminds people of Chinese interest in chime-bells. The year 1987, when Zhang's opera-film was made, celebrated the ninth anniversary of the 1978 excavation of Marquis Yi's chime-bells, which revived the Chinese instrumental tradition of playing chime-bells.

Because of its distinctive sonorities and *minyue-ized* performance practices, the *c-yue* in Zhang's opera-film should have triggered intense debate, but it did not. It sharply contrasted with the hybridized sounds of revolutionary operas that lingered on in post–Cultural Revolution China of the 1980s. In addition, the *c-yue* does not draw excessive attention to itself; it only guides audiences to focus on Zhang's mesmerizing enactment of idealized Chinese femininity. Thus, the innovative features in the instrumental music in Zhang's opera-film of 1987 are conveniently easy to gloss over.

In 1998–1999, the Lincoln Center in New York staged a pathbreaking production of the *Peony Pavilion*,[26] featuring *t-yue* that realized eighteenth-century notated kunqu music (*t-yue-item 2*). As performed and heard, the music projected kunqu authenticity and/or traditionality. As such, it was favorably received. In addition to this *t-yue*, the Lincoln Center production featured *pingtan* (Suzhou narrative singing) music to sonically enhance the show's storytelling. This use of the vernacular and regional genre of Chinese narrative music elicited harshly negative reactions from traditional kunqu practitioners. They heard it as a "vulgar sound," one that echoed the production's other "undesirable" elements. As a result, the production's traditional features, including *t-yue*, were ignored, while its "pathbreaking" expressions were attacked as culturally misrepresentative and even "offensive." In other words, the show's Chinese critics selectively heard and negatively critiqued the instrumental music in Chen's production; they ignored its *t-yue* and emphasized its atypical sounds, using them to denigrate the director's efforts.

Epilogue

As described here, debates over kunqu instrumental music expose the dynamic nature of the genre's performance and discourse. Its processes and results depend not only on kunqu words, sounds, dances, and visuals but also on the ways specific stakeholders pragmatically de-fuse and re-fuse *yue*-items in fluid *yuescapes*. Inevitably, meanings and understandings vary, and critical questions with no simple answers arise: Who

---

26. For further details about the production, see Chapter 3. Online audiovisual recordings of the Lincoln Center production are accessible online: *Peony Pavilion*, 1999, performance at the Lincoln Center, accessed May 16, 2021, https://www.bilibili.com/video/BV1zs411E7FB?from=search& seid=9542734331279525047.

owns kunqu and thus has the authority to define it in one way or another? Is it a genre of vocal music or opera, a classical legacy of China, a global ICH, or a commercialized tourist attraction? As kunqu practitioners strive to formulate answers, debating with one another, they transform technical arguments about specific kunqu expressions and shows/*yue*-events into abstract ideological claims, generating complex and continually evolving and overlapping phenomena of kunqu as *yue* performance and discourse. Complex and multivalent as the phenomena are, however, they reveal what the stakeholders harbor in their heart-minds as well as demonstrate how they act, feel, and think in their lives and dreams. Because of such revelations and demonstrations, kunqu cannot help but serve as a microcosm of Chinese culture, history, and personhood.

9

Kunqu as a Twenty-First-Century Chinese ICH and World Opera

Introduction

As discussed in the previous chapter, kunqu performance and discourse enfold a multitude of *yue* items, events, stakeholders, *yuescapes*, and agendas as they tell stories about Chinese culture, history, and personhood. Those stories in turn expose various facets of contemporary kunqu, including its transformation into a world opera from China. China today is promoting the genre throughout the world, staging many shows in London, New York, Paris, Tokyo, Seoul, and other cities with diaspora Chinese communities. Audiences the world over have grown to appreciate kunqu performance practices and materials, even becoming dedicated kunqu fans and performing it themselves, viewing it as a significant cultural heritage of China and of the whole world.

To discuss kunqu as classical Chinese opera in the twenty-first-century globalized world, this chapter presents four accounts, each on a specific facet of the genre's recent transformation. The first surveys kunqu overseas performance in order to demonstrate how the genre serves as a tool of cultural exchange and/or soft power—that is, how China is using kunqu to connect itself with Chinese diaspora communities and make international friends. The second analyzes the sinicization of international ICH theories and practices, a process that is shaping Chinese approaches to preserving and developing kunqu. The third compares kunqu with various other Chinese and non-Chinese ICH/performing arts, highlighting how Chinese are packaging kunqu as a classical opera that reflects their contemporary and *qingchun dianya* selves. The fourth reports on Bando Tamasaburo's thought-provoking production of the *Peony Pavilion* (2008–2010), a show that heralds the rise of international kunqu artists and their challenges to China-centered performance of and discourse on the genre.

Overseas Kunqu Performances

Contemporary China is an integral part of the twenty-first-century world; sizable Chinese diaspora communities can be found in cosmopolitan cities in Australia,

172   *Kunqu*

Europe, North America, and Southeast Asia. Many push and pull forces are involved in exporting/importing Chinese culture, including performing arts like kunqu. When kunqu shows are performed outside China, they not only provide operatic entertainment but also build cultural and diplomatic bridges that connect China with the world. For example, Chinese diasporas welcome kunqu shows as operatic confirmations of their ethnic heritage and diaspora identities. At the same time, their non-Chinese compatriots engage with these performances as representations of Chinese culture, history, and personhood, thus demonstrating their benevolence toward Chinese people. Overseas kunqu shows are operatic *yue* events that both Chinese and non-Chinese practitioners/stakeholders can employ tactically to advance their agendas.[1]

Overseas kunqu performances began more than a century ago.[2] In 1919, Mei Lanfang performed Peking Opera and kunqu in Japan, promoting both Chinese opera and his own stardom in what was a rapidly developing East Asian and colonial power. Nine years later, Han Shichang toured Japan as well, displaying his kunqu artistry and stardom, which rivaled Mei's. In 1930 and 1935, Mei toured the US and Russia, generating Western admiration for Chinese operatic aesthetics and performance practices.

In April and May 1958, Yu Zhengfei led a government-sponsored tour of kunqu to twenty-four European cities. The tour presented adapted versions of traditional *zhezixi* like "A Garden Party; Shocking News," "Burying Yang Guifei" ("Maiyu"), and "The Princess Gives Her Lover a Sword" ("Baihua zengjian").[3] Politically charged was the *yuescape* that shaped the tour and was in turn transformed by the tour. In the late 1950s, newly established socialist China set out to woo European nations. At the time, the Korean War had been fought (1950–1953), and China and the US were at odds with each other. To cultivate cultural and diplomatic friendships with European nations, China sent them kunqu, a classical representation of Chinese lives and dreams. Between the mid-1960s and the mid-1980s, however, China was experiencing internal struggles and sent no grand kunqu shows overseas.

In the late 1980s, China resumed sending kunqu shows to friendly nations, staging grand productions in the capitals and major cities of France, Finland, Japan, and South Korea, as well as to Los Angeles and New York. In the 1990s, China repeatedly sent kunqu shows to Japan, a prosperous and technologically advanced East Asian nation that late twentieth-century China wanted to emulate. To demonstrate its friendly intentions and interest in Japanese culture, China created kunqu

---

1. For a study on Chinese operas in cross-cultural exchanges, see Cao Lin, and Yu Jiangan, eds., *Kuawenhua yujing zhong de zhongguo xiqu* (Beijing: Zhongguo xiju chubanshe, 2009).
2. For chronological checklists of overseas kunqu performances, see Wu Xinlei, *Chatuben kunqu shishi biannian*; and Zhou Lijuan, *Zhongguo xiqu yishu duiwai jiaoliu gailan*, 1949–2012 (Beijing: Wenhua yishu chubanshe, 2014), 19–55, 120–138, 177–197, 244–253, and 314–336.
3. For a study of the tour and the *zhezixi*, see Liu Siyuan, "The Case of Princess Baihua: State Diplomatic Functions and Theatrical Creative Process in China in the 1950s and 1960s," *Asian Theatre Journal* 30, no. 1 (2013): 1–29.

shows with Japanese elements. In 1994, BeiKun staged the *Crane (Xihe)*, a contemporary kunqu opera based on a popular Japanese myth. The following year, ShangKun produced its own version of the same story.

In the late 1990s, as China began to prosper and its arts and culture began to attract the First World's attention, two prominent kunqu shows were staged in the West. In May 1998 in Vienna, Peter Sellars opened his avant-garde production of the *Peony Pavilion*, a hybrid show featuring a traditional kunqu *shenduan* performance by Hua Wenyi, a celebrated kunqu star who had immigrated to the US, as well as kunqu-informed contemporary vocal music by Tan Dun, a Chinese-American composer.[4] After the premiere, Sellars took the show to London, Rome, Paris, and Berkeley, CA. Sellars's production was warmly received in the West, though it charmed few Chinese kunqu practitioners. They did not accept the American director's innovative and individualistic presentation as a kunqu work.

The other production was the 1998–1999 Lincoln Center staging of the *Peony Pavilion*.[5] This one began as a "friendship project" between China and the US but ended up fomenting a cultural and diplomatic controversy. Directed by Chen Shizheng, a Chinese-American theater director, the production aspired to present the *Peony Pavilion* as it was originally staged in Ming China. Billed as an authentic performance, the show presented all fifty-five scenes of the drama; it played kunqu music notated in the authoritative *Nashuying qupu* (Ye Tang's library of kunqu scores) published between 1782 and 1794. So that the show would appeal to modern international audience, Chen had introduced many bold artistic innovations. For example, he tried to evoke the classical Chinese landscape by building on his stage a pavilion overlooking a pond on which live ducks swam. The *mis-en-scène* delighted New Yorkers but perplexed connoisseurs of traditional kunqu, who were used to the minimalist kunqu stage, whose standard props were simply a table and two chairs. Chen also evoked historical and ritual China with ghostly characters and sounds and sights from rural China.

Shanghai officials found Chen's innovations disrespectful to and misrepresentative of classical kunqu and historical China. Disagreements between Chen and the officials led to a breakdown in relations. In the summer of 1998, to block Chen's show,

---

4. For a scholarly study of Sellars's work, see Catherine C. Swatek, *Peony Pavilion on Stage: Four Centuries in the Career of a Chinese Drama* (Ann Arbor: Center for Chinese Studies, University of Michigan, 2002), 203–230; and "Boundary Crossings: Peter Sellars's Production of *Peony Pavilion*," *Asian Theatre Journal* 19, no. 1 (Spring 2002): 147–158; see also Min Tian, "Intercultural Theatre at the New *Fin De Siecle*: Peter Sellars's Postmodern Approach to Traditional Chinese Theatre," in *The Poetics of Difference and Displacement: Twentieth-Century Chinese-Western Intercultural Theatre* (Hong Kong: Hong Kong University Press, 2008), 113–137.

5. A video recording of the show is available online: *Peony Pavilion*, 1999, performance at the Lincoln Center, accessed May 16, 2021, https://www.bilibili.com/video/BV1zs411E7FB?from=search&seid=9542734331279525047. For scholarly studies of Chen's work, see Catherine C. Swatek, *Peony Pavilion on Stage*, 231–241. See also David Rolston, "Tradition and Innovation in Chen Shi-Zheng's *Peony Pavilion*," *Asian Theatre Journal* 19, no. 1 (Spring 2002): 134–146.

174   *Kunqu*

the latter forbade the shipping of costumes for the New York performance. Chen had no choice but to postpone that show. A year later, he was able to stage it, but with custom-made costumes and stage props.

Chinese objections to Chen's show underscored the nation's control of kunqu as its cultural capital and nationalistic voice. Officials were most "offended" by Chen's representations of a backward and superstitious China, which included the parading of ghost characters wearing tall conical hats and one-piece gowns—vernacular symbols of the Chinese "underworld." Shocking to the officials was Chen's stage prop in the "Judgment" scene; it showed a woman's legs protruding from a large barrel, as if she had been tortured and was being disposed of.

Traditional kunqu and its cultural, social, and political significances were not unknown in New York. Since 1988, the New York Kunqu Society has been staging traditional kunqu performances in the city, meeting the artistic and cultural needs of the Chinese diaspora in the greater New York area. Many of the shows staged by the society feature leading kunqu artists from mainland China. They come to promote the genre as representative of classical China, socialize with friends and family members, and see the US, the "beautiful country," with their own eyes. They also anticipate that successful overseas performances will further polish their stardom back home. Performances by kunqu stars from China attract Chinese diaspora audiences. Many drive hours to see celebrated performers, whose singing/dancing takes them back to the China they have left but continue to cherish. Needless to say, many also use the shows as opportunities for business transactions and social gatherings.

Non-Chinese audiences at overseas kunqu shows gradually increased after 2001, after UNESCO declared the genre a Masterpiece of the Oral and Intangible Cultural Heritage of Humanity. One overseas kunqu event that excited many American audiences was the 2006 west coast tour of SuKun's *Young Lovers*. As a *yue* event, the tour succeeded for many reasons. Bai Xianyong, its artistic director and organizer, was an internationally known Chinese author and a Professor Emeritus at the University of California, Santa Barbara. He was well-connected to California authorities and patrons. His tour had generous support from the University of California and local institutions and agents, all of whom wanted to showcase authentic Chinese culture and promote friendship between China and the US.

Bai's tour opened a path for staging grand kunqu shows in the US. As it transpired, 2012 was a bountiful year for kunqu in both America and Britain. In March of that year, a group of ShengKun performers presented a program of *zhezixi* and scenes from the *1699 Peach Blossom Fan* in Los Angeles, Irvine, and Downey, CA. The shows were co-sponsored by UCLA and the Western US Kunqu Society (Meixi kunqu she). The educational goals of the former were as clear as the diasporic aspirations of the latter. The choice of shows was practical: the *1699 Peach Blossom Fan* was ShengKun's hit *qingchun dianya* show of the time.

In May 18–20 of the same year, ShangKun performed not only *zhezixi* but also two masterpieces in New York, namely the *Story of the Mountain of Rotten Axe Handle*

(*Lanke shan*) and the *Monkey King: The Journey to the West* (*Xiyou ji*). Sponsored by the Asia Society, the Museum of New York, and the Ministry of Culture of China, these performances celebrated cultural and friendship ties between New York and Shanghai.[6] They also thrilled audiences with many acrobatic acts that US audiences could appreciate without any knowledge of the Chinese language and operatic practices.

On September 28 and 29 of the same year, SuKun performed, in Ann Arbor, Michigan, highlights from the *Young Lovers* and a selection of favorite *zhezixi*.[7] Co-produced by the University Musical Society of the University of Michigan and the Confucius Institute at the University of Michigan, the performances promoted Chinese culture and arts in southeastern Michigan. To help Michiganders understand kunqu as a classical opera of China, the University Musical Society arranged pre-performance lectures and published explanatory program notes.

In November 2012, the New York Metropolitan Museum presented an abridged version (seventy minutes) of the *Peony Pavilion* in its Astor Court, a Chinese garden within the museum compound.[8] Featuring Zhang Jun, a progressive kunqu artist from Shanghai, the show revealed to its American audience the latest Chinese fashion of staging kunqu shows in gardens or on stages built in scenic settings—ironically, the practice had been launched by Chen's show of 1998 and 1999 and had been critically dismissed. As a form of cultural exchange, and as an international dialogue, the museum show served both its Chinese and its US stakeholders. Zhang Jun got to present the kind of kunqu he promoted, and he was handsomely rewarded for doing so—the show helped seal his status as a "Prince of Kunqu" and a UNESCO cultural ambassador. The New York Metropolitan Museum got a unique show that complemented its exhibition of precious Chinese *objets d'art*. Seeing kunqu close-up in a garden setting afforded New Yorkers an opportunity to imagine elite lives in Ming and Qing China.

Successful as the Astor Court show was, its impact as an overseas production and a diplomatic exercise paled by comparison to what took place in the UK that same year. On April 23, 2012, ZheKun performed selected scenes from the *Peony Pavilion* in Stratford-upon-Avon for a British audience. The performance was part of a series of events staged to promote Chinese–British cultural exchange and friendship. Two weeks before the performance in the Bard's hometown, a celebratory kunqu

---

6. For an online announcement of the show, see Asia Society New York, "Three Shanghai Kunqu Performances for New York Audiences," accessed May 6, 2016, http://asiasociety.org/new-york/three-shanghai-kunqu-opera-performances-new-york-audiences.

7. For a description and video recording of the performance in Ann Arbor, see "Zhezixi," 2012 performance at the University of Michigan, accessed May 16, 2021, https://www.youtube.com/watch?v=as4GguYZXcs&t=72s.

8. For a discussion by Tan Dun, the producer, and Maxwell K. Hearn, curator of the museum, see "A Conversation with Tan Dun: A New Peony Pavilion in an Old Context," uploaded by the Met on December 6, 2012; accessed April 23, 2015. A full audiovisual recording of the performance can be viewed at the Museum's website: http://www.metmuseum.org/metmedia.

festival and scholarly conference was held in Suichang, Zhejiang, the town where Tang Xianzu briefly served as a local magistrate. Since 2012, Tang Xianzu and William Shakespeare have become a pair in kunqu discourse; Tang is now being promoted as the bard's Chinese counterpart.[9]

The Chinese pairing of Tang/kunqu with Shakespeare/British drama is pregnant with cultural and historical meanings; it is also a testimonial to Chinese ingenuity in packaging kunqu as a form of Chinese cultural capital and diplomatic soft power. Historically speaking, the kunqu connection between China and Britain resulted from a diplomatic engagement between the two nations.[10] In June 2011, Wen Jiabao, the Chinese prime minister at the time, visited Britain and proposed the forging of stronger cultural ties between the two nations. Wen's proposal was favourably received, and this led to ZheKun's 2012 performance in the UK, the building of a Chinese pavilion in Stratford-upon-Avon, and the launching of a digital kunqu museum at Cambridge University.[11]

Since 2012, kunqu practitioners have produced a number of shows with various Shakespearean elements. These include Ke Jun's *A Shakespearean Handan Dream* (*Tangsha hui handan meng*, 2016); a realization of Tang Xianzu's *Scholar Lu's Brief Dream of A Successful Life* (*Handan meng*), which creatively incorporated dramatically appropriate English lines from several of the Bard's masterpieces; ShengKun's *Belladonna and Intoxicated Hearts* (*Zuixin hua*, 2016 and 2018), a kunqu work based on the *Romeo and Juliet* story; Zhang Jun's *I, Hamlet* (*Woshi hamulaite*, 2017), a one-man show that interpretatively realizes Shakespeare's *Hamlet*; and *Julius Caesar* (*Kaisa*, 2019), a kunqu and Peking opera interpretation of Shakespeare's drama of the same title.[12]

Kunqu with Shakespearean elements is a contemporary *yue* event, but its emergence is culturally and historically grounded. Since the early 1900s, Chinese artists and scholars have been studying Shakespearean dramas as world literature and theater.[13] In 1942, *Hamlet* was performed as a spoken drama in wartime Chongqing.

---

9. For a revealing document on Chinese coupling of Tang Xianzu with Shakespeare, see Hua Zhiwu, ed., *Qihang—Tang Xianzu-Shashibiya wenhua jiaoliu hezuo* (Hangzhou: Zhejiang daxue chubanshe, 2013); see esp. 158–162 and 207–212.

10. For a theoretically informed description of the development, see Alexa Alice Joubin, "Performing Commemoration: The Cultural Politics of Locating Tang Xianzu and Shakespeare," *Asian Theatre Journal* 36, no. 2 (2019): 275–280.

11. The website address of the digital museum is: https://maa.cam.ac.uk/digital-museum-of-global-chinese-kun-opera/.

12. For an anthology of essays on Ke Jun's *A Shakespearean Handan Dream*, see Li Xiaoju and Ke Jun, comp., *"TangShahui" Handanmeng* (Nanjing: Jiangsu Fenghuan meishu chubanshe, 2018). For an online video recording of Zhang Jun's performance, see *I, Hamlet* (*Woshi Hamulaite*), 2017 performance by Zhang Jun, accessed May 16, 2021, https://www.youtube.com/watch?v=c8EhZxUHBn4&t=1149s.

13. For three representative studies, see Liana Chen, "Engaging Tang Xianzu and Shakespeare in the Quest for Self," *Asian Theatre Journal* 36, no. 2 (2019): 327–346, Alexander C. Y. Huang, *Chinese Shakespeares: Two Centuries of Cultural Exchange* (New York: Columbia University Press, 2009); and Li Ruru, *Shashibiya: Staging Shakespeare in China* (Hong Kong: Hong Kong University Press, 2004).

The first professional kunqu rendition of Shakespearean works was, however, ShangKun's *Bloodstained Hands* (*Xueshou ji*), which premiered in 1986 at the First Chinese Shakespeare Festival, held in Shanghai.[14] The following year, the show was presented at the Edinburgh International Festival in Scotland. In 2008, a new version of the same opera was staged; since then, *zhezixi* from the opera have regularly appeared on kunqu stages.

As demonstrated by the *Bloodstained Hands* and the *Belladonna and Intoxicated Hearts*, kunqu practitioners selectively appropriate Shakespearean dramas. What is readily identifiable as Shakespearean in kunqu adaptations seldom goes beyond story outlines or dramatizations of humanity. Clearly, kunqu is a Chinese opera with many established conventions and thus does not readily accommodate foreign elements. For example, kunqu *qupai* melodies and linguistic-literary structures do not readily accommodate translated lyrics. Kunqu operas cannot be composed or performed without their prescriptive *qupai* and stylized melodies and rhythms.

Instrumental music is the only component of kunqu that can accommodate non-Chinese materials without facing insurmountable technical difficulties, as attested by the increasing use of *c-yue* in contemporary kunqu. In fact, *c-yue* often embodies foreign elements in hybridized kunqu shows. For example, the *c-yue* in the *Belladonna and Intoxicated Hearts*, which ShengKun produced with overseas performances in mind, features leitmotifs that musically symbolize characters and dramatic developments. Similarly, in his *I, Hamlet* (2017), which he produced for the Asia Society in New York, Zhang Jun sang in both Chinese and English and used *t-yue* and/or *c-yue* to articulate his innovative one-man performance of the Bard's masterpiece. To overcome casting and other practical challenges, he performed the drama's four protagonists by himself as an actor-singer and as a manipulator of two hand puppets.

As kunqu practitioners hybridize and globalize the genre, they help build a nationalistic kunqu *yuescape*, one that implements a Chinese policy with generous funding from the Chinese government. Since 2012, the Chinese government has been implementing a policy of "Chinese Culture Going Global" ("Wenhua zou chuqu").[15] As a result, kunqu practitioners have had more opportunities and resources to perform abroad, carrying out personal, institutional, and national agendas. Many overseas kunqu shows staged in the last decade throughout the world had been directly or indirectly supported by Chinese funds that covered the performers' international travel as well as their performance expenses.

---

14. For a report on the opera and the Chinese Shakespeare Festival, see Li Ruru, "Chinese Traditional Theatre and Shakespeare," *Asian Theatre Journal* 5, no. 1 (Spring 1988): 38–48. For an analysis of the *Bloodstained Hands*, see Li Ruru, *Shashibiya: Staging Shakespeare in China*, 109–136.

15. For a collection of Chinese articles on the policy, see Ye Fei, ed., *Zhongguo wenhua yishu zouchuqu yanjiu* (Beijing: Beijing daxue chubanshe, 2016). For a study on Chinese efforts to send culture to the world, see Yu Jiangang, ed., *Xiqu kuawenhua jiaoliu rencai peiyang yanjiu* (Beijing: Wenhua yishu chubanshe, 2014).

Kunqu as a Chinese *Feiyi* and a World ICH

In 2001, UNESCO declared kunqu a Masterpiece of the Oral and Intangible Cultural Heritage of Humanity, an international honor that has invigorated Chinese reclamation of the genre while also compelling Chinese to engage with international theories and practices on ICH and devise Chinese interpretations and applications. To tap into the power of the UNESCO honor, Chinese need to subscribe to international theories and practices of ICH. To do so "literally," however, would generate intellectual doubts and nationalists' objections. Is China's preservation and development of kunqu a disingenuous or postcolonial response to a Western and humanist development? Would subscribing to foreign cultural values negatively impact classical kunqu? There are no simple answers to these questions. For the time being, what is clear is that kunqu practitioners have pragmatically interpreted and adjusted international ICH theories and practices to serve their own needs and values.

Chinese interpretations of ICH theories and practices emerged out of a distinctive *yuescape*, once socialist China realized it urgently needed to protect its own culture. In 1972, UNESCO established its World Heritage Program, triggering an idealistic global movement for safeguarding endangered world cultural heritages. The movement aligned with Chinese concerns about protecting the nation's cultural heritage, much of which had been damaged or even destroyed during the Cultural Revolution. In the 1990s, UNESCO's calls for preserving cultural heritage became a practical concern for China; by then it was beginning to prosper and could afford to pay heed. In the late 1990s, when UNESCO announced its ICH program,[16] China responded enthusiastically.

Immediately, kunqu practitioners grasped its significance, and promptly, they sent in a convincing application, one that highlighted the genre's historical background and cultural-social meanings. How kunqu practitioners aligned their facts and values with Western ones becomes apparent from a brief review of UNESCO theories and their Chinese applications/interpretations. In a 2003 convention, UNESCO defined ICH as heritages that are endangered by "globalization and social transformation, alongside the conditions they create for renewed dialogue among communities."[17] The same

---

16. During the years of 2000 through 2005, UNESCO issued three exclusive lists of ICH, each of which is honored as a Masterpiece of the Oral and Intangible Heritage of Humanity. UNESCO dropped the controversial nomenclature of masterpieces after 2005. Nevertheless, kunqu practitioners cherish the nomenclature which underscores their understanding and promotion of the genre as a "masterpiece" of Chinese heritages—proudly, kunqu practitioners declare that kunqu was the only item unanimously chosen in the UNESCO application/competition in 2000. To discuss kunqu in global and theoretical contexts of ICH, the nomenclature of masterpiece will be skipped here.

17. See UNESCO, "Basic Text of the 2003 Convention for the Safeguarding of the Intangible Cultural Heritage, 2010 Edition, " CLT. 2010/WX/17, uploaded UNESCO; accessed January 15, 2020, https://unesdoc.unesco.org/ark:/48223/pf0000189761?5=null&queryId=1973bee0-0612-41ec-932f-eeae40ad45cb.

convention presented four reasons for safeguarding ICH and six guidelines for their selection. The four basic reasons:

1. To safeguard ICH of humanity.
2. To ensure respect for ICH of diverse communities, groups and individuals concerned.
3. To raise awareness at the local, national, and international levels of the importance of ICH, and of ensuring mutual appreciation thereof.
4. To provide for international cooperation and assistance for preservation efforts.

The six guidelines:

1. Outstanding value as masterpieces of human creative genius.
2. Wide evidence of their roots in the cultural traditions or cultural histories of the communities concerned.
3. Affirmation of the identities of the cultural communities concerned.
4. Proof of excellence in the application of skills and technical qualities displayed.
5. Value as unique testimonials to living cultural traditions.
6. Facing risk of degradation or of disappearing.

In broad terms, the definitions and guidelines UNESCO proposed are logical, inclusive, and practical.[18] UNESCO assumes that peoples are diverse, that their traditional cultures are all intrinsically creative, expressive, and meritorious, and that many forms/genres of traditional cultural heritage are being negatively impacted by globalization forces. UNESCO observes that until modern times, most cultural heritages were transmitted directly from ancestors to descendants living in geographically specified lands, thus sustaining communities/traditions defined by artistic, ethnic, historical, linguistic, political, ritual, social, and other natural and human elements. Assuming direct relationships between peoples and their endangered cultures, UNESCO formulated its calls to preserve ICH through local, national, and international efforts.

Upon close scrutiny, UNESCO definitions and guidelines for identifying and preserving ICH have many limitations and thus cannot be uniformly implemented in today's world. For example, involuntary and large-scale movements of people in the twentieth century have rendered conventional definitions of and relationships among cultural heritages, ethnic identities, and geographic and temporal boundaries imprecise and problematic. Attempts to address these issues have opened a Pandora's box of

---

18. There is a wealth of studies on ICH theories and practices. For two representative studies, see Keith Howard, *Music as Intangible Cultural Heritage: Policy, Ideology, and Practice in the Preservation of East Asian Traditions* (London: Ashgate, 2012); Laurajane Smith and Natsuko Akagawa, eds., *Intangible Heritage* (New York: Routledge, 2009).

questions.[19] What is outstanding value for cultural heritage, and how is it defined and exercised? Who has the authority to evaluate excellent skills and expressive qualities? Why and how should local cultural heritages be preserved for global citizens? Do foreign patrons, sponsors, and audiences have the right to shape the preservation of ICH in local, national, and international contexts?

Striving to safeguard kunqu in the ways they desire, the genre's Chinese practitioners have had to adapt UNESCO theories and practices, formulating their own nationalistic and pragmatic solutions. Thus, they have transformed international ideas and efforts into Chinese and *feiyi* theories and practices. *Feiyi* is an acronym carved out of a literal Chinese translation of ICH—*"feiwuzhi* (non-material) *koutou* (oral) *wenhua* (cultural) *yichan* (legacies). As a newly coined bisyllabic term, *feiyi* underscores Chinese priorities and sensitivities; semantically, it highlights the intangibleness (*fei*) of culture and its being a property/capital inherited from the past (*yichan*). *Feiyi* theories and practices differ from those of their UNESCO counterparts in many obvious and hidden ways. For instance, to "rediscover" China's "forgotten" ICH/*feiyi*, China has launched many government-supported and -supervised institutions, such as *feiyi* research centers at the Central Conservatory of Music, Beijing, and the Wuhan Conservatory of Music, Wuhan. Responding to government initiatives, many rural Chinese communities are now vigorously "excavating" their local cultural heritages.

Judging from what kunqu practitioners have said and done, their *feiyi* efforts reflect many conceptual contradictions and performative inconsistencies. For example, whereas kunqu is primarily discussed as a cultural and historical heritage with a fixed repertory and a codified system of virtuoso performance practices and materials, the genre is often "preserved and developed" in ways that reflect contemporary and creative practices. Few kunqu practitioners believe in keeping the genre as it was performed in the past or as it has been rediscovered. Most prefer to "update" or "popularize" the genre as a global and intelligible ICH. As a result, most "excavated" kunqu shows are performatively more contemporary than historical or traditional.

The Chinese approach to kunqu as ICH is idiosyncratic, though it becomes more intelligible when examined through the prism of the Chinese *feiyi yuescape*. Safeguarding kunqu as a cultural heritage is not an imported concern but an urgent national matter. During the Cultural Revolution, much of China's traditional cultural heritage was damaged, if not destroyed—kunqu was banned during that turbulent decade. Since 1978, when post–Cultural Revolution China adopted open-door policies, the nation has rapidly transformed itself from an economically underdeveloped nation into a prosperous one. The cost has been the destruction of numerous tangible and intangible legacies, ranging from historical *hutong*, labyrinths of narrow streets that meander inside old residential areas in Beijing, to traditional genres of

---

19. For a revealing article about ICH in Turkey, see Aykan Bahar, "Whose Tradition, Whose Identity: The Politics of Constructing 'Nevrus' as Intangible Heritage in Turkey," *European Journal of Turkish Studies* 19 (2014), accessed March 15, 2019, https://doi.org/10.4000/ejts.5000.

performing arts. By the 1990s, China had clearly realized how urgent it was to preserve the nation's cultural legacy; otherwise, it would lose more and more ancestral roots, or legitimizing evidence, of China's beautiful, civilized, and productive culture, history, and personhood.

As China strives to preserve and present its past, it finds the international ideal of ICH a timely and convenient tool; it is something China can fruitfully adapt to serve Chinese realities and needs. By promoting kunqu as a UNESCO ICH, China finds a global justification for preserving and developing the genre in ways it wants. By aligning ICH ideals with Chinese notions of local clans/families, schools, and communities, China legitimizes national and regional promotion of local cultures, solidarities, and economies. Traditionally, Chinese identify themselves not only as Chinese but also as sons and daughters of particular geographical-ethnic-social-political entities. For example, a kunqu practitioner born and raised in Suzhou will often present himself as a native of Suzhou. Many Chinese people use local performing arts to project their clan/regional identities and to expand social relationships.

Kunqu practitioners employ *feiyi* theories to consolidate their artistic, social, and political positions.[20] From the ways they use kunqu and the results they generate thereby, practitioners/dominant stakeholders can be divided into four related groups:

1. Officials—individuals who control the political, social, and financial resources required to preserve and develop kunqu inside and outside China.
2. Professionals—producers, actor-singers, instrumentalists, and scholars, who have the knowledge and skills needed to create, perform, and negotiate kunqu in national and international contexts.
3. Avocational performers (*quyou*), critics, and patrons, who critique performances and performers, praising or dismissing the latter's expressions and asserting their personal and communally held views and values.
4. Audiences/fans, who support kunqu shows by paying admission fees and by idolizing individual actor-singers, confirming or rejecting what the officials, professionals, and connoisseurs do and say; individual audiences/fans negotiate from weak positions, but their collective voice rings loud and clear with the help of internet communications.

Chinese officials have dominated the *feiyi* kunqu "industry." Through their control of financial and social resources, they can encourage, if not demand, specific ways of preserving and staging kunqu productions. National and provincial officials tend to support grand shows of "excavated" kunqu works, thus displaying their support for

---

20. For three representative studies on Chinese *feiyi* theories and practices, see Helen Rees, "Intangible Cultural Heritage in China Today: Policy and Practice in the Early Twenty-First Century," in *Music as Intangible Cultural Heritage*, ed. Keith Howard, 23–54; and Zhang Boyu, Yao Hui, and Huib Schippers, "Report: The Rise and Implementation of Intangible Cultural Heritage Protection for Music in China," *The World of Music*, new series, 4, no. 1 (2015): 45–59; and Wang Wenzhang, *Feiwuzhi wenhua yicang gailun* (Beijing: Wenhua yishu chubanshe, 2006).

the genre. Administrative directors and artistic leaders in kunqu troupes, many of whom are appointed by national and provincial authorities, decide what their troupe members will perform. Under the rubric of preserving and developing *feiyi* kunqu, troupes stage politically and/or socially meaningful productions. For example, senior officials in BeiKun chose to stage the contemporary kunqu opera *Swift Crossing of Luding Bridge* (*Feiduo luding qiao*; 2016) to celebrate the ninetieth anniversary of the Red Army's passing over the bridge on May 29, 1935—a critical moment in their Long March against their Chinese rival, the Kuomintang. Similarly, municipally appointed administrators guided KunKun to produce its *Master Gu Yanwu* (2018). A newly created work, it dramatizes the life and political thoughts of Gu Yanwu (1613–1682), a Kunshan gentleman and an influential figure in the Ming–Qing transition.

Senior kunqu actor-singers, particularly those who are politically connected, play equally influential roles. As nationally anointed "people's artists," they embody the genre's artistic excellence, continuous performance tradition, and localized meanings. For instance, Shanghai kunqu masters like Cai Zhengren, Liang Guyin, and Yue Meiti personify and sustain the Shanghai branch of contemporary kunqu. From their exalted positions, they transmit "authentic" kunqu to their disciples, implementing their duties as *feiyi* transmitters, teaching and/or gatekeeping in ways they deem appropriate and productive.

Officials and master performers, however, cannot on their own totally dominate kunqu's development. Visionary patrons and scholarly performers also play critical roles. They have brought kunqu to university campuses, nurturing new generations of young fans. Attending shows and/or learning to sing kunqu as a hobby, these fans identify with the young scholars and charming beauties enacted on stage. To pursue their kunqu lives and/or dreams, they organize or recharge kunqu singing clubs at their schools and in their urban communities. Since 2011, a number of long-renowned noncommercial kunqu institutions of performance, learning, and research, such as Tianyun qushe (Heavenly kunqu music association) in Wuxi and Daohe qushe (Kunqu association of harmonious music and tradition) in Suzhou, have been reactivated. And new ones, such as Zilan qushe (Orchid kunqu club) of the Central Academy of Fine Arts, Beijing, have been launched. Gathering in their clubhouses, members sing kunqu for one another and learn from hired teachers, who are active or retired professionals. Some fans grow into connoisseurs, critics, and even guardians of *feiyi* kunqu. In such roles, they exercise their feeling, thinking, and action-taking Chinese selves.

Singularly and collectively, the four types of dominant kunqu stakeholders described earlier shape contemporary kunqu, rendering it a revealing microcosm of contemporary Chinese lives and dreams. Four features of this microcosm are idiosyncratically revealing and should be briefly highlighted here. First, in their efforts to safeguard and develop the genre, kunqu practitioners have "excavated" (*wajue*) a substantial number of old and forgotten kunqu dramas/*zhezixi*. Such excavations evoke Chinese engagements with historical relics and legacies. In Chinese culture, rediscovered *objets d'art* (*guwan*) from the past are treasured. Since 1949, Chinese archaeology has unearthed many treasures, including the Marquis Yi Chime-Bells. Excavated treasures are often "authentically" copied, generating imitations (*fangzhi*, *fanggu*) or forgeries, some of which are sophisticatedly made and eventually become treasures by themselves. Many "excavated" kunqu works have been staged with rewritten/revised scripts, newly composed tunes, and fashionable acting and singing styles. What is verifiably "excavated" in such works is often little more than their historical titles and story outlines.

Feiyi kunqu are simultaneously historical and contemporary. This paradox is evident in a number of original innovative productions, such as Beikun's *Dream of the Red Chamber* (*Honglou meng*, 2011) and Zhang Jun's *Spring River* (*Chunjiang huayue ye*, 2015). The former relates dramatic episodes from a well-known Chinese novel of the same title. The latter tells a new story inspired by a celebrated Tang dynasty poem of the same title. Whether such newly composed works help preserve six-century-old kunqu has stimulated vigorous debate. Some critics have argued that such works should not be counted as *feiyi*/ICH *yue*-items, even though they can help stimulate efforts to develop the genre.

Second, many contemporary kunqu shows, such as the *Young Lovers* and the *1699 Plum Blossom Fan*, are grand and entertaining. Elaborate productions were not unknown in Ming and Qing China, but these were occasional and exclusive events that average operagoers in historical China could hardly have witnessed. The current trend toward grand kunqu shows, *feiyi* or not, is less an effort to project historical China and more a way to parade *fugui* (rich and privileged) Chinese selves on stage. To be sure, some kunqu practitioners shy away from participating in such displays of ostentatious consumption, but their stance is marginal in contemporary kunqu.

Third, many contemporary kunqu shows feature charming young actor-singers whose performance skills often pale beside those of their mentors or experienced performers. This points to contemporary kunqu's aesthetic turn away from the literary and performative toward the physical and visual. Some critics have argued that *feiyi* kunqu practitioners have focused on the kinetic and visual expressions of the genre at the expense of its music. Other critics, however, have noted how new generations of virtuoso performers, such as Li An, Shan Wen, Shen Fengying, Xia Shiming, Yu Jiulin, and Zhang Jun, have emerged, attesting that Chinese efforts at preserving and developing kunqu are bearing fruit.

Fourth, many contemporary kunqu shows, such as SuKun's *Young Lovers*, ShangKun's *Bloodstained Hands*, and ShengKun's *1699 Peach Blossom Fan*, have incorporated elements from non-Chinese theaters/performing arts. This development is not only a result of the genre's being internationalized but also an indication that young kunqu performers have globalized experiences and visions. As they tour internationally more and more, performers like Yang Yang and Sun Jing of ShengKun learn more and more from world performing arts and aesthetics. Being creatively bold, they do not hesitate to incorporate what they have learned into their latest shows.

184   *Kunqu*

They believe that kunqu must not simply preserve the old; it also needs to explore the unknown.

To realize their dreams of making kunqu a classical opera/ICH/*feiyi* for China and the globalized world, however, they have to secure funding from public and private sources, avoid colliding with the authorities, follow market trends, win professional competitions, and overcome many national and international challenges. Put simply, they have to be pragmatists.

Other Chinese and Non-Chinese ICH

The pragmaticism of kunqu practitioners making the genre serve their needs is plain to see; any comparison of the genre with other Chinese and non-Chinese ICHs would demonstrate this. In addition to kunqu, China boasts three other ICHs—*qin* (seven-string zither) music of Han people, *muqam* music of the Uyghur-Chinese people of Xinjiang, and *urtiin duu* songs of Han Chinese, Mongolian Chinese, and Mongolians. Like kunqu, all three are artistically meritorious, culturally and socially representative, and deserving of preservation by Chinese and international stakeholders. And all three make *yue* phenomena in their own and distinctive ways, thereby reflecting China's long history, diverse cultures, ethnic experiences, and competing selves.

None of these other ICHs, however, projects Han and contemporary Chinese selves the way kunqu does. The reasons why *muqam* does not positively project Han China are obvious. The genre's modal melodies and additive rhythms sonically contrast Uyghur and Uyghur-Chinese against Han Chinese, exposing their historical and contemporary relationships, which were and still are tense.[21] *Muqam* is an ethnic and/or marginalized sound in contemporary and urbanized China. Its *yue* items, events, stakeholders, and *yuescapes* reference more Uyghur and Uyghur-Chinese aesthetics, experiences, and memories than Han Chinese ones. In other words, *muqam* does not and indeed cannot project cultural and historical China as Han Chinese have remembered or idealized it. For that reason, *muqam* is neither protected nor developed the way kunqu has been in twenty-first-century mainland China.

The same applies to *urtiin duu*, which is officially recognized as an ICH of both the Chinese and the Mongolian peoples,[22] whose cultures and histories have intertwined extensively. *Urtiin duu* features expansive melodies, flexible rhythms, and robust vocal practices. Singularly and collectively, they stimulate Mongolian and Chinese

---

21. See UNESCO, "Uyghur Muqam of Xinjiang," uploaded by UNESCO; accessed on October 2, 2020, http://www.unesco.org/culture/ich/index.php?RL=00109. For recent studies on the music, see Wong Chuenfung, "Peripheral Sentiments: Encountering Uyghur Music in Urumchi" (PhD diss., UCLA, 2006); Rachel Harris, *The Making of a Musical Canon in Chinese Central Asia* (London: Ashgate, 2008).

22. See UNESCO, "Urtiin Duu, Traditional Folk Long Song," uploaded by UNESCO; accessed October 2, 2020, http://www.unesco.org/culture/ich/?RL=00115. See also Carole Pegg, *Mongolian Music, Dance, and Oral Narrative: Performing Diverse Identities* (Seattle: University of Washington Press), 2001.

audiences' memories or imaginations about herdsmen roaming across the grasslands beyond the Great Wall. Listening to *urtiin duu* melodies set to Chinese lyrics and sung in Putonghua, Han Chinese audiences will find contemporary expressions of Chinese-Mongolian people and their lives in Mongolian China and Mongolia. *Urtin duu* songs are now commonly performed as ethnic/world/ popular music on Chinese and international stages, where they are commercially promoted as expressions of Mongolian people. A prime example of such *yue* events and objects is provided by Hangai, the world-renowned Chinese-Mongolian music group.[23] At their concerts, audiences find many popularized images of Mongolian culture and people that *urtiin duu* also projects. Because of such images, and their popularity, *urtiin duu* is heard and interpreted as more Mongolian than Chinese-Mongolian. As such, the songs cannot represent Han Chinese.

Like kunqu, *qin* music vividly projects classical Han China. It does not, however, project the *qingchun dianya* Chinese selves that kunqu practitioners claim for themselves. In 2003, UNESCO chose *qin* music as a Chinese ICH because it has "existed for over 3,000 years and represents China's foremost solo musical instrument tradition."[24] Like kunqu, *qin* music struggled to survive in mid-twentieth-century China, but the genre was never threatened with extinction. In the 1950s and 1960s, *qin* music received some national support. *Qin* music masters like Zha Fuxi (1898–1976) and Wu Jinglüe (1907–1987) were invited to teach in the newly created music conservatories. Their students, who include Li Xiangting (b. 1940) and Gong Yi (b. 1941), have emerged as twentieth-century *qin* masters. Their public concerts and students have transformed *qin* music from an elite and intimate mode of music-making into one of public and presentational concertizing.[25] This transformation has marginalized but not terminated the traditional practice of playing *qin* for one's own enjoyment and/or for appreciative friends in private settings.

After the 2003 UNESCO declaration, *qin* music blossomed throughout China, generating a vibrant *yue* phenomenon of *qin* performance and discourse. Since that year, many *qin* teaching studios and social clubs have popped up in Chinese cities. As a result, the number of *qin* players and audience has rapidly increased, stimulating a robust demand for concerts, media productions, and scholarly discussions.

---

23. For writings on Hangai and audiovisual clips of their shows, google "Hangai."
24. UNESCO, "Qin," accessed October 3, 2020, http://www.unesco.org/culture/ich/index.php?RL=00061. For further information on *qin* music, see Hans Van Gulik, *The Lore of the Chinese Lute: An Essay on the Ideology of the Ch'in* (Tokyo: Sophia University, 1940); Zhang Huaying, *Guqin* (Hangzhou: Zhejiang renmin chubanshe, 2005); and Xu Jian, *Qinshi xinbian* (Beijing: Zhonghua shuju, 2012).
25. For two ethnographic studies on contemporary *qin* performance and transmission activities, see Shi Yong, *Xianwai zhiyin—dangdai guqin wenhua chuancheng shilu* (Beijing: Guangming ribao chubanshe, 2011), 200–223; and Bell Yung, "An Audience of One: The Private Music of the Chinese Literati," *Ethnomusicology* 61, no. 3 (Fall 2017): 506–539.

For practical reasons, however, *qin* as a UNESCO ICH has not garnered Chinese national attention the way contemporary kunqu has. Four can be listed here. First, *Qin* recitals are quite intimate events; a *qin* concert might sometimes attract a couple of hundreds of dedicated music lovers. In contrast, most kunqu shows staged in grand theaters easily attract audiences of 1,000 or more. And whereas appreciation of *qin* music, a "sound" art, demands attentive listening, kunqu, a multimedia expression, can be enjoyed singularly or collectively as words, sounds, and/or dance.

Second, *qin's* service as a tool of engagement with historical China has been financially curtailed. The cost of antique *qin* instruments has skyrocketed. An authentic Song or Tang dynasty *qin*, for example, can easily fetch a seven-figure price in US dollars. Antique *qin* instruments make not only desirable tools/objects for performers and music lovers but also profitable additions to investors' portfolios. For Chinese with modest resources, antique *qin* instruments, even those that are barely a hundred years old, are unattainable luxuries. By comparison, kunqu objects, such as paintings, costumes, and manuscripts, are relatively inexpensive and thus affordable to all varieties of fans and collectors. And as staged on commercial stages, six-century-old kunqu is accessible to all who can afford the price of admission. In other words, kunqu makes a cultural heritage that is economically and socially much more accessible than *qin* music is.

Third, new *qin* music does not generate nationwide controversies of the sort that the *c-yue* of kunqu has provoked. Many new *qin* compositions, including "rearrangements" of historical works played with ensemble or orchestral accompaniment, are being created. However, most are composed and played with traditional or neo-traditional techniques that do not conflict with contemporary music aesthetics and values.

Fourth, *qin* music does not tell China's past theatrically. Even when *qin* compositions tell Chinese stories, their narratives are more abstract than realistic. A case in point is the *qin* work titled "Nie Zheng Assassinates the King of the Han State" ("Guanglinsan").[26] Listening to the music, the audience can interpret distinct melodic and rhythmic expressions as sonic representations of intense emotions or even murderous acts. Few, however, can directly connect the story's dramatic details and/or emotions with contemporary Chinese experiences and values. Kings and assassinations do not figure prominently in contemporary and cosmopolitan Chinese lives. As culturally and historically representative as *qin* music is, it can hardly serve as a fount of *qingchun dianya* China and Chinese selves.

In contrast, kunqu can. Indeed, by bringing celebrated Chinese individuals to life on stage, it builds a unique bridge between China's past and present. To illustrate this function of kunqu, a brief comparison of kunqu, Peking opera, and Cantonese opera will suffice. As operas that tell Chinese stories with words, music, and dance, the three genres have much in common. Being the oldest, kunqu is a source for many

---

26. For a musicological introduction to the piece, see Xu Jian, *Qinshi xinbian*, 57–64 and 170–172. Many audio or audiovisual recordings of the composition are available online.

expressive and performative features in Peking and Cantonese operas. The three genres, however, do have many critical differences. For example, their stylized singing of arias and playing of musical instruments render them recognizable as distinctive genres of Chinese opera.

Sung with melodious tunes and energetic rhythms, Peking opera has been continuously and popularly performed since the turn of the eighteenth and nineteenth centuries.[27] From the 1920s through the 1980s, it was the dominant genre of Chinese opera. During the Cultural Revolution, the genre's revolutionary model operas (*geming yangban xi*) and their characteristic use of Chinese and Western musical instruments/musical sounds permeated socialist China. Peking opera is still regularly performed, and calls for its preservation and promotion are not unknown.

In twenty-first-century China, Peking opera competes against kunqu for national attention and resources. The former cannot, however, challenge the latter's function as a representation of classical China and its *qingchun dianya* people. This is partly a result of kunqu stakeholders' tactics for promoting kunqu at the expense of Peking opera. Three such tactics are noteworthy. First, kunqu practitioners claim that their genre is the "mother" of all Chinese theater, an argument that perfectly matches international interest in old and "endangered" heritages and conveniently underscores that Peking opera is younger and more populist than kunqu. Prototypes of Peking opera formally entered the *yuescape* of operatic Peking in 1792, two hundred or more years after kunqu became a national pastime. As a younger genre of Chinese opera, Peking opera extensively borrowed storylines, *shenduan* practices, role-types, and other dramatic and performance elements from kunqu. Mature Peking opera, however, offered much to sustain late nineteenth- and early twentieth-century kunqu, a development the latter genre's practitioners tend to gloss over.

Second, kunqu participants spotlight the genre's *ya* features, a discursive strategy that has some empirical grounds. Kunqu lyrics are more literary than those of Peking opera, a fact that any comparison of kunqu and Peking opera renditions of the same stories or scenes, such as "Autumn Farewell" ("Qiujiang") of the *Jade Hairpin*, would reveal. As music and as text composed according to preexisting *qupai*, kunqu arias make structurally complex and through-composed tunes, the artistry and expressions of which can be opaque to those who know little about the genre. In contrast, Peking opera is readily intelligible and unmistakably entertaining. Peking opera lyrics are written in straightforward vernacular that most Chinese, even those with little education, can readily understand. Also, Peking opera arias are composed according to formulaic tune types (*banqiang*) and are thus readily recognizable and/or singable even by casual audiences.[28] Pulsating and relatively quick, Peking opera rhythms

---

27. For two scholarly studies on Peking opera, see Nancy Guy, *Peking Opera and Politics in Taiwan* (Urbana: University of Illinois Press, 2005) and Elizabeth Wichmann, *Listening to Theatre: The Aural Dimension of Beijing Opera* (Honolulu: University of Hawai'i Press, 1991).

28. For an analytical study of Peking opera aria structures and patterns, see Rulan Chao Pian, "Text Setting with the Shipyi Animated Aria," in *Words and Music: The Scholar's View*, ed. Laurence Berman

188   *Kunqu*

perfectly support the genre's *shenduan*, which are more realistic, and thus self-explanatory, than those of kunqu.

Third, kunqu practitioners call attention to the genre's tragic experiences, such as the ones suffered by the Chuanzibei Masters and other legendary performers over the last hundred or so years. Repeatedly, the practitioners describe how the genre was resuscitated by heroic "white knights" who appeared at critical moments and miraculously revived the genre while it was on its deathbed. The stories of kunqu being saved by Mu Ouchu in the 1920s, and by the central government in 1950s, appeal to Chinese audiences, who have experienced hardship in their own lives. Stories of kunqu declines and sufferings, one notes, are often told as allegories of nineteenth- and early twentieth-century China's trampling by Western and colonial powers.

For different reasons, Cantonese opera cannot compete with kunqu as a microcosm of contemporary Chinese lives and dreams.[29] Cantonese opera does, however, make a highly revealing statement of late imperial and modern Chinese experiences and memories. The genre developed into a local opera in nineteenth-century Guangzhou and Hong Kong and soon spread to Southeast Asia and North America when Cantonese migrated to those places as they fled natural and human-made disasters in China. This history of Cantonese opera, however, does not and cannot cover up the genre's "deficiencies." The genre's aesthetics and linguistic-musical practices are regional and dialectic. Performed in the Cantonese dialect the genre is only intelligible to Cantonese speakers in the Guangzhou, Hong Kong, and overseas Cantonese communities. Cantonese opera performance scripts, if written, are neither literary nor widely circulated as in print outside the genre's home base.

In early and mid-twentieth century, Cantonese opera blossomed in Hong Kong, a British colony from 1842 through 1997. This *yuescape* stimulated the genre to incorporate many Western/Westernized performance practices and materials. Violins, saxophones, and other Western instruments were commonly played in early and mid-twentieth-century Cantonese opera productions. Cantonese opera tunes and instrumental music were contemporaneously played as dance music in nightclubs and other entertainment venues in Hong Kong and Shanghai. As a result, Cantonese opera was until recently known as a modernized and hybridized genre of Chinese opera. Western elements are no longer prominently featured or practiced in current performances of Cantonese opera, but suspicions about its authenticity and hybridity linger on.

No such suspicions are hurled at kunqu. Its assessment as a classical opera of China and its realistic projection of *qingchun dianya* China and Chinese people are cemented by accounts of its history and personalities and by its creative and

---

(Cambridge, MA: Harvard University Press, 1972), 237–270.

29. For English references on Cantonese opera, see Rong Shicheng, *Xunmi yueju shengying: Cong hongchuan dao shuiyindeng* (Hong Kong: Oxford University Press, 2012); Wing Chung Ng, *The Rise of Cantonese Opera* (Urbana: University of Illinois Press, 2015); and Bell Yung, *Cantonese Opera: Performance as Creative Process* (London: Cambridge University Press, 1989).

re-creative shows. Kunqu's function as a *yue* performance and discourse of Chinese culture, history, and personhood is unique. Among the world cultural heritages/performing arts that UNESCO has made known throughout the globalized world, *noh*, a culturally and historically distinguished genre of Japanese theater and literature that UNESCO declared an ICH in 2001, is the only genre that can be meaningfully compared to kunqu. However, *noh* does not stage beautiful, civilized, productive, and youthful Japanese people the ways kunqu does in China.

Noh first blossomed in Japan of the fourteenth and fifteenth centuries with patronage from the shogunate and elite warriors.[30] Like *chuanqi*/kunqu scripts, *noh* scripts are literary works that relate representative Japanese lives and dreams. And like kunqu performance practices and materials, those of *noh* are codified and sustained by virtuoso performers and dedicated connoisseurs. Since the 1950s, the genre has been promoted as a national treasure of Japan. In 1983, the National Noh Theater was founded to provide a stable base for the genre's performance and training of future performers and audiences. Currently, a vibrant community of professional *noh* actors, amateur performers, patrons, and fans is working together to safeguard and develop the genre inside and outside Japan. Many educated and cultivated Japanese still learn to sing *noh* arias as a hobby and as a means to link themselves with classical Japanese literature and culture. Many Japanese and international scholars conduct research on *noh* performance and texts as evidence of Japanese culture, history, and personhood.

Noh connects Japan's past and present in ways that are more retrospective than practical, a fact that three distinctive features in *noh*'s *yuescape* underscore. First, *noh* operates with a conservatism that defines and is defined by the genre's performance schools/lineages. School heads (*iemoto*) have exclusive rights to rank school members and to grant them tiered licenses to practice and teach *noh* performance. Unless approved by their school heads, *noh* performers cannot change performance content and practices of their shows at will. Those who want to perform according to their own visions must create new schools or troupes, thereby forfeiting their claims to artistic authenticity and lineage. As a result, *noh* displays an institutionalized and tenacious conservatism that kunqu does not have.

Second, *noh* school heads, or gatekeepers, do not easily yield to external forces that demand change, and most contemporary Japanese *noh* practitioners do not harbor an urgent desire to "update" their shows, even though they face many financial and other practical challenges in their Japanese *noh yuescape*. As stakeholders, *noh* artists do not prioritize present and practical needs over the desire to preserve cultural heritages as they have been transmitted. New and experimental *noh* plays and performance

---

30. For the UNESCO description of noh, see UNESCO, "Nôgaku Theatre," accessed January 24, 2019, http://www.unesco.org/culture/ich/index.php?RL=00012. For a comparison of noh and kunqu, see Akamatsu Norihiko, Komatsu Ken, and Yamazaki Yoshiyuki, *Nogaku to konkyoku—Nihon to chugoku no koten yangeki wo tanoshimu* (Tokyo: Kyuko shoin, 2009). For a general description of *noh* music and history, see William Malm, *Traditional Japanese Music and Musical Instruments*, new ed. (Tokyo: Kodansha, 2000), 119–148.

practices are not unknown, but they do not dominate the genre's contemporary operations. Commercial and populist uses of *noh* as an icon of Japanese culture and people are common, but those uses hardly occupy the genre's center stage.

Third, even though *noh* presents many iconic characters in Japanese culture and history, these portrayals tend to be more imaginative than realistic—thus, the characters do not readily serve as models for contemporary life. As scripted and enacted, many *noh* characters live on earth/stage as youthful and charming men and women but spend their afterlives in hell. There, many male warriors (*samurai*) and charming beauties are transformed into vengeful ghosts or pitiful souls, personifying Japanese aesthetics of *aware* (grief) and Buddhist karma on life and afterlife. As such, *noh* characters hardly make desirable models for Japanese people, who are or aspire to live like their *qinchun dianya* Chinese counterparts.

Epilogue: Bando Tamasaburo's Japanese-Chinese Du Liniang

Contemporary Japanese, needless to say, have their own means to perform and discourse on their desired lives and dreams. One such tool is kunqu: some young, China-friendly, arts-loving Japanese find the genre appealing, as well as instrumental for their expressive and performative needs. Japanese kunqu fans, one notes, are arguably the most dedicated and informed international practitioners and audiences of the Chinese opera. Japanese have a century-long history of engaging with kunqu. Since the early decades of the twentieth century, Japan has repeatedly invited kunqu performers. Since the 1990s, China has sent many kunqu productions to Japan. A number of Japanese scholars have studied kunqu in China. Some Japanese connoisseurs and amateur performers have even mounted their own kunqu productions and organized their own kunqu clubs and study groups.[31]

A case in point is Bando Tamasaburo's (b. 1950) Chinese-Japanese production of the *Peony Pavilion* (2008–2010), in which he played Du Liniang.[32] Tamasaburo is an internationally renowned female impersonator in Japan's *kabuki* theater. His performance artistry is representative of Japanese aesthetics and performing arts and is celebrated the world over. His kunqu performance of Du Liniang is less celebrated but immensely significant for the genre's prospects as a globalized Chinese ICH. Extensively covered by Chinese and Japanese media, Tamasaburo's performance has not only produced a personalized kunqu *yue*-item but also generated a Chinese-Japanese *yuescape* for the genre's internationalizing developments. Tamasaburo has a

---

31. For chronological information on Japanese kunqu activities in China, see Wu Xinlei, *Chatuben kunqu shishi biannian* (Shanghai: Guji chubanshe, 2015), 265–404. For a general Japanese account of Chinese opera, see Akamatsu Norihiko ed., *Chugoku no dento bungei engeki ongaku* (Kyoto: Geijutsu gakusha, 2014); see in particular, 81–104 and 141–152.

32. See *Peony Pavilion*, 2008–2010 performance by Bando Tamasaburo and SuKun, accessed May 16, 2021, www.youtube.com/watch?v=J8AB-Y1DfVY. Many audiovisual materials and verbal reports are accessible to readers who subscribe to the *Japan Times*, and Japanese media.

Figure 9.1: Bando Tamasaburo as Du Liniang. Source: Pamphlet of Bando Tamasaburo's 2010 Shanghai performance of the *Peony Pavilion*.

long-time interest in Peking opera, and he once studied it with Mei Baojiu (1934–2016), a celebrated Peking opera female impersonator and a son of Mei Lanfang. In 1986, Tamasaburo attended Zhang Ziqing's kunqu performance in Tokyo and was smitten with what he saw. He then developed a desire to learn kunqu and incorporate its expressive practices into his kabuki shows. In 2007, Tamasaburo visited SuKun and expressed his wish to learn kunqu and do a kabuki version of the *Peony Pavilion*. In the process of explaining and demonstrating kunqu to Tamasaburo, SuKun artists convinced him that it was more practical for him to stage his *Peony Pavilion* in Chinese and as kunqu—they argued that the genre's performance practices and materials could not be meaningfully transplanted. Tamasaburo accepted their challenge and decided to learn kunqu acting, dancing, and singing from Zhang Ziqing so that he could perform Du Liniang himself.

In March 2008, with the help of SuKun, he premiered a Japanese-Chinese version of the *Peony Pavilion* in Beijing and Kyoto. On those stages, Tamasaburo brought his Du Liniang alive in his personal way, mesmerizing Chinese and Japanese audiences. In 2009, Tamasaburo performed the show in Suzhou, a historical center of kunqu and the nexus of its current development. In the summer of 2010, he performed his show again in Shanghai as an artistic-cultural program at the Shanghai Exposition. As an international *yue* event, the performance attracted not only Chinese and Japanese operagoers living in Shanghai but also the artist's Japanese fans; some flew to Shanghai to see him perform kunqu. To experience Tamasaburo's sensational show, some kunqu practitioners flew in from Hong Kong, Taiwan, and the US.

Tamasaburo's kunqu production is unprecedented and thought-provoking in many ways. He does not speak Chinese, and he is no China specialist. Nevertheless, he managed to learn the role of Du Liniang by rote, sang her feminine songs in Chinese, and brought the character, an idealized Chinese woman, to life on stage. In the process, he creatively and judiciously injected into the character his artistic self and kabuki aesthetics. As a result, his Du Liniang is unmistakably his and noticeably Chinese-Japanese. His *shenduan*, and in particular his facial expressions and subtle bodily movements, reveal kabuki elements and sensibilities. His singing is accented— he speaks kunqu as a foreign language.

Tamasaburo's kunqu show elicited strong and contrasting reactions from diverse audiences. Japanese audiences applauded it; they proudly viewed Tamasaburo's personal success as a national achievement. Some Chinese audiences concurred, noting that the Japanese artist's Du Liniang was more "feminine" and "real" than those enacted by less talented Chinese performers. However, some Chinese slighted Tamasaburo's performance as a gimmick. Some even suggested that he desperately needed something exotic to bolster his declining stardom in Japan. However it is viewed, Tamasaburo made a long-lasting impact on kunqu: his performance helped revive Chinese acceptance of the art of female impersonation, a traditional practice that socialist China has discouraged since the 1950s. Emboldened by Tamasaburo's success, several young Chinese male kunqu performers, such as Dong Fei, have openly declared themselves to be *nandan* (female impersonators). Should such Chinese acceptance of kunqu female impersonation continue, the genre may rediscover a forgotten past and explore an uncharted future.[33]

Tamasaburo's sensational kunqu endeavor raises many fundamental questions about the genre's internationalization and popularization. How can kunqu be preserved and developed as a classical Chinese opera or world opera by non-Chinese but talented and hard-working artists like Tamasaburo? They have something meaningful to offer to the genre, do they not? Do they have the right to perform, or change, the genre as they desire? Should hybridized kunqu, such as works by Peter Sellars, Chen Shizheng, and Tamasaburo, be welcomed inside and outside of China? What and whose culture, history, and personhood do they perform and discourse? How can Chinese kunqu practitioners say they want to share their opera with the world when they resist non-Chinese packaging of the genre?

---

33. For a study on the contemporary practice of kunqu female impersonation, see Joseph S. C. Lam, "Kunqu Cross-Dressing as Artistic and/or Queer Performance," in *The Oxford Handbook of Music and Queerness*, ed. Fred Maus and Sheila Whiteley (New York: Oxford University Press, 2019), 539–558.

10
Kunqu at a Crossroads

Continuities, Changes, and Explorations

Introduction

In the third decade of the twenty-first century, kunqu is no longer merely a revived genre of classical Chinese opera and an ICH; it is also an opera in transition.[1] Kunqu has arrived at a crossroads, just as China now has. Its practitioners have preserved and developed their genre for Chinese and international audiences, staging traditional and contemporary productions, expanding codified performance practices and materials, and justifying their actions and aspirations with facts and claims. As a result, kunqu practitioners have brought their genre to a crossroads—today they must not only review their past achievements and failures but also plan ahead for challenges that may or may not materialize. Can, or should, kunqu, the classical opera of today's transforming China, stay the course? What kind of kunqu does today's China desire, or need? To examine kunqu in transition—a fitting topic to end this monograph—this chapter presents an overview of the genre's most recent developments, highlighting the ways they embody overarching continuities and bold explorations.

Continuities

Twenty-first-century kunqu has succeeded in reconnecting with historical performance practices and materials, if the genre's artistic and cultural continuities are measured only in terms of quantifiable data. Many contemporary kunqu shows tell stories derived from recently rediscovered scripts. Many kunqu arias sung nowadays features lyrics and melodies similar to those notated in Qing China by Prince Yin Lu,

---

1. For annual reports of contemporary kunqu events, see Zhongguo kunqu nianjian bianzhuan weiyuanhui, ed., *Zhongguo kunqu nianjian* (Suzhou: Suzhou daxue, 2012–present). For a survey of major productions in the last two decades, see Ming Yang, "The Modernization of Chinese Xiqu with a Case Study of Major Kunqu Produtions in Mainland China, 2001–2013," in *Modernization of Asian Theatre: Process and Tradition*, ed. Yasuhi Nagata and Ravi Chaturvedi (Singapore: Springer, 2019), 165–186.

Ye Tang, Yin Guishen, and other historical kunqu practitioners. Many *shenduan* performed today on stage echo what mid-twentieth-century paintings and photographs have preserved. However one examines it, contemporary kunqu's connections with its past are substantive. They are especially impressive when we examine them against the transformations China has experienced over the past sixty or so years. The connections are, however, less convincing when we compare current kunqu music and dances with those preserved in pre-1970 audiovisual recordings.

Broad continuities between contemporary kunqu and its historical predecessors can be summarized into the following threads. The first relates to the repertory of *zhezixi*. Any comparison of current and historical kunqu productions will demonstrate that more or less the same *zhezixi* repertory is being performed and critiqued today as in the past. The traditional favorites still performed nowadays include "Dog Exit," "Flee by Night," "Happy Time," "Kneeling by the Pond," "Taken Alive," "Searching for the Dream," "Strolling; Dreaming," and "Yearning for the Secular World."

A number of *chuanqi*/kunqu dramas that were frequently performed and discussed in late Qing and Republican China are still being staged with adapted scripts. Their titles include the *Butterfly Dream*, the *Fifteen Strings of Coins*, the *Jade Hairpin*, the *Palace of Everlasting Life*, and the *Story of the Western Wing*. Some seminal kunqu shows that fell out of favor in late nineteenth- and early twentieth-century China have been "excavated" or restored. Their titles include the *Dames in Love*, the *Peach Blossom Fan*, and the *Story of the White Rabbit*.

The second thread of continuity between traditional and contemporary kunqu relates to the genre's historicism. Many new kunqu productions tell old Chinese stories and/or reference historical memories and imaginations. Representative of such shows are the *Story of General Gongsun Zidu* (2008), the *Dream of the Red Chamber* (2011), the *Kunqu Sage: Wei Liangfu* (2017; Qusheng, Wei Liangfu), and the *Story of Gu Yanwu* (2018; Gu Yanwu). The same historicism manifests itself in the genre's debates about historical performances, performers, and documents.

A third thread of continuity has to do with the genre's theoretical practices. Any comparative reading of historical and current treatises on kunqu history and theory will find the same set of fundamental issues, such as the linguistic attributes of the words sung or spoken in kunqu shows, *qupai* identities and attributes, prescriptions for proper singing techniques, and definitions of musical modes and scales. Even when the issues are discussed with reference to contemporary shows, the goals and structures of the discussions do not deviate substantively from traditional ones.

The fourth and most significant continuity between traditional and contemporary kunqu concerns the genre's transmission of performance practices and materials. There have been many celebrated cases of effective kunqu transmission between mentors and disciples. A prominent line of contemporary kunqu transmission is, for example, the Yu School of kunqu singing, a practice that Yu Sulu (1847–1930) supposedly learned from a disciple of Ye Tang (1722?–after 1792) and passed on to his son, Yu Zhengfei (1902–1992). The young Yu fine-tuned it during his many decades of performing and teaching kunqu and then passed it on to his students, who included Cai Zhengren (b. 1941) and Yue Meiti (b. 1941). Both are now leading kunqu masters and pedagogues; it was they who groomed Li An, Yu Jiulin, Zhou Xuefang, and other current kunqu stars. Another celebrated route of successful transmission involves the Chuanzibei Masters. They flowed their artistry to their students, who are now senior masters and pedagogues. Any comparative viewing of performances by Liang Guyin, Ji Zhenhua, and Shi Xiaomei and other kunqu masters who learned from the Chuanzibei Masters will find broad but identifiable similarities.

The kunqu continuities described here are possible because they take place in a relatively stable *yuescape*, one that the genre's dominant stakeholders—national institutions and officials, dedicated practitioners, and visionary patrons—have constructed in order to revive kunqu as a classical opera and ICH of China, and one that shapes, in turn, their kunqu performances and discourse. For example, the eight professional kunqu troupes collaborate with one another to preserve and develop the genre, even though their personal, institutional, and regional agendas are dissimilar. Many leading kunqu professionals have repeatedly led transmission projects, conducting performance workshops for professional and semiprofessional actor-singers, offering classes for amateurs and fans, and presenting lectures on kunqu aesthetics, history, and theory. Pursuing kunqu as a hobby or a cultural-historical activity, many focus their energies on sustaining kunqu as a classical opera and ICH. Liu Run'en of Shanghai, an erudite connoisseur of kunqu, for example, has strived to demonstrate and sustain traditional kunqu as he has learned and envisioned it.[2]

All of these continuities can be found in SuKun's 2018 production of the *Lute: Cai Bocai (Pipa ji: Cai Bojie)*, a much condensed and newly rewritten version of Gao Ming's the *Lute*, the classical and historical *nanxi* masterpiece that was promoted by Zhu Yuanzhang, the founder of the Ming dynasty. As crafted by Zhang Hong (b. 1947), a leading dramatist of contemporary kunqu, the script of the SuKun production focuses on the drama's main story—the separation and reunion of the scholar and filial son, Cai Bojie, with his virtuous wife, Zhao Wuniang. To make a long story short and to give it new narrative twists, Zhang has deleted some favorite scenes and dramatic developments, such as the newly married couple's farewell and Zhao's eating of fibrous husk of rice grain but highlighted others, such as the wife's singing of *pipa* ballads and the husband's playing of *qin* music. Zhao's singing serves as a dramatic tool that enables Cai to recognize his virtuous wife, and Cai's playing of *qin* music affords him moments to express his intense yearning for home and conflicted emotions about his old and new wives. In terms of performance practices, the SuKun show features traditional singing and *shenduan* acting. However, to musically stage the union of Zhao and her husband, the production has the wife sing a soulful *pipa*

---

2. Liu has posted many of his restorative performances online; see, for example, "Liu Runen zhi kunqu changshengdian tanci quan chu," accessed October 15, 2020, https://www.bilibili.com/video/av838290799.

ballad. Its melody echoes *pingtan* music, a vernacular genre that did not appear on late imperial kunqu stages but would have been performed by itinerant female musicians of the time. In terms of cultural and operatic discourse, the SuKun version highlights not only the traditional patrilineal filial piety that Gao Ming's text dramatizes but also a contemporary Chinese approach to female agency and virtues. In short, SuKun's the *Lute: Cai Bojie* is a creative continuation of traditional kunqu practices.

Changes

However much contemporary kunqu emphasizes continuity, it also has to change. Otherwise, it will not survive in twenty-first-century China, a nation/society that has been hugely transformed since the Open Door Policy of the 1980s. Even if contemporary kunqu productions are, and can be, staged with the genre's "original sauce and taste," their expressive and performative details cannot literally repeat what was performed five or more decades ago. To satisfy contemporary audiences, kunqu has had to change somehow.

In broad terms, some of these changes have been unmistakable. Contemporary kunqu tends to tell dramatically condensed stories with vernacular lyrics and dialogue, short but tuneful arias, mimetic *shenduan*, fashionable costumes and makeup, and technologically advanced stage sets. Many shows are staged with particular goals and for targeted audiences. For example, the *Belladonna and Intoxicated Hearts* of ShengKun, a creative adaptation of Shakespeare's *Romeo and Juliet*, was staged in 2016 to celebrate the 400th anniversary of the passing of the Bard and Tang Xianzu. As a hybridized work, the opera features dramatic episodes, lyrics, music, and *shenduan* that deviate subtly from traditional practices. For example, the rapid alternation between intimate and crowd scenes in the opera is not a traditional kunqu feature. As an attempt to explore historical sites and spatial effects for artistic and commercial purposes, the *Six Vignettes of A Floating Life* (SuKun 2018; *Fusheng liuji*) was performed not on a stage but in actual rooms and yards in different parts of the Blue Wave Pavilion (Canglang ting), a historically celebrated Suzhou garden and a UNESCO World Heritage Site.

Efforts to stage productions that are both creative and marketable have pushed kunqu in different directions. Five can be highlighted here. First, contemporary shows have become more *kunju* than kunqu—the former prioritizes the dramatic telling of fast-paced stories, while the latter emphasizes the singing of kunqu arias that showcase the characters' emotional states. As a result, most contemporary kunqu shows unfold with six to eight scenes of rapid dramatic development. And featured in those scenes are relatively long speeches and short arias. Second, tendencies toward *kunju* have rendered dramatic/narrative intelligibility a primary concern. As a result, kunqu lyrics and speeches are now written in simple Chinese that the average Chinese audience can readily grasp. To help audiences understand sung lyrics, their Chinese subtitles are displayed on large LCD monitors installed stage left and right. In Shanghai and Beijing, the monitors display subtitles in both Chinese and English.

At a Crossroads

Third, to sonically project characters' emotions, contemporary kunqu employs many newly composed pieces of kunqu instrumental and nondiegetic music. Performed as overtures, interludes, postludes, and even background music to accompany dialogues, these *c-yue* compositions feature recurring motifs. Fourth, most contemporary kunqu shows cast attractive young actor-singers who don elaborate and dramatically expressive costumes. The visuals and visual effects in contemporary kunqu productions often become attractions in and of themselves. Publicity stills of performers in dramatic costumes striking glamorous poses are now integral to kunqu advertisements. Fifth, to excite all senses of the audience, contemporary shows employ the latest staging technologies, including illustrative stage backdrops, large and realistic props, shifting colored lighting, and realistic sound effects, such as chirping birds and rolling thunder.

The five directions of change outlined above can emerge in any contemporary kunqu performance, as attested by recent productions of the *Spring River* and the *Belladonna and Intoxicated Hearts*. As authored by Luo Zhou, a forty-something and much awarded dramatist, these two operas tell dramatically concise stories with expository dialogue and expressive lyrics set to traditional and neotraditional *qupai*. The tragic love story of the *Spring River* has characters constantly crossing back and forth between the human and supernatural realms: carried to the underworld by mistake, a talented poet continues to pursue a living woman whom he has seen briefly only three times, while rejecting an angel's amorous advances. Bringing the fanciful story to life on stage are young and physically attractive actor-singers in fanciful costumes, who dance and sing on and by a bridge that links the human and supernatural worlds. And inviting audiences to enter that magical world is Sun Jian'an's *c-yue*. It features flowing melodies, energetic rhythms, and contemporary timbres played on Western and Westernized Chinese musical instruments.

Compared to the *Spring River*, the *Belladonna and Intoxicated Hearts* looks and sounds neotraditional. For example, the production's minimalist stage setting is quite traditional; the stage props—chairs with extremely tall backs—are, however, unmistakably avant-garde. Narratively, the drama more or less follows the story of *Romeo and Juliet*. Its script, however, features many verbal allusions to Chinese love stories and romantic memories. Luo Zhou, the author, declared that she had scripted a Chinese love story, not a translation of a British drama.[3] The opera's melodies and *shenduan* differ from traditional ones only subtly.

What highlights the opera's contemporary and populist hybridity is its extensive use of nondiegetic instrumental music to accompany, or parallel, the protagonists' long dialogues and expressive *shenduan*. For instance, a *c-yue* composition with dramatic rhythms and contrasting sonorities played by *pipa*, *zheng*, *erhu*, and percussion instruments marks the moment when Ji Can/Romeo finds Ying Ling/Juliet's altar in a

---

3. Luo Zhou, "Zuixin hua, woshou xie woxin," accessed October 10, 2019, https://weibo.com/ttarticle/p/show?id=2309404052531151029245.

nunnery. There and then, he confesses his love for her, offers a round of sacrificial wine to her soul, and kills himself.[4]

Changes and innovations in contemporary kunqu are significant, pointing to twenty-first-century Chinese realities and sensibilities. For example, scripts with dramatically straightforward stories underscore not only contemporary Chinese audiences' understanding of drama but also their unfamiliarity with traditional stories, many of which narratively meander with "unessential" twists. Similarly, the use of fancy costumes both reflects kunqu's long tradition of elaborate costumes and contemporary audiences' pursuit of material and visual pleasure. Luxurious kunqu costumes are not an isolated development in contemporary Chinese performing arts. Many Chinese singers and instrumentalists, especially female ones, perform in spectacular dresses, rendering their concerts *de facto* fashion shows.

To understand the significance of these changes/innovations in particular contemporary kunqu works and/or shows, they must be analyzed as specific *yue* events that individualistic kunqu practitioners/stakeholders perform in fluid *yuescapes*. In those *yuescapes*, they dynamically interact with one another, making maximum use of available resources, showcasing their talents, pleasing their audiences, and advancing their agendas. A prime example of a contemporary kunqu production pregnant with meanings is the controversial staging of the *Masters' Performance of the Peony Pavilion* (*Dashi ban Mudang ting*; hereafter the *Masters' Performance*), in Beijing (December 13 and 14, 2014) and Shanghai (October 31 and November 1, 2015).

Superficially, the show was all about sustaining traditional kunqu, and not about its innovations; nevertheless, it still made changes, projecting new expressions/meanings that contrasted with traditional ones. Produced by BeiKun in partnership with several national and cultural offices, the show was as much an operatic presentation as a cultural-social celebration.[5] Its *cause célèbre* was its cast of twenty senior kunqu artists who had formally retired from the stage but had chosen to participate in a *yue* event that could never be repeated. Pre-performance promotion for the show was extensive, and ticket sales were robust. It attracted many who wanted to see the celebrated artists perform in person.[6] Post-performance discussions were heated, manifesting not only

---

4. A complete audiovisual recording of the opera is accessible online; see "Kunqu Fleur de L'ivresse du Coeur 1," https://www.youtube.com/watch?v=Fxwlb8CaL00; "Kunqu Fleur de L'ivresse du Coeur 2," https://www.youtube.com/watch?v=a7WLJP-ZdFs; "Kunqu Fleur de L'ivresse du Coeur 3," https://www.youtube.com/watch?v=Yp6bdXPqoSw&t=1365s; all were accessed on November 21, 2021. The dramatic music being discussed here is played in "Kunqu Fleur de L'ivresse du Coeur 3," 19'17" to 22'18.

5. The offices are Wenhuabu yishusi (Arts Division of the Ministry of Culture), Guojia kunqu yishu changjiu, baohu, he fuchi gongcheng bangongshi (National Office for Salvaging, Protecting, and Sustaining Kunqu), and Beijing shi wenhua ju (Culture Bureau of the Municipal Government of Beijing).

6. This discussion of the *Masters' Performance* is based on what I witnessed in November 2015 in Shanghai. Audiovisual recordings of the show are now available online, see *The Peony Pavilion*, 2014–2015 Masters' Performance (*Kunqu Dashiban Mudanting*), accessed January 15, 2018, https://www.bilibili.com/video/av9595586.

At a Crossroads

diverse reactions to the show but also the crossroads at which kunqu had found itself.

The *Masters' Performance* elicited strong reactions because it was presented as an authentic and authoritative production of the *Peony Pavilion*, one that allowed the masters to demonstrate their artistry, showcase the practices they had learned from their mentors, polished over their long careers, and taught to their disciples. This *yue* agenda vividly manifested itself in scenes like the "Infernal Judgment" ("Mingpan").[7] As scripted by Tang Xianzu, the scene unfolds with five episodes, presenting Du Liniang in an underworld court, declaring her purity in front of an infernal judge, who sends her back to the human world to reunite with her husband, Liu Mengmei. Playing the role of the judge, a character different from the martial heroes he so often enacts, Hou Shaokui (b. 1939) made the *zhezixi* a showcase for both his stardom and his talent as he gave new meanings to the character and the *zhezixi*.[8] Hou achieved that by stretching the introductory episode 1, which dramatizes the judge's travel to the underworld court with his entourage of ghost-attendants, giving it sixteen out of a total of thirty-three minutes of performance time. Wearing bright-red costumes and striking green makeup, Hou performed a sequence of physically demanding *shenduan* on the expansive stage. His actions/dances included walking sideways, kicking up his legs and stretching his arms, and riding a (symbolic) horse. Hou's stage assistant/companion, who played the role of a horseman, also performed spectacular acrobatics.

In addition, Hou sang, chanted, and spoke the words Tang Xianzu scripted with a resonant voice, demonstrating his personal grain of voice. His singing of the northern aria "Rouged Lips" ("Dian jiangchun") at the beginning of the scene was a tour de force performance that won enthusiastic applause. The instrumental music accompanying Hou's singing was typical *t-yue*: its blended sounds articulated Hou's spectacular *shenduan* without drawing undue attention to themselves. With episode 1 thus extended, the rest of the scene was squeezed. Episode 2 was skipped; episode 3, which shows Du Liniang's encounter with the judge (12 minutes), unfolded as scripted; Episodes 4 and 5 were briefly performed (about 4 minutes) to wrap up the scene.

Hou's atypical rendition of the "Infernal Judgment" underscores traditional kunqu players' efforts to creatively express themselves at the expense of scripted texts and established performance routines. As I have observed and learned from my research partners, Hou's performance baffled many contemporary critics. They found his show dramatically unbalanced, if not incoherent—episode 1 was too long, they felt, and showed nothing but the master performer's acrobatics. Yet the same production won

---

7. For an informative study of the social and political meanings of the *zhezixi*, see Thomas Kelly, "Putting on a Play in an Underworld Courtroom: The 'Mingpan' (Infernal Judgment) Scene in Tang Xianzu's *Mudan ting (Peony Pavilion)*," *Chinoperl: Journal of Chinese Oral and Performing Literature* 32, no. 2 (December 2013): 132–155.

8. For this discussion's convenience, Hou's performance in the *Masters' Performance* is examined as his creative work. A comprehensive discussion of the creative processes of the unique production is beyond the scope of this chapter.

enthusiastic applause from Hou's fans and casual audiences. Many had bought expensive tickets to see Hou perform; they wanted to see his legendary artistry with their own eyes and ears.

Contrasting responses to Hou's performance underscore not only stakeholders' competing aesthetics but also what kunqu continuities and changes may signify. To illustrate, the following analysis of the *Masters' Performance* will suffice. The show unfolded as it did because Beikun yielded to the celebrated masters' artistic and personal wishes—given their seniority and stardom, they could perform whatever and however they wanted. Their artistry was the rare and treasured commodity that many audience members would pay to see. BeiKun then seized on that audience demand to make an aesthetic point and to help satisfy the institution's practical needs. Until the production of the *Masters' Performance*, BeiKun had not produced any popular renditions of the *Peony Pavilion*. Until its 2011 production of *Dream of the Red Chamber* (*Honglou meng*), Beikun had presented no nationally and internationally successful shows.[9]

To produce a hit, and to create a market niche for itself, Beikun presented the *Master's Performance* as a historical and commercial show. It would generate profit and recognition for the troupe, help with kunqu transmission, and, above all, satisfy the audience's desire to see the senior masters perform while they still could. Revealingly, some of the audience called the senior stars "big pandas" (*da xiongmao*), that is, national treasures of China whose natural charm is irresistible and whose presence on earth is endangered—see them before they disappear!

However one interprets the *Masters' Performance*, it was an artistic, commercial, and social success as well as a seminal event in contemporary kunqu history. Its distinctive blend of continuities and changes raised critical questions: Do authoritative master performers have the license to change classical *zhezixi* as they like? Is their creative use of codified performance practices and materials a continuation or a change? Can kunqu be coherently preserved if it is merely what performers want to play or what audiences want to see?

Such questions resonate in the world of twenty-first-century kunqu, in which conventional wisdom is being challenged in multiple ways. A vivid documentation of this reality is the *Kunqu baizhong dashi shuoxi* (One hundred kunqu masterpieces: master performers' lecture-demonstrations on their signature shows; hereafter *The Lecture-Demonstrations*, 2014).[10] A monumental collection of 110 DVD recordings of presentations by twenty-nine master kunqu performers, with five volumes of edited transcriptions of the presentations, the collection comprehensively relates what the

---

9. For further information on the show, see Wang Wenming and Yang Fengyi, eds., *Honglou xinmeng, konggu youlan: kunqu Hongloumeng pinlun ji* (Beijing: Zhongguo xiju chubanshe, 2015).

10. Ye Shaoxin coordinated (*cehua*), *Kunqu baizhong: dashi shuoxi*, 5 vols. and 110 DVDs (Changsha: Hunan dianzi yinxiang chubanshe and Yuelu shushe, 2014). For a summary review of the publication, see Kim Hunter Gordon, "*Kunqu Baizhong, Dashi Shuixi* (One Hundred Pieces of Kunqu, Master Performers Talk about Their Scenes): A Review Essay," *Chinoperl* 35, no. 2 (2016): 143–152.

masters have learned from their mentors and how they have fine-tuned that knowledge for artistic and personal reasons. The collection also projects a kunqu world that is more fluid and complex than the genre's pragmatic history implies.

The twenty-nine presenters of the collection are all kunqu masters and stars; all command sizable cohorts of fans. All except three were born in the 1940s and had lessons/rehearsals with the Chuanzibei Masters, Yu Zhenfei, and other mentors. All have taught a number of professional and amateur disciples, some of whom have become stars in their own right. The three exceptions are Wang Fang (b. 1963; SuKun), Lin Weilin (b. 1964; ZheKun), and Ke Jun (b. 1965; ShengKun).

Every presentation in the collection focuses on one specific *zhezixi*, explaining its creative and performance features and tracing its development as the lecturer's signature show.[11] Collectively, the presentations register a wealth of biographical and historical details about kunqu and raise many fundamental questions about the genre's past, present, and projected future. To illustrate, a brief review of the representation by Shi Xiaomei's (b. 1949) and her "Writing on the Fan" ("Tihua") from the *Peach Blossom Fan* will suffice. With plain words and illustrative acts of singing and dancing, Shi, a kunqu male impersonator, explains the process of her creative restoration of the *zhezixi* and its distinctive expressions.[12]

The process began with her decision to perform the "Writing on the Fan" at a national competition in 1988, a *zhezixi* that the *Liuye qupu* (An anthology of kunqu arias from the Liuye Studio), a late nineteenth-century source, has preserved.[13] To realize her staging of the *zhezixi* Shi researched its performance and reception history. To her surprise, she learned that despite its fame, the *Peach Blossom Fan* had rarely been staged and its historical performances were scantily documented; she found little about the *zhezixi*. She then consulted experts on kunqu and Chinese literature. Her kunqu teacher, Shen Chuanzhi (1906–1994), a Chuanzibei Master, did not offer anything concrete; he could not remember ever seeing or performing "Writing on the Fan" himself.

Thus, Shi concluded that she and her artistic partner and husband, Zhang Hong, would have to knead (*nie*) the preserved script and notated music of the *zhezixi* into a show by themselves. To create the stage set of her show, one that would physically evoke the love story related in the *Peach Blossom Fan*, Shi visited the Qinhuai area, the historic entertainment quarter in Nanjing, where Hou Fangyu and Li Xiangjun, the protagonists of the historical love story, had actually lived. There, Shi supposedly

---

11. For a translation of the lecture by Zhang Jiqing, see Joseh Stenberg, "An Annotated Translation of Zhang Jiqing's Lecture on Playing Cui-shi in *Chimeng* (The Mad Dream): A Sample Lecture from *Kunqu Baizhong, Dashi Shuoxi* (One Hundred Pieces of Kunqu, Master Performers Talk about Their Scenes)," *Chinoperl* 35, no. 2 (2016): 153–175.

12. Shi Xiaomei, "Taohuashan: Tihua," in *Kunqu baizhong: dashi shuoxi*, Vol. 3, 341–352; DVD #65. Shi has also discussed her recreation of "Writing on the Fan" in other lectures and occasional audiovisual recordings, some of which are available on YouTube; to access, Google Shi Xiaomei or "Tihua."

13. Zhang Yusun, ed., *Zengji liuye qupu* (Reprint, Taipei: Zhonghua shuju, 1977).

found the lovers' historical residence—a living room flanked by a bedroom and a game room. Inspired by the physical layout of the place, Shi envisioned not only her stage for "Writing on the Fan" but also the *shenduan* she would perform. She would use the traditional props of one table and two chairs for her enacting of Hou's sneaking into the garden surrounding the residence and climbing the staircases that led to Li's boudoir.

To define the stage/mise-en-scène as a feminine space, Shi draped light green brocade over the staged table and chairs. Shi rejected pink, the traditional color for a courtesan's residence, because it could not adequately project Li as a courtesan with moral integrity. To complement the green she had chosen, Shi dressed Hou in deep blue. Having designed her stage and costume, Shi performed the "Writing on the Fan" as a *zhezixi* of four episodes and five arias, singing her interpretation of the melodies and rhythms preserved in the late nineteenth-century score.

As Shi recounts, her creative process for "Writing on the Fan" was a mix of library research, fieldwork, personal experiences, and interpretations/claims. The process is much more complex and nuanced than suggested by generalized kunqu history and theory. The *zhezixi* Shi created/re-created was a success; it won her a Plum Blossom Award in 1988. Shi's account in the *Lecture-Demonstrations* ends with a call for exploration, arguing that kunqu artists should not only practice and transmit what they have learned from their mentors to the next generation but also create new shows for themselves and their successors.

As a representative chapter in the *Lecture-Demonstrations*, Shi's account draws attention to concerns and questions that many kunqu practitioners share. Four can be highlighted here. First, kunqu artistry and history are much more complex than conventional and pragmatic narratives have told. Gaps in the pragmatic narrative of the genre's history need to be filled. Second, as senior kunqu performers become socially elevated, they are no longer merely actor-singers; they now have to serve as administrators-artistic directors, give lectures on kunqu appreciation, conduct performance workshops for professional and amateur actor-singers, and interact with the media to promote the genre and their own stardom. How the performers' new roles will positively or negatively impact the future of kunqu is a concern that many stakeholders have voiced.

Third, the *Lecture-Demonstrations* poignantly highlights the roles played by private and visionary patrons in the development of kunqu. Given the extent to which Chinese officials have influenced the genre's recent developments, many kunqu practitioners believe that the genre's future depends on national policies and resources. Challenging that belief is the *Lecture-Demonstrations*, which was financed by a single dedicated and generous connoisseur, Mr. Ye Zhaoxin.[14] He wanted to have the

---

14. There are few public documents about Ye Zhaoxin. The speech he presented on September 29, 2014 at the closing ceremony of his project is informative. I did not listen to his speech in person but was privileged to receive, via email, a copy of his text.

At a Crossroads   203

performers' artistry and knowledge widely disseminated, a goal he began to pursue after attending kunqu lecture-demonstrations at the Chinese Civilisation Centre of the City University of Hong Kong.[15] Ye's goal is noble, and his success has been impressive. Nevertheless, his publication raises questions about the power that stakeholders/patrons can wield to shape kunqu performance and discourse. For example, one can ask how Ye's patronage shaped the content of his seminal publication. Had it more governmental, or national, support, would it include presentations by kunqu composers, arrangers, and instrumentalists? Does their expertise on kunqu music deserve the same dissemination as enjoyed by master actor-singers?

Fourth, the format of the *Lecture-Demonstrations* underscores that technology has critically impacted contemporary kunqu performance and appreciation—the global *yuescape* of kunqu is very much what Appadurai theorized as a *technoscape*. If technology has enhanced kunqu preservation and development, it has also generated a number of practical concerns. Some kunqu critics have noted that audiovisual aids have negatively affected young performers' training; some novice actor-singers have relied on audiovisual aids and learned to perform their arias and *shenduan* without grasping the meanings of what they are performing. And because they depend on technology to amplify their singing, some young performers are focusing on their *shuenduan* acting and have neglected to develop resonant voices that can fill large performance venues. Paradoxically, sound amplification highlights singers' imperfect enunciation, phrasing, and other aspects of vocal performance.

Technology may also unnecessarily objectify kunqu performance and expressions. The standardizing effects of audiovisual recordings can be seen in the broad dissemination of audiovisual recordings and media productions of the *Young Lovers*. The show's distinctive performance style is now so well-known that intentionally or not, some audiences use it as a yardstick for their kunqu viewing and listening. The same can be said about the two Taiwanese series of kunqu videotapes made in the 1990s, which are now viewed as authoritative records of traditional kunqu.[16]

The *Lecture-Demonstrations* is becoming an authoritative reference on kunqu performance and discourse. It will be critically studied and its data will be compared with what is offered by the *Complete Compendium of Kunqu Resources* (*Kunqu yishu dadian*; hereafter the *Compendium*, 2016).[17] A monumental compilation of kunqu resources, and the result of a multiyear nationally sponsored project, the *Compendium* presents 149 volumes of texts and graphics, 100 hours of audio recordings of kunqu singing

---

15. Zheng Peikai, "Bu xiaoxin chengjiu di dashi", in *Kunqu baizhong dashi shuoxi: booklet of catalogue and congratulatory essays*, comp. Zhongguo yishu yanjiu yuan (Hefei: Shidai chuban chuanmei gufen youxian gongsi and Anhui wenyi chubanshe, 2014), 42–45.

16. For a list of the videotapes, see "Fulu jiu: Taiwan zhizuo zhi kunqu luying dai mulu," in *Kunqu cidian*, Vol. 2, 1322–1326.

17. This description is based on my communications with the editors and on data presented in *Kunqu yishu dadian*, comp. Zhongguo yishu yanjiu yuan (Hefei: Shidai chuban chuanmei gufen youxian gongsi and Anhui wenyi chubanshe, 2016).

made before 1966, and 350 hours of audiovisual documentation made between 1950 and 2000. Preserving historical sights and sounds of legendary performers from the early decades of the twentieth century, the historical recordings are treasures that kunqu connoisseurs and scholars will diligently examine for many years to come. Together, the *Lecture-Demonstrations* and the *Compendium* have monumentalized kunqu's past achievements, embodied its current operations and evolving expressions, and shaped the paths leading to kunqu of the future.

Explorations

Some of the paths into the future are being explored by forward-looking kunqu practitioners. They ask what kunqu will or should become and how it will shape future Chinese lives and dreams. Among kunqu practitioners who have boldly challenged the genre's status quo with innovative performance practices and materials, Danny Yung (b. 1943) of Hong Kong and his ShengKun collaborators stand out. They have produced a series of avant-garde kunqu works under the rubric of *One Table Two Chairs* (*Yizhuo liangyi*; hereafter 1T2C), works that have deconstructed kunqu's long-codified practices by hybridizing them with non-Chinese elements.

Yung and his collaborators work both inside and outside the kunqu world and in doing so have generated a cross-genre, intercultural and international *yue* phenomenon. In 2015, Yung's kunqu labor vividly manifested itself with the *Toki International Arts Festival 2015: Bridge the Traditional and the Contemporary | Cross Cultures and Boundaries*, a festival of performances, workshops, and discussions on traditional Chinese kunqu and experimental-transnational theater (hereafter the Toki Festival). Held in Nanjing during the week of October 25–31, 2015, the festival was co-organized by Zuni Icosahedron (Hong Kong), which Yung directs, ShengKun, the Nanjing Museum, and the Japan Foundation, four prominent institutions of Asian culture and performing arts. The Toki Festival presented a rich program: (1) two presentations of experimental Asian theatrical works; (2) two formal performances of 1T2C works by ShengKun artists; (3) two formal performances of classical dances from India and Indonesia; (4), four lecture-demonstrations by senior Chinese and non-Chinese performers, introducing classical Indian dance from Hyderabad, classical Javanese dance from Yogyakarta, Indonesia, kunqu from Nanjing, and *noh* from Tokyo; and (5), four roundtable discussions about kunqu, Asian performing arts, ICH, and related issues.

The festival became an annual event of the Toki Project, a UNESCO-supported enterprise that Yung launched in 2010 with Makoto Sato (b. 1943) of Japan. Their overall goal is to preserve and develop Asian performing arts that are in danger of being homogenized through globalization. Yung and Sato first teamed up to coproduce *Toki*, a multimedia show for the Japan Pavilion at the 2010 Shanghai Exposition. Blending Chinese kunqu and Japanese *noh* performance practices, that work served as an artistic and humanist call to protect the world's natural environment and traditional

Asian performing arts. Like the endangered *toki* birds, which once flew freely over East Asia and left many traces in Chinese and Japanese memories, traditional Asian performing arts are in peril; efforts to preserve them are urgently needed.

Yung's *1T2C* works implement an intellectual-cultural-social-political ideal that he has been developing since the late 1970s. Yung is an award-winning creative polymath: simultaneously, he is a much-published author and editor, a prolific director and producer of experimental theater works, a celebrated cartoonist, an active creator of visual and installation art works, and an intellectual-activist based in Hong Kong. Yung's artistic outlook and ideology are cosmopolitan and deeply rooted in the history and culture of Hong Kong, a British colony between 1842 and 1997 as well as a vortex of local, national, and international forces.

Yung's *1T2C* works simultaneously honor and dismiss hallowed kunqu aesthetics and practices.[18] For example, the works are performed on a minimalist stage, a design that echoes the traditional Chinese practice of employing one table and two chairs as the sole stage props. *1T2C* works highlight traditional kunqu norms by deconstructing them. For instance, some *1T2C* works are not narrative, as kunqu was and still is. Some even dispense with onstage singing by actors and actresses, even though singing is a defining element of traditional kunqu. Performers of *1T2C* works do not always wear role-specific costumes or character-defining makeup.

Many conservative kunqu audiences are puzzled by Yung's experimental works and performances. Many also find the mix of Chinese and non-Chinese elements in the works unacceptably dissonant. Audience members sometimes leave in the middle of *1T2C* shows, acting out their rejection of Yung's experiments. For example, in a post-performance discussion at the Toki Festival, a clearly agitated middle-aged woman loudly challenged Yung and his performers, demanding to know what they thought they were doing and urging them to perform traditional kunqu as she knew it.

An *1T2C* work that vividly manifests Yung's deconstructionist aesthetics and experiments is his internationally acclaimed "Flee by Night" ("Yeben"; hereafter "*1T2C* Flee by Night"). A contemporary take on the classical kunqu *zhezixi* of the same title, Yung's masterpiece premiered in Norway in 2004, celebrating fifty years of Chinese–Norwegian diplomatic ties. Since then, the show has been performed successfully in Hong Kong (2010, 2012), Taipei (2011), Singapore (2010), Germany (2015), and Ann Arbor and Toronto (2017). Featuring Ke Jun and his disciple Yang Yang as lead performers, this evolving experimental production makes audiences wonder what kunqu was, is, and can become.

---

18. For two revealing reports by the Toki participants, see Ke Jun, Rong Nianzeng and Wang Xiaoying, eds., *Zhuhuan ji /Story of the Toki Project* (Nanjing: Jiangsu fenghuang kexue jishu chubanshe, 2015), and Sun Rongjie ed., *Yizhuo liangyi: "Yeben"* (Nanjing: Fenghuang chuban chuanmei, 2015). For an study on the Toki Project in English, see Rossella Ferrara, "Asian Theatre as Method: The Toki Experimental Project and Sino-Japanese Transnationalism in Performance," *TDR: The Drama Review* 61, no. 3 (Fall 2017): 141–164.

Figure 10.1: Yang Yang performs Lin Chong in Ann Arbor, Michigan. Photography by J. Lam, 2017. Courtesy of Yang Yang.

As published in 2010,[19] "*1T2C* Flee by Night" has nine scripted scenes. As performed in March 2010 and preserved in an audiovisual recording, scenes 7 and 8 are particularly dramatic and thought-provoking. In scene 7, Ke Jun plays the wronged hero, Lin Chong. He wears not a traveling soldier's costume but a plain *magua*, a formal gown worn by late nineteenth- and early twentieth-century Chinese men. Two minutes into the scene, Ke unbuttons his gown, baring his chest. Then he does a series of martial but contemporary *shenduan*, such as having his whole body falling to the stage floor. Ke neither sings nor chants in the scene, as is done in traditional shows. Accompanying Ke's actions and dances is a recorded musical work that echoes mid-twentieth-century and international electronic music. This use of music is unmistakably deconstructionist and unexpectedly communicative. It underscores the importance of music and tradition in kunqu by suppressing them—paradoxically, the lack of vocal music in "*1T2C* Flee by Night" underscores the centrality of singing in traditional kunqu productions, and the use of electronic sounds in the contemporary work raises questions about what and how kunqu should sound like.

Scene 8 of "*1T2C* Flee by Night" is titled "A Letter Home." As performed in Ann Arbor, Michigan, in April 2017, it features Yang Yang as a bare-chested man, doing various kinds of martial *shenduan* as well as poses that echo traditional ones. As Yang performs, subtitles projected on the backdrop ask reflective questions one after another: "Am I not proactive enough?"; "Am I seeing enough?"; "Am I rather pessimistic, not thinking enough?"; and so forth. The questions provoke audiences to

---

19. The performance script and performance photos are published in Wang Xiaoying, ed., *Yizhuo liangyi/ One Table Two Chairs: Yeben/Flee by Night* (Nanjing: Jiangsu fenghuang kexue jishu chubanshe, 2015), 165–297.

think about the characters, storylines, performances, institutions, and social-political meanings inherent in elitist kunqu.

Searching for interpretive references, some *1T2C* critics would recall what Ke Jun has publicly and repeatedly declared: he feels like he is the kunqu character featured in "Flee by Night." However, he is being chased not by murderous enemies but rather by a strong sense of duty to preserve and develop kunqu. As a senior kunqu master and an administrator of ShengKun, the only commercially run kunqu troupe in mainland China, Ke faces a daunting task. He must ask himself what he can and should do to preserve and develop the genre and its tradition. Having worked with Danny Yung since 2000, Ke now believes that to bring kunqu into the future, a binary strategy is needed. It should simultaneously preserve what has been inherited from the past and explore what can be created for the future.

As a leading stakeholder of kunqu in China, Ke practices what he preaches. He and his disciples and junior colleagues in ShengKun explore new artistic frontiers, but they never stop performing traditional shows. They find their old and new kunqu efforts complementary. As Sun Jing, a young ShengKun and *1T2C* performer, noted, what they have learned from Yung and other foreign masters has deepened their understanding of traditional kunqu and expanded their creative horizons.[20]

As intellectually convincing and theatrically stimulating as they are, *1T2C* works have attracted only a relatively small community of enthusiasts. By contrast, populist-experimental works by Zhang Jun (b. 1974) have attracted many fans, a fact that was demonstrated at the Shanghai Contemporary Kunqu Festival (hereafter the Shanghai Festival) held on December 7–12, 2015. A week-long *yue* event held at the Shanghai Grand Theater, the festival embodied not only Zhang Jun's creative mix of traditional, contemporary, and experimental kunqu but also his collaboration with colleagues inside and outside the kunqu world. Significantly, the festival involved four different kunqu institutions: (1) Zhang's kunqu center, a private commercial company that produces and markets kunqu shows; (2) ShengKun, the kunqu institution of Nanjing that Ke Jun directs; (3) Zuni Icosahedron, a Hong Kong not-for-profit institution of contemporary theater that Danny Yung directs; and (4) KunKun, the kunqu troupe founded in Kunshan in 2015.

Revealingly, the festival presented six stylistically contrasting shows: (1) a performance of Zhang's signature *zhezixi*, showcasing his traditional artistry in the young male role; (2) a performance of traditional *zhezixi* by Zhang's students; (3) a performance of traditional *zhezixi* by young ShengKun performers; (4) a traditional performance of the *Story of the Horse Trader* (*Fanma ji*) featuring three celebrated stars: Zhang, Li Hongniang of ShengKun, and Wei Haimin, a kunqu actress from Taiwan; (5) a performance of *1T2C* works performed by Zhang and ShengKun artists; and (6) Zhang's *Shuimo xindiao* (New water-polished kunqu music), a performance of experimental, populist-style kunqu singing and instrumental playing. As a *yue* event,

---

20. Conversation with Sun Jing and other Shengkun performers in Nanjing in May 2019.

Figure 10.2: A moment from "Dreams Long and Short." Photograph by J. Lam, 2015. Courtesy of Zhang Jun and Xu Sijia.

the festival showcased not only artistic and ideological differences among top kunqu stakeholders but also the crossroads where kunqu currently finds itself.

The 1T2C performance that dramatically challenged festival audiences to imagine what kunqu could become was the *Dreams Long and Short* (*Mengchang mengduan*), an innovative feminist take on the traditional "Strolling; Dreaming." Throughout its running time of almost thirty minutes, Zhang Jun, who played the male protagonist, lay on a couch as a man dreaming of love, making minimalist gestures sporadically. Meanwhile, Xu Sijia, a talented young ShengKun performer of the young female role, acted and danced on stage. Neither performer sang; instead, throughout the show, a recorded montage of Zhang's stylized uttering of the Chinese word *meng* (dream) was played, as sounds that evoked traditional kunqu chanting and speaking. In terms of performed sounds, movements, and sights, *Dreams Long and Short* could not be more different from traditional kunqu shows. Nevertheless, it evokes what elite kunqu connoisseurs cherish—a classical Chinese opera that seamlessly integrates verbal, sonic, and choreographic expressions into a sensually expressive and intellectually stimulating show.

Dreams Long and Short points to a future for kunqu that will serve cerebral audiences. It bears no resemblance to Zhang's hybridized and populist works that feature his new kunqu music—melodies that flow like traditional *qupai* tunes but are sung with *c-yue* played by a mixed band of *erhu*, *pipa*, violin, saxophone, guitars, drums and so forth. Zhang's new kunqu music clearly appeals to young, cosmopolitan Chinese: some arias of Zhang's experimental and populist kunqu shows have become his trademark songs, songs he often sings in his guest appearances on Chinese TV.

By staging traditional and experimental kunqu shows, the Shanghai Festival projected different routes and vistas for kunqu. Some retrospectively connect with the genre's past, while others head for uncharted futures. Their diversity reflects the multitude of solutions that have been proposed in answer to this fundamental question: how kunqu should be preserved and developed, and why, and for whom?[21] Will the genre split into multiple sub-genres for elite and commoner audiences, or will it transform into something that is simultaneously Chinese and globalized? How will the genre perform and discourse on Chinese and non-Chinese lives and dreams? What will this signify for world performing arts and ICH?

Epilogue

At present, kunqu participants have no master plan for preserving and developing the genre. Yet they know that the need to project a positive Chinese image for themselves and for their international partners has become more critical. In the third decade of the twenty-first century, traditional Chinese cultural and social values are being challenged, if not forgotten, within China; the nation's rise as a superpower is being resisted. And as *qingchun* China matures, it realizes that in addition to youth, beauty, and riches, it will also need ideals and values that will sustain Chinese people's humanity. It is significant that between 2015 and 2018, China saw a number of kunqu shows that performed and discoursed on Chinese anxieties. In 2018, for example, ShangKun and SuKun produced their own distinct versions of the *Lute*, indexing national and social debates about filial piety, loyalty, and other traditional Chinese virtues. Similarly, new productions of the *White Silk Robe* (*Bailuo shan*; SuKun, 2016, and ShengKun, 2018) highlighted conflicting emotions about what is humanly right. The drama tells the story of an adopted son who finds out that the person who has lovingly raised him is the murderer of his biological father. Should he kill one to avenge the injustice done to the other?

As contemporary kunqu tells Chinese lives and dreams with literary words, flowing music, and elegant dances, it performs and discourses on *qingchun dianya* China and Chinese people of the past and the present while connecting them with their global partners. But for the genre to carve itself a stable niche in the globalized world of competing cultures, histories, and peoples, its practitioners will have to find ways past the crossroads they have recently encountered. To identify paths forward, kunqu practitioners will have to reflect on what they have achieved, on whether they have missed opportunities, and on how they can make more effective and productive use of available resources in future and uncharted *yuescapes*. And they will have to find solid answers to many perplexing questions. What can kunqu become? A heavenly opera of China? An earthly ICH of twenty-first-century China? What stories will it tell? For whom? *Qingchun dianya* citizens of the Chinese and/or globalized world? How?

---

21. For an insightful discussion regarding Shanghai kunqu performers and expressions of their artistic selves, see Liana Chen, "Engaging Tang Xianzu and Shakespeare in the Quest for Self," *Asian Theatre Journal* 36, no. 2 (2019): 327–346.

Appendix 1
Current Kunqu Scholarship

A Sketch

Since 2001, many general and specialized studies about kunqu have been published, registering a wealth of facts and theories about the genre's biographies, performance scripts, histories, current developments, and social-political significances. To present an overview of these studies, which have guided my research, and which demonstrate the strengths and limitations of conventional kunqu scholarship, I present this sketch—publication data for the studies referenced here will, however, be presented in "Works Cited."

Currently, there are five multivolume and substantive references on kunqu that bring together conventional scholarship:

1. *Kunqu congshu* [Kunqu monographs], two series of monographs edited by Hong Weizhu and published since 2002; they include, for example, *Kunqu yanjiu ziliao suoyin* [An annotated index of kunqu research materials] and *Kunqu yanyijia qujia ji xuezhe fangwen lu* [Interviews with kunqu performers, music masters, and scholars].

2. *Kunqu yu chuantong wenhua yanjiu congshu* [Research monographs on kunqu and traditional Chinese culture], 10 volumes, written by multiple authors, and published in 2005; two representative monographs from the series are: Wu Xinlei, *Ershi shijie qianqi kunqu yanjiu* [Early twentieth-century kunqu studies]; and Zhou Yude, *Kunqu yu Ming Qing shehui* [Kunqu and Ming Qing society].

3. *Kunqu jingbian jumu diancang* [A collection of critically edited performance scripts for 300 *zhezixi*], edited by Tang Xiaobo; the collection was originally prepared as performance scripts for teaching and rehearsals at the Shanghai Academy of Theatre.

4. *Kunqu baizhong: dashi shuoxi* [One hundred kunqu masterpieces: Master performers' lecture-demonstrations on their signature shows] of 2014; a set of five books and 110 DVDs published with Ye Zhaoxin's sponsorship and coordination efforts, it preserves twenty-nine senior kunqu masters' creative and performance experiences with their celebrated *zhezixi*.

5. *Kunqu yishu dadian* [A comprehensive compendium of kunqu resources], edited and published in 2016 by the Zhongguo yishu yanjiuyuan; a gigantic collection of 149 volumes of printed words and illustrations, and 100 hours of early twentieth-century audio recordings, and 350-plus hours of audiovisual recordings of mid- and late twentieth-century performances.

There are two monumental dictionaries on kunqu. The first is Wu Xinlei's *Zhongguo kunqu dacidian/Dictionary of Chinese Kunqu Opera*, a tome of 1,149 pages. It covers practically every important topic on kunqu and provides a wealth of primary data, including representative music scores and rare photographs of historical performers and performances. The second encyclopedic reference is Hong Weizhu's *Kunqu cidian* [Kunqu dictionary], a two-volume work of 1,615 pages. In addition to concise descriptions on all important kunqu topics, it includes a chronology of kunqu history and informative catalogs on repertories, audiovisual recordings, and historical performance venues.

The number of single-volume works on kunqu history and theory is increasing. Noteworthy ones include: Chen Fong's study on kunqu performance and transmission; Hu Ji and Liu Zhizhong's panoramic account of kunqu developments; Lu Eting's pioneering work on kunqu performance history; Tian Shaodong's study of kunqu singing practices; Wu Xinlei's topical studies of kunqu history; and Zhou Qin's narrative of kunqu in Suzhou.

Since the early 2000s, many anthologies of kunqu aria lyrics, performance scripts, and notated scores have been published. Some of these are reprints of seminal works compiled or published around the turn of the nineteenth and twentieth centuries. These include notated anthologies by Wang Zhenglai, Yu Zhenfei, Zhou Qin, and other authoritative performers and scholars. Publications about kunqu choreography, costumes, and stage designs are limited. Two informative ones are Liu Yuemei's study on kunqu costume, and Ma Changshan's introduction to kunqu staging arts.

There are many kunqu autobiographies, biographies, and essay collections by individual writers. To mention but a few, they include the martial actor Hou Shaohui's autobiography; Tang Baoxiang's critical biography of Yu Zhenfei; Sang Yuxi's biographies of the Chuanzibei Masters; Zhang Weidong's essays on kunqu preservation and modernization; and Zhang Yunhe's kunqu diary.

Biographical works seldom elaborate on kunqu music and its technical features, a lacuna that has been somewhat remedied by the 2014 publication of the *Kunqu baizhong: dashi shuoxi* mentioned above. There are, however, some informative studies, which include Liu Minglan's musicological studies on kunqu composition and performance practices; Wang Shoutai's discussion of kunqu *qupai* structures and uses; Wu Junda's analyses and theories on kunqu music structures and styles, and Zhu Kunhuai's study of kunqu as a vocal performance art.

An increasing number of master's theses and doctoral dissertations are being produced in mainland China and Taiwan. Noteworthy ones include, but are not limited to, Xuan Leilei's dissertation on current kunqu scholarship; Pan Yanna's examination of the ShangKun production of *The Palace of Everlasting Life*; Ke Fan's study of contemporary kunqu transmission and development; and Chen Chunmiao's historical study of kunqu scores published in late nineteenth- and early twentieth-century China.

Many kunqu studies have appeared in academic journals and conference proceedings. Two leading kunqu serials are: the *Zhongguo kunqu luntan* (Chinese kunqu discussions), published since 2010, and the *Zhongguo kunqu nianjian* (Yearbook of kunqu opera—China), published since 2012. Many papers presented at occasional kunqu conferences

Appendix 1

are published in single-volume anthologies. Two representative examples are Hua Wei's *Kunqu, chunsan eryue tian: miandui shijie de kunqu yu Mudanting* (Kunqu, springtime: kunqu and *The Peony Pavilion* facing the globalized world), and Liu Zhen's *Beifang kunqu lunji* (Essays on northern kunqu). A profusion of short and journalistic writings on kunqu have appeared on personal blogs and institutional websites. The veracity and significance of kunqu facts and insights preserved in these non-academic essays, however, awaits critical assessment.

Western scholarship on kunqu remains underdeveloped, even though a small number of scholars have published some substantive studies. Their names include Andrea Goldman (cultural-social history of Chinese theatre), He Yuming (Ming culture, literature, and performance), Joseph Lam (kunqu history, music, and repertory), Lindy Li Mark (kunqu history and performance), Richard Strassberg (kunqu librettos and performance), Catherine Swatek (kunqu performance and literature), Isabel Wong (kunqu sources and performance), Xu Peng (kunqu history and resources), and Judith Zeitlin (kunqu literature, history, and performance).

Currently, there are only seven monographs in English that comprehensively or thematically discuss kunqu. The first one is Catherine Swatek's *Peony Pavilion Onstage: Four Centuries in the Career of A Chinese Drama*. Written from literary and performance perspectives, it gives a panoramic view of the performance and reception history of *The Peony Pavilion* since its premiere in the 1590s. The second is Xiao Li's *Chinese Kunqu Opera*, a translation of a short historical account written in Chinese by the author, and a presentation of many informative photographs of kunqu performances. The third is *Writings on the Theory of Kun Qu Singing* (2006) by Koo Siusun and Diana Yue. In four volumes, this work presents original Chinese texts of four seminal treatises of kunqu theories, their English translations, and bilingual annotations. The fourth is A.C. Scott's *Traditional Chinese Plays, Vol. 2: Longing for Worldly Pleasures/Ssu Fan and Fifteen Strings of Cash/Shi Wu Kuan*. This work presents full English translations of two seminal kunqu plays as well as informative introductions on their performance practices. The fifth is William Dolby's *A History of Chinese Drama*, which is not a dedicated discussion of kunqu, but rather a general account of historical Chinese theater. Its chapters on kunqu history in Ming and Qing China are concise and informative. The sixth is Andrea Goldman's *Opera and the City: The Politics of Culture in Beijing, 1770–1900*, a cultural and social history of Chinese theatre in Beijing, the Qing capital where kunqu once blossomed. The seventh is Daphne Lei's *Alternative Chinese Opera in the Age of Globalization: Performing Zero*, which includes a chapter on kunqu in global contexts.

There is a small collection of kunqu theses and dissertations written in English and other non-Chinese languages. Four were written before 2000: Wang Guangqi's 1934 dissertation for Bonn University, Germany, an introduction to kunqu; Majorie Bong-ray Liu's "Tradition and Change in Kunqu Opera," a 1976 dissertation for UCLA; Jean-Marie Fégly's "Théatre chinois: survivance, développement et activité du kunqu au Xxe siècle," a 1986 dissertation for Université de Paris VII; and Luo Qin's "Kunju, Chinese Classical Theater and Its Revival in Social, Political, Economic and Cultural Contexts," a 1997 dissertation for Kent State University.

Nine dissertations written in English were recently completed: Kim Hunter Gordon's "Contesting Traditional *Luzi* (Choreographic Paths'): A Performance-Based Study of Kunqu" (Royal Holloway, University of London, 2016); Shih-huang Hsu's "Chinese Kunqu in Contemporary Times and Self-Orientalism: Inheritance and Reinvention of Traditional Art in An Economic Age" (Royal Holloway, University of London, 2018); Juliane Jones's "Contemporary Kun Opera Composition" (University of British Columbia, Vancouver, 2014); Da Lin's "The Political Economy of Kun Opera in China (1940s–2015)" (University of Pittsburgh, 2017); Min Yen Ong's "Kunqu in Twenty-First Century China: Musical Change and Amateur Practices" (SOAS University of London, 2013); and Xu Peng's "Lost Sound: Singing, Theater, and Aesthetics in Late Ming China" (University of Chicago, 2014); Ju-Hua Wei's, "Kunqu in Practice: A Case Study," (University of Hawai'i, 2019); Ming Yang, "Return of the Soul: In Heritance and Innovation in the Process of Artistic Creation in Major Kunqu Productions in the People's Republic of China, 2001–2015" (University of Hawai'i, 2019), and Wei Zhou's "A *Peony* Transplanted: Pai Hsien-yung and the Preservation of Chinese *Kunqu*, dissertation," (University of Edinburgh, 2011).

At least two are in progress. They are: Minlei Ye's dissertation on kunqu in early twentieth-century Shanghai (Princeton University) and Yihui Sheng's "Beyond the Text: Excavating a New Understanding of *Chuanqi* in Early Modern China" (University of Michigan).

In addition to these English monographs and dissertations, a number of publications written in French, German and Japanese are available. Regarding French publications of kunqu, Luo Shilong has published his "Kunqu zai faguo de chuanbo, fazhan, yu yanjiu" [Kunqu transmission, development, and research in France), an informative survey. Representative German and Japanese publications include, for example, *Studie zum Kunqu in Geschichte und Gegenwart* by Mei Wei; *Kunqu: Die Klassische Chinesische Oper Des 16–19 Jahrhundert* by Rudolf Brandl and Qu Liuyi; and *Nogaku to Konkyoku: Nihon to Chugoku no koten engeki wo tanoshimu* (Noh and kunqu: An appreciation of classical theatres of Japan and China) by Akamatsu Norihiko, Komatsu Ken, and Yamazaki Yoshiyuki. Wei's work is a case study of several kunqu arias (*qupai*); Brandl and Qu's monograph is a survey. The Japanese publication compares *noh* and kunqu by contrasting their histories, acting and dancing practices, and scripts. Though short and selective, it heralds a productive methodology for comparing kunqu and its Japanese counterpart.

Providing an abundance of contextual and pertinent information about kunqu is a large collection of scholarly and English publications on Chinese expressive culture, including its theatrical traditions. Representative monographs in these studies include but are not limited to those published by Joshua Goldstein, Nancy Guy, Colin Mackerras, Siu-Leung Li, Jonathan Stock, David Rolston, Elizabeth Wichmann, and Bell Yung. There are some informative articles by Andrea Goldman, He Yuming, Joseph S. C. Lam, Lindy Li Mark, François Picard, Grant Shen, Xu Peng, and Judith Zeitlin. Goldman's article on "Yearning for the Secular World," for example, sheds light on the show's historical and social-political meanings. He Yuming's "Difficulties of Performance: The Musical Career of Xu Wei's *The Mad Drummer*" provides an innovative and practical model for probing

Appendix 1

historical kunqu composition and performance. François Picard's "*Qupai* in Kunqu: Text-Music Issues," which he co-authored with Kar Lun Alan Lau, presents a concise introduction to a musically technical topic.

Collectively, Chinese and international kunqu scholarship is substantive and is rapidly expanding. It not only describes the genre's historical and current manifestations but also demonstrates its relevance to scholarship about Chinese and world cultures and performing arts. Nevertheless, current kunqu scholarship still has obvious lacunae and limitations; for example, the dearth of technical studies of the genre's repertory and composition and performance practices is painfully obvious and should be remedied as soon as possible.

Appendix 2
Titles of Kunqu Dramas, *Zhezixi*, and *Qupai*

I. Drama

14:28	*Earthquake at 14:28*
1699 Taohua shan 1699 桃花扇	*1699 Peach Blossom Fan*
Bailuo shan 白羅衫	*White Silk Shirt*
Baitu ji 白兔記	*The Story of the White Rabbit*
Baojian ji 寶劍記	*The Story of the Precious Sword*
Changsheng dian 長生殿	*The Palace of Everlasting Life*
Chunjiang huayue ye 春江花月夜	*Flowers and Moonlight by the River in Spring; Spring River*
Dandao hui 單刀會	*The Story of Guan Yu's Visiting His Rival's Camp Barely Armed*
Dongchuang shifa 東窗事發	*The Story of a Crime Plotted by the East Window*
Dou'e yuan 竇娥冤	*Injustice Done to Woman Dou E*
Fanma ji 販馬記	*A Horse Trader's Tragedy*
Feidu luding qiao 飛渡瀘定橋	*The Swift Crossing of Luding Bridge*
Fengyun hui 風雲會	*Heroes Gathering at a Turbulent Time*
Gongsun Zidu 公孫子都	*The Story of General Gongsun Zidu*
Gu Yanwu 顧炎武	*The Story of Gu Yanwu*
Handan meng 邯鄲夢	*Scholar Lu's Brief Dream of a Successful Life*
Honglou meng 紅樓夢	*The Dream of the Red Chamber*
Hudie meng 蝴蝶夢	*The Butterfly Dream*
Lanke shan 爛柯山	*The Story of the Mountain of Rotten Axe Handle*
Lianxiang ban 怜香伴	*Dames in Love*
Mudan ting 牡丹亭	*The Peony Pavilion*
Nanke meng 南柯夢	*Chunyu Fen's Dream*
Niehai ji 孽海記	*World of Sins*

Appendix 2

Pipa ji 琵琶記	*The Lute*
Pipa ji: Cai Bojie 琵琶記：蔡伯喈	*The Lute: Cai Bojie*
Qianli song Jingniang 千里送京娘	*Escorting Lady Jing Home*
Qianzhong lu 千鐘戮	*Killing of Patriots*
Qingchunban Mudan ting 青春版牡丹亭	*The Peony Pavilion, the Young Lovers' Edition; The Young Lovers*
Qusheng: Wei Liangfu 曲聖魏良輔	*The Kunqu Sage: Wei Liangfu*
Shihou ji 獅吼記	*The Lioness Roars*
Shiwu guan 十五貫	*The Fifteen Strings of Coins*
Tangsha hui Handan meng 湯沙會邯鄲夢	*A Shakespearean Handan Dream*
Taohua shan 桃花扇	*The Peach Blossom Fan*
Wansha ji 綄紗記	*The Story of Washing Silk*
Woshi hamulaite 我是哈姆來德	*I, Hamlet*
Xihe 夕鶴	*The Crane*
Xixiang ji 西廂記	*The Story of the Western Wing*
Xiyou ji 西遊記	*Journey to the West*
Xueshou ji 血手記	*The Blood-Stained Hands*
Yanzi jian 燕子箋	*Swallow Letters*
Yuzan ji 玉簪記	*The Jade Hairpin*
Zichaij i 紫釵記	*The Purple Hairpin*
Zuixinhua 醉心花	*Belladonna and Intoxicated Hearts*

II. Zhezixi

"Baihua zengjian" 百花贈劍	"The Princess Gives Her Lover a Sword"
"Beijie" 別姬	"Farewell to the Concubine"
"Chikang" 吃糠	"Eating Husk"
"Chimeng" 痴夢	"Idiotic Dreams"
"Chuangai" 傳概	"Introduction"
"Chuange" 傳歌	"Music Lesson"
"Cihu" 刺虎	"Killing a Warlord"
"Dexin; Zhongyuan" 得信；重圓	"Message Received; Reunion"
"Dingqing" 定情	"Pledging Love"
"Duanqiao" 斷橋	"Reunion at the Broken Bridge"
"Fang Pu" 訪普	"Emperor Taizu Visits Zhao Pu"
"Fangcui" 訪翠	"Visiting the Beauties"

"Fubing" 伏兵 — "Mollifying Troops"

"Goudong" 狗洞 — "Dog Exit"

"Guichi" 跪池 — "Kneeling by the Pond"

"Hewei" 合圍 — "Hunting Games"

"Huozhuo" 活捉 — "Taken Alive"

"Jiandu" 見都 — "An Audience with the Censor"

"Jiaqi" 佳期 — "Happy Time"

"Jishan" 寄扇 — "Sending the Fan"

"Jizi" 寄子 — "Wu Yuan Entrusts His Son to a Friend"

"Kuiyu" 窺浴 — "Peeping at Imperial Bathers"

"Kuxiang" 哭像 — "Lamenting in front of Yang Guifei's Wooden Statue"; "Lamenting"

"Maiyu" 埋玉 — "Burying Yang Guifei"

"Mengchang mengduan" 夢長夢短 — "Dreams Long and Short"

"Mingpan" 冥判 — "Infernal Judgment"

"Mishi" 密誓 — "Intimate Pledge"

"Qintiao" 琴挑 — "Zither Seduction"

"Qiujiang" 秋江 — "Autumn Farewell"

"Sao Qin" 掃秦 — "Scolding Qin Kui"

"Shanghe" 賞荷 — "Viewing Lotus Blossom"

"Shanmen" 山門 — "The Drunken Monk Shatters the Gateway"

"Shuang xiashan" 雙下山 — "The Young Nun and Monk Leave for the Secular World"

"Shuguan" 書館 — "Reunion in the Studio"

"Shuoqin" 說親 — "Marriage Proposal"

"Sifan" 思凡 — "Yearning for the Secular World"

"Songshou" 嵩壽 — "Birthday Gifts for Yan Song"

"Tai Bai zuixie" 太伯醉寫 — "Li Bai Composes Poetry While Drunk"

"Tanci" 彈詞 — "Ballad Singing"

"Tihua" 題畫 — "Writing on the Fan"

"Tiqu" 題曲 — "Commenting on *The Peony Pavilion*"

"Toushi" 偷詩 — "Snatching Manuscripts"

"Wenyue; Zhipu" 聞樂 制譜 — "Yang Guifei Dreams and Notates the Music of *The Rainbow Dress of Feather*"

"Wenyue" 聞樂 — "Yang Guifei Dreams of Heavenly Music"

"Wupen" 舞盆 — "Dancing on a Disk"

"Xianfa" 獻髮 — "A Gift of Hair"

Appendix 2

"Xianguan" 獻館   "Surrendering to the Rebels"
"Xiansheng" 先聲   "Introduction by the Story-Teller"
"Xiaoyan jingbian" 小宴驚變   "A Garden Party; Shocking News"
"Xiaoyan" 小宴   "Casual gathering"
"Xiezhen" 寫真   "Painting a Self-Portrait"
"Xunmeng" 尋夢   "Searching for the Dream"
"Yeben" 夜奔   "Flee by Night"
"Yougou" 幽媾   "Nightly Rendezvous"
"Youyuan jingmeng" 遊園驚夢   "Strolling; Dreaming"
"Zheliu yangguan" 折柳楊關   "Bidding Farewell with Willow Twigs"
"Zhipu" 制譜   "Notating Music"

III. *Qupai*/Musical Works

"Chaoyuange" 朝元歌
"Desheng ling" 得勝令
"Dian jiangchun" 點絳唇
"Dou anchun" 斗鵪鶉
"Fendie'er" 粉蝶兒
"Guanglingsan" 廣陵散
"Huangying'er" 黃鶯兒
"Huolang'er" 貨郎兒
"Jinong" 寄弄
"Jinshe kuangwu" 金蛇狂舞
"Ji xianbin" 集賢賓
"Lanhuamei" 懶畫眉
"Lizhixiang" 荔枝香
"Nichang yuyi qu" 霓裳羽衣曲
"Qinqu" 琴曲
"Qi yanhui" 泣顏回
"Shanbo yang" 山坡羊
"Shi'erhong" 十二紅
"Tuobushan" 脫布衫
"Xiaoxiang shuiyun" 瀟湘水雲
"Yan'er lou" 雁兒落
"Zaimeibian" 在梅邊
"Zao luopao" 皂羅袍

Appendix 3
Music Examples

These music examples are notated to demonstrate structural features of the kunqu arias being discussed. Melodic, rhythmic, and linguistic-tonal details and phrasal divisions reflect traditional interpretations that Wang Zhenglai, Yu Zhenfei, and Zhou Qin have presented in their *gongche* and/or *cipher* scores of kunqu music, which are, respectively, the *Quyuan zhuiying*, the *Zhenfei qupu*, and the *Cunxin qupu*. Romanizations of Chinese words in the lyrics are provided to facilitate comparison of different singers' kunqu-stage pronunciation with *Putonghua* of contemporary China. Music Examples 1 through 7 and 9 were notationally created with Sibelius by my assistants, Casper Chan, Huang Jingyun, and Conner VanderBeek. Musical Example 8 is a transcription by Ye Yancheng. Music Example 10 is taken from Zhou Youliang's published score.

Appendix 3

Music Example 1: "Pink Butterfly" ("Fendie'er") Aria 1 in "A Garden Party; Shocking News."

Music Example 2: "Taking the Cloth Shirt Off" ("Tuobushan"), "Short Liangzhou" ("Xiao Liangzhou"), and "Repeat," Arias 4 through 6 in the "Lamenting."

Appendix 3

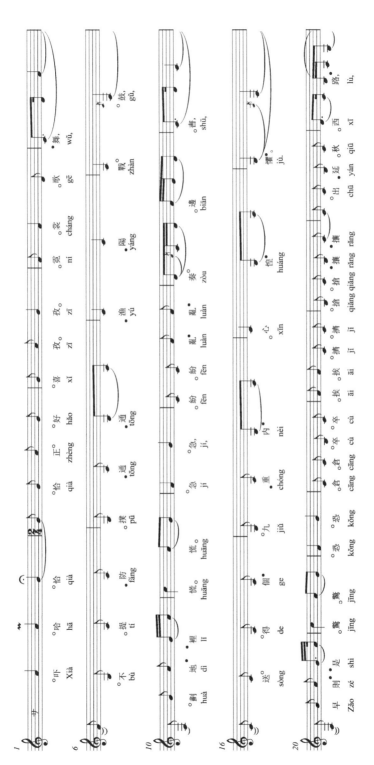

Music Example 3: "The Peddler, the Sixth Variation" ("Huolang'er, liuzhuan"), Aria 8 in the "Ballad Singing."

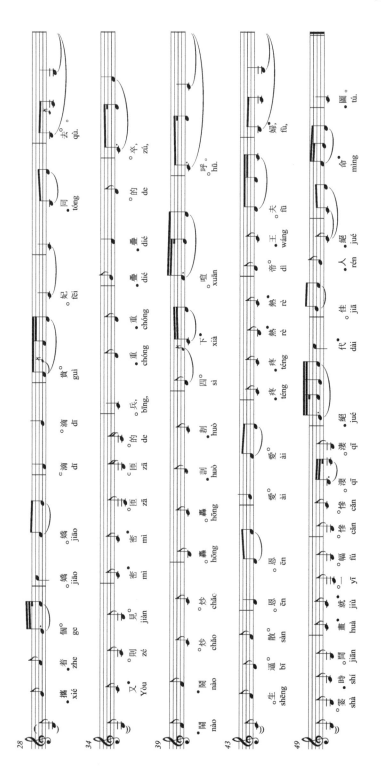

Music Example 3 (continued)

Appendix 3

Music Example 4: "The Peddler, the Seventh Variation" ("Huolang'er, qizbuan"), Aria 9 in the "Ballad Singing."

Music Example 5: "Sheep on the Slope" ("Shanbo yang"), Aria 1 in "Yearning for the Secular World."

Appendix 3

Music Example 5 (continued)

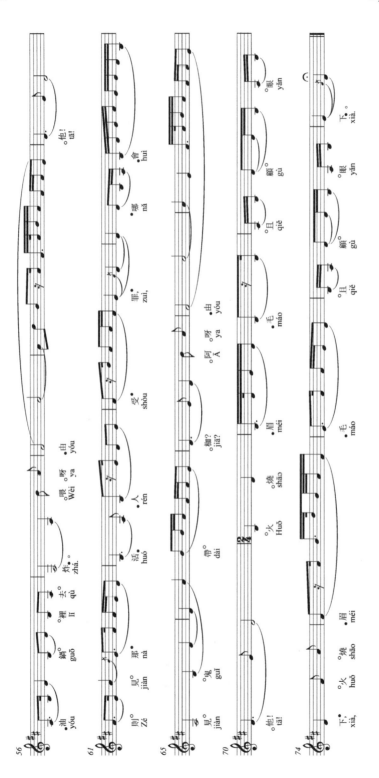

Music Example 5 (continued)

Appendix 3

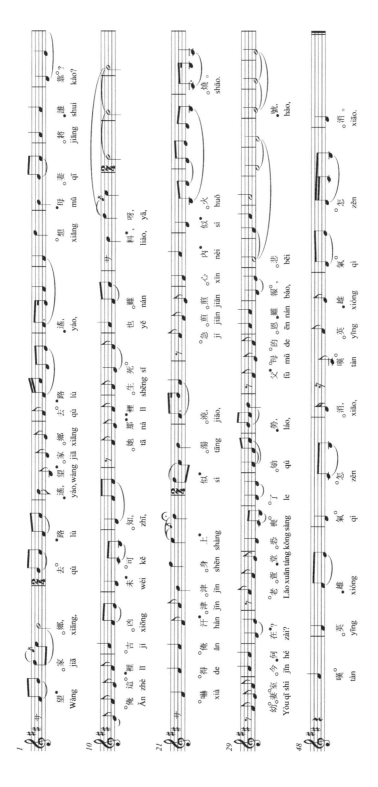

Music Example 6: "Geese Descending from the Sky" ("Yan'er luo") and "Being Victorious" ("Desheng ling"), Aria 6 in "Flee by Night."

Music Example 7: "Lazy Bird" ("Lanhuamei"), Arias 1 to 4 in the "Zither Seduction."

Appendix 3

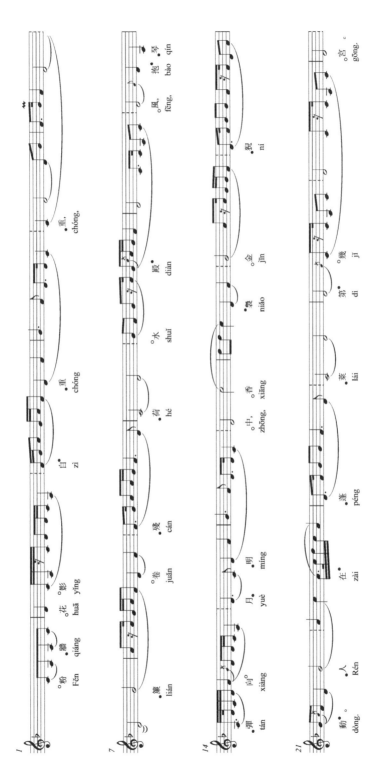

Music Example 7 (continued)

232

Music Example 7 (continued)

Appendix 3

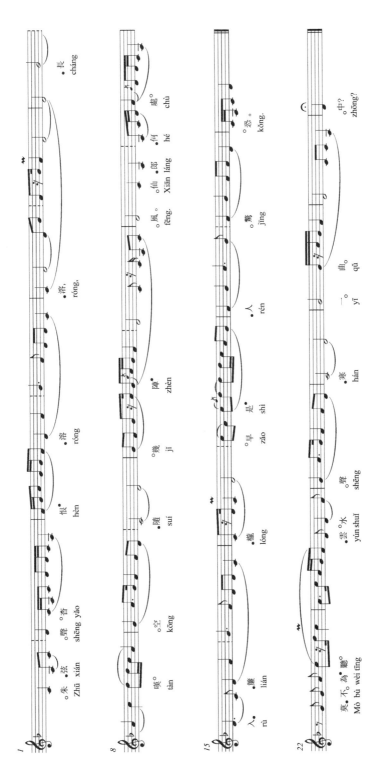

Music Example 7 (continued)

234 Appendix 3

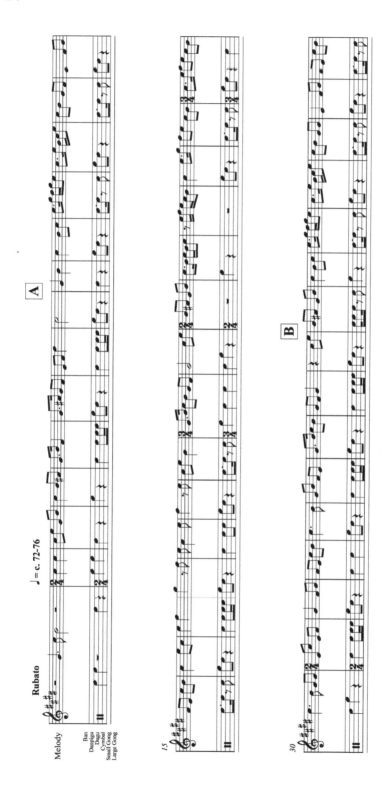

Music Example 8: "Pipa Tune," incidental music in the "Audience" scene of the *Fifteen Strings of Coins.*

Appendix 3

Music Example 8 (continued)

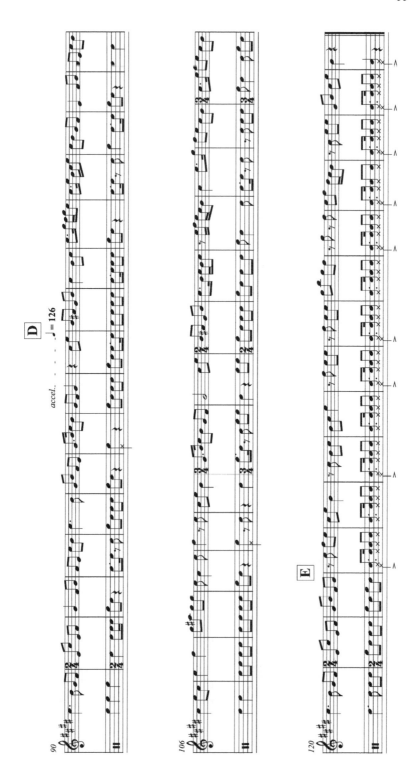

Music Example 8 (continued)

Appendix 3

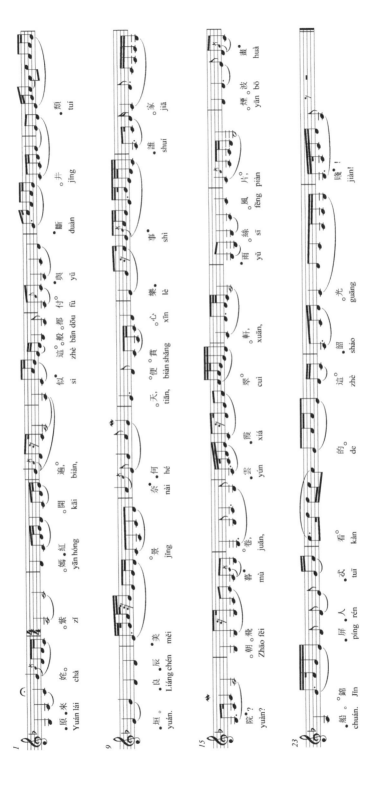

Music Example 9: "Dark Silk Robe" ("Zaoluopao"), Aria 4 in "Strolling; Dreaming."

Music Example 10: "'Jingmeng huashen' wudao yinyue zongpu" (Orchestral Score for the Flower Angels' Dance in the "Strolling; Dreaming" scene in the *Young Lovers*). Source: Zhou Youliang, *Qingchunban Mudanting quanpu* (Suzhou: Suzhou daxue chubanshe, 2015), 210–212.

Appendix 3

239

Music Example 10 (continued)

Appendix 4

Links to Online Audiovisual Kunqu Recordings

"*1699 Taohuashan* juzhao." Accessed September 25, 2020. http://image.haosou.com/i?src= rel&q=%E6%98%86%E6%9B%B2%E6%A1%83%E8%8A%B1%E6%89%871699%E5 %89%A7%E7%85%A7.

"*1699 Taohuashan* juzhao." Accessed September 25, 2020. http://image.haosou.com/i?src= rel&q=%E6%98%86%E6%9B%B2%E6%A1%83%E8%8A%B1%E6%89%871699%E5 %89%A7%E7%85%A7.

"Dog Exit" ("Goudong"), performance by Wang Chuansong. Accessed September 20, 2019. https://www.youtube.com/watch?v=GJWNaesxaAE.

"Flee by Night" ("Yeben"), singing by Hou Yongkui (sound; 1954) and acting by You Shaokui (2000). Accessed May 17, 2021. https://www.youtube.com/watch?v= XBcB7IE4djs&t=7s.

"Liu Runen zhi kunqu changshengdian tanci quan chu" [Liu Run'en Sings "Tanci" from the *Palace of Everlasting Life*]. Accessed October 15, 2020. https://www.bilibili.com/video/ av838290799/.

"Marriage Proposal" ("Shuoqin") from the *The Butterfly Dream*, performance by Liu Yilong and Xing Jingsha. Accessed May 16, 2021. https://www.youtube.com/watch?v= pBpkKWMlDY4.

"New Shuimo xindiao," performance by Zhang Jun. Accessed May 17, 2021. https://www. youtube.com/watch?v=WGuaKCb-LPU.

"*Peony Pavilion* with English Subtitle," performance by SuKun. Accessed November 23, 2021. www.youtube.com/watch?v=AV1JMA1CwrI.

"Scolding Qin Hui" ("Sao Qin"), 1998 performance by Wang Chuansong. Accessed March 20, 2018. www.youtube.com/watch?v=QbcuUwPcOJ0.

"Scolding Qin Kui" ("Sao Qi"), performance by ShangKun. Accessed March 10, 2018. www. youtube.com/watch?v=QbcuUwPcOJ0.

"Tai Bai Writes Poetry While Drunk" ("Taibai zuixie"), performance by Yu Zhenfei. Accessed May 16, 2021. https://www.youtube.com/watch?v=oliJFMuo_JM.

"Taken Alive" ("Huozhuo"), performance by Liang Guyin and Liu Yilong. Accessed May 16, 2021. https://www.youtube.com/watch?v=sqcrXxn_Zek&t=86s.

"Wu Yuan Entrusts His Son to a Friend," performance by Zheng Chuanjian and Fang Chuanyi. Accessed November 23, 2021. https://www.youtube.com/results?search_query=%E5% B4%91%E6%9B%B2%E5%AF%84%E5%AD%90.

"Yearning for the Secular World" ("Sifan"), performance by Liang Guyin. Accessed May 15, 2021. https://www.youtube.com/watch?v=hrBAOqDMXnA&t=777s.

Appendix 4 241

"Yearning for the Secular World" ("Sifan"), performance by Shen Shihua. Accessed May 15, 2021. https://www.youtube.com/watch?v=MaNfIn4Hvbc&list=RDMaNfIn4Hvbc&start_radio=1.

"Yu Sulu Sings Kunqu," 1921 performance by Yu Sulu. Accessed May 17, 2021. https://www.youtube.com/watch?v=4LVNuNvrJ-g.

"Zai meibian," performance by Wang Leehom. Accessed May 15, 2021. https://www.youtube.com/watch?v=2YFDMXXf3ws.

1699 Peach Blossom Fan, 2006 performance by ShengKun. Accessed May 16, 2021. https://www.youtube.com/watch?v=CUPkUkLT69Y&t=7984s.

600 Years of Kunqu Opera, the (*Kunqu 600 nian*). Accessed May 15, 2021. https://www.youtube.com/results?search_query=600+years+of+kunqu.

Belladonna and Intoxicated Hearts (*Zuixinhua*). Accessed July 23, 2020. https://www.youtube.com/watch?v=Fxwlb8CaL00; https://www.youtube.com/watch?v=a7WLJP-ZdFs; https://www.youtube.com/watch?v=Yp6bdXPqoSw&t=1365s.

Book 1: https://www.youtube.com/watch?v=kn1du7m-vj8&t=3637s

Book 2: https://www.youtube.com/watch?v=rcYkExD7Szc&t=50s

Book 3: https://www.youtube.com/watch?v=MwFUbkkbuDQ&t=106s

Fifteen Strings of Coins, the (*Shiwuguan*), 1956 opera-movie by ZheKun. Accessed April 23, 2021. https://www.youtube.com/watch?v=2jjNDkbCVTk&t=4134s.

I, Hamlet (*Woshi, Hamulaite*), 2017 performance by Zhang Jun. Accessed May 16, 2021. https://www.youtube.com/watch?v=c8EhZxUHBn4&t=1149s.

Jade Hairpin (*Yuzan ji*), 1950s performance by Bai Yunsheng and Han Shichang. Accessed September 28, 2019. https://www.bilibili.com/video/av13811300/.

Jade Hairpin, 1957 performance by Yu Zhenfei and Yan Weizhu. Accessed January 18, 2016. www.youtube.com/watch?v=O9mEo0muk-o.

Jade Hairpin, 1981 performance by Yu Zhenfei and Zhang Xian. Accessed on January 18, 2016. http://v.youku.com/v_show/id_XMzc4NjQ2MjQ4.html.

Jade Hairpin, 1985 performance by Hua Wenyi and Yue Meiti. Accessed May 16, 2021. www.youtube.com/watch?v=pqLYPefnV3g.

Jade Hairpin, 1988 performance by Wang Shiyu and Wang Fengmei. Accessed on May 16, 2021. https://www.bilibili.com/video/av56425644/.

Jade Hairpin, 2004 performance by Yue Meiti and Zhang Jingxian. Accessed May 16, 2021. www.youtube.com/watch?v=-flPnhK3hyM.

Jade Hairpin, 2009 performance by Shen Fengying and Yu Jiulin. Accessed May 16, 2021. www.youtube.com/watch?v=URmZI1YaT6Q.

Lioness Roars (*Shihao ji*), 2004 performance by Yue Meiti and Zhang Jingxian. Accessed May 16, 2021. https://www.youtube.com/watch?v=K7x6hxfB-10&t=5777s.

Lute (*Pipaji*), 2018 performance by ShangKun. Accessed March 18, 2021. https://www.youtube.com/watch?v=hPxoFHA9F-8&t=400s.

Lute: Cai Bojie, 2019 performance at the Michigan State Theater, Ann Arbor. Accessed May 16, 2021. https://www.youtube.com/watch?v=4Zp6eX0ikTQ&t=217s.

Palace of Everlasting Life (*Changsheng dian*), 2004 performance by SuKun. Accessed May 16, 2021. https://www.bilibili.com/video/av12636683/.

Palace of Everlasting Life (*Changsheng dian*), 2007 performance by Cai Zhengren and Zhang Jingxian. Accessed May 16, 2021. https://www.youtube.com/watch?v=sS9lLXb951M.

242   Appendix 4

Palace of Everlasting Life (*Changsheng dian*), 2018 performance by ShangKun. Accessed May 16, 2021.
  Book 1: https://www.youtube.com/watch?v=qTzPhRUTnxQ&t=229s
  Book 2: https://www.youtube.com/watch?v=28-5frwFYP8&t=7201s
  Book 3: https://www.youtube.com/watch?v=Xjwr6xl28XM&t=4892s
  Book 4: https://www.youtube.com/watch?v=xAUw7rFLn-4&t=267s
Peach Blossom Fan (*Taohuashan*): "Writing on the Fan" ("Tihua"), performance by Shi Xiaomei. Accessed March 15, 2018. www.youtube.com/watch?v=FpDQEbWkqs4.
Peach Blossom Fan, 2018 performance by ShengKun. Accessed May 16, 2021. https://www.youtube.com/watch?v=yI3LJ2qOMJY.
Peony Pavilion (*Mudan ting*), 1960 performance by Mei Lanfang, Yan Huizhu, and Yu Zhenfei. Accessed May 16, 2021. https://www.youtube.com/watch?v=nNydt77MhzQ&t=2759s.
Peony Pavilion, 1987 performance by Zhang Jiqing. Accessed May 16, 2021. www.youtube.com/watch?v=VWuEZkjK7ak.
Peony Pavilion, 1989 performance by Cai Zhengren Zhang Xunpeng. Accessed March 28, 2009. www.youtube.com/watch?v=vDTEooXzqI4.
Peony Pavilion, 1999, performance at the Lincoln Center. Accessed May 16, 2021. https://www.bilibili.com/video/BV1zs411E7FB?from=search&seid=9542734331279525047.
Peony Pavilion, 2004 performance by SuKun. Accessed May 16, 2021.
Peony Pavilion, 2008–2010 performance by Bando Tamasaburo and SuKun. Uploaded by Tamasaburo on May 9, 2008. Accessed May 16, 2021. www.youtube.com/watch?v=J8AB-Y1DfVY.
Peony Pavilion, 2012 performance by Zhang Jun at the Astor Court, NY Metropolitan Museum. Accessed September 2016. https://metmuseum.org/media/video/concerts/peony-pavilion.
Peony Pavilion, 2014–2015 Masters' Performance (*Kunqu Dashiban Mudanting*). Uploaded by Bilibili April 3, 2017. Accessed May 16, 2021. https://www.bilibili.com/video/av9595586/.
Story of General Gongsun Zidu (*Gongsun Zidu*), performance by ZheKun. Accessed April 23, 2018. Youtube.com/watch?v/=D5kia8H5NKY.
Story of Guan Yu's Visiting His Rival's Camp Barely Armed (*Dandaohu*), performance by Hou shaohui. Accessed May 15, 2021. https://www.bilibili.com/video/av17317932/.
Story of the Mountain of Rotten Axe Handle, the (*Lanke shan*), performance by Zhang Jiqing. Accessed September 23, 2019. https://www.youtube.com/watch?v=rLqhmPPr1V8.
Story of the White Rabbit, the (*Baitu ji*), performance by XiangKun. Accessed May 16, 2021. https://www.bilibili.com/video/av4637119/.
Zhezixi, 2012 performance at the University of Michigan. Accessed May 16, 2021. https://www.youtube.com/watch?v=as4GguYZXcs&t=72s.
Zhezixi, performance for the New York Kunqu Society, featuring ShangKun artists. Accessed March 28, 2019. http://asiasociety.org/new-york/three-shanghai-kunqu-opera performances-new-york-audiences.

Glossary

Note: Common nouns are in italics; proper nouns are marked with actual dates or the adjective of "contemporary"; character names are not dated.

Ah Jia 阿甲 (1907–1994)
aibu 矮步
An Lushan 安祿山 (703–757)
Bai Chongxi 白崇熙 (1893–1966)
Bai Juyi 白居易 (772–846)
Bai Pu 白樸 (1226–after 1306)
Bai Xianyong 白先勇 (b. 1937)
Bai Yusheng 白雲生 (1902–1972)
Baimao nü 白毛女
baimian 白面
baishi li 拜師禮
ban 板
Bando Tamasaburo 坂東玉三郎 (b. 1950)
bangzou 伴奏
banqiang 板腔
Bao Hansuo 包涵所 (fl. 1630s)
baohu 保護
baoyin 爆音
Bei Jinmei 貝晉眉 (1887–1968)
beiguan 北管
beikun 北崑
BeiKun 北崑 (Beifang kunju yuan) 北方崑劇院
beiqu 北曲
ben 本
bense 本色

bianju 編劇
biaoyan jia 表演家
biaoyan yishu jia 表演藝術家
Cai Zhengren 蔡正仁 (b. 1941)
caizi 才子
Canglang ting 滄浪亭
Cao Shaohua 蔡少華 (contemporary)
caokun 草崑
celü 策略
chang 唱
Chang Tongching 張冬青 (contemporary)
changqiang chuangzuo 唱腔創作
changqiang zhengli 唱腔整理
chayuan 茶園
Chen Jichang 陳季常
Chen Mei-e 陳美娥 (contemporary)
Chen Miaochang 陳妙常
Chen Yi 陳怡 (b. 1953)
Chen Yuanyuan 陳圓圓 (1623–1695)
chenghuang 城隍
chengji 承繼
chou 丑
chu 齣
chuanben 串本
chuancheng 傳承
chuangcheng ban 傳承版

244 Glossary

chuancheng jihua 傳承計畫

chuangxin 創新

chuanqi 傳奇

chuantong 傳統

Chuanyi zhongxin 傳藝中心

Chunxiang 春香

chun 春

chushen renhua 出神入化

cishadan 刺殺旦

Cui Shi 崔氏

cui 啐

da xiongmao 大熊貓

dabaiguang 大白光

daiqiang 帶腔

damian 大面

dan 旦

danpi gu 單皮鼓

Daohe qushe 道和曲社

daoma dan 刀馬旦

daoyan 導演

dashi 大師

Datong yuehui 大同樂會

dawo 大我

Daya 大雅

Dazhang 大章

dazhong 大眾

dianqiang 墊腔

dianya 典雅

diban 底板

Ding Ling 丁玲 (1904–1986)

dingwei 定位

dizi 笛子

Dong Fei 董飛 (contemporary)

Du Fu 杜甫 (712–770)

Du Liniang 杜麗娘

duqu 度曲

erhu 二胡

Fang Yang 方洋 (b. 1940)

fan 犯

fanggu 仿古

fangzhi 仿製

fazhan 發展

feiwuzhi wenhua yichan 非物質文化遺產

feiyi 非遺

fengguan 鳳冠

fengjian 封建

fengliu 風流

fensi 粉絲

fo 拂

Fu Chai 夫差 (?–473 BCE)

Fu Xihua 傅惜華 (1907–1970)

fugui 富貴

fuguiyi 富貴衣

fumo 副末

Fuwang 福王 (1607–1646)

fuwu 服務

fuzhuang sheji 服裝設計

gaige kaifang 改革開放

gaige 改革

gailiang 改良

Gao Lian 高濂 (1573–1620)

Gao Lishi 高力士

gaohu 高胡

ge 歌

gehu 革胡

geming yangban xi 革命樣板戲

Gong Yi 龔一 (b. 1941)

Gongsu Zidu 公孫子都 (fl ca. 700 BCE?)

gongche 工尺

Gu Chuanjie 顧傳玠 (1910–1965)

Gu Dehui 顧德輝 (1310–1369)

Gu Duhuang 顧篤璜 (b. 1933)

Gu Jian 顧堅 (fl. 1360s?)

Gu Tiehua 顧鐵華 (contemporary)

Gu Xin 顧欣 (b. 1956)

Gu Yanwu 顧炎武 (1613–1682)

guansheng 官生

guanyi 官衣

Glossary

gudian 古典

guibu 鬼步

guifu shengong 鬼斧神功

Guo Xiaozhuang 郭小莊 (contemporary)

guochang yinyue 過場音樂

guomen 過門

guoqu 過曲

gushi 鼓師

guwan 古玩

guxitai 古戲台

ha 哈

Han Shichang 韓世昌 (1898–1976)

Hantan yuefu 漢唐樂府

hao 好

haohan 好漢

haohua 豪華

haokan 好看

haoting 好聽

Hong Sheng 洪昇 (1645–1704)

Hong Weizhu 洪維助 (b. 1934)

Hou Fangyu 侯方域 (1618–1655)

Hou Shaokui 侯少奎 (b. 1939)

Hou Yongkui 侯永奎 (1911–1981)

Hou Yushan 侯玉山 (1893–1996)

Hua Wenyi 華文漪 (b. 1941)

huabu 花部

huadan 花旦

huali 華麗

Huangjia liangcang 皇家糧倉

huayin 花音

huiyan 匯演

huo 活

iemoto 家元

Ji Can 姬燦

Ji Zhenhua 計鎮華 (b. 1943)

jia 假

jiaben 家班

Jiang Fucong 蔣復璁 (1898–1990)

jianzhi 監製

Jiao Chengyun 焦承允 (1902–1996)

jiaota shidi 腳踏實地

jiaren 佳人

jin 斤

jing 淨

jinghua ban 精華版

jingshen wuyan 精神污染

jingying 精英

jingzi 鏡子

jinsheng 巾生

jinshi 進士

jiqu 集曲

jiu 舊

Jixiu ban 集秀班

ju 劇

jueji 絕技

juren 舉人

juzuo jia 劇作家

kaimen 開門

Ke Jun 柯軍 (b. 1965)

Kong Shangren 孔尚任 (1648–1718)

Kuang Zhong 況鐘 (1383–1442)

kulian 苦練

kundi 昆笛

Kunju chuanxi suo 崑劇傳習所

KunKun 崑崑 (Kunshan dangdai kunju yuan 崑山當代崑劇院)

Kunqu chuanxi jihua 崑曲傳習計畫

Kunqu yishu jie 崑曲藝術節

kunshan qiang 昆山腔

lanhuazhi 蘭花指

Lanting kunju tuan 蘭亭崑劇團

Lao Xiang 老象 (contemporary)

laodan 老旦

Laolang miao 老郎廟

laosheng 老生

Li An 黎安 (b. 1976)

Li Bai 李白 (701–762)

Li Dong 李東 (contemporary)

Li Fanggui 李方桂 (1902–1987)
Li Guinian 李龜年 (fl. 750)
Li Kaixian 李開先 (1502–1568)
Li Longji 李隆基 (685–762)
Li Shujun 李淑君 (1930–2011)
Li Xiangjun 李香君 (1624–1654)
Li Xiangting 李翔霆 (b. 1940)
Li Yu 李漁 (1610–1680)
Li Yu 李玉 (1591–1671?)
Liang Chenyu 梁辰魚 (1521–1591)
Liang Guyin 梁谷音 (b. 1942)
liangxiang 亮相
liantao 聯套
Lin Chong 林沖
Lin Huaimin 林懷民 (b. 1947)
Lin Jifan 林繼凡 (b. 1946)
Lin Weilin 林為林 (b. 1964)
Liu Mengmei 柳夢梅
Liu Run'en 劉潤恩 (contemporary)
Liu Sanji 劉三姐
Liu Tianhua 劉天華 (1895–1932)
Liu Yilong 劉異龍 (b. 1940)
liudan 六旦
liuli 流麗
Liushi 柳氏
liushui ban 流水板
liuye qin 柳葉琴
longtao 龍套
Lu Zhishen 魯智深
luantan 亂彈
luo 鑼
Luo Zhou 羅周 (contemporary)
luogu 鑼鼓
luogu chuangzuo 鑼鼓創作
luogu dianzi 鑼鼓点子
Lü Fuhai 呂福海 (contemporary)
Lü Jia 呂佳 (contemporary)
mabian 馬鞭
magua 馬褂

Mei Baojiu 梅葆玖 (1934–2016)
Mei Langfang 梅蘭芳 (1984–1961)
Meihuajiang 梅花獎
meiren 美人
Meixi kunqu yanjiushe 美西崑曲研究社
mei 美
miao 妙
minyue 民樂
mo 末
moguishi xunlian 魔鬼式訓練
Mu Ouchu 穆藕初 (1876–1943)
nankun 南崑
nanlü gong 南呂宮
nanqu 南曲
nanxi 南戲
nan 難
nian 念
nianbai 念白
noh 能
Ouyang Yuqian 歐陽于倩 (1889–1962)
paixian 拍先
Pan Bizheng 潘必正
paolong tou 跑龍套
peiqi 配器
peiyue 配樂
pei 帔
Peng Tianxi 彭天錫 (fl. 1640s)
piaoyou 票友
pingfan 平凡
pingtan 評彈
pinpai 品牌
Pu Tong 溥桐 (1877–1952)
Qi Biaojia 祁彪佳 (1602–1645)
Qian Nanyang 錢南楊 (1899–1987)
Qian Yi 錢熠 (contemporary)
Qiandeng 千燈
qiangjiu 搶救
Qianrenshi 千人石
Qin Hui 秦檜 (1090–1155)

Glossary

qin 琴

qing 請

qing 情

qingchang 清唱

qingchun 青春

qingge miaowu 清歌妙舞

qinggong 清工

qiongsheng 窮生

qu 曲

Qu Binbin 屈斌斌 (contemporary)

quanben 全本

Quanjin huiguan 全晉會館

qudi 曲笛

qujia 曲家

qujiu lai 取酒來

qupai 曲牌

qupu 曲谱

qusheng 曲聖

qushe 曲社

qushi 曲師

quyou 曲友

Ren Erbei 任二北 (1897–1991)

renjian 人間

renmin yishu jia 人民藝術家

ruan 阮

Ruan Dacheng 阮大鋮 (1587–1646)

sanban 散板

sanxian 三弦

Sanya yuan 三雅園

Sashiliu yuanyang guan 卅六鴛鴦館

Sekong 色空

Shan Wen 單雯 (contemporary)

Shanghai shi xiqu xuexiao 上海市戲曲學校

ShangKun 上崑 (Shanghai kunju tuan 上海崑劇團)

shangxin leshi 賞心樂事

Shen Chuanzhi 沈傳芷 (1906–1994)

Shen Fengying 沈豐英 (b. 1979)

Shen Gang 沈剛 (contemporary)

Shen Guofang 沈國芳 (contemporary)

Shen Jing 沈璟 (1553–1610)

Shen Shixing 申時行 (1535–1614)

Shen Shoulin 沈壽林 (1825–1890)

Shen Yuequan 沈月泉 (1865–1936)

shen 神

shenduan 身段

sheng 生

sheng 笙

ShengKun 省崑 (Jiangsu sheng kunju yuan 江蘇省崑劇院)

shenpin 神品

Shenzong 神宗 (reigned 1572–1620)

shi 實

Shi Kefa 史可法 (1601–1645)

Shi Xiaomei 石小梅 (b. 1949)

shicheng 師承

shijing 實景

shishang hua 時尚化

shiyan 實驗

Shuimo quji 水磨曲集

shuimoqiang 水磨腔

shuixiu 水袖

shujuanqi 書卷氣

shuo 說

sida shengqiang 四大聲腔

Siku quanshu 四庫全書

SiMa Xiangru 司馬相如 (179 BCE–117 BCE)

sizhu 絲竹

Song Yu 宋玉 (298 BCE?–222 BCE?)

souqiang 擻腔

su 俗

Su Dongbo/Su Shi 蘇東坡/蘇軾 (1037–1101)

Suichang 遂昌

SuKun 蘇崑 (Jiangsu sheng Suzhou kunju yuan 江蘇省蘇州崑劇院)

Sun Jian'an 孫建安 (contemporary)

Sun Jing 孫晶 (contemporary)

suona 嗩吶

suyue 俗樂

Suzhou liyuan gongsuo 蘇州梨園公所

Suzhou xiqu bowuguan 蘇州戲曲博物館

Taida kunqushe 台大崑曲社

Taiwan kunjutuan 台灣崑劇團

taizi 太子

Tan Dun 譚盾 (b. 1957)

Tang Minghuang 唐明皇 (685–762)

Tang Rong 唐榮 (contemporary)

Tang Xianzu 湯顯祖 (1550–1616)

tanhua 談話

taxian 踏先

Tian Qinxin 田沁鑫 (contemporary)

tian 天

tiancai 天才

tiandi da wutai 天地大舞台

tiandiren 天地人

tianlai 天賴

tianshang 天上

tianxia 天下

tianxian 天仙

tianyi 天意

Tianyun she 天韻社

tianzi 天子

ting 聽

tiqin 提琴

touban 頭板

tudi gong 土地公

wai 外

waihang 外行

wajue 挖掘

Wang Chuansong 王傳淞 (1906–1987)

Wang Fang 王芳 (b. 1963)

Wang Fengmei 王奉梅 (b. 1945)

Wang Guowei 王國維 (1877–1927)

Wang Jielie 王季烈 (1873–1952)

Wang Shiyao 王世瑤 (1939–2020)

Wang Shiyu 汪世瑜 (b. 1939)

wawasheng 娃娃生

Wei Haimin 魏海敏 (contemporary)

Wei Liangfu 魏良輔 (fl. 1522–1573)

wenchang 文場

Weng Yuxian 翁育賢 (contemporary)

Wenhua jiang 文華獎

wenhua wuran 文化污染

wenhua zou chuqu 文化走出去

Wenjianhui 文建會

Wenquanfuban 文全福班

Wu Mei 吳梅 (1884–1939)

Wu Jinglüe 吳景略 (1907–1987)

Wu Wanqing 吳婉卿 (1847–1926)

Wu Yuan 伍員 (d. 484 BCE)

wuchang 武場

wumei 舞美

wumei sheji 舞美設計

wusheng 武生

wutai 舞台

wutai xiao tiandi 舞台小天地

xi 戲

Xi Shi 西施 (b. 506–?)

Xia Huanxin 夏煥之 (1905–1988)

Xian Yuzhi 鮮于之

xian 縣

xiandai 現代

xiandai hua 現代化

Xiang Yu 項羽 (232 BCE–202 BCE)

XiangKun 湘崑 (Hunan sheng kunju tuan 湖南省崑劇團)

xianyue 仙樂

xianzi 弦子

xiao baimian 小白面

xiaoluo 小鑼

xiaosheng 小生

xiaowo 小我

xigong 戲工

Xinxiang wenjiao jijin hui 新象文教基金會

Glossary

xiqu 戲曲

xiqu dianying 戲曲電影

xiqu pindao 戲曲頻道

xiucai 秀才

xiu 繡

Xizong 熹宗 (reigned 1572–1620)

Xu Lingyun 徐凌允 (1888–1966)

Xu Sijia 徐思佳 (contemporary)

Xu Yanzhi 徐炎之 (1898–1989)

Xu Ying 徐櫻 (contemporary)

xu 虛

xuexi 學習

xungen 尋根

ya 雅

yaji 雅集

Yan Huizhu 言慧珠 (1916–1966)

Yan Song 嚴嵩 (1480–1567)

yan 眼

Yang Guifei 楊貴妃 (719–756)

Yang Guozhong 楊國忠 (700–756)

Yang Hanru 楊汗如 (contemporary)

Yang Jisheng 楊繼勝 (1516–1555)

Yang Xueqin 楊學勤 (contemporary)

Yang Yang 楊洋 (contemporary)

Yang Yinliu 楊蔭瀏 (1899–1994)

yanhuole 演活了

yanyuan 演員

Yao Chuanxiang 姚傳薌 (1912–1996)

yaoban 腰板

Yayun yishu chuanbo youxian gongsi 雅韻
藝術傳播有限公司

ya 呀

Ye Zhaoxin 葉肇鑫 (contemporary)

yiban sanyan 一板三眼

yiban yiyan 一板一眼

yichan 遺產

Yin Guishen 殷桂深 (1825?–?)

yinpeixiang 音配像

Ying Ling 贏令

yingsheng 鶯聲

yinjian 陰間

yinsheng 淫聲

yinxiang dengguang sheji 音響燈光設計

yinyue chuangzuo 音樂創作

yishu biaoyanjia 藝術表演家

yishu zongjian 藝術總監

yiyang qiang 弋陽腔

Yongjia kunqu chuanxi suo 永嘉崑曲傳習
所

You Caiyun 尤彩雲 (1887–1955)

Yu Ji 虞姬 (233 BCE–202 BCE)

Yu Jiulin 俞玖林 (b. 1978)

Yu Sulu 俞粟廬 (1847–1930)

Yu Zhenfei 俞振飛 (1902–1993)

Yuan Hongdao 袁宏道 (1568–1610)

Yuan Xuefen 袁雪芬 (1922–2011)

yuanchang 圓場

yuanlin ban 園林版

yuanzhi yuanwei 原汁原味

yuanzuo 原作

yue 樂

Yue Fei 岳飛 (1103–1142)

Yue Meiti 岳美緹 (b. 1941)

yueju 越劇

yueshi 樂師

Yunmen wuji 雲門舞集

Yushan shengjing 玉山勝境

yuyao qiang 余姚腔

zaju 雜劇

Zeng Yongyi 曾永義 (b. 1941)

zengban 增板

Zha Fuxi 查阜西 (1898–1876)

Zhang Chonghe 張充和 (1913–2015)

Zhang Dai 張岱 (1597–1689)

Zhang Geng 張庚 (1911–2003)

Zhang Hong 張弘 (b. 1947)

Zhang Jingxian 張靜嫻 (b. 1947)

Zhang Jiqing 張繼青 (1939–2022)

Zhang Weidong 張衛東 (contemporary)

Zhang Xian 張嫻 (1915–2006)

Zhang Xiaoxiang 張孝祥 (1132–1169)

Zhang Xunpeng 張洵澎 (b. 1941)

Zhang Yetang 張野塘 (fl. 1550s.)

Zhang Yuanhe 張元和 (1907–2003)

Zhang Yunhe 張允和 (1813–2015)

Zhang Zidong 張紫東 (1881–1951)

Zhao Kuangyin 趙匡胤 (927–976)

Zhao Wenlin 趙文林 (contemporary)

Zhao Wuniang 趙五娘

ZheKun 浙崑 (Zhejiang sheng kunju tuan 浙江省昆劇團)

zhen 真

Zheng Chuanjian 鄭傳鑑 (1910–1996)

Zheng Jinwen 鄭瑾文 (1872–1935)

Zheng Peikai 鄭培凱 (contemporary)

Zheng Qian 鄭騫 (1905–1992)

Zheng Zhenduo 鄭振鐸 (1989–1959)

zhengban 正板

zhengdan 正旦

Zhengyici 正乙祠

zheng 箏

zhezixi 折子戲

Zhilan qushe 芝蘭曲社

zhiti yuyan 肢體語言

Zhong Kui 鍾馗

Zhongguo xijujia xiehui 中國戲劇家協會

zhonghu 中胡

Zhongyang guangbo minzu guanxian yuetuan 中央廣播民族管弦樂團

Zhongyang daxue 中央大學

Zhongzhou yun 中州韻

Zhou Chuanying 周傳瑛 (1912–1988)

Zhou Enlai 周恩來 (1898–1976)

Zhou Long 周龍 (b. 1953)

Zhou Qin 周秦 (b. 1949)

Zhou Xuefeng 周雪峰 (contemporary)

Zhou Youliang 周友良 (contemporary)

Zhu Chuanming 朱傳銘 (1909–1974)

Zhu Guoliang 朱國亮 (1900–1960)

Zhu Maichen 朱賣臣 (?–115 BCE)

Zhu Yingyuan 朱櫻瑗 (contemporary)

Zhu Yuanzhang 朱元璋 (1328–1398)

zhuanchang 專場

zhuangyuan 狀元

Zhuangzi 莊子 (369 BCE?–286 BCE?)

zhuanjia 專家

zhuliu hua 主流化

Zhuo Wenjun 卓文君

Zhuozheng yuan 拙政園

zhuti yinyue 主題音樂

zhuxuanlü 主旋律

ziran 自然

Zuo Liangyu 左良玉 (1599–1644)

zuojia 作家

Works Cited

I. Primary Sources: Dramatic Scripts, Notated Music, and Historical Writings

Cai Yi 蔡毅, ed. *Zhongguo gudian xiqu xuba huibian* 中國古典戲曲序跋匯編 [A collection of prefaces and colophons in historical prints and manuscripts of classical Chinese opera]. Jinan: Qilu shushe, 1989.

Gao Jingchi 高景池. *Kunqu chuantong qupai xuan* 崑曲傳統曲牌選 [A selection of traditional kunqu instrumental music]. Edited by Fan Buyi 樊步義. Beijing: Renmin yinyue chubanshe, 1981.

Gao Lian 高濂. *Yuzanji* 玉簪記 [*Jade Hairpin*]. Beijing: Zhonghua shuju, 1959.

Guan Dequan 關德權, and Hou Ju 侯菊, comp. *Hou Yushan kunqu pu* 侯玉山崑曲譜 [Hou Yushan's kunqu music scores]. Beijing: Zhongguo xiju chubanshe, 1994.

Hong Sheng 洪昇. *Changsheng dian* 長生殿 [*Palace of Everlasting Life*]. Reprint, Beijing: Renmin wenxue chubanshe, 1983.

Kong Shangren 孔尚任. *Taohua shan* 桃花扇 [*Peach Blossom Fan*]. Reprint, Beijing: Renmin wenxue chubanshe, 1980.

Li Yu 李漁. *Xianqing ouji* 閒情偶記 [Occasional notes for leisurely living]. In *Zhonguo gudian xiju lunzhu jicheng* [A compendium of classical treatises on Chinese operas], Vol. 7, 1–114. Compiled by Zhongguo xiju yuan. 10 vols. Reprint, Beijing: Zhongguo xiju chubanshe, 1980.

Li Yu 李漁. *Xianqing ouji* 閒情偶記 [Occasional notes for leisurely living]. Beijing: Yanshan chubanshe, 1988.

Liang Chenyu 梁辰魚. *Liang Chenyu ji* 梁辰魚集 [Collected works of Liang Chenyu], edited by Wu Shuyin. Shanghai: Shanghai guji chubanshe, 1998.

Lin Ping 林萍 and Wang Weimin 王衛民. *Han Shichang kunqu biaoyan yishu* 韓世昌崑曲表演藝術 [Han Shichang's kunqu performance artistry]. Beijing: Zhongguo xiju chubanshe, 2012.

Mao Jin 毛晉 ed . *Liushi Zhong qu* 六十種曲 [Sixty Ming dramas]. Reprint, Beijing: Zhonghua shuju, 2007.

Pu Tong 溥侗. *Hongdou guanzhu paizheng ciqu yicun* 紅豆館主拍正詞曲遺存 [Pu Tong's preserved *kunqu music* manuscripts]. Beijing: Shangwu, 2012.

Qian Decang 錢德蒼. *Zhui bai qiu* 綴百裘 [A collection of kunqu *zhezixi* performance scripts]. Reprint, Beijing: Zhonghua shuju, 2005.

Shen Chongsui 沈寵綏. *Duqu xuzhi* 度曲須知 [Essential knowledge for composing and singing arias]. In *Zhongguo gudian xiqu lunzhu jicheng* 中國古典戲曲論著集成 [A comprehensive collection of theoretical writings on classical Chinese operas], Vol. 5, 183–319. 10 Vols. Reprint, Beijing: Zhongguo xiju chubanshe, 1980.

Suzhou kunju chuanxisuo 蘇州崑劇傳習所, ed. *Kunju chuanshi yanchu zhenben quanbian* 崑劇傳世演出珍本全編 [A comprehensive collection of rare and preserved kunqu scripts and music scores]. 5 vols. Shanghai: Renmin chubanshe, 2011.

Tang Xianzu 湯顯祖. *Tang Xianzu xiquji* 湯顯祖戲曲集 [Collection of Tang Xianzu's libretti]. Edited by Qian Nanyang 錢南楊. Shanghai: Shanghai guji chubanshe, 1978.

Tang Xianzu 湯顯祖. *Mudan ting* 牡丹亭 [*Peony Pavilion*, with illustrations,] edited by Xu Shuofang 徐朔方 and Yang Xiaomei 楊笑梅. Reprint, Beijing: Renmin wenxue chubanshe, 2005.

Tang Xiaobo 唐小波, ed. *Kunqu jingbian jumu diancang* 崑曲精編劇目典藏 [A collection of critically edited performance scripts for 300 *zhezixi*]. 20 Vols. Shanghai: Wenyi chubanshe, 2011.

Wang Chiu-kui 王秋桂, comp. *Shanben xiqu congkan* 善本戲曲叢刊 [Rare books of Chinese dramas]. 6 Series and 104 Vols. Taipei: Xuesheng shuju, 1980s.

Wang Jilie 王季烈. *Jicheng qupu* 集成曲譜 [A comprehensive collection of kunqu scripts and music scores]. Beijing: Commercial Press, 1925.

Wang Jilie 王季烈. *Yinlu qutan* 螾廬曲談 [Wang Jilie talks about kunqu music]. Shanghai: Shangwu yinshuguan, 1934.

Wang Wenzhang 王文章, ed. *Kunqu yishu dadian* 崑曲藝術大典 [A comprehensive compendium of kunqu resources]. 149 Vols. Hefei: Anhui wenyi chubanshe, 2016.

Wang Xiaoying 王曉映, ed. *Yizhuo liangyi/One Table Two Chairs: Yeben/Flee by Night*. Nanjing: Jiangsu fenghuan kexue jishu chubanshe, 2015.

Wang Xichun 王錫純. *Eyunge qupu* 遏雲閣曲譜 [Kunqu scores of the Studio of Soaring Singing]. Shanghai: Zhuyi tang, 1893.

Wang Zhenglai 王正來. *Quyuan zhuiying* 曲苑綴英 [A selection of celebrated kunqu arias]. Hong Kong: Xianggang zhonghua wenhua chujin zhongxin, 2004.

Wei Liangfu 魏良輔. *Qulü* 曲律 [Principles of kunqu composition and singing]. In *Zhongguo gudian xiqu lunzhu jicheng*, Vol. 5, 1–14. 10 Vols. Reprint, Beijing: Zhongguo xiju chubanshe, 1980.

Wu Jinya 吳錦亞. *Kunqu luogu* 崑曲鑼鼓 [Kunqu drum and gong music]. Suzhou: Guwuxian chubanshe, 2009.

Xu Dachun 徐大椿. *Yuefu chuansheng* 樂府傳聲 [Traditional *qu* aria singing]. In *Zhonguo gudian xiju lunzhu jicheng*, Vol. 7, 145–188. Compiled by Zhongguo xiju yuan. 10 vols. Reprint, Beijing: Zhongguo xiju chubanshe, 1980.

Xu Fuming 徐扶明. *Mudan ting yanjiu ziliao kaoshi* 牡丹亭研究資料考釋 [Research materials on the *Peony Pavilion*, with annotations]. Shanghai: Shanghai guji chubanshe, 1987.

Xu Wei 徐渭. *Nanci xulu* 南詞敘錄 [An account on the rise of southern arias]. In *Zhonguo gudian xiju lunju jicheng*, Vol. 3, 233–256. Compiled by Zhongguo xiju yuan. 10 vols. Reprint, Beijing: Zhongguo xiju chubanshe, 1980.

Ye Tang 葉堂. *Nashuying qupu* 納書楹曲譜 [Ye Tang's library of kunqu scores]. In *Shanben xiqu congkan*, Vols. 82–86. Facsimile, Taipei: Xuesheng shuju, 1984.

Works Cited

Yi'an zhuren 怡庵主人. *Huitu jingxuan kunqu daquan* 繪圖精選崑曲大全 [A comprehensive and illustrated collection of selected kunqu plays]. Reprint, Taiyuan: Shanxi renmin chubanshe and Sanjin chubanshe, 2018.

Yu Weichen 俞維琛, and Gong Ruifeng 龔瑞豐. *Mingxin jian* 明心鑒 [A mirror for actors' heart-minds]. In *Xiqu yanchang lunzhu zhushi*, edited by Zhou Yibai, 176–208. Beijing: Shogun xiqu chubanshe, 1962.

Yu Zhenfei 俞振飛, ed. *Sulu qupu* 粟廬曲譜 [Yu Sulu's scores of kunqu arias]. Reprint, Taipei: N.p.; n.d.

Yu Zhenfei 俞振飛. *Zhenfei qupu* 振飛曲譜 [Yu Zhenfei's scores of kunqu music]. Shanghai: Shanghai wenyi chubanshe, 1982.

Yun Lu 允祿, ed. *Jiugong dacheng nanbeici gongpu* 九宮大成南北詞宮譜 [A comprehensive and notated formulary of northern and southern arias in nine musical modes]. 1746. In *Shanben xiqu congkan*, Vols. 87–104. Facsimile, Taipei: Xuesheng shuju, 1980s.

Zhang Chonghe 張充和. *Zhang Chonghe shouchao kunqu pu* 張充和手抄崑曲譜 [Zhang Chonghe's manuscripts of kunqu performance scripts and music scores]. Compiled by Anna Chen. Shanghai: Shanghai cishu chubanshe, 2012.

Zhang Dai 張岱. *Tao'an mengyi* 陶庵夢憶 [Zhang Dai's dreams and reminiscences]. Annotated by Lin Bangjun 林邦鈞. Shanghai: Shanghai shiji chuban gufen youxian gongsi, 2014.

Zhang Yusun 張余蓀. *Zengji liuye qupu* 增輯六也曲譜 [An expanded collection of kunqu scores from the Liuye Studio]. Reprint, Taipei: Zhonghua shuju, 1977.

Zhang Zidong 張紫東. *Kunju shouchao quben yibaice* 崑劇手抄曲本一百冊 [One hundred fascicles of handwritten kunqu scripts and music notation, in facsimile]. Compiled by Zhongguo kunqu bowuguan. Yangzhou: guangling gujie keyinshe, 2009.

Zheng Zhengduo 鄭振鐸 et al. *Guben xiqu congkan* 古本戲曲叢刊 [Collection of historical manuscripts and prints of Chinese dramas]. 10 series and multiple volumes. Beijing: Guojia tushuguan chubanshe, 2016.

Zhongguo xiqu yanjiuyuan 中國戲曲研究院, ed. *Zhongguo gudian xiqu lunzhu jicheng* 中國古典戲曲論著集成 [A comprehensive collection of theoretical writings on classical Chinese operas]. 10 Vols. Beijing: Zhongguo xiju chubanshe, 1959.

Zhongguo yishu yanjiuyuan 中國藝術研究院, comp. *Kunqu yishu dadian* 崑曲藝術大典 [A complete compendium of kunqu resources]. Heifei: Shidai chuanbo chuanmei gufen youxian gongsi, and Anhui wenyi chubanshe, 2016.

Zhongguo yishu yanjiuyuan yinyue yanjiusuo 中國藝術研究院音樂研究所 et al., ed. *Tianyun she qupu* 天韻社曲譜 [Kunqu score of Tianyun she]. Facsimile edition. Beijing: Wenhua yishu chubanshe, 2019.

Zhongyang yinyue xueyuan minzu yinyue yanjiusuo 中央音樂學院民族音樂研究所, comp. *Kunqu chuida qupai* 崑曲吹打曲牌 [Kunqu *qupai* for wind and percussion instruments]. Beijing: Yinyue chubanshe, 1956.

Zhou Qin 周秦, ed. *Cunxin shuwu qupu* 寸心書屋曲譜 [A collection of kunqu scores from the Cunxin Studio]. 2 vols. Suzhou: Suzhou daxue chubanshe, 1993.

Zhou Qin 周秦, comp. *Kunxi jicun* 崑戲集存 [A collection of preserved kunqu performance scripts and music scores]. 12 vols. Hefei: Huangshan shushe, 2016.

Zhou Xuehua 周雪華. *Kunqu—Tang Xianzu Linchuan simeng quanji Nashuying qupu ban* 崑曲一湯顯祖《臨川四夢》全集納書楹曲譜版 [Kunqu: Transcriptions of the *Nashuyin qupu* version of notated music for Tang Xianzu's four dream operas]. Shanghai: Shanghai jiaoyu chubanshe, 2008.

Zhou Youliang 周有良. *Qingchunban Mudanting quanpu* 青春版牡丹亭全譜 [A complete score of the *Peony Pavilion, the Young Lovers' Edition*]. Suzhou: Suzhou daxue chubanshe, 2015.

II. Translation of Chuanqi Libretti/Kunqu Performance Scripts

Birch, Cyril, trans. *Peony Pavilion*. Reprint, Boston: Cheng and Tsui, 1994.

Chen Shih-hsiang, and Harold Acton. *Peach Blossom Fan* by Kong Shangren. With the collaboration of Cyril Birch. Berkeley: University of California Press, 1976.

Mulligan, Jean, trans. *Lute: Kao Ming's P'i-p'a chi*. New York: Columbia University Press, 1980.

Scott. A. C. *The Classical Theatre of China*. Reprint, New York: Dover Publications, 2001.

Scott, A. C. *Traditional Chinese Plays*, Vol. 1. Madison: University of Wisconsin Press. 1967.

Wang Hong, Wang Rongbei, and Zhou Qin, trans. *Gems of Kunqu Opera*. Suzhou: Suzhou daxue chubanshe, 2006.

Wang, Ben. *Laughter and Tears: Translation of Selected Kunqu Dramas*. Beijing: Foreign Languages Press, 2009.

Yang Hsien-yi, and Gladys Yang, trans. *Palace of Eternal Youth* by Hong Sheng. Beijing: Foreign Language Press, 1955.

III. Chinese Studies

Bai Xianyong 白先勇, ed. *Bai Xianyong shuo kunqu* 白先勇說崑曲 [Bai Xianyong talks on kunqu]. Guilin: Guangxi shifan daxue chubanshe, 2004.

Bai Xianyong 白先勇, ed. *Mudan huanhun* 牡丹還魂 [*The Peony Pavilion* revived]. Shanghai: Wenhui chubanshe, 2004.

Bai Xianyong 白先勇. *Niezi* 孽子. Reprint, Taipei: Yunchen chubanshe, 1989.

Bai Xianyong 白先勇, ed. *Chazi yanhong kaibian: Qingchunban* Mudan ting *xunyan jishi* 姹紫嫣紅開遍：青春版《牡丹亭》巡演紀實 [A colorful blossom: A witness report on the US performance tour of Bai Xianyong's the *Young Lovers*]. Taipei: Tianxia yuanjian chuban, 2005.

Bai Xianyong 白先勇, ed. *Sedan baotian Yuzanji—qinqu shuhua kunqu xin meixue* 色膽包天 《玉簪記》——琴曲書畫崑曲新美學 [*Jade Hairpin*, a drama of bold love: New aesthetics on Chinese *qin* music, kunqu, calligraphy, and painting]. Taipei: Tianxia yuanjian, 2009.

Cai Xinxin 蔡欣欣. "Kunqu zai Taiwan fazhan zhi lishi jingguan" 崑曲在台灣發展之歷史 景觀 [A historical view of kunqu developments in Taiwan]. *Zhonghua xiqu* 38 (2008): 184–230.

Cai Zhongde 蔡仲德. *Zhongguo yinyue meixue shi* 中國音樂美學史 [A history of Chinese music aesthetics]. Beijing: Renmin yinyue, 2004.

Cao Lin 曹林, and Yu Jiangang 于建剛, eds. *Kuawenhua yujing zhong de zhongguo xiqu* 跨文化 語境中的中國戲曲 [Chinese opera in cross-cultural discourse]. Beijing: Zhongguo xiju chubanshe, 2009.

Works Cited

Chen Chunmiao 陳春苗. "WanQing Minguo qupu yanjiu 晚清民國曲譜研究/A Study on Kunqu Scores Produced in Late Qing and Republican China." Dissertation, Chinese University of Hong Kong, 2017.

Chen Fang 陳芳. *Kunju de biaoyan yu chuancheng* 崑劇的表演與傳承 [Kunqu performance and its transmission]. Taipei: Guojia chubanshe, 2010.

Chen Jun 陳均. *Jingdu kunqu wangshi* 京都崑曲往事 [Kunqu stories from historical Beijing]. Taipei: Xiuwei zixun keji, 2010.

Chen Jun 陳均. *Xianyue piaomiao: Li Shujun pingzhuan* 仙樂縹緲：李淑君評傳 [Heavenly music flows: A critical biography of Li Shujun]. Shanghai: Guji chubanshe, 2011.

Chen Jun 陳均. 京都聆曲錄 [Kunqu listening in Beijing]. Beijing: Shangwu yinshu guan, 2016.

Chen Kaihua 陳凱華. *Cong antou dao qushu*: Mudan ting *MingQing wenren zhi quanshi gaibian yu wutai yishu zhi dijin* 從案頭到氍毹：《牡丹亭》明清文人之詮釋改編與舞臺藝術之遞進 [From the desk to the stage: Ming Qing interpretations and revisions of the *Peony Pavilion* and development of its performance on stage]. Taipei: Taida chuban zhongxin, 2013.

Chen Yi 陳益. *Zhengsheng jibaisui* 正聲幾百歲 [Kunqu as a centuries-old music]. In *Kunshan chuantong wenhua yanjiu kunqu juan* 崑山傳統文化研究崑曲卷 [Studies in traditional culture in Kunshan; kunqu], Vol. 1. Shanghai: Renmin chubanshe, 2009.

Cong Zhaohuan 叢肇桓. *Cong Zhaohuan tanxi* 叢肇桓談戲 [Cong Zhaohuan talks on opera]. Taipei: Xiuwei zhixun keji, 2015.

Ding Sheng 丁盛. *Dangdai kunqu chuangzuo yanjiu* 當代崑劇創作研究 [A study of contemporary writing of kunqu libretti]. Shanghai: Guji chuabanshe, 2017.

Ding Xiuxun 丁修詢. *Kunqu biaoyan xue* 崑曲表演學 [Kunqu performance practices]. Nanjing: Jiangsu fenghua jiayu chubanshe, 2014.

Fu Jin 傅瑾. "Kunqu *Shiwuguan* xinlun" 崑曲十五貫新論 [A new view on the *Fifteen Strings of Coins*]. In *Xinhuo xiangchuan: Feiwuzhi wenhua yichan baohu di lilun yu shijian* 薪火相傳：非物質文化遺產保護的理論與實踐 [Fire and wood transmission: Theory and practice on preservation of intangible cultural heritage], 265–289. Beijing: Zhongguo shehui kexue chubanshe, 2008.

Fu Jin 傅謹. "Yinyue yu minyue" 音樂與民樂. In *Xi zai shuwai: Xiju wenhua suibi* 戲在書外：戲劇文化隨筆 [Essays on Chinese opera culture], 147–153. Beijing: Beijing daxue chubanshe, 2014.

Fu Xueyi 傅雪漪. *Kunqu yinyue xinshang mantan* 崑曲音樂欣賞漫談 [Random talks on kunqu music and appreciation]. Beijing: Renmin yinyue chubanshe, 1996.

Gao Houyong 高厚永. *Minzu qiyue gailun* 民族器樂概論 [An introduction to Chinese instrumental music]. Reprint, Taipei: Danqing tushu youxian gongsi, 1988.

Gu Lingsen 顧聆森. *Kunqu yu renwen Suzhou* 崑曲與人文蘇州 [Kunqu and cultural Suzhou]. Shenyang: Chunfeng wenyi chubanshe, 2005.

Gu Lingsen 顧聆森. *Li Yu yu kunqu Suzhou pai* 李玉與崑曲蘇州派 [Li Yu and the Suzhou school of kunqu dramatists]. Yangzhou: Guangling shushe, 2011.

Gu Lingsen 顧聆森. *Yeben xiang liming: Ke Jun pingzhuan* 夜奔向黎明：柯軍評傳 [Running towards dawn: A critical biography of Ke Jun]. Shanghai: Shanghai guji chubanshe, 2011.

Gu Lingsen 顧聆森 et al., eds. *Shen Jing yu kunju wujiang pai* 沈璟與崑劇吳江派 [Shen Jing and the Wujiang school of kunqu dramatists]. Shanghai: Shanghai wenyi chubanshe, 2006.

Guo Chenzi 郭晨子. *Kunqu: Jinsheng kandao de qianshi* 崑曲：今生看到的前世 [Kunqu: Historical Chinese lives seen through current kunqu shows]. Beijing: Xinxing chubanshe, 2006.

Guo Yingde 郭英德. *Ming Qing chuanqishi* 明清傳奇史 [A history of Ming and Qing *chuanqi* dramas]. Beijing: Renmin wenxue chubanshe, 2011.

Han Jia'ao 韓家鰲. *Kunqu ziyin* 崑曲字音 [Kunqu enunciation]. Hong Kong: Hongkong Zhonghua wenhua cujin zhongxin, 2001.

Hong Weizhu 洪惟助, ed. *Kunqu yanyijia, qujia, ji xuezhe fangwen lu* 崑曲演藝家、曲家及學者訪問錄 [Interviews with kunqu performers, music masters, and scholars]. Taipei: Guojia chubanshe, 2002.

Hong Weizhu 洪惟助, ed. *Kunqu cidian* 崑曲辭典 [*A Dictionary of Kunqu*]. Yilan: Guoli chuantong yishu zhongxin, 2002.

Hong Weizhu 洪惟助, ed. *Kunqu yanjiu ziliao suoyin* 崑曲研究資料索引 [An annotated index of kunqu research resources]. Taipei: Guojia chubanshe, 2002.

Hou Shaokui 侯少奎, and Hu Mingming 胡明明. *Dawusheng—Hou shaokui kunqu wushi nian* 大武生一侯少奎崑曲五十年 [The grand martial actor: Hou Xiaohui's kunqu career of fifty years]. Beijing: Wenhua yishu chubanshe, 2007.

Hou Yongkui 侯永奎. "Wo de kunqu wutai shengyai" 我的崑曲舞台生涯 [My career on the kunqu stage]. In *Yandu yitan*, compiled by Anonymous, 50–58. Beijing: Beijing chubanshe, 1985.

Hou Yushan 侯玉山. *Youmeng yiguan bashinian* 優孟衣冠八十年 [Eighty years of acting on stage]. Beijing: Zhongguo xiju chubanshe, 1991.

Hu Ji 胡忌, and Liu Zhizhong 劉致中. *Kunju fazhan shi* 崑劇發展史 [A history of kunqu developments]. Beijing: Zhongguo xiju chubanshe, 1989.

Hua Wei 華瑋, ed. *Tang Xianzu yu Mudanting* 湯顯祖與牡丹亭 [Tang Xianzu and his *Peony Pavilion*]. Taipei: Zhongyang yanjiuyuan zhongguo wenzhe yanjiusuo, 2005.

Hua Wei 華瑋, ed. *Kunqu·Chunsan eryue tian: Miandui shijie de kunqu yu* Mudan ting 崑曲・春三二月天：面對世界的崑曲與《牡丹亭》[Kunqu, springtime: Kunqu and the *Peony Pavilion* facing the globalized word]. Shanghai: Shanghai guji chubanshe, 2009.

Hua Zhiwu 華治武, ed. *Qihang—Tang Xianzu-Shashibiya wenhua jiaoliu hezuo* 啟行：湯顯祖——沙士比亞文化交流合作 [Taking off: Cultural exchange and cooperation through performance of Tang Xianzu and Shakespeare dramas]. Hangzhou: Zhejiang daxue chubanshe, 2013.

Jiangsu sheng yanyi jituan 江蘇省演藝集團, ed. *1699 Taohua shan: Zhongguo chuanqi dianfeng* 1699・桃花扇：中國傳奇巔峰 [The 1699 *Peach Blossom Fan*: A pinnacle of Chinese *chuanqi* theatre]. Nanjing: Jiangsu meishu chubanshe, 2006.

Ke Fan 柯凡. *Shuying youlan—zhongguo kunqu de dangdai chuancheng yu fazhan* 疏影幽蘭——中國崑曲的當代傳承與發展 [Dabbled shadows and lone orchids: Transmission and development in contemporary kunqu]. Beijing: Wenhua yishu chubanshe, 2014.

Ke Jun 柯軍, Rong Nianzeng 榮念曾, and Wang Xiaoying 王曉映, eds. *Zhuhuan ji* 鵡環記 [Story of the Toki Project]. Nanjing: Jiangsu fenghuang kexue jishu chubanshe, 2015.

Works Cited

Ke Jun 柯軍, ed. *Zheng Chuanjian ji qi biaoyan yishu* 鄭傳鑒及其表演藝術 [Zheng Chuanjian and his kunqu performance artistry]. Nanjing: Hedong daxue chubanshe, 1995.

Lei Jingxuan 雷競璇, ed. *Kunju hudie meng—yibu chuantong xi de zaixian* 崑劇蝴蝶夢——一部傳統戲的再現 [*Butterfly Dream*: The remaking of a traditional kunqu opera]. Hong Kong: Oxford University Press, 2005.

Lei Jingxuan 雷競璇. *Kunju Zhu Maichen xiuqi—Zhang Jiqing Yao Jikun yanchu banben* 崑劇朱賣臣休妻——張繼青姚繼焜演出版本 [Zhu Maichen divorces his wife—the kunqu version by Zhang Jiqing and Yao Jikun]. Hong Kong: Oxford University Press, 2007.

Li Bin 李斌. "Shilun Taiwan kunqu chuanbo" 試論台灣崑曲傳播 [A preliminary study of kunqu transmission in Taiwan]. *Zhongguo xiqu xueyuan xuebao* 30, no. 1 (February 2009): 32–37.

Li Bin 李斌. "Hongqushu jieyuan hulianwang" 紅氍毹結緣互聯網——崑劇研究學術網站探略 [The stage connects with the web: An exploration of kunqu websites as research tools]. In *Guanzhu xingjin zhong de kunju: Jiangsu sheng kunju yanjiu hui 2010 nian lunwen ji* 關注行進中的崑劇：江蘇省崑劇研究會2010年論文集 [Paying attention to the transforming kunju: Proceedings from 2010 conference of the Jiangsu Province Kunju Research Association], edited by Liu Junhong 劉俊鴻 and Gu Lingsen 顧聆森, 154–172. Beijing: Zhongguo xiju chubanshe, 2011.

Li Liqing 李瀝青. *XiangKun wangshi* 湘崑往事 [Memories of XiangKun]. Zhenzhou: Hunan renmin chubanshe, 2014.

Li Xiao 李曉. *Kunqu wenxue gailun* 崑曲文學概論 [An introduction to kunqu literature]. Shanghai wenhua chubanshe, 2014.

Li Yi 李熠. "Suzhou yuanlin yu kunqu wutai" 蘇州園林與崑曲舞台 [Suzhou gardens and kunqu stages]. MA thesis. Shanghai xiju xueyuan, 2012.

Li Zhongyao 李中耀. "Yuzangji di zuozhe, gushi yanbian ji banben liuchuan 玉簪記的作者，故事演變，版本流傳 [*The Jade Hairpin*: Its author, story, editions, and transmission]. *Xinjiang daxue xuebao zhexue shehui kexue xuebao* 新疆大學學報哲學社會科學學報 19, no. 3 (1991): 85–91.

Liao Ben 廖奔. *Zhongguo xiqu shengqiang yuanliu shi* 中國戲曲聲腔源流史 [A history of Chinese operatic music and repertories]. Taipei: Guanya wenhua shiye youxiangongsi, 1992.

Liao Ben 廖奔 and Liu Yanjun 劉彥君. *Zhongguo xiqu fazhanshi* 中國戲曲發展史 [A history of Chinese operas]. Taiyuan: Shanxi jiaoyu chubanshe, 2003.

Lin Cuiqing 林萃青. "Shijie yinyue wenhua quanqiuhua duihua zhong de kunqu yinse yu yinxiang tizhi" 世界音樂文化全球化對話中的崑曲音色與音响體質 [Kunqu music tone colors and textures as performance-discourse in globalization of world music]. In *Kunqu·Chunsan eryue tian: Miandui shijie de kunqu yu Mudanting*, edited by Hua Wei, 152–164. Shanghai: Shanghai guji chubanshe, 2009.

Lin Pin 林萍, and Wang Weimin 王衛民. *Han Shichang kunqu biaoyan yishu* 韓世昌崑曲表演藝術 [The performance artistry of Han Shichang]. Beijing: Zhongguo xiju chubanshe, 2012.

Liu Jianchun 劉建春, and Jiang Haofeng 姜浩峰. *Zhongguo kunqu ditu* 中國崑曲地圖 [A map of kunqu developments and performances]. Shanghai: Shanghai wenhua chubanshe, 2009.

Liu Junhong 劉俊鴻, and Gu Lingsen 顧聆森, eds. *Guanzhu xingjin zhong de kunju* 關注行進中的昆劇 [Tracking current kunqu developments in Jiangsu Province, China]. Beijing: Zhongguo xiju chubanshe, 2011.

Liu Minglan 劉明瀾. "Lun kunqu changqiang de yishumei" 論崑曲唱腔的藝術美 [On the art of kunqu as vocal music and performance]. *Zhongguo yinyuexue* (1993/3): 27–38.

Liu Shuiyun 劉水雲. *Ming Qing jiayue yanjiu* 明清家樂研究 [A study of household opera troupes in Ming and Qing China]. Shanghai: Shanghai guji chubanshe, 2005.

Liu Yuchen 劉宇宸, ed. *Bai Yunsheng wenji* 白雲生文集 [Collected kunqu writings by Bai Yunsheng]. Beijing: Zhongguo xiju chubanshe, 2002.

Liu Yuemei 劉月美. *Zhongguo kunqu yixiang* 中國崑曲衣箱 [Kunqu costume]. Shanghai: Shanghai cishu chubanshe, 2010.

Liu Zhen 劉禎. *Xiqu lishi yu shenmei bianqian* 戲曲歷史與審美變遷 [A history of Chinese opera and aesthetics]. Beijing: Zhzongguo wenlian chubanshe, 2015.

Liu Zhen 劉禎, and Gu Haohao 谷好好, eds. *Changsheng dian kunju quanben chuangzuo pinglun ji: Chaihe qingyuan yu lishi xingwang de shendu chengxian* 長生殿崑劇全本創作評論集：釵盒情緣與歷史興亡的深度呈現 [An anthology of criticisms and discussions on the creation of the comprehensive version of the *Palace of Everlasting Life*: A deep representation of imperial love and dynastic rise and fall]. Shanghai: Guji chubanshe, 2014.

Liu Zhen 劉禎, Liu Yuchen 劉宇宸, and Cong Zhaohuan 叢兆桓, eds. *Beifang kunqu lunji* 北方崑曲論集 [Essays on northern kunqu]. Beijing: Wenhua yishu chubanshe, 2009.

Lu Eting 陸萼庭. *Kunju yanchu shigao* 崑劇演出史稿 [A draft history of kunqu performance]. Shanghai: Shanghai wenyi chubanshe, 1980.

Lu Eting 陸萼庭. "Yin Guishen yu *Yuqingtang qupu*" 殷桂深與余慶堂曲譜 [Yin Guishen and his kunqu scores]. *Zhongguo kunqu luntan* (2003): 180–185.

Luo Qin 洛秦. "Chengshi yinyue de lishi jidian, shengtai jiegou ji qi yanjiu de jizhixing yinsu—lun Mingmo zhi minguo Suzhou yinyue wenhua de lishi fazhan ji qi tezheng" 城市音樂的歷史積澱、生態結構及其研究的機制性因素——論明末至民國蘇州音樂文化的歷史發展及其特徵 [From the late Ming dynasty to the early Republic of China: History and characters of Suzhou's musical culture]. *Yinyue yishu* 2 (2020): 68–84.

Luo Shilong 羅仕龍. "Kunqu zai faguo de chuanbo, fazhan, yu yanjiu" 崑曲在法國的傳播、發展、與研究 [Kunqu transmission, development, and research in France]. *Huawen wenxue* 5 (2021): 1–23.

Luo Zheng 駱正. *Zhongguo kunqu ershijiang* 中國崑曲二十講 [Twenty lectures on kunqu]. Guilian: Guangxi chubanshe, 2007.

Ma Changshan 馬長山. *Kunju wutai meishu gailun* 崑劇舞台美術概論 [A introduction to kunqu staging arts]. Shanghai: Shanghai wenhua chubanshe, 2017.

Mei Lanfang 梅蘭芳. "Wo yan 'Youyuan jingmeng'" 我演《遊園驚夢》 in *Mei Lanfang wenji*, edited by Zhongguo xijujia xiehui, 60–79. Beijing: Zhongguo xiju chubanshe, 1982.

Mei Lanfang 梅蘭芳. *Wutai shenghuo sishi nian* 舞台生活四十年 [Forty years of performing on the stage]. Documented by Xu Jichuan 徐姬傳. Reprint, Hong Kong: Open Page Publishing, 2017.

Miao Tianrui 繆天瑞, Ji Liankang 吉連抗, and Guo Nai'an 郭乃安. *Zhongguo yinyue cidian* 中國音樂辭典 [A Chinese music dictionary]. Beijing: Renmin yinyue chubanshe, 1985.

Mu Fanzhong 穆凡中. *Kunqu jiushi* 崑曲舊事 [Historical reports on kunqu]. Zhengzhou: Henan renmin chubanshe, 2006.

Pan Xinghua 潘星華. *Chunse ruxu: Qingchunban kunqu* Mudan ting *renwu fangtan lu* 春色如許：青春版崑曲《牡丹亭》人物訪談錄 [Spring colors like these: Interviews with producers and performers of the *Young Lovers*]. Singapore: Global Publishing, 2007.

Pan Yanna 潘妍娜. "'Huigui chuantong' de liniang yu shijian—Shanghai kunju tuan quanben *Changsheng dian* yanjiu" '回歸傳統' 的理念與實踐——上海崑劇團全本《長生殿》研究" [The idea and practice of "returning to the tradition"—a case study on the full version of the *Palace of Eternal Youth*] by the Shanghai Kunqu Opera. PhD diss., Shanghai Conservatory of Music, 2011.

Qian Ying 錢瓔, and Gu Duhuang 顧篤璜, eds. *Shengshi liufang: Jizibei congyi liushi nian qinghe yanchu jinian wenji* 盛世流芳：'繼' 字輩從藝六十年慶賀演出紀念文集 [A lasting legacy: Essays for Jizibei kunqu masters' celebration performance on the sixtieth anniversary of their career]. Suzhou: Gu Wuxuan chubanshe, 2015.

Qiao Jianzhong 喬建中. *Tudi yu ge: chuantong yinyue wenhua ji qi dili lishi beijing yanjiu* 土地與歌：傳統音乐文化及其地理歷史背景研究 [Earth and song: A study of traditional musical culture and its geographical and historical contexts]. Revised edition. Shanghai: Shanghai Conservatory of Music, 2009.

Rong Shicheng (Yung Saishing) 容世誠. *Xunmi yueju shengying: cong hongchuan dao shuiyin deng* 尋覓粵劇聲影：從紅船到水銀燈 [From red boat to silver screen: Visual and sonic culture of Cantonese opera]. Hong Kong: Oxford University Press, 2012.

Sang Yuxi 桑毓喜. *Kunju chuanzibei pingzhuan* 崑劇傳字輩評傳 [A critical biography of the Chuanzibei masters]. Shanghai: Shanghai guji chubanshe, 2010.

Shanghai shi lishi bowuguan 上海市歷史博物館, comp. *Shuimo chuanxing: Haishang kunqu wenwu shuzhen* 水磨傳聲：海上崑曲文物敘珍 [Introduction to the cultural relics of Kunqu opera in Shanghai]. Shanghai: Xuelin chubanshe, 2011.

Shen Bin 沈斌. *Pinlan tanyou: kunju daoyan zhilu* 品蘭探幽：崑劇導演之路 [Appreciating and finding kunqu: My journey as a kunqu director]. Shanghai: Dongfang chuban zhongxin, 2018.

Shen Buchen 沈不沉. *Kuntan ouyun: Yongjia kunju renwu pingzhuan* 崑壇甌韻：永嘉昆劇人物 [The Wenzhou style in Kunqu performance: Critical biographies Yongjia kunju performers]. Shanghai: Guji chubanshe, 2011.

Shi Jian 史建. *Nichang yayun yongting fangfei: Shanghai kunju tuanqing sishi zhounian jinian* 霓裳雅韻榮庭芳菲：上海昆劇團團慶四十周年紀念 [A commenorative book for the fortieth anniversary of the founding of the Shanghai Kunqu Opera Troupe, 1978–2018]. Shanghai: Shanghai Kunju Opera Troupe, 2017.

Shi Yong 史咏. *Xianwai zhiyin—dangdai guqin wenhua chuancheng shilu* 弦外之音——當代古琴文化傳承實錄 [The investigation of guqin cultural inheriting in the contemporary era]. Beijing: Guangming ribao chubanshe, 2011.

Sun Huizhu 孫惠柱. *Shehui biaoyan xue* 社會表演學 [Studies of social performance]. Beijing: Shangwu yinshuguan, 2009.

Sun Rongjie 孫榮潔, ed. *Yizhuo liangyi : "Yeben"* 一桌兩椅：夜奔 [One table two chairs: "Flee by Night"]. Nanjing: Fenghuang chuban chuanmei, 2015.

Suzhou kunju chuanxisuo 蘇州崑劇傳習所, ed. *Suzhou kunju chuanxisuo jinian ji* 蘇州崑劇傳習所紀念集 [A collection of essays for celebrating the 85th anniversary of Suzhou kunju chuanxisuo]. Suzhou: Suzhou kunqu yichan qiangjiu baohu cujinhui, 2006.

Suzhoushi wenhua guangbo dianshi guanli ju 蘇州市文化廣播電視管理局. *Sukunju chengzibei* 蘇崑劇承字輩 [The *cheng*/inheritance students of the Chuanzihei Masters]. Suzhou: n.p., 2007.

Tang Baoxiang 唐葆祥. *Qingfeng yayun bo qianqiu:Yu Zhenfei pingzhuan* 清風雅韵播千秋：俞振飛評傳 [Everlasting elegance and music: A critical biography of Yu Zhenfei]. Shanghai: Shanghai guji chubanshe, 2010.

Tang Shifu 唐斯復, and Guo Yu 郭宇, eds. *Changsheng dian wutai liuying* 長生殿舞台留影 [Memories and images from the Shangkun performance of the *Palace of Everlasting Life*]. Shanghai: Wenyi chubanshe, 2009.

Tang Xiangyin 唐湘隱. *Lanyun jiumeng: wode xiangkun yisu shengya yu qingjie* 蘭韻舊夢：我的湘崑生涯與情結 [Old dreams from Lanyuan: My career at and feelings for XiangKun]. Beijing: Zhongguo xiju chubanshe, 2010.

Tang Yulin 湯鈺林, and Zhou Qin 周秦, eds. *Zhongguo kunqu luntan* 中國崑曲論壇 [Chinese kunqu discussions]. Suzhou: Guwuxuan chubanshe, 2010–present.

Tian Shaodong 田韶東. *Kunqu yanchang yishu yanjiu* 崑曲演唱藝術研究 [A study of the art of kunqu singing]. Hangzhou: Zhejiang daxue chubanshe, 2013.

Wang Ankui 王安葵, and He Yuren 何玉人. *Kunqu chuangzuo yu lilun* 崑曲創作與理論 [Kunqu composition and theory]. Shenyang: Chunfeng wenyi chubanshe, 2005.

Wang Anqi 王安祈. *Mingdai chuanqi zhi juchang jiqi yishu* 明代傳奇之劇場及其藝術 [Stage and staging craft of Ming *chuanqi* dramas]. Taipei: Taiwan xuesheng shuju, 1986.

Wang Chuansong 王傳淞. *Chouzhong mei: Wang Chuansong tanyi lu* 丑中美：王傳淞談藝錄 [A clown's charm: Wang Chuansong on his performance artistry]. Documented by Shen Zu'an 沈祖安and Wang Deliang 王德良. Shanghai: Wenyi chubanshe, 1987.

Wang Dao 王道. *Yisheng chonghe* 一生充和 [Zhong Chonghe's kunqu life]. Beijing: Sanlian shudian, 2017.

Wang Guangqi 王光祁. *Lun Zhongguo gudian geju* 論中國古典歌劇 [A study of classical Chinese opera]. In *Zhongguo gudai yueqikao; lun zhongguo gudian geju* . Changchun: Jilin chuban jituan, 2010.

Wang Ning 王寧. *Kunqu zhezixi yanjiu* 崑曲折子戲研究 [A study of *kunqu zhezixi*]. Hefei: Huangshan chuban chuanmei gufen youxian gongsi, 2013.

Wang Shide 王世德. *Shiwuguan yanjiu* 十五貫研究 [A study on the *Fifteen Strings of Coins*]. Shanghai: Wenhua chubanshe, 1981.

Wang Shoutai 王守泰. *Kunqu gelü* 崑曲格律 [Kunqu aria structure]. Suzhou: Jiangsu renmen chubanshe, 1982.

Wang Shoutai 王守泰. *Kunqu qupai ji taoshu fanli ji* 崑曲曲牌及套數范例集 [Studies of kunqu southern *qupai* and suites]. Shanghai: Shanghai wenyi chubanshe, 1994.

Wang Weimin 王衛民. *Quxue dacheng houshi shibiao: Wu Mei pingzhuan* 曲學大成後世師表：吳梅評傳 [A scholar and teacher of kunqu aria studies: A critical biography of Wu Mei]. Shanghai: Guji chubanshe, 2010.

Wang Wenming 王蘊明, and Yang Fengyi 楊鳳一, eds. *Honglou xinmeng, konggu youlan: kunqu Hongloumeng pinlun ji* 紅樓新夢空谷幽蘭崑曲紅樓夢評論集 [A new dream and a fragant orchid: A collection of criticism about *The Dream of the Red Chamber*]. Beijing: Zhongguo xiju chubanshe, 2015.

Wang Wenzhang 王文章. *Feiwuzhi wenhua yichan gailun* 非物質文化遺產概論 [An introduction to the intangible cultural heritage]. Beijing: Wenhua yishu chubanshe, 2006.

Wang Xiaoying 王曉映, ed. *Yizhuo liangyi: Zhuhuanji* 一桌兩椅：朱媛記 [One table and two chairs: The Toki story]. Nanjing: Jiangsu fenghuang kexu jishu chubanshe, 2015.

Wu Mei 吳梅. *Wu Mei Ciqu Lunzhuji* 吳梅詞曲論著集 [A collection of Wu Mei's writings on *ci* and *qu*], edited by Jie Yufeng. Nanjing: Nanjing daxue chubanshe, 2008.

Wu Junda 武俊達. *Kunqu changqiang yanjiu* 崑曲唱腔研究 [A study of kunqu aria composition and performance]. Beijing: Renmin yinyue chubanshe, 1993.

Wu Xinlei 吳新雷, ed. *Chatuben kunqu shishi biannian* 插圖本崑曲史實編年 [A chronology of historical kunqu activities, with illustrations]. Shanghai: Shanghai guji chubanshe, 2015.

Wu Xinlei 吳新雷. *Ershi shiji qianqi kunqu yanjiu* 二十世紀前期崑曲研究 [Early twentieth-century kunqu studies]. Changchun: Chunfeng wenyi chubanshe, 2005.

Wu Xinlei 吳新雷. *Kunqushi kaolun* 崑曲史考論 [Studies in kunqu history]. Shanghai: Guji chubanshe, 2015.

Wu Xinle 吳新雷. *Kunqu yanjiu xinji* 崑曲研究新集 [A new collection of kunqu studies]. Taipei: Xiuwei zixun keji, 2014.

Wu Xinlei 吳新雷, ed. *Zhongguo kunju dacidian* 中國崑劇大辭典 [*A Dictionary of Chinese Kunqu Opera*]. Nanjing: Nanjing daxue chubanshe. 2002.

Wu Zhiwu 吳志武. *Xinding jiugong dacheng nanbeici gongpu yanjiu* 新訂九宮大成南北詞宮譜研究 [A study of the *Xinding jiugong dancheng nanbeici gongpu*]. Beijing: Renmin yinyue chubanshe, 2017.

Xie Boliang 謝伯梁, and Gao Fumin 高福民. *Qiangu qingyuan*: Changsheng dian *guoji xueshu yantao hui lunwen ji* 千古情緣：《長生殿》國際學術研討會論文集 [A thousand-year-old romance: Proceedings of the international conference on the *Palace of Everlasting Life*]. Shanghai: Shanghaiguji chubanshe, 2006.

Xie Boliang 謝伯梁, and Niu Junyi 紐君怡. *Yabu zhengyin guansheng kuishou: Cai Zhengren zhuan* 雅部正音官生魁首：蔡正仁傳 [An authentic voice of classical kunqu and a leading actor of the official male role: A biography of Cai Zhenren]. Shanghai: Shanghai guji chubanshe, 2012.

Xu Huaizhi 許懷之. "Gao Lian Yuzanji yanjiu—cong wenxue juben dao kunqu yanchu" 高濂玉簪記研究——從文學劇本到崑曲演出 [A study on Gao Lian's *Jade Hairpin*—from literary script to kunqu performance]. MA thesis. Guoli Zhongyang daxue, 2010.

Xu Jian 許建, *Qinshi xinbian* 琴史新編 [A new narrative of *qin* music history]. Beijing: Zhonghua shuju, 2012.

Xu Lingyun 徐凌雲. *Kunju biaoyan yide; kanxi liushinian* 崑劇表演一得；看戲六十年 [Xu Lingyun's insights on performing kunqu; sixty years of attending kunqu shows]. Compiled and edited by Guan Ji'an 管際安 and Lu Jianzhi 陸兼之. Suzhou: Guwuxian chubanshe, 2009.

Xuan Leilei 軒蕾蕾. "Xin shiqi kunqu xueshu shilun" 新時期崑曲學術史論 [A historical essay on kunqu opera research of the recent thirty years]. Dissertation. Chinese National Academy of Arts. 2010.

Yang Baochun 楊寶春. *Pipaji de changshang yanbian yanjiu* 琵琶記的場上演變研究 [A study of historical changes in staging the *Lute*]. Shanghai: Sanlian shuju, 2009.

Yang Shousong 楊守松. *Kunqu zhilu* 崑曲之路 [Paths in kunqu history]. Beijing: Renmin wenxue chubanshe, 2009.

Yang Yinliu 楊蔭瀏. "Yuyan yinyue xue chutan" 語言音樂學初探 [A preliminary exploration into linguistic-musicological studies]. In *Yuyan yu yinyue*, edited by Anonymous, 1–96. Beijing: Yinyue chubanshe, 1983.

Yang Yinliu 楊蔭瀏. *Zhongguo gudai yinyue shigao* 中國古代音樂史稿 [A draft history of Chinese music]. Beijing: Renmin yinyue chubanshe, 1981.

Ye Changhai 葉長海, ed. *Changsheng dian: Yanchu yu yanjiu* 長生殿：演出與研究 [*The Palace of Everlasting Life*: Performance and research]. Shanghai: Shanghai wenyi chubanshe, 2009.

Ye Changhai 葉長海, and Liu Qing 劉慶, eds. *Hunqian kunqu wushinian* 魂牽崑曲五十年 [Soulfully connected for fifty years: Biographies of Shangkun performers]. Beijing: Zhongguo xiju chubanshe, 2000.

Ye Fei 葉飛. *Zhongguo wenhua yishu zouchuqu yanjiu* 中國文化藝術走出去研究 [The research on the "going-global" strategy of Chinese culture and art]. Beijing: Beijing daxue chubanshe, 2016.

Ye Zhaoxin 葉肇鑫, coordinated. *Kunqu baizhong: dashi shuoxi* 崑曲百種：大師說戲 [One hundred kunqu masterpieces: Master performers' lecture-demonstrations on their signature shows]. 149 vols.; 110 DVDs. Changsha: Hunan dianzi yinxiang chubanshe and Yuelu shushe, 2014.

Yu Dan 于丹. *Youyuan jingmeng: Kunqu zhimei* 遊園驚夢崑曲之美 [Kunqu's charms]. Taipei: Lianjing, 2008.

Yu Jiangang 于建剛, ed. *Xiqu kuawenhua jiaoliu rencai peiyang yanjiu* 戲曲跨文化交流人才培養研究 [A study on training talents for promoting cultural exchanges with operatic arts]. Beijing: Wenhua yishu chubanshe, 2014.

Yu Zhenfei. *Yu Zhenfei yishu lunji* 俞振飛藝術論集 [A collection of Yu Zhenfei's writings on kunqu performance]. Edited by Wang Jiaxi 王家熙 and 許寅 Xu Yin. Shanghai: Shanghai wenyi chubanshe, 1985.

Yue Meiti 岳美緹. *Linfeng duqu: Yue Meiti kunju jinsheng biaoyan yishu* 臨風度曲：岳美緹，崑劇巾生表演藝術 [Gentlemanly Performance: Yue Meiti's artistry as a performer of kunqu young man characters]. Edited by Yang Hanru 楊汗如. Taipei: Shitou, 2006.

Yue Meiti 岳美緹. *Jinsheng jinshi: Yue Meiti kunqu wushinian* 巾生今世：岳美緹崑曲五十年 [My life as a kunqu man: Yue Meiti's kunqu career of fifty years]. Beijing: Wenhua yishu chubanshe, 2008.

Zeng Yongyi 曾永義. *Cong qiangdiao shuodao kunju* 從腔調說到崑劇 [Essays on kunqu music and drama]. Taipei: Guojia chubanshe, 2002.

Zhang Chonghe 張充和, narrated, and Sun Kangyi 孫康宜, ed. *Quren hongzhua benshi*: Zhang Chonghe quren benshi 曲人鴻爪：張充和曲人本事 [Traces of kunqu personalities]. Guilin: guangxi shifan daxue chubanshe, 2010.

Zhang Faying 張發穎, ed. *Zhongguo jiayue xiban* 中國家樂戲班 [Household operatic troupes in historical China]. Beijing: Xueyuan chubanshe, 2002.

Zhang Geng 張庚. "Cong Zhang Jiqing de biaoyan kan xiqu biaoyan yishu di jiben yuanli" 從張繼青的表演看戲曲表演藝術的基本原理 [Reviewing principles of Chinese opera performance practices with Zhang Jiqing's shows]. In *Qing chu yu lan: Zhang Jiqing kunqu 55 nian*, edited by Zhu Xi and Yao Jikun, 150. Beijing: Wenhua yishu chubanshe, 2009.

Zhang Geng 張庚, and Guo Hancheng 郭漢城. *Zhongguo xiqu tongshi* 中國戲曲通史 [A general history of Chinese opera]. Beijing: Zhongguo xiju chubanshe, 1981.

Zhang Huaying 章華英. *Guqin* 古琴 [An introduction to *guqin* music]. Hangzhou: Zhejiang renmin chubanshe, 2005.

Zhang Jun 張軍. *Woshi xiaosheng* 我是小生 [I am a kunqu *xiaosheng*]. Shanghai: Shanghai cishu chubanshe, 2008.

Zhang Weidong 張衛東. *Shanghua you shi duqu youdao—Zhang Weidong shuo kunqu* 賞花有時，度曲有道——張衛東論崑曲 [A time for viewing flowers and a path for making kunqu: Zhang Weidong discusses kunqu]. Beijing: Shangwu yinshu guan, 2013.

Zhang Xiuyun 張岫雲. *Buyuan jiushi* 補園舊事 [Memories of kunqu people and events in Buyuan]. Suzhou: Guwuxuan chubanshe, 2005.

Zhang Yunhe 張允和. *Kunqu riji* 崑曲日記 [Zhang Yunhe's kunqu diary]. Beijing: Yuwen chubanshe, 2004.

Zhao Heping 趙和平, and Zhou Yude 周育德. *Linghun de jiushu: Kunju* Gongsun zidu *chuangzuo pinglun ji* 靈魂的救贖：崑劇《公孫子都》創作評論集 [Essays on the kunqu opera *Gongsun Zidu*]. Beijing: Zhongguo xiju chubanshe, 2010.

Zhao Shanlin 趙山林. *Zhongguo xiqu guanzhongxue* 中國戲曲觀眾學 [A study of Chinese operatic performance, audience, and their aesthetics.] Shanghai: Huadong shifan daxue chubanshe, 1990.

Zhao Shalin 趙山林, and Zhao Tingting 趙婷婷. *Mingdai yong kunqu shige xuanzhu* 明代咏崑曲詩歌選注 [An annotated anthology of poems on kunqu]. Taipei: Xiuwei zixun keji, 2014.

Zheng Chuanyin 鄭傳寅. *Chuantong wenhua yu gudian xiqu* 傳統文化與古典戲曲 [Traditional culture and classical drama]. Taipei: Yangzhi wenhua, 1995.

Zhongguo kunqu nianjian bianzhuan weiyuanhui 中國崑曲年鑑編撰委員會, ed. *Zhongguo kunqu nianjian* 中國崑曲年鑑 [The yearbook of kunqu opera—China]. Suzhou: Suzhou daxue, 2012–present.

Zhongyang yinyue xueyuan minzu yinyue yanjiusuo 中央音樂學院民族音樂研究所, ed. *Kunju chuida qupai* 崑劇吹打曲牌 [Wind and percussion music of Chinese kunqu opera]. Beijing: Yinyue chubanshe, 1956.

Zhou Bing 周兵, and Jiang Wenbo 蔣文博. *Kunqu liubai nian* 崑曲六百年 [Six centuries of kunqu]. Beijing: Zhongguo qingnian chubanshe, 2008.

Zhou Chuanying 周傳瑛. *Kunju shengya liushi nian* 崑劇生涯六十年 [A sixty-year career as a kunqu actor-singer]. Documented by Luo Di 洛地. Shanghai: Wenyi chubanshe, 1988.

Zhou Lijuan 周麗娟. *Zhongguo xiqu yishu duiwai jiaoliu gailan, 1949–2012* 中國戲曲藝術對外交流概覽 [A survey on overseas Chinese opera performances as cultural exchange activities, 1949–2012]. Beijing: Wenhua yishu chubanshe, 2014.

Zhou Qin 周秦. *Suzhou kunqu* 蘇州崑曲 [Kunqu in Suzhou]. Taipei: Guojia chubanshe, 2002.

Zhou Qin 周秦. *Huawu disheng: Cunxin shuwu kunqu suibi* 花塢笛聲：寸心書屋崑曲隨筆 [Flowered dock and flute music: Occasional writings from the Cuxin Studio]. Jinan: Shandong huabao chubanshe, 2012.

Zhou Yibai 周貽白. *Zhongguo xiju shi* 中國戲劇史 [A history of Chinese opera]. Beijing: Zhonghua shuju, 1953.

Zhou Yude 周育德. *Kunqu yu MingQing shehui* 崑曲與明清社會 [Kunqu and Ming Qing society]. Changchun: Chunfeng wenyi chubanshe, 2005.

Zhu Jianming 朱建明, comp. Shenbao *Kunju ziliao xuanbian*《申報》崑劇資料選編 [Selected kunqu documents from the *Shenbao*]. Shanghai: Shanghai Kunjuzhi bianjibu, 1992.

Zhu Jianming 朱建明. *Mu Ouchu yu kunqu: Minchu shiyejia yu chuantong wenhua* 穆藕初與崑曲：民初事業家與傳統文化 [Mu Ouchu and kunqu: An early twentieth-century industrialist and traditional Chinese culture]. Taipei: Xiuwei zixue keji, 2013.

Zhu Junling 朱俊玲. *Kunqu zai beifang di liuchuan yu fazhan* 崑曲在北方的流傳與發展 [Transmission and development of kunqu in Northern China]. Beijing: Zhongguo shehui kexue chubanshe, 2015.

Zhu Kunhuai 朱崑槐. *Kunqu qingchang yanjiu* 崑曲清唱研究 [A study of kunqu singing]. Taipei: Da'an chubanshe, 1991.

Zhu Lin 朱琳. *Kunqu yu jiangnan shehui shenghuo* 崑曲與江南社會生活 [Kunqu and social lives in Jiangnan]. Guilin: Guangxi shifan daxue chubanshe, 2007.

Zhu Xi 朱禧, and Yao Jikun 姚繼焜. *Qingchu yulan: Zhang Jiqing kunqu wushiwu nian.* 青出於藍：張繼青崑曲五十五年 [A flower above all: Zhang Jiqing's kunqu career of fifty-five years]. Beijing: Wenhuayishu chubanshe, 2009.

Zhu Xiajun 朱夏君. *Ershi shiji kunqu yanjiu* 二十世紀崑曲研究 [Twentieth-century kunqu studies]. Shanghai: Guji chubanshe, 2015.

Zou Yuanjiang 鄒元江. *Tang Xianzu xinlun* 湯顯祖新論 [A new interpretation of Tang Xianzu]. Shanghai: Shiji Chuban jituan, 2015).

Zou Yuanjing 鄒元江. *Mei Lanfang biaoyan meixue tixi yanjiu* 梅蘭芳表演體系研究 [A study on Mei Lanfang's aesthetics and performance practices]. Beijing: Renmin chubanshe, 2018.

IV. Japanese and Western Studies

Akamatsu, Norihiko, ed. *Chugoku no dento bungei engeki ongaku* 中国の伝統文藝・演劇・音楽 [Traditional Chinese performing arts, theatre, and music]. Kyoto: Geijutsu gakusha, 2014.

Akamatsu, Norihiko, Komatsu Ken, and Yamazaki Yoshiyuki. *Nogaku to konkyku—Nihon to chugoku no koten engeki wo tannoshimu* 能樂と崑曲—日本と中國古典演劇を楽しむ [Noh and Kunqu—appreciation of Chinese and Japanese classical theaters]. Tokyo: Kyuko shoin, 2009.

Alexander, Jeffrey. "Cultural Pragmatics: Social Performance between Ritual and Strategy." *Sociological Theory* 22, no. 4 (2004): 527–573.

Ames, Roger T., Thomas P. Kasulis, and Wimal Dissanayake, eds. *Self as Person in Asian Theory and Practice.* New York: SUNY Press, 1994.

Appadurai, Arjun. *Modernity at Large: Cultural Dimensions of Globalization.* Minneapolis: University of Minnesota Press, 1996.

Becker, Howard. *Art Worlds.* Rev. ed. Berkeley: University of California Press, 2008.

Berger, Harris M. "Horizons of Melody and the Problem of the Self." In *Identity and Everyday Life: Essays in the Study of Folklore, Music, and Popular Culture*, edited by Harris M. Berger and Giovanna P. DelNegro, 43–88. Middletown: Wesleyan University Press, 2004.

Birch, Cyril. *Scenes for Mandarin: The Elite Theater of the Ming.* New York: Columbia University Press, 1995.

Works Cited

Brandl, Rudolf, and Qu Liuyi. *Einführung in das Kunqu—die klassische chinesische Oper des 16. bis 19. Jahrhunderts*. Göttingen: Cuvillier Verlag, 2007.

Certeau, Michel de. *The Practice of Everyday Life*. Berkeley: University of California Press, 1984.

Chang, Dongshin. "Borrowing the Fan: An Example of Actable Plays (*Zhezixi*) for the Kunqu Stage." *Asian Theatre Journal* 34, no. 2 (2017): 259–283.

Chen, Fuyan. "Principles of K'un-Ch'ü Singing." *Asian Music* 8, no. 2 (1977): 4–25.

Chen, Liana. "Engaging Tang Xianzu and Shakespeare in the Quest for Self." *Asian Theatre Journal* 36, no. 2 (2019): 327–346.

Chen, Liana. *Staging for the Emperors: A History of Qing Court Theatre, 1683–1923*. Amherst: Cambria Press, 2021.

Chin, Annping. *Four Sisters of Hofei: A History*. New York: Scribner, 2001.

Cook, Scott. "'Yueji'—*Record of Music*: Introduction, Translation, Notes, and Commentary." *Asian Music* 26, no. 2 (Spring–Summer, 1995): 1–96.

DeNora, Tia. *Music in Everyday Life*. Cambridge: Cambridge University Press, 2000.

Dolby, William. *A History of Chinese Drama*. London: Paul Elek, 1976.

Fégly, Jean-Marie. "Théâtre chinois: survivance, d´veloppement et activité du kunju au Xxe siècle." PhD diss., Université de Paris VII, 1986.

Fei, Faye Chunfang. *Chinese Theories of Theater and Performance: From Confucius to the Present*. Ann Arbor: University of Michigan Press, 2002.

Ferrara, Rossella. "Asian Theatre as Method: The Toki Experimental Project and Sino-Japanese Transnationalism in Performance." *TDR: The Drama Review* 61, no. 3 (Fall 2017): 141–164.

Frankel, Ch'ung-ho Chang. "The Practice of K'un-Ch'u Singing from the 1920's to the 1960's." *Chinoperl* 6, no. 1 (1976): 82–92.

Fung Yu-lan. *A History of Chinese Philosophy*. Translated by Derk Bodde. Princeton: Princeton University Press, 1983.

Gardner, Daniel K. *Confucianism: A Very Short Introduction*. New York: Oxford University Press, 2014.

Goldman, Andrea S. "The Nun Who Wouldn't Be: Representations of Female Desire in Two Performance Genres of 'Si Fan.'" *Late Imperial China* 22, no. 1 (June 2001): 71–138.

Goldman, Andrea S. *Opera and the City: The Politics of Culture in Beijing, 1770–1900*. Stanford: Stanford University Press, 2012.

Goldstein, Joshua. *Drama Kings: Players and Publics in the Re-creation of Peking Opera, 1870–1937*. Berkeley: University of California Press, 2007.

Gordon, Kim Hunter. "Contesting Traditional *Luzi* ('Choreographic Paths'): A Performance-Based Study of Kunqu." PhD diss., Royal Holloway, University of London, 2016.

Gordon, Kim Hunter. "*Kunqu Baizhong, Dashi Shuoxi* (One Hundred Pieces of Kunqu, Master Performers Talk about Their Scenes): A Review Essay." *Chinoperl: Journal of Chinese Oral and Performing Literature* 35, no. 2 (December 2016): 143–152.

Gulik, Hans van. *The Lore of the Chinese Lute: An Essay on the Idealogy of the Ch'in*. Tokyo: Sophia University, 1940.

Guy, Nancy. *Peking Opera and Politics in Taiwan*. Urbana: University of Illinois Press, 2005.

Hanan, Patrick. *The Invention of Li Yu*. Cambridge, MA: Harvard University Press, 1988.

Harris, Rachel. *The Making of a Musical Canon in Chinese Central Asia*. London: Routledge, 2008.

He, Yuming. "Difficulties of Performance: The Musical Career of Xu Wei's *The Mad Drummer*." *Harvard Journal of Asiatic Studies* 68, no. 2 (2008): 949–984.

Howard, Keith. *Music as Intangible Cultural Heritage: Policy, Ideology, and Practice in the Preservation of East Asian Traditions*. London: Ashgate, 2012.

Howard, Vernon A. "Virtuosity as a Performance Concept: A Philosophical Analysis." *Philosophy of Music Education Review* 5, no. 1 (1997): 42–54.

Hsu, Immanuel. *The Rise of Modern China*. 6th ed. New York: Oxford University Press, 2000.

Hsu, Shih-huang. "Chinese Kunqu in Contemporary Times and Self-Orientalism: Inheritance and Reinvention of Traditonal Art in an Economic Age." PhD diss., Royal Holloway, University of London, 2018.

Huang, Alexander C. Y. *Chinese Shakespeares: Two Centuries of Cultural Exchange*. New York: Columbia University Press, 2009.

Huang, Martin W. "Sentiments of Desire: Thoughts on the Cult of *Qing* in Ming-Qing Literature." *Chinese Literature: Essays, Articles, Reviews (CLEAR)* 20 (1998): 153–184.

Huang, Yan. *Pragmatics*. New York: Oxford, 2007.

Jones, Juliane. "Contemporary Kun Opera Composition." PhD diss., University of British Columbia, 2014.

Joubin, Alexa Alice. "Performing Commenoration: The Cultural Politics of Locating Tang Xianzu and Shakespeare." *Asian Theatre Journal* 36, no. 2 (2019): 275–280.

Kelly, Thomas. "Putting on a Play in an Underworld Courtroom: The 'Mingpan' (Infernal Judgment) Scene in Tang Xianzu's *Mudan ting (Peony Pavilion)*." *Chinoperl: Journal of Chinese Oral and Performing Literature* 32, no. 2 (December 2013): 132–155.

Kile, Sarah E. "Sensational Kunqu: The April 2010 Beijing Production of *Lianxiang ban* (*Women in Love*)." *Chinoperl Papers* 30, no. 2 (December 2011): 215–222.

Koo Siusun, and Diana Yue. *Wei Liang-fu: Rules of Singing Qu*. In *Writings on the Theory of Kun Qu Singing*. Hong Kong: Oxford University Press, 2006.

Lam, Joseph S. C. "Chinese Music and Its Globalized Past and Present." *Macalester International* 21 (Summer 2008): 29–77.

Lam, Joseph S. C. "Eavesdropping on Zhang Xiaoxing's Musical World in Early Southern Song China." In *Senses of the City: Perceptions of Hangzhou and Southern Song China*, edited by Joseph Lam, Shuen-fu Lin, Christian de Pee, and Martin Powers, 25–54, 1127–1279, Hong Kong: Chinese University of Hong Kong Press, 2017.

Lam, Joseph S. C. "Escorting Lady Jing Home: A Journey of Chinese Gender, Opera, and Politics." *Yearbook for Traditional Music* 46 (2014): 117–141.

Lam, Joseph S. C. "Impulsive Scholars and Sentimental Heroes: Contemporary Kunqu Discourse of Traditional Chinese Masculinities." In *Gender in Chinese Music*, edited by Rachel Harris, Rowan Pease, and Shzr Ee Tan, 86–106. New York: Rochester University Press, 2013.

Lam, Joseph S. C. "Kunqu Cross-Dressing as Artistic and/or Queer Performance." In *The Oxford Handbook of Music and Queerness*, edited by Fred Maus and Sheila Whitely, 539–558. New York: Oxford University Press, 2022.

Lam, Joseph S. C. "A Kunqu Masterpiece and Its Interpretations: *Tanci* (the Ballad) from Hong Sheng's *Changsheng Dian (Palace of Everlasting Life)*." *Chinoperl: Journal of Chinese Oral and Performing Literature* 33, no. 2 (December 2014): 98–120.

Works Cited

Lam, Joseph S. C. "Musical Confucianism: The Case of 'Jikong yuewu.'" In *On Sacred Grounds: Culture, Society, Politics, and the Formation of the Cult of Confucius*, edited by Thomas A. Wilson, 134–172. Cambridge, MA: Harvard University Asia Center, 2002.

Lam, Joseph S. C. "Musical Wantons, Chauvinistic Men, and Their Kunqu Discourse in Traditional China." In *Wanton Women in Late Imperial China*, edited by Wu Cuncun and Mark Stevenson, 81–104. New York: Brill, 2017.

Lam, Joseph S. C. "Notational Representation and Contextual Constraints: How and Why Did Ye Tang Notate His Kun Opera Arias?" In *Themes and Variations: Writings on Music in Honor of Rulan Chao Pian*, edited by Bell Yung and Joseph S. C. Lam, 26–35. Cambridge, MA, and Hong Kong: Department of Music, Harvard University, and the Institute of Chinese Studies, Chinese University of Hong Kong, 1994.

Lam, Joseph S. C. "The *Southern Story of the Western Wing (Nan Xixiang)*: Traditional Kunqu Composition, Interpretation, and Performance." In *How to Read Chinese Drama*, edited by Patricia Sieber and Regina S. Llamas, 191–211. New York: Columbia University Press, 2022.

Lam, Joseph S. C. "*Ya* kunqu in Late Ming and Early Qing China." *China Arts Quarterly* 6 (September 2019): 68–94.

Lam, Joseph S. C. "Zhang Dai's (1597–1680) Musical Life in Late Ming China." In *Ming China*, edited by Kenneth Swope, 343–365. New York: Routledge, 2019.

Lau, D. C., trans. *Confucius: The Analects (Lunyu)*. London: Penguin Book, 1979.

Lei, Daphne. *Alternative Chinese Opera in the Age of Globalization: Performing Zero*. London: Palgrave Macmillan, 2011.

Li, Hsiao-T'i. *Opera, Society, and Politics in Modern China*. Cambridge, MA: Harvard University Asia Center, 2019.

Li, Ruru. "Chinese Traditional Theatre and Shakespeare." *Asian Theatre Journal* 5, no. 1 (Spring 1988): 38–48.

Li, Ruru. *Shashibiya: Staging Shakespeare in China*. Hong Kong: Hong Kong University Press, 2004.

Li, Sui Leung. *Cross-Dressing in Chinese Opera*. Hong Kong: Hong Kong University Press, 2003.

Li Xiao. *Chinese Kunqu Opera*. San Francisco: Long River Press, 2005.

Lin, Da. "The Political Economy of Kunqu Opera in China (1940s–2015)." PhD diss., University of Pittsburgh, 2017.

Liu, Lydia. "A Folksong Immortal and Official Popular Culture in Twentieth-Century China." In *Writing and Materiality in China*, edited by Judith T. Zeitlin and Lydia H. Liu, 553–612. Cambridge, MA: Harvard University Asia Center, 2003.

Liu, Majorie Bong-ray. "Tradition and Change in Kunqu Opera." PhD diss., UCLA, 1976.

Liu, Majorie Bong-ray. "Aesthetic Principles and Ornamental Style in Chinese Classical Opera-Kun." *Selected Reports in Ethnomusicology* 4 (1983): 29–61.

Liu, Siyuan. "The Case of Princess Baihua: State Diplomatic Functions and Theatrical Creative Process in China in the 1950s and 1960s." *Asian Theatre Journal* 30, no. 1 (2013): 1–29.

Lo, Andrew. "Textual Representations of the Sixteenth-Century Chinese Drama *Yuzan ji (The Jade Hairpin)*. *Oral Tradition* 20, no. 2 (2005): 335–361.

Luo Qin. "Kunju, Chinese Classical Theater and Its Revival in Social, Political, Economic, and Cultural Contexts." PhD diss., Kent State University, 1997.

Mackerras, Colin. "Performance Review: The Imperial Granary Production of *Mudan ting* (*The Peony Pavilion*)." *Chinoperl* 26 (2010): 209–216.

Mackerras, Colin. *The Performing Arts in Contemporary China*. London: Routledge and Kegan Paul, 1981.

Mackerras, Colin. "Tourism and Musical Performing Arts in the First Decade of the Twenty-First Century: A Personal View." *Chinoperl* 30 (2011): 155–182.

Malm, William. *Traditional Japanese Music and Musical Instruments*. New ed. Tokyo: Kodansha, 2000.

Mark, Lindy Li, trans. "Argosies of Wonder on the Rivers and Lakes: Memories of the Quanfu Troupe by Yunhe Zhang and Qixiang Tan." *Chinoperl* 14 (1986): 77–95.

Mark, Lindy Li. "From Page to Stage: Exploring Some Mysteries of Kunqu Music and Its Melodic Characteristics." *Chinoperl* 32, no. 1 (July 2013): 1–29.

Mark, Lindy Li. "The Role of Avocational Performers in the Preservation of Kunqu." *Chinoperl* 15 (1990): 95–114.

Mark, Lindy Li. "Tone and Tune in Kunqu." *Chinoperl Papers* 12 (1983): 9–60.

Murck, Alfreda. "Golden Mangoes: The Life Cycle of a Cultural Revolution Symbol." *Archives of Asian Art* 57 (2007): 1–21.

Ng, Wing Chung. *The Rise of Cantonese Opera*. Urbana: University of Illinois Press, 2015.

Ong, Min Yen. "A Report on the 2010 Tiger Hill Amateur Kunqu Festival." *Chinoperl* 30 (2011): 259–264.

Ong, Min Yen. "Kunqu in 21st Century China: Musical Change and Amateur Practices." PhD diss., School of Oriental and African Studies, University of London, 2013.

Pegg, Carole. *Mongolian Music, Dance, and Oral Narrative: Performing Diverse Identities*. Seattle: University of Washington Press, 2001.

Pian, Rulan Chao. "Text Setting with the Shipyi Animated Aria." In *Words and Music: The Scholar's View*, edited by Laurence Berman, 237–270. Cambridge, MA: Harvard University Press, 1972.

Picard, François, and Kar Lun Alan Lau. "*Qupai* in Kunqu: Text-Music Issues." In *Qupai in Chinese Music: Melodic Models in Form and Practice*, edited by Alan Thrasher, 119–154. New York: Routledge, 2016.

Rebull, Anne. "Locating Theatricality on Stage and Screen: Rescuing Performance Practice and the Phenomenon of *Fifteen Strings of Cash* (*Shiwuguan*; 1956)." *Chinoperl* 36, no. 1 (2017): 46–71.

Rees, Helen. "Intangible Cultural Heritage in China Today: Policy and Practice in the Early Twenty-First Century." In *Music as Intangible Cultural Heritage*, edited by Keith Howard, 23–54. London: Ashgate, 2012.

Rice, Timothy. *Modeling Ethnomusicology*. New York: Oxford University Press, 2017.

Riley, Jo. *Chinese Theatre and the Actor in Performance*. Cambridge: Cambridge University Press, 1997.

Rolston, David. "Tradition and Innovation in Chen Shi-Zheng's Peony Pavilion." *Asian Theatre Journal* 19, no. 1 (Spring 2002): 134–146.

Schafer, R. Murray. *The Soundscape: Our Sonic Environment and the Tuning of the World*. Rochester: Destiny Books, 1977.

Smith, Laurajane, and Natsuko Akagawa, eds. *Intangible Heritage*. New York: Routledge, 2009.

Schechner, Richard. *Performance Studies: An Introduction*. 2nd ed. London: Routledge, 2006.

Works Cited

Schwarz, Vera. *The Chinese Enlightenment: Intellectuals and the Legacy of the May Fourth Movement of 1919*. Berkeley: Center for Chinese Studies, University of California, 1990.

Scott, A. C. *Traditional Chinese Plays, Vol. 2: Longing for Worldly Pleasures/Ssu Fan and Fifteen Strings of Cash/Shi Wu Kuan*. Madison: University of Wisconsin Press, 1969.

Seeger, Anthony. *Why Suya Sing: A Musical Anthropology of an Amazonian People*. Urbana: University of Illinois Press, 2004.

Shen, Grant. "Acting in the Private Theatre of the Ming Dynasty." *Asian Theatre Journal* 15, no. 1 (Spring, 1998): 64–86.

Shih, Chung-wen. *The Golden Age of Chinese Drama: Yüan Tsa-chü*. Princeton: Princeton University Press, 1976.

Siu, Wang-Ngai, and Peter Lovick. *Chinese Opera: The Actor's Craft*. Hong Kong: Hong Kong University Press, 2014.

Small, Christopher. *Musicking: The Meanings of Performing and Listening*. Middletown: Weslyan University Press, 1998.

Stenberg, Josh. "An Annotated Translation of Zhang Jiqing's Lecture on Playing Cui-shi in Chimeng (The Mad Dream): A Sample Lecture from *Kunqu Baizhong, Dashi Shuoxi* (One Hundred Pieces of Kunqu, Master Performers Talk About Their Scenes)." *Chinoperl* 35, no. 2 (2016): 153–175.

Stock, Jonathan. *Huju: Traditional Opera in Modern Shanghai*. London: British Academy, 2003.

Strassberg, Richard E. "On Singing Techniques of K'un Ch'ü and their Musical Notation." *Chinoperal Papers* 6 (1976): 45–81.

Struve, Lynn A. *The Dreaming Mind and the End of the Ming World*. Honolulu: University of Hawai'i Press, 2019.

Sun, Mei. "Nanxi: The Earliest Form of *Xiqu* (Traditional Chinese Theatre)." PhD diss., University of Hawai'i Press, 1995.

Sun, Mei. "Performances of Nanxi." *Asian Theatre Journal* 13, no. 2 (Autumn 1996): 141–166.

Sutcliffe, Bret. "Kunqu Concert at Lion Hill and Kunqu Amateur Convention at Suzhou, November 2001." *Chinoperl* 24 (2002): 133–136.

Swatek, Catherine. "Boundary Crossings: Peter Sellars's Production of *Peony Pavilion*." *Asian Theatre Journal* 19, no. 1 (Spring 2002): 147–158.

Swatek, Catherine. *The Peony Pavilion on Stage: Four Centuries in the Career of a Chinese Drama*. Ann Arbor: Center for Chinese Studies, University of Michigan, 2002.

Tian, Min. *The Poetics of Difference and Displacement: Twentieth-Century Chinese-Western Intercultural Theatre*. Hong Kong: Hong Kong University Press, 2008.

Tu Weiming. "Embodying the Universe: A Note on Confucian Self-Realization. In *Self as Person in Asian Theory and Practice*, edited by Roger T. Ames, Thomas P. Kasulis, and Wimal Dissanayake, 177–186. New York: SUNY Press, 1994.

Turino, Thomas. *Music as Social Life: The Politics of Participation*. Chicago: University of Chicago Press, 2008.

Volppe, Sophie. "The Literary Circulation of Actors in Seventeenth-Century China." *Journal of Asian Studies* 61, no. 3 (2002): 949–984.

Wang, Ayling. "Music and Dramatic Lyricism in Hong Sheng's *Palace of Eternal Life*." In *Text, Performance, and Gender in Chinese Literature and Music, in Honor of Wilt Idema*, edited by Maghiel van Crevel, Tian Yuan Tan, and Michel Hockx, 233–262. Leiden: Brill, 2009.

Wang, Jing. *High Culture Fever: Politics, Aesthetics, and Ideology in Deng's China*. Berkeley: University of California Press, 1996.

Wei, Juhua. "Kunqu in Practice: A Case Study." PhD diss., University of Hawai'i, 2019.

Wei, Mei. *Studie zum Kunqu in Geschichte und Gegenwart*. Göttingen: Cuvillier Verlag, 2009.

Wei, Zhou. "A *Peony* Transplanted: Pai Hsien-yung and the Preservation of Chinese *Kunqu*." PhD diss., University of Edinburgh, 2011.

Wichmann, Elizabeth. *Listening to Theatre: The Aural Dimension of Beijing Opera*. Honolulu: University of Hawai'i Press, 1991.

Wichmann-Walczak, Elizabeth. "Ma Bomin and the Question of Creativity Authority in the *Peony Pavilion* Controversy." *ACMR Reports* 11 (1998): 107–110.

Wong, Chuenfung. "Peripheral Sentiments: Encountering Uyghur Music in Urumuchi." PhD diss., UCLA, 2006.

Wong, Isabel. "The Printed Collections of K'un-Ch'ü Arias and their Sources." *Chinoperl* 8, no. 1 (1978): 100–129.

Wood, Francis, trans. "The Traditional Gardens of Suzhou" by Li Dunzhen. *Garden History* 10, no. 2 (Autumn 1982): 108–141.

Wu, Hung. "The Painted Screen." *Critical Inquiry* 23, no. 1 (1996): 37–79.

Xu, Peng. "Lost Sound: Singing, Theater, and Aesthetics in Late Ming China, 1574–1644." PhD diss., University of Chicago, 2014.

Xu, Peng. "The Music Teacher: The Professionalization of Singing and the Development of Erotic Vocal Style During Late Ming China." *Harvard Journal of Asiatic Studies* 75, no. 2 (December 2015): 259–297.

Yang, Ming. "Return of the Soul: Inheritance and Innovation in the Process of Artistic Creation in Major Kunqu Productions in the People's Republic of China, 2001–2015." PhD diss., University of Hawai'i, 2019.

Yang, Ming. "The Modernization of Chinese *Xiqu* with a Cast Study of Major Kunqu Productions in Mainland China, 2001–2013." In *Modernization of Asian Theatre: Process and Tradition*, edited by Yasuhi Nagata and Ravi Chaturvedi, 165–186. Singapore: Springer, 2019.

Yung, Bell. "An Audience of One: The Private Music of the Chinese Literati." *Ethnomusicology* 61, no. 3 (Fall 2017): 506–539.

Yung, Bell. *Cantonese Opera: Performance as Creative Process*. Cambridge: Cambridge University Press, 1989.

Zhang Boyu, Yao Hui, and Huib Schippers. "Report: The Rise and Implementation of Intangible Cultural Heritage Protection for Music in China." *The World of Music*, new series, 4, no. 1 (2015): 45–59.

Zeitlin, Judith. "Shared Dreams: The Story of the Three Wives' Commentary on the *Peony Pavilion*." *Harvard Journal of Asiatic Studies* 54, no. 1 (June 1994): 127–179.

Zeitlin, Judith. "My Year of Peonies." *Aisan Theatre Journal* 19, no. 1 (Spring 2002): 124–133.

Zeitlin, Judith. "Music and Performance in Hong Sheng's *Palace of Lasting Life*." In *Text, Performance, and Gender in Chinese Literature and Music: Eassys in Honor of Wilt Idema*, edited by Maghiel van Crevel, Tian Yuan Tan, and Michel Hockx, 263–292. Leiden and Boston: Brill, 2009.

Works Cited

271

V. Online Documents

Anonymous. *"1699 Taohuashan juzhao"* 1699桃花扇劇照 [Performance pictures of *1699 Peach Blossom Fan*]. Accessed September 25, 2020. http://image.haosou.com/i?src=rel &q=%E6%98%86%E6%9B%B2%E6%A1%83%E8%8A%B1%E6%89%871699%E5% 89%A7%E7%85%A7.

Anonymous. "Tian Qinxin." Accessed September 15, 2020. https://baike.baidu.com/item/ %E7%94%B0%E6%B2%81%E9%91%AB/10366199.

Asia Society New York. "Three Shanghai Kunqu Kunqu Performances for New York Audiences. Accessed May 6, 2016. http://asiasociety.org/new-york/three-shanghai-kunqu-opera-performances-new-york-audiences.

Aykan Bahar. "Whose Tradition, Whose Identity: The Politics of Constructing 'Nevrus' as Intangible Heritage in Turkey." *European Journal of Turkish Studies* 19 (2014). Accessed March 15, 2019. https://doi.org/10.4000/ejts.5000.

Feng Qifeng 馮起鳳. *Yinxiang tang qupu* 吟香堂曲譜 [Kunqu music from the Studio of Singing and Fragrance]. 1789. Digital Facsimile. Accessed May 15, 2021. http://www. guoxuemi.com/shumu/303169o.html.

Luo Zhou 羅周. *"Zuixin hua, woshou xie woxin"* 醉心花我手寫我心 [*Belladonna and Intoxicated Hearts*; my hand writes what my heart tells]. Accessed October 10, 2019. https://weibo.com/ttarticle/p/show?id=2309404052531151029245.

UNESCO. "Basic Text of the 2003 Convention for the Safeguarding of the Intangible Cultural Heritage, 2010 Edition." CLT. 2010/WX/17. Accessed January 15, 2020. https://unesdoc.unesco.org/ark:/48223/pf0000189761?5=null&queryId=1973bee0-0612-41ec-932f-eeae40ad45cb; uploaded UNESCO.

UNESCO. "Nôgaku Theatre." Accessed January 24, 2019. http://www.unesco.org/culture/ ich/index.php?RL=00012.

UNESCO. "Qin." Accessed October 3, 2020. http://www.unesco.org/culture/ich/index. php?RL=00061.

UNESCO. "Urtiin Duu, Traditional Folk Long Song." Accessed October 2, 2020. http:// www.unesco.org/culture/ich/?RL=00115.

UNESCO. "Uyghur Muqam of Xinjiang." Accessed October 2, 2020. http://www.unesco.org/ culture/ich/index.php?RL=00109.

Wenhuabu. "Wenhuabu caizhengbu guanyu yinfa 'Guojia kunqu yishu qiangjiu, baohu he fuchi gongcheng shishi fangan' de tongzhi" 文化部財政部關於印發 "國家崑曲藝術搶救，保護和扶持工程實施方案" 的通知 [A notice on the proclamation of the policy on salvaging, protecting, and developing kunqu by the Finance Department of the Ministry of Culture]. Accessed February 23, 2016. https://e.cacanet.cn/cpll/law7292.shtml.

"Meihua jiang" 梅花獎 ["Plum Blossom Prize]. Accessed May 20, 2016. http://www.xijucn. com/html/jingju/20081208/6427.html.

"Nandu fanhui jingwu tujuan" 南都繁會景物圖卷 [A view of busy and prosperous Nanjing, the southern capital]. Accessed May 16, 2021. http://www.chnmuseum.cn/enlarge. html?path=/tilegenerator/aggregate/004/069/069.xml.

"Shi daxu" 詩大序 [Preface to the *Classic of Poetry*]. Accessed May 16, 2021. https://baike. baidu.com/item/%E8%AF%97%E5%A4%A7%E5%BA%8F#2.

"Tian Qinxin." Accessed on September 15, 2020. Baike.baidu.com/item Tian Qinxin.

"Zhongguo xiju meihuajiang ji lijie huojiang mingdan 中國戲劇梅花獎及歷屆獲獎名單 [The Plum Blossom Prize and a list of winners]. Accessed January 10, 2019. http://www.xijucn.com/html/jingju/20081208/6427.html.

"Yueji" 樂記 [*Record of Music*]. Accessed May 16, 2021. https://ctext.org/liji/yue-ji/zh.

VI. Institutional Websites

Digital Kunqu Musuem at Cambridge University: maa.cam.ac.uk/digital-museum-of-global-chinese-kun-opera.

Fan-theatre: www.fan-theatre.com.

Kunqu Society [of New York]: www.kunqusociety.org.

New York Metropolitan Museum: www.metmuseum.org/metmedia.

Suzhou Musueum of Chinese Operas: www.kunopera.com.cn.

Zhengyici Theatre: theatrebeijing.com/theatres/zhengyici_theatre.

VII. Commercial DVDs

Changsheng dian by ShangKun. 4 DVDs. ISRC CN-AA02-08-0056-0/V.J9.

DVD attached to *Kunju Zhu Maishen xiuqi—Zhang Jiqing Yao Jikun yanchu banben*, edited by Lei Jingxuan. Hong Kong: Oxford University Press, 2007.

The Lark from the East: Yang Xuejin Solo Concert at Vienna; ISRC CMN-E02-12-318-09V-J6.

Index

1699 Peach Blossom Fan, The: backdrop, 42; comparison with *Young Lovers, The*, 126–27; criticism, 124–26; production, 120–23; publicity, 36. *See also* "Writing on the Fan"

Academy for the Teaching and Preservation of Kunju, 62, 99. *See also* Chuanzibei Masters

acrobatics and martial arts, 32, 40, 199. See also *shenduan*

actor-singers: active before 1970, 71, 92–94, 103, 111, 114, 145, 172; active between 1970 and 2000, xiv, 130, 146–47; active after 2000, 94, 125, 183, 207. *See also* Bando Tamasaburo; Cai Zhengren; Hou Shaokui; Hua Wenyi; Mei Lanfang; Shi Xiaomei; Yu Zhanfei; Yue Meiti; Zhang Jingxian; Zhang Jiqing

arias, analyzed: "Attending a Court Audition" ("Chaoyuange"), 142; "Dark Silk Robe" ("Zao luopao"), 167–69, Music Examples 9 and 10; "Fighting Quails" ("Dou anchun"), 51; "Geese Descending from the Sky"("Yan'er lou"), 107, Music Example 6; "Lazy Bird" ("Lanhuamei"), 141, Music Example 7; "Peddler, The" ("Huolang'er"), 5, 53, Music Examples 3 and 4; "Pink Butterfly" ("Fendie'er'), 48–49; "Sheep on the Slope," ("Shanbo yang"), 105–6, Music Example 5; "Taking the Cloth Shirt Off" ("Tuobushan"), 53, Music Example 2

arias, general: 16, 24, 54, 63, 86. *See also* music, vocal; *qupai*; *shuimoqiang*

audience, 6–7, 15, 20, 86, 148, 150

Bai Xianyong, 100–102. See also *Young Lovers, The*

"Ballad Singing" ("Tanci"), 53–54, Musical Examples 3 and 4

Bando Tamasaburo, 3–4, 190–92

Cai Zhengren, 5, 49, 51–52, 82n5, 96, 133. *See also* "Garden Party; Shocking News, A"; "Lamenting"

centers of kunqu operations, Chinese: Beijing, 69, 93; Hangzhou, 69; Kunshan, xii, 65; Nanjing, 120–24; Qiandeng, 65; Shanghai, 5–7, Suzhou 69, 111–14; Taipei, 114–16

characterizations of kunqu, Chinese: continuous tradition, as a, 10, 193–94; cultural legacy, as a, 8, 59, 183; entertainment, as, 10, 49; heavenly music, as, 8, 18, 30–31; *Jiangnan* culture, as, 8, 61, 67; literature, music, and dance seamlessly integrated, as, 48–49, 53, 141–44; mirror of Chinese lives and dreams, as a, xiii, 10, 27, 34, 81–82; mother of Chinese operas, as, 8; soft power, as, 172, 176; virtuoso performance, 19, 32. *See also* keywords and tropes, kunqu

characters, kunqu: popular, 103, 107–8, 131–41; modeled after historical

274 Index

figures, 4–5, 21, 54, 89–90, 104–5, 113, 124

Chen, Shizheng, 2, 78, 101, 169, 173

chuanqi, 22, 33–34, 63, 131

Chuanzibei Masters, 1, 96–99

composers and music arrangers: Dai Peide, 123; Sun Jian'an, 123; Tan Dun, 173; Wang Zhenglai, 220; Yin Guishen, 84, 94; Zhou Qin, 114, 220; Zhou Xuehua, 83n13; Zhou Youliang, 101, 160, 166

Confucian teachings on music/*yue*, 26–27, 35, 62–63, 156. See also *yue* performance and discourse; *yuescape*

connoisseurs and critics, 8, 10, 33, 48, 95, 125, 133, 148–50, 166, 199–200

control of and support for kunqu, national: bureaucratic and institutional, 9, 91–92, 98, 113, 117–19, 176, 182; financial, 3, 8, 117; ideological, 72; scholarship, 119

controversies: authenticity, 2–3, 17–18, 166–67; commercialization and popularization, 17, 51, 124; cultural representation, 173–74; kunqu's social functions, 19, 192; the tradition's pending implosion, 119n24; outsiders' control, 119; preservation and development directions, 17, 193–94; regional differences, 110. See also music, instrumental

costume: 38–39, 83, 124, 131, 198

creativity/recreativity: 38, 128–29, 140–41, 144

dances, group, 74–76

"Dark Silk Robe" ("Zao luopao"), 167–69, Music Examples 9 and 10

directors and producers: Bai Xianyong, 113; Cai Xiaohua, 113; Gu Duhuang, 113; Gu Xin, 120–22; Tian Qinxin, 122; Wang Xiang, 79

"Dog Exit," ("Goudong"), 107–8

dramatists and scriptwriters: Gao Lian, 67, 134; Hong Sheng, 35; Kong Shangren, 125–26; Li Yu 33, 36; Luo Zhou 197; Ruan Dacheng, 108; Shen Jing, 67; Tang Xianzu, 67, 92; Tian Qinxin, 122; Zhang Hong, 195, 201

"Dreams Long and Short," 208

eroticism, kunqu dramatization of, 39, 49, 73, 75, 105, 131, 136, 139, 145

feiyi, 19, 180–84. See also ICH

Fifteen Strings of Coins, The, 1, 62, 71, 150

"Flee by Night" ("Yeben"), xii, 17, 107, 205–7

formulism in kunqu, 132–43

"Garden Party; Shocking New, A" ("Xiaoyan jingbian"): 5, 41, 48–51, 73, 79, 175, 196

gardens as kunqu stages and mis-en-scènes, 41, 50, 55, 79, 196

gender roles/stereotypes, kunqu dramatization of traditional Chinese: xiii, 33, 49, 75, 105–8, 138, 146–47, 192, 202

genealogies, kunqu actor-singers' artistic, 5, 11, 92–98

globalization, kunqu: adoption of Shakespeare dramas, 176–77, 196; Chinese push for, 77, 101; interactions with world artists and audience, 101, 123, 173, 183, 192; overseas tours, 171–78, 192. See also *Peony Pavilion, The*; *Young Lovers, The*

history, kunqu: changes and continuities, 193–209; historiography, 66–67; overview, 1–4; pragmatic narrative, 61–72; revival, 59–61; rise of *zhezixi*, 23, 33, 69. See also controversies, Chuanzibei Masters, *feiyi*, globalization

Hou Shaokui, 94, 199–200

Hua Wenyi, 78, 146

ICH, 178–80, 184–90

impersonation, female, 192. See also Bando Tamasaburo and Mei Lanfang

Index

"Infernal Judgement" ("Mingpan"), 199–200

internet, as a repository of kunqu audio-visual recordings and communications, 4, 7, 89n10, 240–42, 272

interpretation of kunqu, a holistic: 9–11, 135

Jade Hairpin, The, 23, 134–44. *See also* "Zither Seduction"

Ke Jun, 123, 201, 207

keywords and tropes, kunqu, 8, 17–22

"Kneeling by the Pond" ("Guichi"), 104–5

kunqu and kunju, definitions of, 22, 25, 68

"Lamenting" ("Kuxiang"), 51–53, Music Example 2

Liang Chenyu, 66, 89, 91–92

linguistics: dialects, 35; linguistic tones and melodic contours, match of, 53, 87, 143–45; Zhongzhou yun, 43. *See also* oral deliveries; *qupai*; music, vocal

luogu, 45–46, 144. See also *zhezixi* analyzed

make-up, 38, 131

Mei Lanfang: 73–75, 94, 167, 172

minyue, 75, 146–47, 161–65, Table 8.1 and 8.2

morals and social conflicts, kunqu dramatization of, 90, 103, 105, 126, 147, 192, 209

Mu Ouchu, 71, 98–100

museums, 3, 116

music, instrumental: *c-yue* and *t-yue*, 113, 145–48, 197, 208, Tables 8.1 and 8.2, Music Examples 8 and 10; creative processes, 46, 197; functions and types, 45–46, 158–61, 165–67, 177, 197; instruments & ensembles, 43, 45–46, 58; interrelationships with vocal melodies/singing, 35, 88, 145; sonic features and programmatic meanings, 20, 160, 164–65. See also *minyue*, rhythms and tempi

music, vocal: composition, arrangements, and performance, 50–51, 53–54; repertories and styles: 63; theories and practices, 16, 45, 85–88, 143–44; *shida shengqiang*, 63–64. *See also* arias, analyzed

noh, Japanese, 189–90, 204

operas, analyzed. See *1699 Peach Blossom Fan, The; Palace of Everlasting Life, The; Peony Pavilion, The; Young Lovers; Jade Hairpin, The*

Operas, discussed: *Belladonna and Intoxicated Hearts*, 197–98; *Blood-Stained Hands, The*, 177, 183; *Butterfly Dream, The*, 81, 130–31; *Chunyu Fen's Dream*, 81; *Crane, The*, 173; *Dames in Love*, 33, 83; *Dream of the Red Chamber, The*, 183; *Earthquake at 14:28*, 34; *Escorting Lady Jing Home*, 90; *Fifteen Strings of Coins, The*, 1, 62, 71, 150; *Flowers and Moonlight by the River*, 183, 197; *I, Hamlet*, 176; *Journey to the West*, 175; *Kunqu Sage: Wei Liangfu, The*, 91; *Lioness Roars, The*, 103–5; *Lute, The*, 63, 86; *Lute: Cai Bojie, The*, 195–96; *Peach Blossom Fan, The*, 122–23; *Six vignettes of a Floating Life*, 196; *Story of General Gongsun Zidu, The*, 130; *Story of Gu Yanwu, The*, 182; *Story of the Horse Trader*, 207; *Story of the Mountain of Rotten Axe Handle, The*, 90, 174; *Story of the Western Wing, The*, 116; *Story of the White Rabbit*, 131; *Story of Washing Silk, The*, 66, 89; *Swift Crossing of Luding Bridge, The*, 182; *White Silk Shirt, The*, 209

oral deliveries: chanting and speaking, 43; vocables as dramatic expressions, 50, 137, 139–40, 144

Palace of Everlasting Life, The (Changsheng dian): dramatist (Hong Sheng), 35; history and synopsis, 47–48;

Index

ShangKun production, 4–5; Sukun (2004) production 3, 55, 133. *See also* "Ballad Singing," "Garden Party; Shocking News, A," "Lamenting"

patrons: 64, 67–68, 70, 98, 102, 114, 202. *See also* Bai Xianyong, Mu Ouchu

Peony Pavilion, The, 33, 39, 169, 173–76, 198–200

performance practices. *See* oral deliveries, costume, make-up, music, *shenduan*, stages, staging technologies, publicity

performance scripts: literary forms, 23; writing processes, 34–35, 128; performance instructions, 134. See also *chuangqi* and *zhezixi*

performance venues, historical kunqu, 81, 98, 111–12

performers/practitioners, 15–16, 26, 181, 202. *See also* actor-singers, composers and music arrangers, directors and producers, dramatists, and scriptwriters

presentations/shows: functions of, 14–15, 23–25, 80, 118; types of, 14–15, 68, 129, 196

publicity, 35–36

qin: as a dramatic element, 51, 136–37, 141, 148; as a Chinese ICH, 185–86

qingchun dianya, 19–22

qupai: creative process with, 142–43, 177; definition of, 35, 85; identification of, 132–33; instrumental, 46, 159–60. *See also* arias, analyzed

recordings, audio and audio-visual, 15, 94–96, 115–16, 200–201, 203–4

rhythms and tempi, 44, 51, 53

role-types, 36–38. *See also* operas, analyzed and *zhezixi*, analyzed

scholars, Chinese kunqu: 33n8, 70, 93, 102–3, 115, 212–13

Sellars, Peter, 78, 172, 192

shenduan: 24, 39–41, 88–89, 131–32, 140. See also operas, analyzed and *zhezixi*, analyzed.

Shi Xiaomei, 201–2

shuixiu, 39, 140, 148

shujuanqi, 95, 100, 144, 146

sources: dictionaries, 212; dissertations, 212–13; historical accounts, 33n6, 85, 211; multi-media materials, 200–204, 211; notated sources, 78, 84–85, 113, 135, 143, 193–94; performance scripts, 82–83, 211; publications by international scholars, 212–15; theoretical treatises, 85–89; visual illustrations, 83

stages: backdrops, 42, 131, 146, 196; props, 40–41, 131, 139, 202; types, 41–42, 111

staging technologies, 41–42, 173, 196

"Strolling; Dreaming" ("Youyuan jingmeng"), 73–79

supernatural beings/forces, kunqu dramatization of, 4, 18, 51, 58, 75, 90, 97

Tang Xianzu, 67, 92

theories consulted, international: 8–11, 26–28, 135, 152–54, 176

ticket sales, 6, 10, 79

tourism, 6, 9n15, 57, 61, 65, 112, 125

training and transmission, 9, 19, 96, 101, 115, 203. *See also* genealogies, kunqu actor-singers' artistic

troupes: contemporary and professional, 14, 96; historical and professional, 69–70; contemporary and semi-professional, 14, 115, 174, 182

TV documents and screenings of recorded kunqu shows, 61, 80, 119, 203

UNESCO, 3, 72. *See also* ICH

virtuosities, kunqu performance, 31–36, 52

Wei Liangfu, 35, 65, 85–87, 91

"Writing on the Fan" ("Tihua"), 125, 201–2

xiqu, definitions of, 26

Index

ya, 21, 35, 156

yanhuole, xiv, 19, 22, 87, 133

"Yearning for the Secular World" ("Sifan"), 105–6

Young Lovers, The: California tour, 174–75; comparison with *1699 Peach Blossom, the*, 126–27; controversy, 150; instrumental music, 147, 160, 165–67; production, performance, and reception, 3, 38, 101. See also *Peony Pavilion, The*

Yu Zhenfei: overseas tours, 172; performance artistry, 133, 144–45; school of kunqu singing, 194–95; teaching, 133, *shuquanqi*, 144; theories on singing, 43, 95–96

Yue Meiti, 96, 135–36, 146. *See also* "Zither Seduction"

yue performance and discourse, hypothesis of, 28, 155–57, 166–67

yuescape, 28, 110, 119, 157–58, 166, 172, 180–81, 188–89, 195, 198. *See also* centers of kunqu operations, Confucian teachings on music/*yue*

Yung, Danny, 204–7

Zhang Jingxian, 49

Zhang Jiqing, 41, 75, 119, 133–34, 168

Zhang Jun, 79, 116, 207–9

zhezixi analyzed. *See* "Ballad Singing," "Dog Exit," "Dreams Long and Short," "Flee by Night," "Garden Party; Shocking News, A," "Infernal Judgment," "Kneeling by the Pond," "Strolling; Dreaming," "Writing on the Fan," "Yearning for the Secular World," "Zither Seduction"

zhezixi referenced, 4, 34, 43, 83, 89, 90, 94, 99, 131, 142, 172, 182

"Zither Seduction" ("Qintao"): arias, 141–44, Music Example 7; creative process, 140–42; productions, 144–48; *shenduan* and story, 134–37